COMBINED OPERATIONS

An Official History of Amphibious
Warfare Against Hitler's Third Reich,
1940-1945

Introduced by
John Grehan

FRONTLINE
BOOKS

COMBINED OPERATIONS
An Official History of Amphibious Warfare Against Hitler's Third Reich, 1940-1945

Published in Great Britain in 2022 by Frontline Books,
an imprint of Pen & Sword Books Ltd, Yorkshire – Philadelphia

Based on file reference DEFE 2/1773, from a series of records from the Directorate of Military Intelligence, at The National Archives, Kew and licensed under the Open Government Licence v3.0.

Introduction Copyright © John Grehan, 2022
Text alterations and additions © Frontline Books, 2022

ISBN: 978-1-39904-022-8

No part of this book may be reproduced or transmitted in any form or by any means, electronic or mechanical including photocopying, recording or by any information storage and retrieval system, without permission from the Publisher in writing.

Typeset in Chennai, India
by Lapiz Digital Services.

Printed and bound by CPI UK

Pen & Sword Books Ltd incorporates the imprints of Pen & Sword Archaeology, Air World Books, Atlas, Aviation, Battleground, Discovery, Family History, History, Maritime, Military, Naval, Politics, Social History, Transport, True Crime, Claymore Press, Frontline Books, Praetorian Press, Seaforth Publishing and White Owl

For a complete list of Pen & Sword titles please contact:

PEN & SWORD BOOKS LTD
47 Church Street, Barnsley, South Yorkshire, S70 2AS, UK.
E-mail: enquiries@pen-and-sword.co.uk
Website: www.pen-and-sword.co.uk

or

PEN AND SWORD BOOKS
1950 Lawrence Road, Havertown, PA 19083, USA
E-mail: Uspen-and-sword@casematepublishers.com
Website: www.penandswordbooks.com

Contents

Foreword ix
Glossary xi
Introduction by John Grehan xvii

Part I

The History of the Combined Operations Headquarters 1940-1945

Chapter 1	Early History and the Years Prior to the Outbreak of the Second World War 1
	The First World War, 1914 – 1918 5
	Between the Wars, 1919 – 1939 15
Chapter 2	The Early Days, June 1940 – October 1941 20
Chapter 3	Rapid Growth, October 1941 – March 1942 30
Chapter 4	Full Stature, March 1942 – October 1943 49
Chapter 5	The Raid on Dieppe, August 1942 63
	Preparation and Planning 63
	Lessons Learned from the Operation 70
	The Strategic Value of the Operation 73
Chapter 6	The Switch to the Mediterranean, North African and Sicily Campaigns 75
	North Africa, Operation "Torch" 75
	Sicily, Operation "Husky" 83
	The Lessons Learned from Operations "Torch" and "Husky" 87
Chapter 7	Preparation and Planning for the Invasion of North-West Europe 88
Chapter 8	Changes at C.O.H.Q. during 1943 and the Admiralty takes over the Assault Fleet 115
Chapter 9	The Development of the Plan for the Invasion of North-West Europe, Operation "Overlord" 126
Chapter 10	The Far East 131

Part II

The History and Development of Techniques and Equipment for Combined Operations

Chapter 11	The Story of Some Operations Affecting Development of Command and Control	138
Chapter 12	Training and Training Establishments	155
Chapter 13	The Landing Craft and Bases Organisation	169
Chapter 14	Commandos in Combined Operations	183
Chapter 15	Royal Marines in Combined Operations	193
Chapter 16	Close Support and Combined Operations Bombardment Units	203
	Close Support	203
	Combined Operations Bombardment Units	213
Chapter 17	Combined Operations Signals Organisation	225
Chapter 18	The Beach Organisation	240
Chapter 19	Combined Operations Organisation for Experiments, Trials and Development	260
	The Inter-Services Training and Development Centre (I.S.T.D.C.) up to April 1942	260
	The Experimental Section of C.O.H.Q. and the Combined Operations Development Centre (C.O.D.C.), April 1942 – August 1942	269
	The Directorate of Experiments and Staff Requirements (D.X.S.R.), later becoming the Directorate of Experiments and Operational Requirements (D.X.O.R.), August 1942 – October 1943	272
	The Combined Operations Experimental Establishment (C.O.X.E.), August 1942 – October 1943	281
	Reorganisation to Prepare for the War in the Far East, October 1943 to the end of the War	286
Chapter 20	The Development of Ships and Craft	294
	The Development of Ships and Craft up to 1940	295
	The Development of Landing Ships and Major Landing Craft	297
	The Development of Minor Landing Craft	313
Chapter 21	The Development of Material and Resources other than Ships and Craft	321
	Bridging the Water-Gap	321
	Mines, Beach Obstacles and their Clearance; Craft and Vehicle Recovery	334
	Miscellaneous Projects in Preparation for Operation "Overlord"	337

CONTENTS

Appendices

Appendix I	Raiding Operations: Directive to General Bourne	351
Appendix II	Chiefs of Staff Committee: Directive to the Director of Combined Operations	354
Appendix III	Chiefs of Staff Committee: Combined Operations and Raids	357
Appendix IV	Chiefs of Staff Committee: Directive to Adviser on Combined Operations	360
Appendix V	Operations on the Continent	364
Appendix VI	The State of the Combined Operations Naval Organisation	368
Appendix VII	Combined Chiefs of Staff, "Symbol" Conference	374
Appendix VIII	Points arising from "Rattle" Conference	379
Appendix IX	Directive to Adviser on Combined Operations	385
Appendix X	Combined Operations Organisation in India	388
Appendix XI	Formation and Composition – Small Operations Group S.E.A.C.	394
Appendix XII	Combined Operations Beach Organisation	402
Appendix XIII	List of Operation Code Names Showing Objective	406
Appendix XIV	Diary of Events and Important Dates	408

FOREWORD

This book is intended primarily for students of history, for use at staff colleges and similar establishments, and for the benefit of those interested in ministerial machinery for the direction of war.

It is a record of the activities of Combined Operations Command, its origins and functions, its ramifications in overseas theatres and, above all, its contribution towards winning the war. It is a record of solid material achievement and of significant advances in amphibious technique.

Combined Operations Headquarters was a novel element introduced into the British military organisation. It was begun and developed largely through the genius of Sir Winston Churchill and the outstanding ability and forcefulness of Admiral Mountbatten. The work it did to make amphibious operations possible and its value as a continuing contribution to our national defence organisation are set out for all to read. Even if we cannot anticipate the final verdict of history, we must try to establish the facts on which judgement should be based so that the distinctive contribution of Combined Operations will stand out with incontestable validity.

The main story is told in Chapters 1 to 10; the later chapters, which advisedly incorporate some repetition, may be regarded as supplementary to these and describe the varied activities in more detail.

Inevitably, the story of Combined Operations is largely an account of the efforts of Admiral Mountbatten and his team; his personal example and drive gave impetus to all and everything. The measure of achievement by him personally and by Combined Operations Headquarters can be gathered from the signal made to him which is recorded in Sir Winston Churchill's book *Triumph and Tragedy*:

"Today we visited the British and American armies on the soil of France. We sailed through vast fleets of ships with landing craft of many types pouring more and more men and vehicles ashore. We saw clearly the manoeuvre in process of rapid development. We have shared all secrets in common and helped each other all we could. We wish to tell you at this moment, in your arduous campaign, that we realise that much of this remarkable technique and therefore the success of the venture has its origin in developments effected by you and your Staff of Combined Operations. Arnold, Brooke, Churchill, King, Marshall, Smuts."

Amphibious Warfare Headquarters, 1956

GLOSSARY

Abbreviations and Short Titles

A.C.C.O.	Assistant Chief of Combined Operations.
A.C.C.T.	Air Commodore, Combined Training.
A.C.C.T.C.	Air Commodore, Combined Training Centre.
A.C.N.S.	Assistant Chief of Naval Staff.
A.C.N.S. (W.)	Assistant Chief of Naval Staff (Weapons).
A.C.O.	Adviser on Combined Operations.
A.C.S.E.A.	Air Command, South-East Asia.
A.D.O.D. (C.O.)	Assistant Directorate of Operations Division (Combined Operations).
A.D.X.O.R.	Assistant Director of Experiments and Operational Requirements.
A.L.F.S.E.A.	Allied Land Forces, South-East Asia.
A.L.C.	Assault Landing Craft.
A.L.O.s	Army Liaison Officers.
A.N.C.X.F.	Allied Naval Commander, Expeditionary Force.
A.O.C.O.	Air Officer, Combined Operations.
As.C.O. (I.)	Advisers, Combined Operations (India).
B.J.S.M.	British Joint Staff Mission.
B.L.O.	Bombardment Liaison Officer.
B.P.C.	Beach Protection Craft.
C.B.U.	Commander Bombardment Units.
C.C.B.	Combined Communications Board.
C.C.O.	Commodore, Combined Operations (from 16th October until 18th March, 1942).
C.C.O.	Chief Of Combined Operations (from 18th March, 1942).

C.C.O.D.C.	Commandant, Combined Operations Development Centre.
C.C.O.R.	Chief of Combined Operations Representative.
C.D.L.	Canal Defence Lights.
C.G.	Commanding-General.
C.G.S.	Chief of the General Staff.
C.-in-C. (F.C.)	Commander-in-Chief (Fighter Command).
C.-in-C. (H.F.)	Commander-in-Chief (Home Forces).
C.-in-C. (I.)	Commander-in-Chief (India).
C.-in-C. (X.F.)	Commander-in-Chief (Expeditionary Force).
C.M.S.D. (W.)	Chief of Military Staff Duties (Weapons).
C.M.S.F.	Co-ordinator of Ministry and Services Facilities.
C.N.C.T.	Captain, Naval Combined Training.
C.O.B.U.	Combined Operations Bombardment Unit.
C.O.D.C.	Combined Operations Development Centre.
C.O.H.Q.	Combined Operations Headquarters.
C.O.J.P.	Combined Operations Joint Planning.
C.O.L.O.	Combined Operations Liaison Officer.
C.O.P.P.	Combined Operations Pilotage Party.
C.O. (R.)	Combined Operations ("Rattle") Conference.
C.O.S.	Chiefs of Staff.
C.O.S.S.A.C.	Chief of Staff, Supreme Allied Commander.
C.O.X.E.	Combined Operations Experimental Establishment.
C.S.O.	Chief Signal Officer.
C.T.C.	Combined Training Centre.
C.T.E. (M.)	Combined Training Establishment (Mediterranean).
C.X.D.	Co-ordinator of Experiments and Development.
D.C.C.O.	Deputy Chief of Combined Operations.
D.C.O.	Director of Combined Operations.
D.C.O. (I.)	Director of Combined Operations (India).
D.C.O. (Air)	Director of Combined Operations (Air).
D.C.O.D.	Director of Combined Operations Development.
D.C.O.M.	Director of Combined Operations Materials.
D.C.O. (M.E.)	Director of Combined Operations (Middle East).
D.C.O. (Mil.)	Director Combined Operations (Military).
D.C.O. (N.)	Director Combined Operations (Naval).

GLOSSARY

D.C.O.S. (I.T.)	Deputy Chiefs of Staff (Inter-Service Training).
D.C.T.	Director of Combined Training.
D.D.C.O.	Deputy Director Combined Operations.
D.D. of P. (C.O.)	Deputy Director of Plans (Combined Operations).
D.D. Tanks	Duplex Drive Tanks.
D.D.X.O.R.	Deputy Director of Experiments and Operational Requirements.
D.D.X.S.R.	Deputy Director of Experiments and Staff Requirements.
D.M.O.	Director of Military Operations.
D.M.T.	Director of Military Training.
D.N.C.	Director of Naval Construction.
D.N.E. (C.O.)	Director of Naval Equipment (Combined Operations).
D.O.C.P.	Director of Combined Operations Personnel.
D. of S.T.	Director of Sea Transport.
D.R.O. (C.O.)	Directorate of Requirements and Organisation (Combined Operations).
D.U.K.W.	A Wheeled Amphibian.
	D. = Date of manufacture.
	U. = Utility.
	K. = Four-wheel drive.
	W. = Six wheels.
D.X.O.R.	Director of Experiments and Operational Requirements.
D.X.S.R.	Director of Experiments and Staff Requirements.
E.P.S.	Economic Planning Section.
E.T.O.U.S.A.	European Theatre of Operations, United States Army.
F.D.S.	Fighter Direction Ship.
F.D.T.	Fighter Direction Tender.
F.O.B.	Forward Officer Bombardment.
F.O.B.A.A.	Flag Officer British Assault Area.
F.O.C.R.I.N.	Flag Officer Commanding Royal Indian Navy.
F.O.I.C.	Flag Officer in Charge.
F.O.O.	Forward Observation Officer.

G. (1)	Staff Officer (Grade 1).
G.1.S.D.	Staff Officer, Grade 1, Staff Duties.
G.O.C.O.	General Officer, Combined Operations.
H.A.I.S.	Hartley Anglo-Iranian Siemens.
H.C.O.R.	Head of Combined Operations Research.
H.D.M.L.	Harbour Defence Motor Launch.
I.E.F.	Indian Expeditionary Force.
I.S.P.S.	Inter-Service Planning Staff.
I.S.T.D.C.	Inter-Services Training and Development Centre.
J.P.S.	Joint Planning Staff.
L.C.A.	Landing Craft Assault.
L.C.B.	Landing Craft Barge.
L.C.F.	Landing Craft Flak.
L.C.G. (L.), (M.)	Landing Craft (Large), (Medium).
L.C.I. (L.)	Landing Craft Infantry (Large).
L.C.M.	Landing Craft Mechanised.
L.C.O.C.U.	Landing Craft Obstruction – Clearance Unit.
L.C.P.	Landing Craft Personnel.
L.C.P. (L.), (M.), (S.)	Landing Craft Personnel (Large), (Medium), (Small).
L.C.P. (R.)	Landing Craft Personnel (Ramped).
L.C.P. (Sy.)	Landing Craft Personnel (Survey).
L.C.R.U.	Landing Craft Recovery Unit.
L.C.S. (M.)	Landing Craft Support (Medium).
L.C.S. (R.)	Landing Craft Support (Rocket).
L.C.T.	Landing Craft Tank.
L.C.T. (R.)	Landing Craft Tank (Rocket).
L.C.V. (P.)	Landing Craft Vehicle (Personnel).
L.S.C.	Light Support Craft.
L.S.D.	Landing Ship Dock.
L.S.G.	Landing Ship Gantry.
L.S.H.	Landing Ship Headquarters.
L.S.I. (H.)	Landing Ship Infantry (Hand-Hoisting).
L.S.I. (L.), (M.), (S.)	Landing Ship Infantry (Large), (Medium), (Small).
L.S.M.	Landing Ship Medium.
L.S.T.	Landing Ship Tank.

GLOSSARY

L.V.T.	Landing Vehicle Tracked.
L.V.T. (A.)	Landing Vehicle Tracked (Armoured).
M.A.W.	Military Amphibious Warfare Officer.
M.G.B.	Motor Gun Boat.
M.G.C.T.	Major-General, Combined Training.
M.G.C.T.C.	Major-General, Combined Training Centre.
M.G.R.A.	Major-General, Royal Artillery.
M.L.	Motor Launch.
M.L.O.	Military Landing Officer.
M.N.B.D.O.	Mobile Naval Base Defence Organisation.
M.O.L.C.A.B.	Mobile Landing Craft Advanced Bases.
M.T.6	Military Training – 6 (War Office).
N.A.W.	Naval Amphibious Warfare Officer.
N.A.W.1	Naval Amphibious Warfare Officer, Grade 1.
N.L. Pns.	Naval Officer Pontoons.
N.Q.P.	Naval "Q" Planners.
N.S.B.T.	Naval Section Bombardment Troop.
N.S.B.U.	Naval Section Bombardment Unit.
O.S.S.	Office of Strategic Services.
P.A.O.	Principal Administrative Officer.
P.C.	Port Construction.
PLUTO	Pipeline under the ocean.
P.O.L.	Petrol, Oil Lubricants.
P.P.I.	Plan Position Indicator.
R.A.C.	Royal Armoured Corps.
R.A.C.O.B.	Rear-Admiral, Combined Operations Bases.
R.A.L.B.	Rear-Admiral, Landing Craft and Bases.
R.A.P.	Round-Up Administrative Planning Committee.
R.E.M.E.	Royal Electrical and Mechanical Engineers.
R.F.A.	Royal Fleet Auxiliary.
R.I.N.V.R.	Royal Indian Naval Volunteer Reserve.
R.M.A.S.G.	Royal Marine Armoured Support Group.
R.M.B.P.D.	Royal Marines Boom Patrol Detachment.
R.N.B.S.S.	Royal Naval Beach Signal Section.

S.A.C.S.E.A.	Supreme Allied Commander, South-East Asia.
S.B.S.	Special Boat Section.
S.E.A.C.	South-East Asia Command.
S.H.A.E.F.	Supreme Headquarters, Allied Expeditionary Forces.
S.L.C.	Support Landing Craft.
S.N.O.C.O. (N.)	Senior Naval Officer, Combined Operations (Northern Bases).
S.N.O.L.	Senior Naval Officer, Landings.
S.O.A.G.	Senior Officer, Assault Group.
S.O.A.S.C.	Senior Officer, Assault Ships and Craft.
S.O.B.	Staff Officer, Bombardment.
S.O.E.	Special Operations Executive.
S.O. (P.)	Staff Officer (Personnel).
S.P. Arty.	Self-Propelled Artillery.
S.R.U.	Sea Reconnaissance Unit.
T.D.S.	Technical Data Section.
T.L.C.	Tank Landing Craft.
U.S.N.	United States Navy.
V.A.C.T.	Vice-Admiral, Combined Training.
V.A.C.T.C.	Vice-Admiral, Combined Training Centre.
V.C.C.O.	Vice-Chief of Combined Operations.
W.S.	Warning of Surface Craft.
X.S.A. 1, 2	Experimental Scientific Adviser 1, 2

INTRODUCTION

On 4 June 1940, as the last of the troops that had been rescued from Dunkirk were disembarking at Dover after being chased out of France and Belgium by Hitler's blitzkrieg, Britain's new prime minister, Winston Churchill, dictated a note to his military secretary, General 'Pug' Ismay: "The completely defensive habit of mind which has ruined the French must not be allowed to ruin all our initiative, 2 insisted Churchill. "It is of the highest consequence to keep the largest numbers of German forces all along the coasts of the countries they have conquered, and we should immediately set to work to organise raiding forces on these coasts where the populations are friendly. Such forces might be composed of self-contained, thoroughly equipped units of say one thousand up to not more than ten thousand when combined. Surprise would be ensured by the fact that the destinations would be concealed until the last moment."[1]

With that simple memorandum the concept of what would eventually be known as the Commandos was conceived, and they would be the main troops who would engage in the early Combined Operations.

Ten days later, the British Chiefs of Staff Committee appointed Lieutenant-General Alan Bourne RM to the post of 'Commander of Raiding Operations on coasts in enemy occupation, and Adviser to the Chiefs of Staff on Combined Operations'. From this small beginning grew the vast organisation that, on 6 June 1944, almost exactly four years to the day after Churchill's memo, launched the greatest amphibious operation of all time.

Combined Operations and Commando raids were to play a key role in Britain's war strategy. Britain intended to mount a war of attrition by blockading enemy ports, undertaking a heavy air offensive and engaging in every form of propaganda or deception that would

---

[1] Winston S. Churchill, *The Second World War, Volume II, Their Finest Hour* (Cassell, London, 1949), p.214.

confuse the enemy and undermine morale.² The Commandos' part was to strike at enemy-occupied posts and positions, anywhere, at any time, tying down disproportionately large numbers of enemy troops and further weakening enemy morale.

The new body, No.11 Independent Company, was raised on 14 June and ten days later it was engaged in its first operation, codenamed "Collar". On the night of 24/25 June, 115 men were landed from four boats on the French coast south of Boulogne-sur-Mer and Le Touquet. Their objective, officially, was to discover the nature of the German defences, and to bring back prisoners. In reality, it mattered little what they accomplished. It was the fact that British troops could land and attack the Germans which really counted, showing Hitler that Britain was far from beaten.

The men did in fact make contact with German troops. One group became embroiled in a firefight with five of the enemy, and a second group killed two German sentries at a point to the south of Le Touquet.

Though a minuscule affair in terms of the war at large, it enabled the Ministry of Information to issue a highly encouraging communique: "Naval and military raiders, in cooperation with the RAF, carried out successful reconnaissances of the enemy coastline; landings were effected at a number of points and contacts made with German troops. Casualties were inflicted on the enemy, but no British casualties occurred, and much useful information was obtained."³

There was but a little pause before the next raid was mounted, this time against Guernsey on the night of 14/15 July. German forces had occupied the Channel Islands at the end of June, and as early as 2 July, Churchill demanded that "plans should be studied to land secretly by night on the Islands and kill or capture the invaders". This was exactly the kind of exploit for which Combined Operations was created.⁴

Of the three groups which departed Devonport, one failed to reach land, another landed on the wrong island and the third, which reached the correct beach on time, failed to achieve any of its objectives of killing Germans, and destroying enemy aircraft and facilities at Guernsey airport. Heavy seas meant that the boats could not keep close inshore and when the men returned to the beach to reembark, they had to swim some 100 yards to reach the boats. Three of the men could not swim and had to be left behind. In total, four men were captured by the Germans.

---

[2] Brian Loring Villa, *Unauthorized Action, Mountbatten and the Dieppe Raid* (Oxford University Press, 1994), p.65.

[3] Nicholas Rankin, *A Genius for Deception: How Cunning Helped the British Win Two World Wars* (Oxford University Press, 2009), p.250.

[4] The National Archives, PREM 3/330/9.

INTRODUCTION

Churchill was far from impressed with this botched affair, and two days later Bourne was replaced by Admiral of the Fleet, Roger Keyes, in the newly named post of Director of Combined Operations.

This new force quickly began to take shape. Recruits were drawn from the Army, almost entirely men who had volunteered for undisclosed 'Special Duty' all of whom underwent rigorous physical and combat training. By March 1941 the Commandos were ready and the first large-scale Combined Operations raid of the war was undertaken against a small archipelago beyond the Arctic Circle and some 900 miles from Britain – the Lofoten Islands.

Complete surprise was achieved, and the Commandos destroyed important glycerine factories and military installations (resulting in the burning of an estimated 800,000 gallons of oil and petrol) and eleven ships were sunk. The Commandos returned to the UK with 315 volunteers for the Norwegian Navy and Merchant Marine, sixty Quislings and some 228 German prisoners.[5]

Further small operations were carried out, but the very limited nature and uneven achievements of the Commandos prompted criticism from Regular Army generals who claimed that they were largely a "waste of effort" and "could have been better done by a unit of the Field Army". The Army chiefs had never been very supportive of the independent nature of the Commandos, complaining that many of their best men were being lost to the Commandos. They believed that every division should be capable of mounting commando-style operations, not just specially organised units, and had already begun training regular battalions (including, incidentally, my father's battalion) at Inveraray in Scotland in amphibious operations.

Their arguments eventually received some backing from Churchill, and no operation could thereafter be mounted from the UK without the consent of General Sir Alan Brooke, Commander-in-Chief, Home Forces. Admiral Keyes did not like this one bit and so, on 27 October 1941, he was replaced as head of Combined Operations by Lord Louis Mountbatten.

Mountbatten intended to raise the raids to a much higher level and in December 1941, the first of Mountbatten's more ambitious enterprises, Operation "Archery", was undertaken. This was a raid on the Norwegian islands of Vågsøy (spelt Vaagso in the text that follows) and Måløy, which included more than 500 Commandos, a cruiser and four destroyers and, for the first time, the RAF. It was a genuine combined services operation. The main purpose of "Archery" was to destroy the

---

[5] Jon E. Lewis (Ed.), *SAS and Special Forces: True Stories of the Fighting Elite Behind Enemy Lines* (Robinson, London, 2004), p.209.

stores of fish-oil production facilities as the oil was used by the Germans in the manufacture of high explosives. At the same time a diversionary raid was undertaken against the Lofoten Islands by 300 men from No.12 Commando. Both missions included Norwegian troops.

Both attacks were a success, with much damage being done. They prompted the Germans to strengthen their garrisons in Norway, thus reducing the number of soldiers fighting on the critical Eastern Front against the Soviet Union.

Buoyed by these achievements, Mountbatten continued to plan. One of the next raids was undertaken in response to a request from the Air Ministry's Scientific Information Branch for a mission to be undertaken to seize as much instrumentation as could be carried back to the UK of a new machine at the German radar station at Bruneval, a small village on the French coast near Le Havre. The site was close to the cliff edge from which a path led down to an easily accessible beach. The raid was approved by Mountbatten and scheduled for late February.

Rather than launch the assault from the sea, Operation "Biting" was to see a radar specialist and 120 men of 'C' Company, 2nd Battalion The Parachute Regiment, dropped onto the cliffs close to the radar site. On the night of 27/28 February 1942, the small force landed between 1 and 2 miles from the installation. The Paras moved swiftly towards the radar station, encountering fire from German positions in a wooded enclosure some 300 yards to the north. But the radar operators fled. Using screwdrivers, crowbars and brute force, the British team ripped out or dismantled every important component. Flashlight photographs of the mechanism were taken, and notes and hurried drawings made.

The Paras then made their escape with all the material they could carry down to the beach for the pre-arranged rendezvous with the Royal Navy.

While more small raids were carried out, Mountbatten's Combined Headquarters team had laid down plans for the most ambitious raid so far – to destroy the dockyard facilities at Saint-Nazaire in France, the only port on the Atlantic coast with a dry dock able to accommodate the largest of Germany's battleships.

At 14.00 hours on 26 March 1942, the flotilla of Royal Navy vessels left Falmouth and began its long passage to the French port. The operation involved 345 Royal Navy personnel, 257 Commandos, a four-man medical team, three liaison officers and two representatives from the press, in total 611 men. The plan was for the old destroyer HMS *Campbeltown* to be packed with explosives and for her to be rammed into the dock gates. The Commandos would then disembark from the destroyer and accompanying motor launches, MGBs and MTBs to

INTRODUCTION

demolish the dock installations, searchlights, and gun emplacements. The destroyer would then be blown up.

Often described as 'the greatest raid of all', Operation "Chariot" was a resounding success. *Campbeltown* was driven into the lock gates and immediately the Commandos rushed ashore creating mayhem and destruction.

The plan had been to withdraw the troops from the port's Mole on motor launches and transfer them to destroyers waiting out at sea, but most of the small vessels had been destroyed. The Commandos were in a precarious situation for they were surrounded by water on three sides and German reinforcements were descending upon Saint-Nazaire. They could either surrender or attempt to escape. Being Commandos, however, surrender was not an option. They tried to escape but most did not make it.

It was not until noon that the explosives in *Campbeltown* ignited. The massive explosion ripped a huge gap through which the sea burst into the empty dry dock, taking part of the destroyer with it. The port was a scene of utter carnage. The remains of German personnel who had gone onboard *Campbeltown* were blown to the other side of the port. Human remains were found on the roof of the submarine pens across the basin and in other cases up to a mile away.

There was a high price to pay for the success of the raid. Out of 611 men who took part in the operation, 169 were killed and approximately 200 were captured and remained in captivity for the duration of the war. Five Commandos did, however, manage to make their way to the Spanish border where they travelled back home to the UK via Gibraltar.

Such was the magnitude of the destruction, the Germans were never able to use the dry dock again.

The next operation that involved Combined Ops was on a much greater scale than anything that had preceded it – and it was one where my father, Corporal Bernard Grehan of the 1st Battalion, Royal Scots Fusiliers, saw action for the first time.

It had become clear that Britain and, from December 1941, the United States of America, would one day re-invade Europe and come directly to grips with the Germans on the Continent. This would obviously involve a massive amphibious operation, one far beyond specialist formations such as the Commandos. Regular regiments of the Allied armies would have to be trained in amphibious warfare and this included the 29th Infantry Brigade. In May 1942, the brigade was the amphibious assault force which spearheaded the invasion of the French island of Madagascar.

Fearing that the French would allow the Japanese to station submarines in Madagascar which could attack Britain's communications with India, and Australia and New Zealand, a huge task force was assembled. As well as 10-15,000 infantry, artillery, engineers, light and medium tanks and support troops, Operation "Ironclad" included two aircraft carriers, one seaplane carrier, two battleships, six light cruisers, twenty-two destroyers and nineteen other craft, plus more than eighty aircraft. It was another resounding success, the troops seizing the main naval base of Diego Suarez and establishing a firm foothold on the island which eventually came under British control.[6]

The next Combined Operation was anything but a success. The raid upon the French port of Dieppe in August 1942 was a disaster. Of the 6,086 Commandos and infantry that landed at or on the flanks of Dieppe, a total of 3,623, constituting almost 60 per cent, were either killed, wounded, and/or taken prisoner. Enormous amounts of guns and equipment, including all twenty-nine Churchill tanks that were landed, were lost.

The Dieppe raid, Operation "Jubilee", marked the end of such cross-Channel operations until the D-Day landings in Normandy two years later. But Combined Operations Headquarters were actively involved in the invasion of French North Africa in November 1942, Operation "Torch", and the subsequent invasion of Sicily in the summer of 1943, Operation "Husky".

I was pleased to have found this monograph, sitting, long forgotten, in The National Archives at Kew as it details the organisation of the Combined Operations which is not found elsewhere. Rather than re-telling the raids and operations of Combined Ops, which have been the subject of many publications, this book explains how Combined Operations was set up and how it functioned. It also provides information on training, the development of landing craft and ships and other specialist equipment, as well as intriguing projects designed specifically for Operation "Overlord". This monograph has been reproduced here verbatim, other than minor changes and the omission of some less-valuable appendices. Where it states that appendices have been omitted, those were omitted in the original document.

I became a member of the Combined Operations Association in memory of my father and, when circumstances permit, I still wear the association tie adorned with the famous Combined Ops symbol of the three armed forces. I wear it with immense pride.

John Grehan,
March 2022.

---

[6] The story of Operation "Ironclad" can be found in my book, *Churchill's Secret Invasion: Britain's First Large Scale Combined Offensive, 1942*, (Pen & Sword, Barnsley, 2013).

Part I

The History of Combined Operations Headquarters 1940-1945

Chapter 1

EARLY HISTORY AND THE YEARS PRIOR TO THE OUTBREAK OF THE SECOND WORLD WAR

Before the days of mechanised warfare, there was little or no necessity for special ships or craft for the conduct of amphibious operations. Generally, the ships and boats of early times were small and well suited to land infantry on beaches; in fact, a sheltered beach was for thousands of years a perfectly normal landing place for the shipping of the world, except at the largest and most important ports. Moreover, defensive fire power in the modern sense of the word being practically non-existent, the invader was at no great disadvantage compared with the defender.

The defender was at a very real disadvantage because, even supposing his intelligence correctly indicated the actual point of landing, communications difficulties would prevent him from deploying his land forces quickly enough to forestall the descent by a more mobile force from the sea upon the selected beach. Even if the defender overcame this difficulty, his weapons probably gave him no special advantage in a battle against the invaders on the beach itself. One solution to this dilemma of the shore-bound Commander was to take to the sea, thus removing the disadvantage of relative immobility ashore, and fight a land battle at sea. This solution recurred to succeeding defenders of England throughout the Middle Ages and, where properly executed, was invariably successful. Where the anti-invasion fleet was not organised in time, or not provided at all, and the highly organised professional forces of the foreigner or usurper could get ashore, the problem of raising adequate land forces in time, and of defeating him, assumed almost impossible proportions. Examples may be taken from the history of Norse and Danish invaders, William the Conqueror himself, the landing of William of Orange, and the startling initial successes of the '15 and the '45 Rebellions.

The basic military organisation of the Shires of Saxon and even Norman England, enabled English forces to be defeated piecemeal. Only a wealthy and strong monarch could produce a large enough force and effect a sufficiently rapid concentration to defeat the invader once ashore. Harold, having defeated an invading force in Yorkshire, marched south to meet death and defeat at the hands of his new enemy, not on the beaches, but as a result of a common ruse in a set battle behind Hastings. Whoever had been the victor, he would have found himself and his army in an era of fierce local, almost parochial patriotisms, at odds with the English populace. Not because he was foreign but because he had an army, and all armies of either side then lived, with notable lack of tact and self-effacement, off the countryside. To secure the political fruits of a victory, the first essential in England was to get rid of the victorious army, which left the victor dangerously exposed to the machinations of his defeated foe.

The unique military and governmental qualities of the Norman kings and many of their successors enabled them, firstly to appreciate correctly these facts, and secondly to produce the organisation and discipline either to turn them to their advantage or to suppress the more serious manifestations of a widespread and unruly local patriotism. It is only since 1066 that England had enjoyed a relative immunity from invasion. Any serious force, unmet or undefeated at sea, would, once ashore, take the country. In the long period of absence, for political reasons, of an adequate standing army in peace, absolute domination of the narrow seas and acknowledgement of this by gun salutes was no mere piece of arrogance. It was the military prerequisite of the existence and independence of England herself.

Later British Predominance in Maritime and Amphibious Warfare
This local domination of the seas had far-reaching results. Military forces at sea with bigger ships, better sailing and handling techniques, and the cannon, created the Royal Navy. What had started as the only tactical solution to a hitherto insoluble military problem produced

conditions whereby England turned this disadvantage of hers into, as it were, a disadvantage of the whole world *vis-à-vis* herself.

Although British rule abroad had declined in the twentieth century, it should not be supposed that the actual basic British advantage has thereby for this reason declined, or that the United States will always find it convenient, desirable, or even possible in the face of other defence commitments, to bear indefinitely the Trident she has apparently assumed from us. Few informed American Officers will deny, though many normally well-informed British Officers are ignorant of the tremendous British contribution in general experience, material, design and staff organisation to the initial American amphibious efforts, particularly in Europe during the 1939-45 War. The exact extent of that contribution, will, it is hoped, be clear from the succeeding chapters.

Factors Contributing to British Predomination Prior to 1914

The problems of British military and naval Commanders, except for once or twice a century when a particular continental threat reached its peak, were, until 1914, not so much how to prevent invasion of the United Kingdom as how to get ashore on an enemy coast; and very often even less how to get ashore as where to go ashore.

For something over three centuries, the military capabilities of shore and maritime artillery and the musket remained approximately the same. It was true that this placed the well-sited defender of a port or beach at a good tactical advantage, other things being equal, compared with the attacker. However, the British found that very often other things were by no means equal and, from the time that Drake singed the King of Spain's beard at Cadiz until the Dardanelles, the British took calculated risks, pitted their ships if strictly necessary against shore forts and batteries, landed their infantry in open boats, risking musket fire with an accurate range of only some 100 yards, and thus captured the ports and bases required for subsequent military operations.

It did not always succeed, but it was "an operation of war". Further, although gunpowder had cast the die slightly in favour of the defender, the improved mobility of, say, the eighteenth-century man-of-war more than counter-balanced this. The most well-organised post-horse and eighteenth-century continental military road system, although it might give news in Paris of an attack on Toulon slightly quicker than the news went from Ghent to Aix some two centuries before, would not move the infantry to its defence one whit quicker.

Therefore, until 1914, an amphibious assault was largely a matter, firstly, of good intelligence, for it would be an obvious folly to attack a port which superior numbers of first-class enemy infantry could reach before our own forces were well ashore. Secondly, it was a matter of surprise. Both tactical and strategical surprise were largely in the hands of the attacker and the comments of the Hon. Sir Thomas Mackenzie, later in this chapter, on the ill-advised bombardment of the outer Dardanelles forts in November 1914, are relevant. Thirdly, it was a matter of concentrating sufficient conventional forces for the task and making a normal professionally good job of it. Little special material was required and, if it was, it could be improvised satisfactorily locally.

Limited Requirement for Specialised Equipment

The immediate object of an amphibious operation was usually the capture of a port, unless a withdrawal was contemplated when the operation came into the category of what is now known as a raid. A port having been captured, further operations were either of a purely military or of a transport character.

There are, however, historical exceptions to the rule that no special material was required; special improvised material has been used for large scale operations, notably the crossing of the Hellespont by Xerxes in 492 B.C. In this case, pontoon equipment supported by inflated goat skins formed a bridge for the passage of many thousands of men. It is evident that such a plan, which in the event turned out extremely successful, could not have achieved its object under assault conditions and, for this reason, nearly all the early Commanders avoided the issue by marching round the sea obstacle, after the style of Hannibal in the 2nd Punic War, 218 B.C.

During the Middle Ages, the horse came into prominence as the decisive factor in winning land battles, culminating in the supreme achievements in the twelfth century of Genghis Khan and his Golden Horde, which consisted of some 250,000 mounted men manoeuvred under a single command. Nevertheless, neither Genghis nor anyone else attempted amphibious operations, other than river crossings, on any scale with horses between the twelfth century and the present time. Over the whole of this long period, horses were only transported across the sea as part of a build-up and thus became the subject of a transportation problem rather than one of amphibious warfare.

It follows, therefore, that, until World War I, amphibious operations were concerned chiefly with the landing of infantry and artillery without providing for movement thereafter, until a bridgehead had been firmly established. These requirements were met, usually adequately, with the craft already available to the naval forces of the combatants.

The lead in amphibious warfare tactics had been held by Great Britain in the last two and a half centuries, mainly as a result of the use of sea power to conduct numerous small wars. Continental powers were not interested.

Up to 1913, the War Office held all the resources for landing horses and indeed a considerable part of the floating equipment for landing guns, but neither the horse boats not the flats were at all suited for use under assault conditions and they were never intended to be used. After 1913 the Admiralty assumed responsibility, not only for landing troops as heretofore, but also for all ancillary equipment required by the Army. Financial provision to enable amphibious landings to be made efficiently was not made despite this, and the Navy had ready in 1914 only the methods employed by Nelson and his predecessors, with the added disadvantage of having fewer suitable shallow draught vessels available.

Prior to The First World War the last amphibious operations conducted against a major power in Europe had been those carried out by the British and French against the Russians in the Crimea and the basic conditions were the same as had obtained for three centuries. Although this campaign has become famous chiefly for tactical mistakes such as the Charge of the Light Brigade, and logistic and medical difficulties of an acute kind, the basic fact remains that the Allies were able to land where and when they liked, ports were captured and the main battles took place after, not on, landing. Russia, with all her vast manpower, could not garrison her sea coasts.

The First World War, 1914 – 1918

World War I brought the first really basic changes in the factors affecting the application of amphibious strategy and tactics for three centuries. It was the first war fought to attrition by modern industrial states with the material that their factories and productive genius could deliver. It saw the horse being replaced by the internal combustion engine and the arrival of air power. Further, well-developed continental railway systems, operating on interior lines of communication, enabled the Central powers to move forces to the defence of any threatened sector of their sea perimeter almost as quickly as, or quicker than, the maritime powers could build up their attack by sea. Worse still, modern communications, coupled with a good intelligence system, and assisted by a lack of appreciation of what this meant in terms of security and cover plans for future operations, destroyed any great probability of tactical or strategic surprise.

The last straw was the defensive capability of well-handled small arms of the type which had come into the hands of the armies of the world since 1875. The Boer, at the turn of the century, and the Briton, in 1914, used the rifle brilliantly in defence against superior numbers. Continental armies made up in quantity what they often lacked in quality, but before 1915 dawned on the battlefields, the machine-gun was master. The development of artillery was scarcely less spectacular, but the real achievement here lay in the tremendous industrial organisation which enabled such vast quantities of shells and guns to be produced relatively quickly and cheaply.

For the first time in history, not only could the defender obtain information of the attack from the sea in time, but he could move forces, adequate to contain and finally obliterate the bridgehead, quicker than his opponent and he could lay the attackers in bloody heaps on the beach itself or leave their wooden boats, full of the wounded and dead, drifting and sinking before their helpless Commanders.

After forty years, this is easier to see in its proper perspective; but men were not lacking who saw, in part, the problems involved at the time. The following is an extract from the autobiography of Admiral Sir Sydney Freemantle, which deals with a period when he was Head of the War Division at the Admiralty in 1910:

> The functions of the Navy were unfortunately at that time considered very much in isolation from those of the Army, and still more so from those of other government departments, such as the Foreign Office and Board of Trade, which were concerned with National Defence. Our only mutual contact with the War Office was through a naval captain who enjoyed the title of 'Naval Assistant to the Director of Fortifications', but who had become in practice a liaison officer for general purposes between the Admiralty and the War Office. But at the instance of the War College, much interest had been aroused in the study and practice of combined naval and military operations, and during my term of office I found myself the Chairman of two joint Admiralty and War Office Committees, to which was given the work of preparing, respectively, the first handbooks of 'Combined Operations' and of 'Regulations Governing the Entry of Defended Ports in the Time of War'.
>
> The War Office, which had anticipated the Admiralty by many years in the establishment of a General Staff, had given much more attention to these subjects than we had, and they sent very fully qualified representatives to the Committee. We all appreciated the importance, and indeed the urgent necessity of the work before us, and realised our responsibility in the breaking of new ground, so there were no inter-Service jealousies (which in my experience

are of the rarest occurrence in spite of the imaginative references to them in the Press and by lay writers), and the work proceeded apace.

The Handbook of Combined Operations dealt, according to our instructions, with tactical subjects only, and resolved itself therefore into a full detail of the arrangements for the disembarkation of troops on a hostile coast, opposed or otherwise. We discussed the historical examples of such disembarkation, some successful and some unsuccessful and I think those to which we paid the most attention were those at Louisburg, Aboukir, and of Lord Raglan's army in the Crimea. Our book was published in due course, was tried out in an exercise on a fairly large scale at Clacton, and with some few alterations subsequent to that experience formed the tactical basis on which our landing at Cape Helles was effected by 1915.

Historically a unique situation had thus arisen in 1914 as regards amphibious landings. The remainder of this chapter will now briefly trace the history of the Dardanelles campaign in its amphibious aspects and the period between the two world wars.

The Gallipoli Campaign

The outstanding amphibious landing of the 1914-18 War was at the Gallipoli peninsular in 1915. It involved an opposed landing on beaches which were heavily defended and, although it did not attain its aim of enabling the Allied Fleets to enter the Sea of Marmora, it provides us with important lessons worth careful study.

Prior to the entry of Turkey into the war on the side of Germany on 1st November, 1914, the problem of forcing a passage for the Fleet into the Marmora had always been considered to be a full-scale amphibious operation. Plans had been prepared for this but no other preparation or provision of material had been attempted.

Two days after Turkey declared war, a force of Allied warships bombarded the outer forts for a short period. This force was covering the possibility of a break-out by the German battle-cruiser *Goeben* and the light cruiser *Breslau*, which had taken refuge from our warships in Turkish waters just prior to the Turkish declaration of war.

Inception

At the end of December 1914, the Russians appealed to the British Government for help. They were being hard pressed by the Germans and were afraid that the Turks would move against them.

Lord Kitchener, the Secretary of State for War, replied that no troops were available but promised a demonstration against the Turks. Accordingly on 2nd January, 1915, he asked the First Lord of the Admiralty (Mr Winston Churchill) if the Navy could carry out this demonstration.

Lord Fisher, the First Sea Lord, strongly urged an attack on the Dardanelles if it could be carried out at once. Thus, on 3rd January, 1915, the First Lord signalled the Admiral Commanding the Squadron (Vice-Admiral S.H. Carden) at the entrance to the Dardanelles: "Do you consider the forcing of the Straits by ships alone a practicable operation? It is assumed older battleships fitted with mine-bumpers would be used, preceded by colliers as mine-bumpers and sweepers. Importance of results justifies severe loss. Let me know your views."

To this, Admiral Carden replied he did not consider the Dardanelles could be rushed but that they might be forced by extended operations with a large number of ships. In reply to a further signal from the Admiralty, the Admiral proposed that the operation should be undertaken in four phases: (1) Total reduction of the forts at the entrance; (2) Clear the defences inside the Straits up to the Narrows; (3) Reduce the defences at the Narrows; and (4) Clear the minefields, then advance into the Marmora.

War Cabinet Decision

On 13th January, the First Lord explained this plan to the War Cabinet. The latter decided that, "The Admiralty should prepare for a naval expedition in February, to bombard and take the Gallipoli peninsula with Constantinople as its objective".

Reading this, it would appear that the War Cabinet had in mind some form of combined operation if the words "take the Gallipoli peninsula" meant anything at all. However, on 23rd January, the War Council decided that it was to be a purely naval operation and orders were sent our accordingly.

In *Military Operations Gallipoli*, Vol. I, we find: "The decision thus arrived at marks the first great landmark in the Dardanelles campaign. In an effort to satisfy the urgent need of diplomacy, Britain's fleet was to attempt, without the aid of a single soldier, an enterprise which in the earlier days of the war both the Admiralty and the War Office had regarded as a military task. The operation would moreover be many times more difficult than in the early days of the war. The Germans had already had six months in which to improve the defences of the Straits, and the minefields were continually growing. The enterprise was perhaps still capable of accomplishment, if the Government were ready to face the inevitable loss of ships. This was the opinion of the German Admiral von Usedom who knew better than anyone the strength and the weakness of the fortress and the capacity off its defenders. But there must be no indecision, no faltering, no delay. Nothing but iron will and grim determination, both at home and on the spot, could snatch the hazardous victory."

Bombardment
On 20th February, 1915, a bombardment of the outer forts was carried out by battleships of the Allied Fleets. The Turks held their fire until the ships engaged the forts at close range, and were then only silenced after further heavy shelling.

Provision of Troops
The first indication to the Admiral that a combined operation was under consideration in England was information that the General in Egypt had been ordered to hold 10,000 troops in readiness for service at the Dardanelles. Even at this stage no attempt to organise a combined operation was made.

The bombardment was repeated on 25th February, with excellent results. By the late afternoon it appeared that the outer forts were incapable of further resistance and the minesweepers proceeded to sweep the minefields. At the same time demolition parties landed from the inshore squadron to blow up any undestroyed guns.

Military Opinion
On 1st March, General Birdwood arrived at the entrance to the Dardanelles and conferred with the Admiral. His opinion was that "he did not believe that the Fleet alone could force the Dardanelles" and he reported this home.

Lord Kitchener at this time had no intention of undertaking a serious landing and on 4th March, we find him telegraphing to General Birdwood:

"From the Admiral's estimate he expected the Fleet to reach the Marmora by the 20th. The Anzac Corps, the French Division and the Royal Naval Division would be assembled at Mudros by the 18th, but there was no intention of using these troops to take the Gallipoli peninsula unless the Admiral subsequently found it impossible to get through without them .... Extensive operations on the peninsula were not to be undertaken without further orders from home and in this case more troops would probably be sent out from England."

Sweeping Operations
During the first week in March, the Fleet continued the bombardment and the sweeping operations. The latter were not successful owing

to the inexperience of the personnel, the strong current through the Straits and the enemy fire which was mostly from concealed mobile batteries that could not be silenced.

Appointment of General Sir Ian Hamilton as Military Commander

On 14 March, the First Sea Lord sent a telegram to the Admiral stressing the necessity for haste and concluding:

"Sir Ian Hamilton leaves to-night to command the Army and will be with you on Tuesday the 16th."

It is interesting to recall some of the instructions given by Lord Kitchener to General Sir Ian Hamilton:

> 1. The Fleet have undertaken to force the passage of the Dardanelles. The employment of military forces on any large scale for land operations at this juncture is only contemplated in the event of the Fleet failing to get through after every effort has been exhausted.
>
> 3. Having entered on the project of forcing the Straits there can be no idea of abandoning the scheme. It will require time, patience, and methodical plans of co-operation between the naval and military Commanders. The essential point is to avoid a check, which will jeopardise our chances of strategical and political success.
>
> 4. This does not preclude the possibility of minor operations being engaged upon to clear areas occupied by the Turks with guns annoying the Fleet, or for the demolition of forts already silenced by the Fleet. But such minor operations should be as much as possible restricted to the forces necessary to achieve the object in view, and should as far as practicable not entail permanent occupation of positions on the Gallipoli peninsula.
>
> 6. Under present conditions it seems undesirable to land any permanent garrison or hold any lines on the Gallipoli peninsula. Probably an entrenched force will be required to retain the Turkish forces in the peninsula and prevent reinforcements arriving at Bulair, and this force will naturally be supported on both flanks by gun-fire from the Fleet. Troops employed on the minor operations mentioned above (para. 4) should be withdrawn as soon as their mission is fulfilled.
>
> 7. In order not to reduce forces advancing on Constantinople, the security of the Dardanelles passage, once it has been forced is a matter for the Fleet, except as in para. 6 with regard to Bulair. The occupation of the Asiatic side by military forces is to be strongly deprecated.

Change in Naval Command

The naval operations received a setback when Admiral Carden, who had been responsible for the plan, became ill and was relieved by Vice-Admiral Sir John de Robeck. However, the latter was in complete accord with the plan and told the Admiralty so, adding that the operations would proceed, as arranged, on 18th March. On 17th March, a meeting took place at which Admiral de Robeck told Generals Hamilton and d'Amade (the French Commander) that he was confident he could force a passage through the Straits without any large-scale military assistance.

Naval Attack, 18th March

On 18th March, the naval attack took place. At first all went well. The outer forts were silenced, and the Allied Fleet entered the Straits and engaged the forts at the Narrows.

Late in the afternoon, first the French *Bouvet*, then the *Indefatigable*, *Irresistible* and finally the *Ocean* struck mines. The *Indefatigable* managed to beach herself on Tenedos Island but the remainder sank.

The line of mines that caused this damage was one laid by the Turks on the previous night in the area where they had seen our ships operating on previous occasions. These losses seem to have had a profound effect on Admiral de Robeck.

The Combined Attack

To quote from General Sir Ian Hamilton's diary: "On 22nd March, at 10 a.m. we had another conference on the *Queen Elizabeth* ... The moment we sat down de Robeck told us that he was now quite clear he could not get through without the help of all my troops. Before we went on board, Braithwaite, Birdwood and I agreed that whatever we landsmen might think, we must leave the seamen to settle their own job, saying nothing for or against the land operations or amphibious operations until the sailors themselves turned to us and said that they abandoned the idea of forcing the Straits by naval operations alone. They have done so. The fat (that is us) is fairly in the fire ..."

Here, at one stroke, what had started off to be a naval operation had become a combined operation of the first order, but the military force which had been sent was not trained in amphibious warfare, neither were the transports nor the store ships loaded tactically for an assault landing.

With the Admiral's concurrence, General Sir Ian Hamilton had already given orders that the whole military force was to be shipped back from Mudros to Alexandria so as "to shake them out there and re-ship them ready for anything." This was a most glaring example of lack of planning and shows how little study had then been devoted to Combined Operations.

The First Landings, 25th April, 1915

The Army were back at Mudros and ready for a landing by the middle of April. The interval had been used by the Navy to carry out further bombardments and in getting their minesweeping flotillas worked up.

A few practice landings were carried out by the Army at Mudros while waiting for suitable weather to make a landing on the peninsula possible. This did not occur until 25th April, when the assault took place.

Certain of the landings were done in the dark and succeeded with little loss, but the landing at Sedd el Bahr ("V" Beach) was carried out in broad daylight. Here the troops were held up and suffered heavy causalities but, in the end, and by the greatest heroism, a foothold was established. It was here that the famous *River Clyde* was beached full of troops who disembarked from her over a line of barges. This was the first attempt to get troops ashore from a beached ship with the "water gap" bridged. The losses inflicted by the Turks, with small arms fire from entrenched positions, on our troops while they were wading ashore, left a very lasting impression on all who witnessed the scene.

Suvla Bay Landings, 6th August, 1915

The fact that the Turkish forces were still in possession of Achi Baba, a hill that commanded a clear view of all our beaches and entrenched positions, made it impossible for our troops to advance up the peninsula. This was reported to the authorities at home, who decided to send reinforcements. The plan of the Commanders on the spot for the employment of these new troops was to use them in landings well to the northward of the positions gained on the toe of the peninsula and thus take the enemy in the rear. If successful, the Turks, at the south end of the peninsula, would have been cut off by an advance made across the narrow part of the land between Suvla Bay and Maidos.

With all the previous experience to guide them, most careful plans and preparations were made for this operation. Secrecy was well maintained and the landing took place on the night of 6th/7th August. From the point of view of a combined operation this was a success. Little opposition was encountered and the troops got ashore in fairly good order and with few casualties. But there were later misfortunes. Once ashore, the troops did not advance at once and exploit success; the water supply failed and no attempt was made to dig for it. It was now clear that, had this been done, and even allowing for the delay, success might have been achieved. The Turks only had a force of about 3,000 men, some of them Gendarmerie, to oppose our advance.

In this operation, new formations which were untrained in amphibious warfare were used.

Dardanelles Commission Report

The Dardanelles Commission reported on this landing as follows: "The operations at Suvla were a severe trial for a force consisting of troops who had never been under fire, but we think that after taking into consideration and making every allowance for the difficulties of the attack and the inexperience of the troops, the attack was not pressed as it should have been at Suvla on 7th and 8th August, and we attribute this in a great measure to a want of determination and competence in the Divisional Commander and one of his Brigadiers."

The final report of the Dardanelles Commission contains the following finding:

> Viewed as a military enterprise which was undertaken not as a surprise, but after ample warning had been given to the enemy of the probability of a land attack, we are of the opinion that, from the outset, the risk of failure attending the expedition outweighed its chances of success. The conditions of the problem so far as we can judge, were not fully investigated in the first instance by competent experts, and no correct appreciation of the nature and difficulties of the task involved was arrived at. In the absence of such appreciation the authorities responsible for the expedition confidently expected that military action on the peninsula would be short and decisive and the Turkish guns dismounted. The force, which had been landed, would then be available for such operations in the vicinity of Constantinople as might seem appropriate.

A supplementary report by the Hon. Sir Thomas Mackenzie provides, what further experience had proved, a sound summary.

> In my opinion, which I express with all deference, the forcing of the Dardanelles was a practicable proposition had the authorities approached the problem with the recognition of the nature and extent of the difficulties that confronted them and made adequate provision and exhibited the necessary strength of purpose to carry the operation through to the desired end. History has demonstrated and expert opinion supported the view that a combined naval and military attack would ultimately offer the only chance of a favourable issue. The authorities should, I consider, have launched this combined attack only after thorough preparation, and I regard the preliminary bombardment of the outer forts on 3rd November, 1914 – ordered by the Admiralty without consultation with the War Council – as an almost irreparable mistake. Its effect was to draw

the attention of the Turks to the possibility of an attack in force on the peninsula, and there is no doubt it prompted them to make good use of the time which intervened between the November bombardment and the military landing on 25th April, 1915, in the way of improving their defences.

The Blocking of Zeebrugge

Although the blocking of the canal at Zeebrugge, on the night of 23rd April, 1918, was a naval operation in that it was carried out by ships, the diversion on the Mole was entrusted to the Royal Marines; and the Royal Air Force were to carry out a raid with the aim of distracting attention from the real operation. Unfortunately, owing to thick mist and rain the latter were unable to play their part.

Many lessons, which bear on the conduct of Combined Operations, may be learned from this operation.

The aim was clear cut: to block the entrance to the Bruges canal. The landing on the Mole was a diversion to distract the attention of the enemy from the ships as they passed the guns on the breakwater. Special craft and appliances were prepared for the assault. Secrecy was meticulously observed. Finally, the whole organisation was under the command of one-man, Vice-Admiral Keyes, who, as the Chief of Staff to Sir John de Robeck at the Dardanelles, had bitter experience of what a landing in the face of opposition entailed.

Despite the fact that the withdrawal added one more complication to the normal hazards of such a plan, the operation was a success. Losses were comparatively light although the attack was made on the most heavily fortified part of the coastline occupied by the Germans.

A few illustrations of the special preparations necessary for these operations are emphasised hereunder in support of the general principles for the conduct of Combined Operations which will emerge in later chapters.

First and foremost, all the ships and craft used in the operation were specially adapted for their tasks. Secondly the officers and ratings, all volunteers, were assembled about two months prior to "D" Day. On board ship or ashore, they were specially trained, under conditions of the most stringent secrecy. Finally, all training conformed to a carefully thought-out plan prepared by the Admiralty planning staff over which Admiral Keyes presided before being appointed to take command at Dover.

The haphazard methods of Gallipoli were completely absent. The object was clear, full preparation was made, every detail was rehearsed and above all, secrecy was preserved.

Students of combined operations are well advised to study the orders for the operation and to see what provision and pre-vision were put into plan. The detailed work was immense and every eventuality that was foreseeable was considered.

Between the Wars, 1919-1939

The end of the First World War and the prospect of a long peace brought the usual heedless reduction in armament expenditure. The "Ten-Year Rule" (i.e., that no war could take place for ten years) was in force and the money voted to the Services was only sufficient to preserve a static efficiency. There was very little research and experiment.

The war experience of the Army imbued all ranks with a fearful regard for the defensive power of small arms fire. As for Combined Operations, it was regarded as suicidal to approach a defended beach in ships' boats, the only craft available. Further, the awful prospect of having to get out of these open boats to land on an enfiladed beach was not considered, quite rightly, to be "an operation of war." In spite of the successful application of principles in the Zeebrugge operation, it was some time before military thought looked further than the carnage at "V" Beach, Gallipoli, to the deficiencies of material and planning which were its cause, rather than the actual superiority of defensive fire power.

The First Landing Craft

About 1922, the question of the design of a Motor Landing Craft (short title M.L.C.) arose. After considerable discussions as to which Service would have to pay for it, a prototype was constructed; it was a flat-bottomed craft with a square bow and stern and propelled by water jet propulsion.[1] This form of propulsion was designed to avoid damage to screw propellors when the craft grounded. Its unloaded weight was approximately 20 tons.

In the summer of 1927, this craft underwent trials but was not a great success. With the wind astern it made about 6 knots, but the engines were so noisy that all chance of tactical surprise in the assault was extremely doubtful.

In 1930 there were three of these craft in existence.

In 1935 Italy declared war on Abyssinia. This brought amphibious warfare to the fore again as landings in the Red Sea and even in Italy were considered. All that happened was that the existing landing craft

---

[1] A petrol engine drove a centrifugal pump which produced a jet of water and thereby pushed the craft ahead or astern depending upon how the jet was directed.

had bullet-proof plating fitted to the coxswain's position and an order was placed for six more landing craft but it was not until the winter of 1938 that these were delivered.

The Sino-Japanese War
Late in 1937, the Japanese carried out amphibious operations at Tientsin and Shanghai. Our naval forces, who were in the vicinity, saw, much to their surprise, a Landing Craft Carrier (a ship of about 10,000 tons) arrive and launch landing craft over her stern, two at a time. Here was the youngest naval power showing us the way both in design and technique. That great thought and ingenuity had been given to Combined Operations by the Japanese, was clearly shown.

Manual of Combined Operations
Since 1921, the Staff Colleges of the three Services had spent a month of their courses studying Combined Operations, this month usually terminating in a week at Camberley.

The study of Combined Operations was thus kept alive and a manual was gradually complied which was published as an Inter-Service Confidential Book in 1925. This superseded the four paragraphs in the 1914 reprint of the Field Service Regulations. Later editions of the Combined Operations manual were published in 1931 and 1938.

Naval Proposals for the Formation of a Committee and a Centre
On 22nd February, 1936, the Director of the Royal Naval Staff College wrote a letter on the subject of Combined Operations to the Admiral President of the Naval War College.

The document reveals that the Staff College fully realised the importance of the part the Navy would have to play in any amphibious expedition and frankly stated that, as a sea power, the predominant partner in any operation was the Navy. As such the Navy should take the initiative for the design and provision of craft in the organisation required for mounting an overseas expedition and in the supply of any special equipment required.

In forwarding the letter, the Admiral Resident of Greenwich College suggested that a permanent committee should be set up to consider the subject and that a small training and development establishment of the three Services should lead to "real and rapid progress."

Combined Operations Sub-Committee is Appointed
In a paper dated 30th November, 1937, the following note by the Secretary to the Chiefs of Staff Committee appears:

The Deputy Chiefs of Staff agreed, *inter alia*: (ii) That a sub-committee of the Deputy Chiefs of Staff sub-committee should be appointed:

Admiralty – Assistant Chief of the Naval Staff or his representative.

War Office – Director of Military Operations and Intelligence or his representative.

Air Ministry – Deputy Chief of the Air Staff or his representative.

With the following terms of reference:

(a) To study inter-Service exercises and to present collated and agreed reports on the lessons arising from them.

(b) To make recommendations for the study of problems in connection with inter-Service operations and to arrange for the production of schemes for appropriate exercises.

(c) To make recommendations for the development of equipment for inter-Service operations.

(d) To keep under review the Manual of Combined Operations and to draw up amendments to it when required.

This was followed on 9th February, 1938, by a memorandum by the Deputy Chief of the Imperial General Staff supporting the proposal for the formation of an Inter-Services Training and Development Centre. This is a careful and well-thought-out document and brought the whole matter into a very proper perspective.

The Inter-Services Training and Development Centre (I.S.T.D.C.)

After further correspondence, the Deputy Chiefs of Staff in a paper, dated 2nd May, 1938, put forward concrete proposals, the summary of which was:

(1) that the centre should be located at the Portsmouth Division, Royal Marines, Eastney;

(2) that it should consist, initially, of a Captain R.N. (*i.d.c. or p.s.c.*) as Commandant, a General Staff Officer (2nd Grade) and a Wing Commander, with a Royal Marine Adjutant (preferably with a Staff College qualification and with experience with Mobile Naval Base Defence Organisation) and a small civilian clerical staff;

(3) that personnel and equipment should be borrowed as occasion demands from the three Services;

(4) that the Admiralty should be responsible for the administration of the Centre on the same lines as the Imperial Defence College, preliminary arrangements for its establishment being made inter-departmentally between the three Service Departments;

(5) that, if possible, the Centre should be at work before July 1938.

This resulted in the appointment of officers to the Inter-Services Training and Development Centre which was formed at Fort Cumberland, Eastney, Portsmouth.

As one of their duties, the officers witnessed a combined exercise carried out by a cruiser squadron and some destroyers at Slapton Sands. Here, the soldiers were landed in open boats with muffed oars. No progress in technique had taken place since the Crimea.

The staff of the new establishment soon got down to work and laid the foundation for the design of new craft and ships.

Other problems that quickly came under review were contained in a paper dated 2nd June, 1938, which instructed the I.S.T.D.C. to examine:

> The design of craft suitable for landing tanks.
> Beach organisation.
> Beach roadways.
> Floating piers.
> Headquarters ships.
> Landing of tanks.
> Dropping troops by parachute.
> Landing water and petrol in amphibious operations.
> Use of amphibian tanks.
> Methods of crossing under-water obstacles
> Maintenance of supply from the air.
> Provision of landing punts for coastal raids.

State of Readiness, 1939

An interesting paper dated 30th June, 1939; summarises the position as regards amphibious operations just before the outbreak of war as follows:

> To sum up:
>
> (a) With the material at present available it is impossible to stage any landing operation on a hostile shore, with a force of a brigade or more, sooner than six months from the time that the order is given.
>
> (b) In order to reduce this minimum period of preparation to three months the equipment detailed in para. 4 above would have to be provided in peace time at an estimated cost of £344,200.
>
> (c) Even if the equipment referred to in (b) above were provided, the provision of suitable ships to act as transports and landing craft carriers would be extremely difficult unless special carriers were to be constructed.

Notes – Para. 4 makes the following recommendations:

> (a) The construction of 18 small landing craft, 2 support craft, 12 large landing craft and the armament and equipment for 2 additional support craft in addition to those already built or on order.
>
> (b) The construction of 30 sets of gravity davits and winches. It would be necessary to prepare drawings for the installation of the davits and winches in the 14 ships considered suitable for carrying landing craft.
>
> (c) The construction of 2 new M.T. ships (sanction for the building of which had recently been received) in such a manner that they are also suitable for landing M.T. on a beach.
>
> (d) The construction of float undercarriages for three squadrons of aircraft of the type required for landing operations.

The Annex 1, para. 13 of this paper reads as follows:

> There are at present 6 heavy motor landing craft in Home Waters and 3 at Malta. These craft are not very suitable for use in an open anchorage nor are they capable of carrying the maximum load required by the Army. A new type is in design. It would be possible to build the 18 heavy craft required in 16 weeks. There would be no saving in time if only 12 were ordered.

By 1939 therefore, the problems left to us in 1918, which had then only been successfully solved in respect of a relatively small raid on Zeebrugge, had scarcely been touched. We had no means of putting an army ashore in the face of opposition and the technical problems of a greater rate of build-up than the enemy, had scarcely received any attention at all. Any question of tactical or strategic surprise appeared hardly worthy of consideration as any likelihood of it being achieved was remote.

The events of 1940 were to compel rapid and unconventional solutions to all these problems.

Chapter 2

THE EARLY DAYS, JUNE 1940-OCTOBER 1941

After the defeat of the Allied armies in France and the Low Countries in May 1940, it was apparent that the only way of returning to the offensive, other than by bombing, was by means of amphibious operations. In Europe, at this juncture, the policy could only be one of raiding the occupied coasts with the aim of causing the enemy to disperse his forces and equipment uneconomically. Further, the successful execution of a raid is excellent for morale at a time when a country must be strategically on the defensive.

On 14th June, the Chiefs of Staff authorised the appointment of a Commander of Raiding Operations and Lieutenant-General A.G.B. Bourne, who was Adjutant-General, Royal Marines at the time, was given the post.

The directive issued to this officer shows that he was not only appointed Commander of Raiding Operations, but also Adviser to the Chiefs of Staff on Combined Operations.

General Bourne was given operational command of the Independent Companies (later to be known as Commandos), which the War Office had raised under Brigadier C. Gubbins for guerilla operations in Norway. He was also informed that he would have a number of parachutist volunteers placed at his disposal and other irregular Commandos then being raised.

The Inter-Services Training and Development Centres (I.S.T.D.C.) were also placed under his command and he was ordered to expedite the development and production of special landing craft and equipment.

General Bourne set up his headquarters at the Admiralty and an officer of the Royal Air Force was attached to assist with the parachute troops. The latter were just being formed and in a report of his available forces made in October, 1940, mention is made of 100 parachutists under training. Later, when the number expanded, the parachute troops were removed from his command and became the First Airborne Division.

General Bourne's staff at first consisted of one Captain R.N. (Deputy); one Captain R.N. (Intelligence); one Captain R.N. (Operations); and the Army also had a representative.

The Situation – June, 1940

On taking up his appointment, the Commander of Raiding Operations found that his resources were sparse.

On 15th February, 1940, a report had been submitted by the I.S.T.D.C. stating that 90 minor landing craft were built or being built in the United Kingdom with the expected completion date of December, 1940. In this report they asked for certain facilities in the Hayling Island area and as a result Northney Camp (later H.M.S. *Northney*) was requisitioned and subsequently commissioned on 15th June.

In June, 1940, Operation "Collar" was carried out in the Pas de Calais area using adapted craft based on H.M.Y. *Melisande* in the Hamble River. Planning was carried out in the War Office (M.O.9) under Lieutenant-Colonel Dudley Clark, R.A., who had raised the Independent Companies. Some assistance was afforded at this stage by Admiralty and A.C.O. Responsibility for "Collar" was transferred from M.O.9. to the Commander of Raiding Operations on 17th June, 1940, and the raid was staged on 24th/25th June, 1940. This operation proved conclusively that improvised equipment was of no value in the kind of warfare upon which we were now embarking. Further, for this operation the craft were manned by crews inexperienced in running landing craft, an arrangement which was found to be also unsatisfactory. It was realised that special personnel would have to be trained for the purpose. As a result, a six weeks' course of basic naval training in the handling and maintenance of landing craft was inaugurated at H.M.S. *Northney*, on the completion of which the naval personnel were transferred to H.M.S. *Tormentor*, at Warsash, which was commissioned as a raiding base.

Director of Combined Operations (D.C.O.) Appointed

On 17th July, 1940, Admiral of the Fleet Sir Roger Keyes was appointed as Director of Combined Operations (D.C.O.) in succession to General

Bourne. This appointment was made by the Prime Minister, as the following letter shows:

> Prime Minister to General Ismay and Sir Edward Bridges.
>
> I have appointed Admiral of the Fleet Sir Roger Keyes as Director of Combined Operations. He should take over the duties and resources now assigned to General Bourne. General Bourne should be informed that owing to the large scope now to be given to these operations, it is essential to have an officer of higher rank in charge, and that the change in no way reflects upon him or those associated with him. Evidently, he will have to co-operate effectively.
>
> I formed a high opinion of this officer's work as Adjutant-General, Royal Marines, and in any case the Royal Marines must play a leading part in this organisation. Pending any further arrangements Sir Roger Keyes will form contact with the Service Departments through General Ismay as representing the Minister of Defence.

No new directive was issued at this time.

Headquarters moved to Richmond Terrace

Towards the end of August, 1940, Admiral Keyes moved his headquarters to Richmond Terrace and took with him his staff, with the exception of the Naval Operations Section. This latter section remained in the Admiralty and became an Assistant Directorate of the Operations Division (A.D.O.D.(C.O.)) and, under different titles, remained in existence throughout the war.

Almost at once it became clear that it was necessary to have a material section in the Admiralty to deal with combined operational matters and, in consequence, a Department was set up under the Director of Naval Equipment (D.N.E.(C.O.)). This worked under the Controller and in double harness with A.D.O.D.(C.O.). These two entities worked virtually as one organisation in the closest co-operation until well after the end of the war.

The move to Richmond Terrace was decided upon because whilst General Bourne's headquarters remained in the Admiralty, it was looked upon as an Admiralty Division. By having his headquarters outside the Admiralty, Admiral Keyes ensured that the Combined Operations Organisation would be regarded correctly as a Joint Inter-Services Establishment.

The First Combined Training Centre

It soon became apparent that combined training facilities would have to be established. A reconnaissance was made and, as a result, the

THE EARLY DAYS, JUNE 1940-OCTOBER 1941

Combined Training Centre was set up at Inveraray in August, 1940, with Vice Admiral Hallett in charge. (The detailed story of this and other training establishments is given in Chapter 12.)

Forces Available

In July, 1940, the forces under the command of the Director of Combined Operations amounted to about 500 men of the Commandos and 750 men of the Independent Companies: the craft amounted to 15 L.C.A., 4 L.C.M. and various other minor craft.

The Lessons of the Dakar Expedition

At the beginning of August, 1940, a proposal to instal General de Gaulle and his Free French Forces in Dakar came up for consideration. The operation, known as "Menace", was to be supported by British naval and military forces.

The initial plan for the operation was made at short notice by the Inter-Services Planning Staff (the forerunner of the present J.P.S.) and was submitted to the Chiefs of Staff on 9th August, 1940.

The Chiefs of Staff rejected their plan principally because it envisaged British forces leaving Dakar in the care of Free French forces after an unopposed landing, whereas the Chiefs of Staff now required a plan for the capture and holding of Dakar against opposition, British Forces being withdrawn only after General de Gaulle had a firm hold on the country. The Force Commanders, who had been hastily appointed, were now told to produce a plan to suit the new requirement. This was submitted to the Chiefs of Staff on 21st August, 1940. The force sailed from Liverpool on 26th August for Scapa Flow from where, after only four days training, they left for West Africa. Much detailed planning had thus to be completed on the voyage to the assault area.

The story of the operation, which was a failure, is given here to show only the two main lessons learned, as they had an important impact on future developments. These were: (1) The need for a joint organisation to co-ordinate the planning and control of such operations (i.e., Combined Operations Headquarters with executive powers); (2) The need for special Headquarters Ships from which command of an operation could be exercised, as opposed to using a supporting warship which might become involved in a purely naval action.

Raiding Forces Employed in Anti-Invasion Role from September until the end of 1940

During the latter half of 1940, after the return of the forces from the abortive attempt on Dakar, a number of other operations were being considered in Combined Operations Headquarters. Chief among these were "Brisk" (the capture of the Azores), "Shrapnel" (the capture of the Canary Islands) and "Workshop" (the capture of Pantellaria).

These operations competed for the available resources at the disposal of the D.C.O. There was great uncertainty as to the necessity of any or all of the projects and this naturally led to confusion and much wasted effort.

In September all the available Commandos and Independent Companies were placed under the command of the Commander-in-Chief, Home Forces, for an anti-invasion role. This prevented, for the time being, any further raids being carried out because these forces were not released to the D.C.O. until the end of the year, when the direct threat of invasion had passed.

Responsibility for Re-Planning and Control of Operations, Early 1941

On 22nd January, 1941, the Operations Section of Combined Operations Division in the Admiralty was transferred to Training and Staff Duties Division, of which it became a Deputy Directorate, but this made no difference to its relation with D.C.O. on the one hand and the rest of the Admiralty machine on the other. In particular it still retained its close relation with Director of Naval Equipment (Combined Operations), the material implementation department and with the personnel departments.

Other features, however, were introduced during this period, which sowed the germs of instability in the Combined Operations Organisation. For the prospective operations against the Atlantic Islands, it was soon found necessary to establish a Senior Naval Officer Landings (S.N.O.L.) afloat, under the orders of the Force Commander in the mounting area (Clyde), mainly to administer the ships and craft, whilst the Force Commander was planning in London.

When Inveraray was selected as the mounting area, a situation arose where there were two authorities in the same area, one the Vice Admiral Combined Training Centre, and the other the S.N.O.L. who were both engaged in training and the development of amphibious material, then in its infancy. Furthermore, since the Force Commanders' planning teams were not concerned with the long-term requirements and were out of touch with the Combined Operations Section of the Admiralty, considerable friction occurred.

This was not assisted by the fact that the staffs, both in Inveraray and London, were endeavouring to carry out the same functions. Each staff was composed of two Sections, one being concerned with the long-term programme and the fitting of the short-term requirements into it to the best possible advantage, and a second, dealing only with specific operations, which was disinclined to accept any limitations affecting their interests from the long-term planners.

New Directive for the Director of Combined Operations (D.C.O.), March, 1941

The directive issued to General Bourne in June 1940, had never been replaced. Now that the scope of Combined Operations had become larger, the Chiefs of Staff decided that a new directive was necessary for Admiral Keyes. Accordingly on 14th March, 1941 a new one was issued.

This document gave to the D.C.O. the duty of training the Special Service Troops and landing craft personnel. The Independent Companies, which had been raised by the War Office, were renamed Commandos in November, 1940, and ten such Commandos were formed into five Special Service Battalions each of two Commandos. The new directive charged him with the initiation of operations by these Special Service Troops and the responsibility for the planning and execution of raiding operations "which involve not more than 5,000 men."

He was to advise the Chiefs of Staff on the technical aspects of landing operations and be present at their meeting when "that part of the plan is under discussion."

The administration of the Special Service Troops was to be carried out by the War Office, but no mention was made about any ships or craft which might have to be employed in combined operations. Hence it was presumed that the Admiralty undertook this duty in the normal course of business, although the carriers and landing craft for raiding purposes remained under the operational command of the D.C.O.

The Inter-Services Training and Development Centres were also under his command.

Operations Planned in Spring, 1941

The main preoccupation of the Directorate of Combined Operations, at this period, was the plan for the occupation of the Canary Islands. This operation had many names, but it was generally known as Operation "Pilgrim".

The training of the forces required for the operation was carried out in the vicinity of the Combined Training Centre at Inveraray. The transports, as they became available, were used for the accommodation of the forces and a considerable amphibious expedition came into being.

This force was capable of a three Brigade lift and was the beginning of the Overseas Assault Force, which subsequently developed.

Delays were the rule, not only in the fitting out of the ships, but also in their delivery of the landing craft. Building schedules in the bases were never kept, resulting in so much confusion that it was well-nigh impossible to work to any fixed programme.

Operations in the Mediterranean

On 1st February, 1941, certain Special Service Battalions were again split up and Commandos, as units, once more came into being, Nos. 7, 8 and 11 Commandos being despatched on that date to the Middle East. Two Middle East Commandos Nos. 50 and 52 were added, together with a Brigade Headquarters, and the whole was known as "Lay Force", under the command of Brigadier Laycock.

In April and May, 1941, this force, which had only recently arrived on the station, distinguished itself in Greece and Crete. With its special training and the ships and craft it used, it established a name for itself. Unfortunately, the pressure of events was such that it got diverted from its proper role and was divided up and used mainly in evacuation duties, a reversal of the task for which ships and craft had been intended.

The Commandos themselves performed constant and valuable service as rearguards. Mainly equipped with Bren Guns, rifles, tommy-guns and knives, but without mortars, they were unable to force the enemy to deploy and were constantly surrounded or cut off in their efforts to impose a check but contriving to escape by night.

Planning of Long-Term Requirements

Planning for long-term requirements and a return to the Continent had not yet taken shape, but the Admiralty had started a programme for the entry of 115 ratings into the Landing Craft Organisation every three weeks. This was determined by the number of landing craft which were expected to come forward and not with an idea of a great overall expansion. It was a modest beginning, but it sowed the seeds for the eventual large expansion which took place.

There is little to record with regard to the development of the facilities during this period. The work on the bases and training centres progressed slowly in continuation of the plans already made. H.M.S. *Quebec*, the naval wing of the C.T.C. Inveraray, came into use and Dorlin House (near Acharacle) was in constant use as the Advanced Training Establishment for raiding craft and Commando troops.

Raids on the French Coast

Admiral Keyes was very anxious to carry out small raids on the French Coast, which were in accordance with his directive. Craft and personnel for these small operations were always hard to obtain because of the claims made by the Force Commanders of the Overseas Assault Force for every available trained officer and rating; the completion of the assault force ships with landing craft and crews had to be met first.

However, towards the end of June, 1941, one L.C.A. with a trained crew became available at Northney and one of the Commando units provided a raiding party. It was a beginning.

It was decided that when wind, tide and moon served, a raid was to be carried out on the enemy shore at Ambleteuse, near Cape Gris Nez.

The mounting of this operation was quite a problem in itself. The crew and raiding party had to carry out their training and rehearsals at Northney. The craft was then sailed under her own power from Portsmouth to Dover, where she came under the orders of the Flag Officer-in-Charge. He, in his turn, provided the escort and towing craft and decided in consultation with D.C.O. on the best date for the raid. Meanwhile, the Commando troops were sent by road to Dover where they were accommodated in the Barracks.

The raid was carried out on 27th July, 1941, the object being the capture of prisoners and the reconnaissance of beaches. The assault landing craft was observed when some 250 yards from the beach, but the party made a successful landing. Three men scaled the cliff but firing broke out before they could be joined by the remainder. The three men returned to the beach where the remainder of the party had been under fire and the whole force then re-embarked. The raid did not succeed owing to the alertness of the defenders.

Small Operations

Between July and November, five small raids had been planned and carried out by the Special Service Troop under the D.C.O. They had, however, never exceeded the lift available in four L.C.A., and then were carried out under the same general conditions as that employed in the Ambleteuse raid. The object of the raids, with one exception, was the reconnaissance of enemy beaches and defences and the capture of prisoners, the exception being the raid against a four-gun battery position, east of Houlgate. Three of the raids resulted in information being obtained, some Germans being killed and the body of one brought back. On the other two occasions landings were made but, owing to the alertness of the enemy, the objective was not achieved.

Occupation of Canary Islands, Operation "Pilgrim"

During May and June, 1941, the question of whether Operation "Pilgrim" should be carried out or not was constantly under review by the War Cabinet. As planned, it required a dark night and so, if postponed for one month, the force could be brought to longer notice. This enabled the personnel embarked to be granted leave by watches.

It also enabled certain alterations, which were found necessary as the result of experience in exercises, to be made to the transport. It was in this way that a large number of the staff requirements for assault ships and craft were embodied in the specifications which were used later in the war. There had been little previous experience which could provide a guide and the method of trial and error was a hard school.

Gradually the standard of training improved until it was considered that a full-scale exercise employing the whole force could be carried out. In consequence the Force Commanders designate for Operation "Pilgrim" (Lieutenant-General H.G. Alexander and Rear Admiral L.N.K. Hamilton) put forward proposals which were eventually approved. The exercise was given the name "Leapfrog".

Exercise "Leapfrog"

The plan for this exercise was that the whole force should sail from the Clyde area and carry out a full dress rehearsal at Scapa Flow.

After the orders had been prepared and the whole force was on the point of departure, H.M.S. *Keren*, an L.S.I.(L), developed defects which prevented her sailing. She was accordingly adjudged a casualty and the force sailed without her.

The passage from the Clyde to Scapa Flow was made without incident and, early on the morning of 10th August, the convoy anchored in their assigned berths in Scapa Flow.

The weather conditions for the exercise were by no means ideal but were not sufficiently bad to necessitate postponement. In spite of careful training, the mistakes of the past were again apparent. Movement across the beaches was slow, success was not exploited and there were delays in landing the vehicles.

This exercise confirmed a recommendation made after the Dakar operation; the need for a properly equipped Headquarters Ship. This, together with the necessity for better internal communications in the assault ships, were matters that were at once taken up by the staffs of the Services. It was not, however, until March, 1942, that the first ship, H.M.S. *Bulolo*, was put in hand for conversion into a Headquarters Ship.

Another important lesson learned was the requirement for a combined Headquarters where the Force Commanders and their staffs could work together.

Action as the result of "Leapfrog"

On completion of Exercise "Leapfrog", the whole force returned to the Clyde and the ships were taken in hand for such alterations as could be effected within the notice at which the force was kept.

The D.C.O. was critical of the conduct of "Leapfrog" and found himself in disagreement with the Chiefs of Staff, who, largely as a result of their investigations into the shortcomings of the exercise, had recommended to the Prime Minister that the D.C.O. should be issued with a new directive. The Prime Minister endeavoured to persuade Admiral Keyes to accept this proposal, but the latter, finding the terms contrary to his own beliefs, was unable to do so.

In consequence, Admiral Keyes was succeeded by Captain Lord Louis Mountbatten, who was assigned the title of Adviser on Combined Operations and given the rank of Commodore 1st Class. The latter's appointment was dated 14th October but, as he was in command of H.M.S. *Illustrious's* refitting in U.S.A., he did not take up his appointment until 27th October, 1941.

Chapter 3

RAPID GROWTH, OCTOBER 1941-MARCH 1942

Directive to Adviser on Combined Operations (A.C.O.)
The Chiefs of Staff issued a new directive to Commodore Lord Louis Mountbatten on his arrival. It laid emphasis on his position as Adviser on Combined Operations (A.C.O.) whilst he retained command of the training establishments and schools of instruction. He was responsible for all technical information supplied to the Force Commanders, both as to training and planning, and it was incumbent on them to seek his help on all occasions.

The Special Service troops were still under command and could be used for small operations which he might mount.

The General Situation in October, 1941
When Commodore Mountbatten took up his appointment, the general situation with regard to Combined Operations was as follows:

(1) The total staff at his headquarters amounted to twenty-three including typists and messengers. There were no active service naval officers, no regular air force officers and no signals officers.

(2) The three Landing Ships Infantry (*Glengyle, Glenearn* and *Glenroy*) with a full complement of Special Service troops and landing craft were in the Suez Canal Zone. A Combined Training Centre had been set up there, at Kabret, but the ships and troops were not being employed in duties for which they were intended.

(3) The Force earmarked for Operation "Pilgrim" was in the Clyde area, standing by for the capture of the Canary Islands. They were continuously employed on training and developing techniques.
(4) Both the Naval and Military Wings of the C.T.C. at Inveraray were full and plans were being made for increased facilities, notably for training tank crews and larger infantry formations.
(5) The Future Operations Planning Sections of the Joint Planning Staff were just beginning their study of the problems involved in the re-entry into the Continent and the Commander-in-Chief, Home Forces was thinking in terms of the invasion of the Continent rather than a German invasion of the U.K.
(6) The concentration on current operational requirements at the expense of the long-term build-up of forces for the invasion of the Continent began to abate, and with this a better sense of proportion was being achieved.
(7) An examination of the number of ships and craft required for the return to the Continent showed clearly that the building facilities in this country were unequal to the task and, in consequence, the Admiralty were on the point of sending a mission to the United States to lay the problem before the authorities there. This mission took with them the designs for the L.S.T. Mark II, and the Landing Ship Dock.
(8) The question of the intake of personnel into Combined Operations, their accommodation and training was a difficult problem for both the Admiralty and the Combined Operations Organisation.

Control of Combined Operations Forces

During November, 1941, the projected increase in combined operations ships, craft and personnel clearly called for a central authority around which all combined operational activity could be focused. This was represented to the Chiefs of Staff by Commodore Mountbatten and they in their turn directed him to submit proposals.

Accordingly on 3rd December, 1941, Commodore Mountbatten recommended that with the expansion of the Combined Operations Command, involving greater numbers of ships and craft and suitable bases, certain new appointments should be made for their proper control. Rear-Admiral Horan of Combined Operations Headquarters was appointed Rear-Admiral Landing Craft and Bases (R.A.L.B.) and Commodore Warren was appointed Senior Officer Assault Ships and Craft (S.O.A.S.C.), both under Commodore, Combined Operations.

He also recommended the formation of teams of operational staff officers to be lent to Force Commanders to help in planning operations and providing technical advice.

The Chiefs of Staff approved the recommendations which were promulgated in a confidential order acquainting the three Services of the Combined Operations Organisation. They also approved certain amendments to the directive to the Adviser on Combined Operations.

Commodore Mountbatten was to be known as Adviser on Combined Operations (A.C.O.) when advising the Chiefs of Staff or Force Commanders and Commodore Combined Operations (C.C.O.) for administrative command and command of raids.

This new directive was issued on 9th December, 1941. A complete reorganisation of the staff and the work at C.O.H.Q. followed, together with the institution of an Inter-Services Planning Staff, and a purely Naval Administrative Department.

In administrative matters, C.C.O. acted as a retail authority and the Combined Operations Section of the Naval Staff at the Admiralty handled the wholesale business. For example, the Combined Operations Section would calculate the total manpower requirement to provide the forces approved by the Chiefs of Staff and would obtain approval for the necessary programme of personnel intake into combined operational training establishments. C.C.O. would work out the training programme and progress the personnel through the training establishments and control them thereafter. The same applied on the matériel side, in which the Directorate of Naval Equipment, Combined Operations (D.N.E.(C.O.)) was the Admiralty Department concerned.

The relationship between C.O.H.Q., the Combined Operations Section of the Naval Staff and D.N.E. (C.O.) was so close during the ensuing period of rapid expansion that it established an interesting example of two teams working closely together but owing allegiance to different Chiefs. The arrangements might have broken down on divided loyalties, had these existed, but the desire to work together for a common end and the fact that the pace was so fast, meant that there was no time for consideration of anything other than meeting essential requirements or solving the immediate problem in hand. New ground was being broken daily and, as no precedent existed for guidance, a solution had to be found quickly by the few concerned round a table. This decision was immediately acted upon on the assumption that covering approval would be forthcoming in due course.

In the end it resulted in C.C.O. initiating new proposals and the Admiralty Departments progressing them through the Admiralty machine.

RAPID GROWTH, OCTOBER 1941-MARCH 1942

The Administrative Problem

The transfer of ships and training bases to C.C.O. in December, 1941, meant that under the Rear-Admiral Landing Craft and Bases (R.A.L.B.), a Naval Administrative Staff came into being whose duty it was to carry out the day to day naval administration of the Combined Operations Command. It was divided into Personnel, Material and Ships and Craft Sections. For the first three months, most of their time was taken up with the provision of the necessary base and accommodation facilities for the personnel of the command. The story of how these bases were developed is told in Chapter 12.

Raids on the Norwegian Coast

Towards the end of September, 1941, the Chiefs of Staff decided that operations against the Germans occupying the Norwegian coast were to be carried out as soon as possible.

As the ships originally destined for these special operations, namely the *Queen Emma* and the *Princess Beatrix*, had been sent to Freetown for Operation "Pilgrim", the only ships Commodore Mountbatten had available were four of the small Belgian type assault ships, Landing Ships Infantry, Small (L.S.I.(S)). Some doubt was expressed by certain Admiralty Departments as to their suitability for carrying out operations so far afield but this was quickly overcome. In fact, all the ships of this class were subsequently employed in both the Sicilian and Normandy landings and acquitted themselves well.

The eventual plan was that one force should establish a raiding base in the Lofoten Islands and, operating from there, should disrupt the sea communications between Northern and Southern Norway (Operation "Anklet"), while another force was to raid the port and anchorage of Vaagso (Operation "Archery").

For the Lofoten Islands, the two Infantry Assault Ships (L.S.I.(S.)) *Prince Albert* and *Princess Josephine Charlotte* were to be used with No. 12 Commando, Special Operations Executive (S.O.E.) and a small detachment of Norwegian Forces, whilst the *Prince Charles* and *Prince Leopold*, with No. 3 Commando, were detailed for the Vaagso operation.

Reorganisation at C.O.H.Q.

Concurrently with the planning and execution of these operations, the reorganisation of the staff and work at C.O.H.Q., in order to comply with the altered directive, was taking shape.

Broadly speaking, the reorganisation divided the Staff into Operations and Administration Groups. In the former were found the

Intelligence Planning and Training Sections, while the latter consisted of a Naval Staff which dealt with the personnel, material and ships and craft movements. There was a Communications element in both groups.

All the sections of the Operations Group, which are discussed in greater detail below, were inter-Service. This team was later completed with the arrival of United States officers in 1942, thus setting up an historic precedent as the first integrated, Inter-Allied, Inter-Service staff.

Intelligence Section

Quite logically, the first section to be formed was the Intelligence Section. This came into being on 16th December, when Wing Commander The Marquis of Casa Maury, R.A.F.V.R. became the Senior Intelligence Officer. Working under him was an Inter-Services Staff consisting of officers from all three services. They collected the available intelligence from the Intelligence Staffs of the Services Ministries and co-ordinated it so that the most up-to-date joint intelligence was always available to the planners or Force Commanders.

The intelligence collected and co-ordinated was passed to the Target Committee, who recommended the suitable objectives for raids to the planners.

Planning Section

The Planning Section at first dealt with all plans for projected operations or raids, but it was soon found necessary to introduce a form of specialisation. This consisted of dividing the section into those who were principally concerned with long-term or invasion plans, and those whose chief concern was the planning of raids.

Training Section

Both naval and combined training was in the hands of the Vice-Admiral, Combined Training Centre (Vice-Admiral T.J. Hallett) and assisting him was Major-General, Combined Training (Major-General J.S. Drew), the Army representative. At first, their headquarters was at Inverary but it was soon decided to transfer it to Largs, where the headquarters of the Expeditionary Force had been established. They also had offices at C.O.H.Q.

As the result of Exercise "Leapfrog", Lieutenant-General H.G. Alexander had recommended the setting up of an establishment for training a force close to the combined training areas on the west coast of Scotland. C.C.O. enthusiastically supported this and the Hollywood Hotel at Largs was taken over and used throughout the war as the

Headquarters, not only for the Expeditionary Force, but also for the officers controlling the Combined Operations activities on the west coast of Scotland and in the Firth of Clyde.

The Communications Section

In November, 1941, a Committee, consisting of officers of all Services, was sitting at the War Cabinet Offices whose directive was to investigate and report to the Chiefs of Staff on "Communications in Combined Operations." This subject had in the past received little attention but was now one of paramount importance. This Committee was presided over by Captain A.E. Scott-Moncrieff, R.N. and was then at work on its first report on W/T equipment required.

Early in December, 1941, Commander M. Hodges, R.N., was appointed to C.O.H.Q. as Signal Officer Combined Operations. About the same time Captain Scott-Moncrieff was appointed elsewhere so, as a matter of course, Commander Hodges relieved him as Chairman of the Committee. It was soon realised that the scope of the signal work at C.O.H.Q., both in connection with the signals of the growing Combined Operations Organisation and in the development of combined operations communications technique (then practically non-existent), was far too great for one officer. It was therefore decided, with the Chiefs of Staff approval, that the Committee should move to C.O.H.Q. to complete its work and that the naval, military and air force members should join C.O.H.Q. staff under the Chairman, who became Chief Signal Officer, Combined Operations.

During the early days of 1942, the Committee produced reports on Support Communications required in combined operations, Cyphers and Codes, Line Communications with reference to large scale operations on the Continent, and Radar in combined operations.

The Raiding Authority for North-West Europe

The question of command in raids was one to which considerable thought was given. Never before in our history had the question of command in three elements been considered. When, in October, 1941, Commodore Mountbatten took over from Admiral Keyes, a situation had arisen which had no precedent and consequently had to be resolved.

The position then was that C.O.H.Q. controlled, administered and trained all the specialised amphibious forces in the United Kingdom, including the Special Service Brigade (Commandos), and all assault shipping and landing craft. The licence to raid the coast of France and the Low Countries was held by the General Officers Commanding-in-Chief of the various Home Defence Commands. Just as each of the latter had his own sector for the British coast to defend, so also had he a sector of the enemy-occupied coast to mark. The Generals regarded the hostile coast as the front line facing their armies across a watery no-man's-land which they had no means of crossing.

The only area in which Combined Operations forces could operate without infringing on the prerogatives of the Army Commanders was the Norwegian coast.

Far-reaching changes became necessary at the beginning of 1942 when it was decided, as a part of the strategy of the war, that a series of raids, becoming progressively greater in scale, should be undertaken.

In the system finally evolved in May, 1942, C.C.O. became the mounting authority for all raids in North-Western Europe. His functions were as follows:

(1) To prepare an outline plan.
(2) To obtain the approval of the Chiefs of Staff.
(3) To appoint Force Commanders with the approval of the Chiefs of Staff.
(4) To allocate and assemble the requisite specialised forces.
(5) To assist and advise the Force Commanders in the preparation of the detailed plan.
(6) To provide any additional intelligence or equipment which the Force Commanders required.
(7) To assist and advise during the rehearsal and training stage.

On first being appointed, the Force Commanders always worked at C.O.H.Q. where they produced the detailed plan based on the outline plan. As soon as this was completed, they moved to the mounting area to superintend the training and rehearsals and to produce the operation orders.

When it came to the execution of a raid, C.C.O., from the beginning, took the view that the Naval Commander-in-Chief, in whose area the raid lay, must retain overall command in that area and of all ships and craft, including landing ships and craft, and escorts therein. Therefore, although C.C.O. was responsible for making and presenting to the Chiefs of Staff the inter-Service plan for a raid and for supervising the preparations and rehearsals, the final executive order was given by the Naval Commander-in-Chief. For really important occasions C.C.O. always went to the Naval Commander-in-Chief's Headquarters and the decision was made, either to sail or not to sail, jointly.

It was also the responsibility of C.C.O. to arrange any independent air action other than the normal air protection organised by the Combined Area Headquarters. For instance, C.O.H.Q. had to arrange the whole of the air action at Vaagso and the independent bombing of St. Nazaire when the latter port was raided.

Further, the policy was that members of the Planning Section should accompany all raiding forces so that they would have first-hand information of the operation, gain experience and, by their presence, inspire confidence in those taking part. In fact, C.C.O. wanted to make it quite clear that there was no "back seat driving" in any of the operations. C.C.O. himself was forbidden to go on any raids by the Prime Minister, who even reproached him for trying out an early form of a one-man submarine (the Wellman) by himself.

The Raid on St. Nazaire, Operation "Chariot"

In their search for suitable targets on the French coast, the Intelligence Section, early in January, 1942, proposed St. Nazaire. Here was the only dry dock (Forme Ecluse) that could take the German battleship *Tirpitz*. The enemy were using the port as a base for their submarines which were employed in the battle of the Atlantic. Further, a study of the available intelligence revealed a flaw in the defences of the port which had been planned with insufficient regard to the possibility of ships passing over the mud flats at high water spring tides. C.C.O. also learned that, sometime previously, the Admiralty had considered an attack with the object of destroying the big dock, but for various reasons the project had been shelved. However, C.C.O. was determined to carry out this operation and, by the end of January, an outline plan was prepared.

The original plan was for an expendable ship, carrying about two hundred troops and drawing not more than 12 feet, to ram the lock gate. The troops were then to disembark onto the gate and, followed by the ship's company, all were to take cover behind an air raid shelter in the vicinity.

A very heavy charge, built into the ship, and scuttling charges were then to be fired, with the object of blowing a large gap in the outer gate and causing the ship to disintegrate and sink. An M.T.B. was then to pass through the gap and fire her torpedoes at the inner gate. This would render the large basin or wet dock (Bassin de St. Nazaire) tidal, which would be very detrimental to the ships and submarines berthed therein. Immediately after the big explosion, the troops would carry out demolitions within the dockyard subsequently embarking near the entrance to the lock in some six or eight motor launches which were to accompany the expedition for this purpose.

Simultaneously with the amphibious raid, a sustained air raid was to be carried out with the object of creating a diversion.

The plan was quickly approved by the Chiefs of Staff and, on the recommendation of C.C.O., the Commanders were appointed.

Commander R.E.D. Ryder, R.N., was appointed to command the naval craft taking part in the operation and, as the majority of the military forces to be employed were drawn from No. 2 Commando, the Officer Commanding the latter (Lieutenant-Colonel A.C. Newman) became the Military Commander.

As the operation was to be mounted and would take place in his area, the Commander-in-Chief, Plymouth (Admiral of the Fleet Sir Charles Forbes) would exercise the functions of the Naval Commander-in-Chief. C.C.O. invited these officers to meet him at C.O.H.Q. to discuss the plan.

The expendable ship provided by the Admiralty was the ex-American destroyer H.M.S. *Campbeltown* (Lieutenant-Commander S.H. Beattie). The ship had recently been fitted for boom-breaking trials and so could deal with the floating boom which had been shown by air reconnaissance to be in place outside the dock gates.

When the Commanders closely studied the plan, differences of opinion arose. Colonel Newman disliked the idea of having all his troops in one vessel. Commander Ryder was concerned lest the tidal data should prove erroneous and the ship run aground in consequence. The Commander-in-Chief, Plymouth was advised by his staff that the destroyer would bounce off the dock gate. Consequently, an alternative plan was proposed which envisaged the troops being taken in motor launches and, having landed from them, would carry out demolitions including the dock gates.

C.C.O. did not agree with the alternative plan. After consultation with the Engineer who designed the dock gate, he was convinced that the destroyer would not bounce off when she hit the gate. The Commander-in-Chief, Plymouth also insisted that the exploding of the big charge in the *Campbeltown* would kill everyone within half a mile. On this point C.C.O. had been guided by the chief expert on blast of the Ministry of Home Security, who was convinced that the raiders need run no risk from blast.

The Final Plan for Operation "Chariot"

Eventually a new plan, which was in the nature of a compromise, was adopted. The *Campbeltown* was to ram the dock gates, her crew, with certain military details, were to abandon ship over her bow and a delay action fuse to be used for exploding the big charge. This meant that the inner dock gate would not be torpedoed.

The remainder of the military forces were to be taken to the scene of action in motor launches which were also to be used for the withdrawal.

This latter arrangement did not recommend itself to C.C.O. since a single destroyer accompanied by a motor torpedo boat and followed at a discreet distance by the motor launches for the withdrawal, would have excited less attention than the whole force with their escorts steaming in formation.

Results of Operation "Chariot"

The results of the operation are best described in the report of the Commander-in-Chief, Plymouth:

> The principal object of the attack was achieved as the large lock capable of taking the *Tirpitz* should be out of action for a considerable time. (Actually, it was never repaired.) The outer caisson was destroyed by the blowing up of the *Campbeltown* and the demolition parties destroyed the pumping station and the operating mechanisms of the outer and inner caissons.
>
> For success surprise was essential. The unseen passage to the Loire was due partly to favourable weather conditions, which helped to prevent the force being detected from the air, and partly to careful routeing to keep the force out of the track of Zenits and reconnaissance flights by the enemy. It was also due to the almost certain sinking of a U-boat at 0815 on 27th March by H.M.S. *Tynedale*.
>
> That surprise was not complete was principally due to the weather, always a doubtful factor, preventing accurate location of targets by bomber aircraft. Of 62 bombers all but three located the target but only four dropped their bombs. But their presence overhead was sufficient to ensure that every A.A. gun in the neighbourhood was manned and ready to open fire at any moment. As these guns were in no way worried by falling bombs, they were able to concentrate their fire on the M.L. when the alarm was given. The noise of M.L. engines, which on a still night are clearly audible three miles away, was an additional handicap.

A second raid "Myrmidon" with Bayonne as the objective had been planned to synchronise with "Chariot". Owing to unfavourable moon and tide conditions on the date fixed for "Chariot", it was not possible to proceed with "Myrmidon" and it eventually took place on 4th/5th April. Conditions were not too favourable and although landing craft were manned and lowered, the swell proved too high for a landing to be effected.

Capture of Madagascar, Operation "Ironclad"

Concurrently with the planning and preparation for Operation "Chariot", another operation was decided upon by the Chiefs of Staff. This was the capture of Madagascar, which, at the time, was in the hands of the Vichy French.

Towards the end of 1940 the Joint Planning Staff had considered the question of the capture of this island. It was of great strategic importance to us in the conduct of the war, lying as it did on the flank of our sea communications in the Indian Ocean. Other urgent requirements brought the planning of this operation to a standstill and it was not heard of again until the entry of Japan into the war at the beginning of December, 1941.

The plans were reviewed at once and preparations were made to mount an operation which went by the name of "Bonus". With the assistance of the planning staff at C.O.H.Q., the Executive Planning Section of Plans Division of the Admiralty produced a plan which had as its object the capture of Diego Suarez, which was the chief port on the island, and was also a defended anchorage. The outline plan was ready just before Christmas and it envisaged the employment of 102 Royal Marine Brigade under Major-General R.M. Sturges, R.M. in the assault. This Brigade at once started training for its role and carried out a full-scale rehearsal, Exercise "Charcoal".

The project was shelved early in 1942 and it was estimated that it would take a period of ninety-one days from the issue of the preparatory orders before the assault could take place. In the event, the time was fifty-two days.

The success gained by the Japanese in their operations in the Malay Peninsula in December, 1941, and January, 1942, brought the operation to the fore again. It was more important now than ever to make sure that this large island, with its good harbours and facilities, should not be allowed to fall into the hands of the enemy.

Accordingly, the Chiefs of Staff considered the question, this time as a matter of great urgency. They decided to mount the operation at once and to use for the assault the 29th Infantry Brigade in place of the Royal Marines because the former was, at the time, embarked in the assault ships lying in the Clyde, preparatory to carrying out an exercise at Inverary. This decision was taken without the knowledge of C.C.O., who was at Dartmouth inspecting Commandos. However, the Chiefs of Staff decided to retain C.C.O.'s nomination of Major-General Sturges as the Military Commander.

RAPID GROWTH, OCTOBER 1941-MARCH 1942

The actual mounting of the operation is best described by quoting from the report of the Military Commander:

On 12th March, I received orders from H.Q. Expeditionary Force to report to the War Office on the morning of 14th March. When I arrived at the War Office, I was informed that the Chiefs of Staff had decided at 11 o'clock the previous night that the operation subsequently known as "Ironclad" was to be prepared to capture Diego Suarez during the favourable May moon and tide periods, that was between 3rd-8th May. The expedition was to sail with Convoy WS 17 which was to be delayed until 23rd March. Embarkation of vehicles and stores in the four assault ships (*Karanja, Keren, Winchester Castle* and *Sobieski*) was to commence on 18th March and all planning had to be completed to this schedule. After the examination of the new intelligence available, which did not as yet include air photographs, we decided that our previous plans (for "Bonus") were sound and could be carried out with the reduced forces available.

The reduced forces referred to by Major-General Sturges are accounted for in the minutes of a Chief of Staff meeting which reads as follows: "The Chiefs of Staff have re-examined the various methods by which the operation might be carried out and they hit upon a workable solution which obviates any delay.

They propose that the assault should be carried out by the small force which the Chief of Combined Operations suggested, i.e., four Battalions and one Commando, and that one Brigade Group of the 5th Division should be in reserve to support the landing."

By the directive issued to C.C.O. on 9th December, 1941, the preparation of the ships and craft and naval personnel was the responsibility of his Administrative Staff. To assist them was the staff of the Senior Officer, Assault Ships and Craft (Commodore G.L. Warren) who had his headquarters in the same building as the headquarters Expeditionary Force.

There was a very close link between R.A.L.B. and S.O.A.S.C. and the preparations for the sailing of the expedition were completed satisfactorily by the date required.

On this subject the remarks of the Military Commander are of interest: "From 15th March to 19th March my staff was engaged in preparing the necessary plans for loading the ships and completing the necessary preparations for the force to leave the United Kingdom.

A difficult combined problem was to decide in detail the composition of the naval and military forces to be embarked in the four assault ships. To these were to be added H.M.S. *Royal Ulsterman* (L.S.I.) (from the Mediterranean) and H.M.S. *Bachequero* (L.S.T.) (from Sierra Leone). These two ships could not meet the convoy until arrival at Durban, and any troops and vehicles required to make the assault from them had either to be embarked in the four assault ships or to be taken from those units already embarked with 17th Infantry Brigade Group."

Note – The latter were in Convoy WS 17 which was not loaded tactically.

On 18th March I was interviewed by the Chiefs of Staff on my plans for the operation and on 19th March I met the Prime Minister. On the evening of the same day, I left for my Headquarters at Melrose and on 21st March embarked in M.V. *Winchester Castle*. On 23rd March the *Winchester Castle* sailed.

General Conclusion from Operations "Chariot" and "Ironclad"

In both Operations "Chariot" and "Ironclad", the power given to the attackers by amphibious expeditions is well illustrated. The principles of mobility and surprise were used to the full and produced successful results.

Re-entry into the Continent - Operations "Sesame", "Round-up" and "Sledgehammer"

After Dunkirk it was obvious that a return to the Continent by sea was an inevitable operation. For some time, everyone was preoccupied with other problems and it was not until November, 1941, that much attention was given to the matter; it was then that C.-in-C. Home Forces received a directive to "prepare a plan in consultation with C.C.O. and in conjunction with the appropriate Naval and Air Commanders-in-Chief" for "a large scale raid of some duration" which eventually was named Operation "Sesame".

From then on, the tempo of work and planning increased and the Combined Operations Organisation quickly grew. Throughout, C.O.H.Q. played a major part in solving the multitudinous problems and in working out the plans.

Home Forces, in accordance with the November directive, studied and reported on the plan for a large-scale raid, "Sesame". The J.P.S. produced their paper in December entitled Operation "Round-up", a plan for re-entry into the Continent. In January, 1942, the Chiefs of Staff asked C.-in-C. Home Forces to examine this paper, consulting as necessary A.O.s. C.-in-C. Bomber Command and Fighter Command and C.-in-C. Portsmouth. In March, "Sledgehammer" (an operation to threaten the enemy and ease pressure on Russia) appeared and

C.-in-C. Home Forces, A.O. C.-in-C. Fighter Command and C.C.O. were directed to work on it. In April, planning for "Round-up" and "Sledgehammer" was brought into line.

The Combined Commanders

All through this the naval representatives, in what came to be known as the Combined Commanders, varied and was not really clear until Admiral Ramsay was appointed Flag Officer Expeditionary Force in May. This was done at the request of C.C.O. in order to avoid him having to give purely naval advice to the prejudice of his position as an impartial Combined Commander. In June, 1942, C.C.O. ceased to be a Combined Commander and the Naval C.-in-C. became third member.

The methods employed naturally varied as the system built up. Generally, it amounted to teams from the headquarters concerned preparing papers and plans for the Combined Commanders who submitted their recommendations to the Chiefs of Staff. The whole set-up was clearly defined in June, 1942, in a paper from which date the "Round-up" planners became a definite entity and so remained until the appointment of C.O.S.S.A.C. in April, 1943.

References to many operations appear and disappear such as "Tinder", "Imperator", "Super Round-up", but the only one that remained throughout was "Round-up" until it became "Overlord".

Current Work

The J.P. paper of 24th December, 1941, recommended that the study should: "(a) Be taken as a basis of preparation, organisation, and production by the Service Departments; (b) Be submitted to the Commander-in-Chief, Home Forces, for detailed study in conjunction with the Special Operations Executive and also the appropriate Naval and Air Force Commanders."

The Chiefs of Staff at their meeting on 2nd January: "(a) Invited the Commander-in-Chief, Home Forces, in consultation with the Commander-in-Chief, Portsmouth and the Air Officer Commanding-in-Chief, Bomber and Fighter Commands, to examine and comment on the report; (b) Invited the Commander-in-Chief, Home Forces, in the light of (a) above, to prepare an outline plan for operations on the Continent in the final phase and to review the plan periodically with a view to being able to put it into effect if a sudden change in the situation should appear to merit such a course."

On 24th January, G.H.Q. Home Forces submitted a report on plan "Sesame" in which the opinion was expressed that the enemy ports in

Brittany were the only worthwhile objectives for a large scale raid and that this would not be possible in the spring of 1942, owing to lack of landing craft and trained troops. The Joint Planners in considering this report thought that effort should be concentrated on "Round-up" and that plans for a large scale raid should be kept up to date.

Another name that appeared at this time was "Tinder" which provided for a hasty return against crumbling opposition in 1942.

The Chiefs of Staff at their meeting on 13th February (49th) agreed that the policy of small raids should be pressed vigorously and agreed the following new directive to C.-in-C. Home Forces which replaced that of November:

(1) German morale and strength in the West may deteriorate at any time in the future to a degree that will permit us to establish forces on the Continent. You are, therefore, to plan and prepare for a return to the Continent to take advantage of such a situation.

(2) At a very early stage in planning, you, in conjunction with the Admiralty and Air Ministry, are to make recommendations to the Chiefs of Staff regarding the system of command, so that the Commanders for the operation may be appointed as soon as possible and detailed planning begun.

(3) All the military resources under your command will be available for the operation.

(4) You are to assume that all the assault and special shipping in this country will be available for the training of your forces, subject to the continuance of a vigorous policy of small raids.

(5) You should continue your study of a major raiding operation against one of the main French Atlantic ports in case it becomes desirable to carry one out, but no preparations for such an operation are to be allowed to delay your preparations for your primary task.

(6) The Adviser on Combined Operations to be consulted at all stages of the planning.

It was not until the end of 1941, when C.O.H.Q. was reconstituted, that the magnitude of the problem became really apparent, nowhere more quickly than in C.O.H.Q. itself. C.C.O.'s task from then on was to keep this problem constantly before the Chiefs of Staff and later explain its magnitude to the Americans.

His success in this sphere can be judged by the fact that as early as 20th February, 1942, the Chiefs of Staff, on the advice of C.C.O. sent a telegram to the Joint Staff Mission in Washington suggesting that the construction of additional landing craft was essential and asking them to do everything possible to accelerate the programme put forward by the Admiralty representatives when they visited the U.S.A. in November-December, 1941.

This was the time that the new Admiralty design of Landing Ship Tank (L.S.T.), later known as the L.S.T. (2), was put forward and also that of the Landing Ship Dock (L.S.D.) which was something quite novel in ship construction. Two hundred of the former and seven of the latter had been considered at the time to be the maximum that American shipyards were capable of undertaking and this order was placed only after some difficulty in persuading the American Naval Authorities of its vital necessity.

Operation "Sledgehammer"

About this time, the position in Russia gave rise to considerable concern and the question of giving some assistance by action in the West arose. The Joint Planners, in a paper of 7th March, suggested "a major diversion in the West designed to upset German plans and divert German forces from the East." This was discussed at a meeting of the Chiefs of Staff on 10th March, at which C.C.O. was present. The operation was called "Sledgehammer". As a result of this meeting the Joint Planners in conjunction with A.C.O. produced a more detailed paper examining the various areas for attack which rejected the Pas de Calais and Le Havre in favour of the Channel Islands and Cherbourg peninsula. It is clear from the Chiefs of Staff meeting on the 17th March, 1942, that no one liked the look of the operation, nevertheless a further paper and directives for planning were ordered.

The Admiralty and Ministry of War Transport were invited to examine and report on the implications of speeding up the production of landing craft and of giving a higher priority to the allocation of shipping space for landing craft from America. Also, the Admiralty was invited, in consultation with other departments concerned, to begin the construction of suitable hards for the embarkation of armoured vehicles and motor transport into landing craft.

Meeting at C.O.H.Q., 26th February, 1942

Apart from the contribution made to these first rapid studies in connection with "Sledgehammer", C.O.H.Q. was following up the plans on "Sesame" and "Round-up", and on 26th February, a meeting was called at C.O.H.Q. by C.C.O. the object of this was to find out what work and organisation was required to make the south coast of England capable of acting as a springboard from which to launch the forces necessary to invade the Continent.

The main fact that emerged was that a very large amount of work in the nature of preparation would have to be undertaken before anything could be attempted. What this work involved can best be judged from the fact that, prior to January, 1942, many parts of the coasts of the U.K. had been put in a state of defence against invasion. Beaches had strongly constructed defences and many were extensively mined. Beach exits were blocked, piers dismantled and anything that might be of assistance to the enemy removed or made unusable. Particular attention had been given to the south coast of England from the Wash to the Bristol Channel.

Further, owing to the activities of the German Air Force, the large ports like London and Southampton had been very much reduced in work and capacity. The only sea traffic that used the English Channel and the Straits of Dover was restricted to small coastal ships, sailing in convoys, with local escorts. To enable the west coast ports to compete with the ocean traffic diverted to them, they were equipped with cranes, lighters, and tugs, which were transferred from the south and east coasts as was the dock labour.

Therefore, before any re-entry into the Continent became a possibility, not only would the facilities on the south coast have to be restored but they would also have to be greatly augmented. To speed the build-up of any operations, the beaches and beach exits would not only have to be cleared but transit areas and assembly and embarkation points would have to be made in their vicinity.

As a result of the meeting, a paper was prepared for the Chiefs of Staff. On 21st March, the Chiefs of Staff again discussed "Sledgehammer". They concluded that the main limiting factors were going to be landing craft and the difficulty of air support other than in the Pas de Calais. They went on to discuss C.C.O.'s paper and the procedure for planning Cross-Channel Operations.

Procedure for Planning Cross-Channel Operations
It was agreed at this meeting of the Chiefs of Staff on 21st March, 1942, that the planning of Cross-Channel Operations, including the larger scale raids in Home Waters, should be undertaken by the staffs of C.-in-C. Home Forces, C.-in-C. Fighter Command (and where applicable Bomber Command) and the staff of C.O.H.Q., in close consultation.

Once an operation or directive for planning had been approved in outline by the Chiefs of Staff Committee, it was agreed that the Joint Planning Procedure should be adopted.

At the same time the Chiefs of Staff Committee: (1) Invited the Chief [previously Commodore] of Combined Operations, the Commander-in-Chief, Home Forces and the Commander-in-Chief, Fighter Command to prepare a brief appreciation, in accordance with the terms of the directive, with the object of diverting German Air Forces from the Russian front; (2) Approved the proposal for the development of the facilities and defences of the south coast ports, and instructed the Secretary to submit a Minute to the Prime Minister accordingly; (3) Agreed that arrangements should be made for the accommodation of the Assault Commanders in the Headquarters of the Naval C.-in-C., Portsmouth, and at Dover Castle; [and] (4) Instructed the C.O.S. (A.A.) Sub-Committee to prepare in due course, detailed proposals for augmenting the air defences of the south coast area.

The directive, which indicates the trend of thought, was as follows:

Directive

To: C.-in-C., Home Forces.
A.O.C.-in-C., Fighter Command.
Chief of Combined Operations.

(1) You have been appointed to plan operations with the following object: "To make Germany continuously employ her air forces in active operations and to cause protracted air fighting in the West in an area advantageous to ourselves, in order to reduce German air support available for the Eastern Front as early as possible.
(2) It is intended that these operations should include a major deception plan designed to threaten the Germans with a permanent return to the Continent.
(3) Planning is to commence forthwith. You should report to the Chiefs of Staff at the earliest possible date the forces which will be practicable and desirable to employ and your views on the probability of success.
(4) The Controlling Officer and the Special Operations Executive should be associated with you in both the planning and the preparation of the operation.
(5) You should assume that the full support of the Bomber, Fighter and Army Co-operation Commands will be available for this operation and for any advance operations you may deem desirable to assist your plan.

(6) You may find, in the early stages of planning, that certain immediate preparations should be undertaken. You are authorised to initiate these in advance of the final approval of your plans.

This directive shows in paras. 2 and 6 why the concentration of available landing craft in the south already referred to was set in motion.

Chapter 4

FULL STATURE, MARCH 1942-OCTOBER 1943

On 18th March, 1942, the Chiefs of Staff had before them a memorandum by General Ismay, the relevant paragraphs of which read as follows:

(3) The title of the appointment of 'Adviser on Combined Operations' has been altered to 'Chief of Combined Operations.' The appointment will in future carry with it the rank of Vice-Admiral in the Navy, Lieutenant-General in the Army and Air Marshal in the Royal Air Force.

(4) The Chief of Combined Operations will attend meetings of the Chiefs of Staff as a full member whenever major issues are in question and also, as heretofore, when his own Combined Operations, or any special matters in which he is concerned, are under consideration.

From this time onwards, the Chief of Combined Operations (C.C.O.) attended all Chiefs of Staff meetings when he was available and also those of the Vice-Chiefs of Staff.

Consequent on this decision, a confidential order was issued to all three Services, which shows clearly what the Combined Operations Organisation had now become.

Preliminaries for Invasion
After carefully reviewing the requirements for any form of Cross-Channel Operation on a large scale, C.C.O. foresaw that there would be a far greater requirement for craft than even the most optimistic estimates could provide. Further, the time available was short and no

matter what exertions could be made in construction, the shortage of craft would always be a governing factor.

Administrative Problems

Other problems that emerged from a study of the effort required to return to the Continent were the provision of accommodation for the personnel required for the reliefs of crews of landing craft, the collection of spares, not only for the engines but also for the craft, and the setting up of depots where these spares could be conveniently stored.

Above all was the overriding consideration of where to house the officers and men being trained for the landing craft and the selection of suitable areas where they could be trained to the required standard in the minimum amout of time.

The possession of the base originally built by the Americans at Rosneath in the Gare Loch and the enlargement of the facilities at Inveraray and Castle Toward were soon found to be insufficient to compete with the intake and so where next to open up establishments was a constant source of concern to the Administrative Staff.

The improvisation and subterfuge that were forced on the Command will soon become apparent.

Assembly of Craft for "Sledgehammer"

Most of the craft available in the United Kingdom were, at this time (April, 1942), fully employed in the Clyde area in the training of formations in amphibious warfare.

With the emergence of the "Sledgehammer" plan, it at once became necessary to concentrate them in the southern ports. At the same time the deliveries of craft from the U.S.A. were beginning to arrive at our west coast ports in the ships sailing in convoy.

The move of the craft from the north, combined with the reception of the craft from overseas, gave the Administrative Staff a rather complicated problem. It is of interest to note that, not only was this concentration of craft carried out by lifts in the ships under the command of C.C.O., but also by road in motor lorries. It was not possible to use the railways as the beam of the craft would not come within the loading gauge.

As the deliveries to the west coast ports increased, it became necessary to use the canal system and in this way canals, which had been disused for years, came once more into use. As certain of the canals in the Midlands ran through low tunnels, it was impossible for the landing craft to go through them under their own power owing to the exhaust fumes fouling the atmosphere. It was therefore the custom for the ferry crews to lie on their backs on the craft and walk them through by using their feet on the roof of the tunnel. In these many ways the concentration of craft was gradually built up in the southern bases during the months of May, June and July.

Co-operation with the United States

At the end of December, 1941, the Prime Minister paid a visit to the President of the United States. Accompanying him were the Chiefs of Staff and, for a period of about a fortnight, very important conferences took place on the highest level. The general trend of the future strategy to be employed against the enemy powers was formulated.

As a direct result of these deliberations, United States officers came to England to co-operate in the Combined Planning work.

Representatives from C.O.H.Q. took part in these staff discussions and its Planning Staff contributed both useful ideas and important information to all the deliberations.

So far, no long-term arrangements had been made to prepare England for either the reception of the American reinforcements or for its role as a base from which continental operations could be launched. In fact, many prominent people considered that a landing was impossible against the heavily defended coast of France.

Co-ordinator of Ministry and Services Facilities (C.M.S.F.)

For the preparation for the re-entry into the Continent, it would be necessary for not only the Service Departments but also many of the other Ministries to play a part. For the preliminary work the question of the provision of raw materials and labour would have to be studied and allowed for in the allocation of both to the forces and industry. Accordingly, C.C.O. obtained the approval of the Prime Minister, through the Chiefs of Staff, to have Brigadier Sir Harold Wernher appointed to the staff at C.O.H.Q. with the title of Co-ordinator of Ministry and Services Facilities (C.M.S.F.) This became effective on 3rd April. His role was to bring together the authorities involved in any project and, having explained the matter to them, to co-ordinate and follow the progress of the work. Among the first tasks given to him by C.C.O., was the provision of loading hards to augment the available port facilities, and the fitting of derricks to coasters for the carriage of motor transport.

Brigadier Wernher was duly appointed Chairman of the C.M.S.F. Committee which was at first composed of officers from the Admiralty, War Office and Ministry of War Transport. Later the committees over which he presided had members of nearly all Government Departments working in them from time to time.

Sir Harold Wernher records in his book: "I felt at the time that a number of the members thought that much time was being wasted by going into the many problems which came up at the meetings, but I was gratified to hear from the most sceptical, after the Invasion took place, that they considered that all the effort which had been involved was fully justified and that without the preliminary arrangements which we had initiated it would have been impossible to meet the staff requirements of the various Services."

As an example of the work undertaken by C.M.S.F., another of his earlier duties was a reconnaissance of the entire port capacity from the Wash to the Bristol Channel. A complete inventory of every berth was taken and embodied in a document which became the basis for all future planning. Also, on the east and south coasts it was necessary to make arrangements for the assembly of a large military force. Accordingly, the areas were defined as follows:

> Concentration Area: 25 to 30 miles from the coast.
> Assembly Area: 5 to 10 miles from the coast.
> Transit Areas: On the coast.
> Camps, roads and hard standings for vehicles were either constructed or widened throughout the Eastern, South-Eastern and Southern Commands.

The other activities, which fell to the lot of the C.M.S.F Committees, will be covered in the course of the narrative and it will be seen that Brigadier Wernher as C.M.S.F. was eventually absorbed into S.H.A.E.F.

Development of Combined Operations Headquarters

The responsibilities and work of C.C.O. and his staff were considerably increased and there is no doubt that, for the next three years, pressure was great. Not only was C.C.O. the head of an organisation that was growing fast, but he was also a member of the Chiefs of Staff Committee and, for some months, a Combined Commander.

At this time, therefore, C.O.H.Q. may be said to have emerged as an important entity in the conduct of the war. It had started as a Directorate with little or no executive authority and with practically no resources either of men or material, it had now become an important Command. Further, the training staff and establishments in the Command were the acknowledged experts on the technique of a type of warfare which had become an integral part of our strategy. It was plain that our re-entry into the continent of Europe was largely dependent on amphibious warfare and that the more the subject was studied the clearer it became and that the efforts required, both in research and preparation, would have to be on a very large scale.

On top of all this there was the question of training the personnel for the work. As an example, the first duty of a seaman had always been to keep his ship or craft from going ashore. In amphibious operations, it was the role of these same seamen to learn how to ground their ships and craft. It was particularly difficult to overcome the prejudices of the senior officers of both the Royal Navy and the Royal Naval Reserve in this matter.

Further, the amount of repair work entailed in keeping ships and craft serviceable on account of continual groundings was not readily appreciated by the various authorities. Progress was at first slow but, in the end, success was achieved.

The fact that the operations that had been planned and mounted under C.C.O. were successful showed that, providing sufficient thought and ingenuity were used, the matter was not a black art.

With these increases of work there was naturally need for a larger staff and during the first quarter of 1942, C.O.H.Q. grew by 25 per cent These additions were generally distributed amongst the existing branches as were the U.S. officers who joined in May.

Co-ordinator of Experiments and Developments

By his directive C.C.O. was responsible for Amphibious Warfare technique. Originally this was undertaken by the Inter-Services Training and Development Centre (I.S.T.D.C.), but at about this time it was apparent that, not only were new designs for ships and craft necessary, but there was also a demand for other facilities and novel forms of warfare. Accordingly, on 13th April, 1942, a department was set up at C.O.H.Q. under Captain T.A. Hussey, R.N., who was known as the Co-ordinator of Experiments and Developments (C.X.D.). With him were officers of all three Services and, in addition, three scientists, Professors Bernal and Zuckerman and Mr. Pyke. In August the title was changed to Director of Experiments and Staff Requirements (D.X.S.R.).

Liaison in Washington

In April, 1942, Captain J. Knox, R.N. with an inter-Services staff was sent to the United States where he joined the British Joint Staff Mission with the title of Combined Operations Liaison Officer (C.O.L.O.). This title was changed in March, 1943, to Chief of Combined Operations Representative (C.C.O.R.).

The Alternatives - Cherbourg Peninsula or the Pas de Calais

The planning continued mainly on operation "Sledgehammer". On 26th March, 1942, C.C.O. produced a short paper on the acquisition of dumb barges for the carriage of motor transport.

On 27th March the report from C.-in-C., Home Forces, A.O.C.-in-C., Fighter Command and C.C.O. was sent to the Chiefs of Staff. It stated:

(1) Our broad conclusions are as follows: (a) The limited object given by the Chiefs of Staff can be achieved by air action alone; (b) Unless German morale is broken, we do not consider that a re-entry into France with the resources at our disposal in 1942 is likely to be successful; (c) Should, however, circumstances force us to take military action on the Continent during 1942 we lean towards the Pas de Calais but, before coming to a final decision, we require further time to investigate other possibilities. These investigations are being pressed on as rapidly as possible.

(2) We wish to draw attention to the fact that, if a combined operation is to be carried out at all this summer, a decision will have to be made without any further delay.

The choice of the Pas de Calais area was dictated by the range of fighter support but opinion at C.O.H.Q. was not in favour of a landing in this area for the following reasons:

(1) This operation would entail a direct frontal assault on the part of the coastline which was most heavily defended by the Germans. Their gun defences dominated the narrow strip of water through which our ships and craft would have to sail.

(2) The road and rail communications in this area would enable the enemy to concentrate forces very quickly.

(3) Any forces landed would have to be supplied across open beaches, exposed to the full effect of the prevailing wind in the Channel and to the greatest rise and fall of the tide.

(4) Only the most perfectly trained personnel could have a hope of succeeding against the opposition that was to be expected and it was thought that, with the little training they had had up to date, they were not fit for the task.

However, so as to be prepared for the operation, training was intensified in all the establishments in the Combined Operations Command.

The Chiefs of Staff considered these two reports at their meeting on 28th March. The following remarks were made by C.C.O.:

C.C.O. said he fully realised the arguments in favour of the Pas de Calais area but there were certain points about the Cherbourg operations which he though merited further examination. He was not yet in a position to say that a landing on the scale proposed in the Pas de Calais area was a practical operation and he added that, with the lines of communication which would be available, it seemed that the re-embarkation would be a very difficult task. We should certainly have to leave behind most of the equipment and probably many of the personnel. He suggested therefore that the operation in the Cherbourg peninsula should be examined in further detail. This he thought would not interfere with the Pas de Calais project.

The meeting asked for a further report and agreed in principle to the requisitioning of a thousand dumb barges.

In the next few days reports were submitted by the Admiralty on the availability of Tank Landing Craft and the provision of naval forces. On 7th April, the three Commanders reported again and concluded "that the operation is practicable against the present scale of defences, provided that the maintenance problem can be successfully overcome." They also called attention to numerous risks. Among the recommendations they made were:

(1) Planning for an alternative operation should be carried on concurrently with "Sledgehammer". Raids on a scale larger than hitherto carried out should take place during the assembly and training period.
(2) Operation "Round-up" should be based on Operation "Sledgehammer" as it might become imperative to merge the one operation into the other.
(3) Force Commanders should be appointed forthwith.
(4) Priority to be given for such work and equipment essential to the operation.

This report was taken to the Chiefs of Staff meeting on 8th April, 1942. In commenting on the Report, the C.I.G.S. (General Sir Alan Brooke) said:

In the original directive for planning Operation "Sledgehammer", the object laid down was to make Germany employ continuously her air forces in the West in conditions advantageous to ourselves, in order to reduce German air support available for the Eastern Front. In the report which was before them, the object was stated to seize and hold a bridgehead within the advantageous area of fighter cover. Furthermore, judging by the size of the force that was to be employed, it was inferred that the danger of the invasion of this country no longer existed. He did not agree with this change of object or with the assumption.

Later he goes on to say:

> It was suggested that, although the conditions under which Operation "Sledgehammer" could take place were unlikely to present themselves, it might be advisable to have plans prepared in case conditions similar to those needed for Operation "Round-up" were obtained in the latter part of the year.

The Committee therefore invited, (1) The C.-in-C., Home Forces, the A.O.C.-in-C. Fighter Command, and the Chief of Combined Operations to investigate what action could be taken by the armed forces in the West to help Russia in the event of her being hard pressed by the Germans this summer; (2) The A.O.C.-in-C., Fighter Command, in consultation with the A.O.C.-in-C., Bomber Command to prepare an appreciation under the following terms of reference: "How to inflict by air action the greatest possible wastage of German Air Force in the West immediately after the launching of the German spring offensive, to assess this wastage and to estimate the air situation resulting from it."

Later in the same meeting, the following decisions were recorded: "The Committee approved the proposal that the responsibility for planning Operation 'Round-up' should be brought into line with that for Operation 'Sledgehammer.' i.e., it should be transferred to the C.-in-C., Fighter Command (and other R.A.F. Commands as necessary) and the Chief of Combined Operations, the Naval Staff being fully consulted."

On 14th April, the Commanders replied on the question of help to Russia and said that, excluding air action alone, the possibilities of which were being considered separately, a series of medium sized raids was the only practical solution.

On 16th April, the Chiefs of Staff ordered the preparation of a memorandum for planning and procedure, and agreed the appointment of the Force Commanders, namely Vice-Admiral B.H. Ramsay, Lieutenant-General E.C.A. Schreiber and Air Marshal T Leigh Mallory. They were accommodated at C.O.H.Q. in Richmond Terrace.

The Combined Commanders were still divided as to the best locality on the French coast for either "Round-up" or "Sledgehammer". It will be recalled that the Army and the R.A.F. favoured the Pas de Calais because of the fighter cover that could be guaranteed in that area, whereas the opinion held by tC.C.O. and the staff at C.O.H.Q. was that the French coast from the River Canche to Cherbourg should be the scene either of one or both operations, and that the fighter aircraft could be fitted with long range tanks to make them capable of operating in the Cherbourg and/or Baie de la Seine areas. Further, the "Habbakuk" project was being investigated; this had as one of its objectives the provision of floating airfields in any area of operations. C.O.H.Q. was firmly opposed to an attack in the Pas de Calais where the Germans had developed a really powerful coast defence system, which could dominate ships in that area, and had established defence in depth from the coast which, from our air reconnaissance, appeared to be very formidable.

At the Combined Commanders' Meetings, C.C.O. repeatedly pointed out these facts and he was at pains to show that the continental channel ports from Le Havre to the eastward were all shallow ports with narrow entrances and capable of complete protection by minefields. On the other hand, the ports to the westward, notably Cherbourg, were deep-water ports with wide entrances, which could not be so easily mined and which were not nearly so well defended. In fact, the Pas de Calais project did not take into account the advantage given to our forces by the possession of the local command of sea communications, as did the western area.

Another point of difference between C.C.O. and his military and air force colleagues was that he was of the opinion that the Army, on landing in the Baie de la Seine, should turn westward and capture Cherbourg (and possibly other western ports) so as to ensure a rapid and steady build-up of the invading forces. When this build-up had been achieved, the break-out could be made and the advance eastward in strength begun, with the great deep-water ports of Cherbourg, Brest and St. Nazaire in our hands. This would ensure that the supplies for the Army on the Continent could be maintained.

Another point that C.O.H.Q. favoured was the fact that the road and rail communications ran parallel to the coast in the area to the eastward of Cherbourg whereas, in the Pas de Calais, all converged on the coast, thus making it easier for the enemy to bring up his reinforcements quickly.

Visit of Mr. Harry Hopkins and General Marshall, April, 1942

When Mr. Harry Hopkins and General G.C. Marshall, Chief of the U.S. Army Staff, visited London at the beginning of April, 1942, they brought with them the American Chiefs of Staff's views concerning the future conduct of the war.

At the first meeting with the Chiefs of Staff, which was held on 9th April, General Marshall outlined his ideas on how the American and British Forces could be combined to invade France as, in his opinion, Germany could only be beaten by military forces on land. The Chiefs of Staff, who by that time included C.C.O., pointed out that they had been planning for an operation to be called "Round-up" with precisely this end in view. They doubted however whether there was any real prospect of carrying out a re-entry into the Continent in 1942 and would not commit themselves by saying that they would be ready in 1943.

Towards the end of the first meeting, the First Sea Lord, the C.I.G.S. and the C.A.S. invited General Marshall to visit their Service Ministries and placed all their facilities at his disposal. General Marshall then expressed a desire to visit C.O.H.Q. first and on the following day he arrived there, accompanied by his staff officer, Lieut.-Colonel A.C. Wedemeyer.

C.C.O. explained the organisation and gave General Marshall some idea of what the Combined Operations Command was trying to achieve, on the conclusion of which the General expressed his pleasure at finding an organisation already in being for dealing with the problems he had come over to discuss. Before he left C.O.H.Q., General Marshall said he would like to send some of his officers to join C.C.O. staff and work in C.O.H.Q. This was endorsed in the report of the Chiefs of Staff meeting on 10th April, as follows:

"The Committee invited the Chief of Combined Operations, after consultation with the American Authorities, to make arrangements for American Planning Officers to gain experience in planning Combined Operations with his staff."

Nine American naval, army and air force officers, under Brigadier-General L. Truscott, were appointed to the staff at C.O.H.Q., and joined on 11th May, 1942, thus making C.O.H.Q. the first integrated inter-allied inter-services headquarters of the war.

It was during the meeting at C.O.H.Q. that C.C.O. suggested that British orders for landing ships and craft, already placed in the U.S.A., should be doubled so that the American Forces would have some for their own use. C.C.O. explained his ideas for a completely new design of landing craft for the conveyance of infantry in the assault. This was the Landing Craft Infantry (Large) (L.C.I.(L)) which was adopted by both nations and used for the first time in the landings in Sicily (Operation "Husky").

The visit of General Marshall and Mr. Harry Hopkins had other repercussions for the Combined Operations Organisation. While they were in England, they stayed with the Prime Minister at "Chequers" and it was there that C.C.O., who was one of the party, explained to Mr. Harry Hopkins the difficulty in getting the engines for the Thames barges (L.C.B.). Mr. Hopkins then and there promised to see that the engines were provided.

In addition, C.C.O. seized the opportunity of explaining to both General Marshall and Mr. Hopkins a scheme proposed by Mr. Pyke (a scientist on the staff of C.O.H.Q.) for dropping an airborne party into northern Norway to carry on a war of attrition against the German lines of communication. For this task a special vehicle was required which could be dropped by parachute and which could also out-run any German vehicles across the snow. This project was given the code name "Plough" and the vehicle required for the operation was known as the "Weasel".

As a result of this discussion, Mr. Pyke was sent to the U.S.A., accompanied by a Brigadier. With the agreement of General McNaughton, the G.O.C. 1st Canadian Army, the project became a Canadian/United States joint effort and the force, which was finally raised, was under the command of Brigadier-General Frederick of the U.S. Army. The vehicle was developed under Dr. Vannevar Bush, Director of Scientific Research, U.S.A., and, although it arrived too late for operations in Norway, it proved its value crossing muddy foreshores of South-East Asia.

"Round-up" and "Sledgehammer"

On 4th May, 1942, the Force Commanders reported to the Combined Commanders that, on account of its dependency on the weather, the difficulties of maintenance and the lack of sufficient special landing craft, "Sledgehammer", with the resources available, was not a sound military operation.

The Combined Commanders sent this report to the Chiefs of Staff on 6th May, generally agreeing with it and recommending:

(a) That the Force Commanders should be instructed to prepare a detailed plan for "Sledgehammer", to be carried out this year if German morale cracks.
(b) That all preparations which will not cause serious dislocation should be continued.
(c) That the policy of large scale raids should be intensified.

At their meeting on 8th May the Chiefs of Staff decided "To maintain the plans for Operation 'Sledgehammer' in a state of preparedness," and also invited the Combined Commanders "to initiate the preparation of the best plan possible for a major raid on the French coast within the area of fighter protection. The raid should be planned to take place about the middle of July."

This date was in relation to the expected Russian offensive.

In April and May the organisation for planning "Round-up" was under review and the lack of proper naval representation was put right by the appointment, on 15th May, of Vice-Admiral Ramsay as Flag Officer Commanding Expeditionary Force. This was an addition to his being Force Commander for "Sledgehammer".

C.C.O.'s position was also difficult, because he had six distinct functions:

A Chief of Staff,
A Combined Commander with major planning responsibilities,
A Commander of Special Forces,
Controller of small raids,
Adviser on technical development, and
Training for Amphibious Warfare.

On 16th June, 1942, C.C.O., at his own suggestion, ceased to be a Combined Commander but, as he and his staff had much to contribute to the planning and preparation, they were consulted at every stage and worked on innumerable Committees.

On 18th June, Vice-Admiral Ramsay was promoted Admiral and appointed C.-in-C. Expeditionary Force and on 27th June he was added to the authorities for planning "Sledgehammer". Shortly afterwards, a new Force Commander, Rear-Admiral H.T. Baillie-Grohman, was appointed as Rear-Admiral Expeditionary Force.

While the Combined Commanders and C.C.O. (now no longer a Combined Commander) and their planning staffs were busily engaged on operational planning, the logistics aspects were also being examined. The administrative arrangements to be established on the far shore were the responsibility of the Administrative Sections of these planning staffs, but a separate organisation was required in the U.K., the near shore.

The arrangements for the reception of the United States forces in the U.K. was the responsibility of the Bolero Committee on which at this time Brigadier Wernher (C.M.S.F.) represented C.C.O. All other logistical planning was in the hands of the Principal Administrative officers, who in May, 1942, set up the "Round-up" Administrative Planning Staff in Norfolk House. This planning staff was under the chairmanship of Major-General Gale, then M.G.A., Home Forces, and comprised representatives from Home Forces, Admiralty, War Office, Air Ministry, C.O.H.Q., Naval C.-in-C., Expeditionary Force, and the U.S. Navy, Army and Service of Supply. Their task was defined as follows:

"To co-ordinate the detailed administrative arrangements which must be made by the Service Departments and staffs of the Combined Commanders and C.C.O. in order to enable the plans of the Combined Commanders for offensive operations on the continent of Europe to be carried out."

The detailed work was done by Sections, of which at one time there were over forty, and C.O.H.Q. was represented on twenty-nine of them.

As time went on, it became increasingly evident that "Sledgehammer" was unlikely to take place and, on 10th July, 1942, C.C.O. was invited by the Chiefs of Staff to assume responsibility for alternative operations to take the place of "Sledgehammer". General Eisenhower was to be associated as necessary with the planning. The Controlling Officer, in consultation with C.O.H.Q., was required to put into effect the best possible deception plan.

On 17th July, in order to clear up any doubts about "Sledgehammer", the Chiefs of Staff decided that the outline plan as it stood should be submitted for approval and then kept in such a state that it could be implemented if the opportunity offered. It was referred to frequently afterwards until it was absorbed into Plan "Rankin", an operation for use in the event of a crack in German morale. As a diversionary operation it was finally abandoned at the meeting between the Prime Minister and General Marshall on 22nd July.

As interest in "Sledgehammer" waned, so "Round-up" received more attention and the machinery for tackling this enormous problem gradually took shape.

Raids in 1942

From the outset, one of the primary responsibilities of C.O.H.Q. was raiding the coastline of Europe but, on account of the shortage of men and material, and the claims of major operations, no great progress had been made. The staff was not adequate for the amount of work involved, but, when Commodore Mountbatten was appointed and had succeeded in building up the headquarters to a size which was better able to cope, much more attention was given to raiding problems. In fact, no less than twenty-five raids of various sizes were studied in the first three months of 1942 and during the first six months, eight were carried out, namely:

"Curlew" at St. Laurent,
"Biting" at Bruneval,
"Huckaback" at Herm,
"Backchat" at Anse de St. Marten,
"Abercrombie" at Hardelot,
"J.V." at Boulogne,
"Lighter" at Kupho Nisi,
"Bristle" at Boulogne.

These were in addition to the bigger operations of St. Nazaire, Bayonne and Diego Suarez. Five more were mounted, including "Rutter" for Dieppe. With the background of "Sledgehammer" and a diversion in the West, large raids were considered on the Channel Islands and Cherbourg peninsula. The former was turned down in May, 1942, mainly on account of the difficulties of air support.

The general policy for 1942 was to produce a raid once a month, but in the latter part of the year the demands of "Torch" (North Africa) took precedence. Nevertheless, raiding problems alone put a tremendous amount of work on C.O.H.Q. and there is no doubt that, as the war and combined operations developed, much of the effort bore fruit in some form.

Chapter 5

THE RAID ON DIEPPE, AUGUST 1942

During the studies on various raids and "Round-up", there were discussions on the tactics to be employed in the major operation, the invasion of Europe.

Preparation and Planning
At this stage, it was considered that attacks, each of about divisional strength, should be made on various ports with two brigade groups in the assault and one in reserve. It was in order to test these tactical conceptions and to learn more of the technique required that the Dieppe raid was conceived. Against this background, it was a success and provided the key to many problems which had to be solved before the invasion of the Continent could be launched.

Operation "Rutter"
When the requirement was clear, a plan was evolved in C.O.H.Q. for a large scale raid to correspond in some measure to these tactical ideas. The troops for the assault were to be provided by the C.-in-C., Home Forces and the operation was to be known as "Rutter". It was decided that the most favourable target for this raid was the port of Dieppe. Early in April, 1942, the Target Committee at C.O.H.Q. first examined the project and a week or so later the Planning Staff at C.O.H.Q. began work on an outline plan under the general direction of the Naval Adviser to C.C.O. (Captain J. Hughes-Hallet, R.N.), who was subsequently made the Naval Force Commander for the operation that eventually took place ("Jubilee").

It was realised at the outset that, although intelligence reports showed that Dieppe was not very heavily defended, a town of its size could only be successfully raided if the number of troops used was considerable. It was estimated that as many as six battalions would be necessary and this was the size of the force required for a trial on a reasonable scale.

The question of adequate support at once arose and the use of tanks was considered very early in the planning.

Outline Plan for "Rutter"

A frontal assault was not contemplated by the C.O.H.Q. Planning Staff. They thought that the best places for landing would be on each flank: at Quiberville, some 6 miles to the west of Dieppe, and at Criel-sur-Mer, about twice that distance to the east. At Quiberville, the beach was deemed suitable for tanks; once ashore they would have only a short distance to go towards the aerodrome of St. Aubin and to the high ground to the south-west of the town, both of them suitable objectives, the capture of which would secure Dieppe from the west. The main obstacles, which the tanks would encounter, would be the Rivers Saâne and Scie. The bridges across them would therefore have to be seized and held to enable the tanks to cross. These rivers are sluggish and may be compared with the Sussex rivers, Adur and Cuckmere.

On 14th April, representatives of the General Staff, Home Forces, joined the Planning Syndicate in accordance with the procedure agreed by the Chiefs of Staff on 30th March, 1942, whereby, in any raid involving forces within the Home Forces Command, a small number of selected staff officers from within the Home Forces Command were to be associated with the preparation of the plans. The C.-in-C., Home Forces, shortly afterwards delegated his authority in this matter to Lieutenant-General B.L. Montgomery, then G.O.C.-in-C., South Eastern Command. From that moment, the latter became closely associated with the military side of the planning and attended the principal meetings of the planners. When Canadian troops were chosen to carry out the raid, the G.O.C.-in-C., First Canadian Army, and his representatives became associated with the planning. He designated Lieutenant-General H.D.G. Crerar, G.O.C. 1st Canadian Corps, to concert Canadian arrangements with C.O.H.Q.

Two plans were produced. The first, sponsored by C.O.H.Q. Planners, was to make no frontal assault, but to land two battalions at Puits and two at Pourville keeping two battalions as a floating reserve, whilst a seventh battalion was to land with a battalion of tanks at Quiberville.

The second plan, sponsored by the Home Forces Planners, was that Dieppe should be assaulted by a frontal attack delivered against the beaches of the town itself and supported by two flank attacks, one at

Puits, 1.75 miles east of Dieppe, and the other at Pourville, 1.5 miles to the west. Simultaneously, or shortly before, parachute and gliderborne troops were to capture two heavy batteries of coast defence guns, one of which was situated near the village of Berneval, some 6 miles to the east, and the other near Varengeville-sur-Mer, some 3.5 miles to the west.

On 18th April, 1942, a meeting took place with the Vice-Chief of Combined Operations (Major-General J.C. Haydon) in the Chair. It was attended by the Deputy-Chief of the General Staff (Major-General Gregson Ellis) and Brigadier-General Staff (Plans), Home Forces (Brigadier McNabb) and by the G.O.C. Airborne Division (Major-General F. Browning). The pros and cons of the various points of landing were discussed and the conclusion was reached that a frontal assault would have to be included in the plan. It was considered that this assault should be made only after the two flank attacks had been successfully made in darkness against the two heavy batteries. The frontal attack was to be preceded by heavy air bombardment. The reasons in support of these conclusions are discussed in more detail below. The naval opinion was that, although a frontal attack was hazardous, it was perfectly feasible so far as the Navy was concerned. C.C.O. personally expressed his dislike of the frontal assault but was prepared to let Home Forces decide.

On 25th April, the first formal meeting was held to consider the plans for the operation with C.C.O. in the Chair. The Deputy-Chief of the General Staff, Home Forces, attended and the question of a frontal assault was discussed.

The army representatives explained the reasons which led them to favour this form of assault. In the first place, to land any forces as far west as Quiberville would make a surprise attack on Dieppe more difficult to achieve. In the second place, tanks landed on that beach would have to cross two rivers which might prove to be formidable obstacles. In these circumstances, the bridges over them would have to be seized at a very early stage in order to make sure that they were not demolished by the enemy. Thirdly, all available intelligence at that time showed that Dieppe was lightly held by a single low-category battalion supported by about ten A.A. guns, three or four light anti-aircraft guns, one four-gun dual-purpose battery and four coast defence batteries.

Furthermore, the troops in Dieppe, numbering, it was thought, not more than 1,400 in all, could not be strongly reinforced for some time. It was considered that after five hours, the total number of reinforcements which could reach them would not exceed 2,500 men; only from the eighth hour of the attack onwards might important reserves begin to arrive, mainly from Rouen and from the east. Thus, at the end of fifteen hours, the maximum number of enemy troops which might, in the most favourable circumstances, be brought into action, would be in the neighbourhood of 6,500 men.

Despite these considerations, the naval Planners still expressed doubt about the frontal assault, but not on naval grounds. C.C.O. supported the naval Planners and only yielded after pressure from the Home Forces representatives. It was again emphasised that the frontal assault would be preceded by a bombing attack on the town just before the craft, carrying the assaulting troops, touched down. This bombardment would be of maximum intensity and it was thought that the defence would be too confused by it, and by subsequent attacks from low-flying aircraft, to be in a position to offer stout or prolonged resistance. The bombing was to be carried out both from high and low level, the high-altitude attack being made against the sea front and beach defences. The question of fighter cover and air support for the land forces was debated at some length for it was realised that support from the air would be of paramount importance.

The plan, which included a frontal assault, preceded by bombing, was then adopted.

On 9th May, 1942, the outline plan for the operation was submitted to the Chiefs of Staff Committee and on 13th May, that Committee approved the plan as the basis for the detailed planning which was to be carried out by the Force Commanders. The proposal of the C.-in-C., Home Forces, that the troops to be used should come from the Canadian Forces was approved, and the Military and Air Force Commanders were appointed. They were Major-General Roberts, Canadian Army, and Air Vice-Marshal Leigh Mallory, R.A.F. The naval forces were to be under the command of Rear-Admiral H.T. Baillie Grohman, who was, at that time, on his way home from Alexandria, where he had been in charge of combined operations activities.

In forwarding the Outline Plan to the Chiefs of Staff on 9th May, C.C.O. made the following remarks:

(1) I forward herewith the outline plan for a raid on Dieppe to be carried out during the latter part of June.
(2) This operation will be of great value as training for Operation "Sledgehammer" or any other major operations as far as the actual assault is concerned. It will not, however, throw light on the maintenance problem over beaches.
(3) The plan has been drawn up in consultation with the General Officer Commanding-in-Chief South-Eastern Command, who

concurs in it. I ask the approval of the Chiefs of Staff: (i) For the outline plan; (ii) For permission to assemble and train the requisite forces; (iii) For the appointment of Force Commanders and their staffs to date 12th May, 1942.

The Chiefs of Staff gave their approval.

Proposed Air Attack on Dieppe gets Cabinet Approval

On 19th May, 1942, a minute was sent to the Prime Minister pointing out that, under the present Cabinet ruling, targets in occupied France could only be bombed when weather conditions were such that accurate attack could be expected and that this restriction had already proved a handicap to combined operations. The example of the attack on St. Nazaire on 28th March was quoted.

On that occasion, aircraft of Bomber Command arrived over the town and woke up the defences, but were debarred by their orders from creating the diversion, which was an important part of the plan, because low cloud conditions prevented them from seeing the dock area which was their objective. The memorandum went on to explain that such conditions might recur and, therefore, the Chiefs of Staff hoped that the Cabinet ruling might be relaxed in so far as combined operations were concerned. On 1st June, the Chiefs of Staff were informed that the Prime Minister was still opposed to the indiscriminate bombing of French towns at night, but that an exception would be made in the case of a coastal raid.

On 5th June, an important change in the plans was made. At a meeting attended by the Force Commanders, representatives from C.O.H.Q. and Lieut.-General Montgomery, G.O.C.-in-C., South-Eastern Command, who took the Chair, it was decided to abandon the project of a high-level bombing of Dieppe. The Air Force Commander was of the opinion that the bombing of the port itself during the night of the assault would not be the most profitable way of using bombers and might only result in putting the enemy on the alert. In the view of the Military Commander, the destruction of large numbers of houses and the setting on fire of a considerable portion of the town would prevent tanks operating in streets choked with debris. High-level bombing was therefore abandoned in favour of diversionary air attacks.

Intention and Plan

The intention of the operation, as given to the Force Commanders in the outline plan, was as follows: "A force of Infantry, Airborne Troops and Armoured Fighting Vehicles will land in the area of Dieppe to seize the town and vicinity. This will be held during daylight while the tasks are carried out. The force will then re-embark. The operation will be supported by fighter aircraft and bomber action."

Briefly the plan adopted by the Force Commanders consisted of flank attacks by parachute troops on the batteries to the East and West of the harbour entrance and, 30 minutes after these attacks, a frontal assault on the port by the main body.

The withdrawal was to take place on a rising tide just before dark and the naval craft required for the withdrawal were to remain in the vicinity of the port until required and then make their own way back.

Preparation and Rehearsal

The provision of the necessary ships and craft for the operation entailed the concentration in the Solent of the five Belgian L.S.I. (S), the two Dutch L.S.I. (M) and the L.S.I. (L) *Glengyle* which was on her way home after taking part in Operation "Ironclad".

In addition, twenty-four L.C.T. and twenty L.C.P. (L) were also required to facilitate the training of the troops, certain of the latter were based at Newhaven where the Coastal Force base provided facilities for maintenance and accommodation.

This concentration was in all respects complete by 1st June, 1942.

Two full-scale rehearsals were carried out using the small harbour of West Bay (Bridport) on 13th June and 23rd June. The second rehearsal was ordered by C.C.O. because the Military Commander represented that the standard of precision of the landing craft was not good enough for an operation of this complexity. This second rehearsal, which was attended by C.C.O., proved more successful and he decided to carry out the operation on the first favourable date after 24th June.

Postponement and Cancellation

During the last week in June and the first week in July, the weather deteriorated and on 5th July, the operation was postponed, but the weather continued to be unfavourable which resulted in the operation being cancelled on 7th July. Early on that morning, the *Princess Josephine Charlotte* and *Princess Astrid* had been bombed and both ships were hit, the damage to the former being severe.

Consequent upon the cancellation, the military forces returned to their various training areas in Sussex and Surrey. General Montgomery, as G.O.C.-in-C., Southern Command, was opposed to remounting the operation, but the Prime Minister was most insistent that a large scale operation should take place during the summer of 1942 and the C.I.G.S.

was most emphatic that the planning for the main invasion could not proceed until an operation of that scale had taken place.

A raid on Bayonne had been mounted but, on arrival of the landing craft off the harbour bar, the swell was found to be too great. Operation "Blazing" against Alderney had been prepared in May but the raiding force had not landed; now "Rutter" had been cancelled. This was virtually defeat, all this work and nothing to show for it; it was bad for morale.

Although this interval might have led to a loss of security, the extraordinary steps taken to ensure secrecy were effective and when the operation came off, on 19th August, 1942, the enemy were taken completely by surprise.

New Directive – Operation "Jubilee"

On 27th July, 1942, a new directive for a raid on Dieppe was given by the Chiefs of Staff to C.C.O. which ran as follows:

> The outline plan for a raid is to be prepared by the Chief of Combined Operations who will then obtain the agreement or comments of the Commanders-in-Chief concerned or their representatives and the Assistant Chief of the Naval Staff (Home). The outline plan with these comments will then be submitted by the Chief of Combined Operations to the Chiefs of Staff committee. If approved, Force Commanders will then be appointed and made responsible under the Chief of Combined Operations for the detailed planning of the raid.
>
> When the detailed plan and the orders of the Force Commanders are completed, they are to be approved by the Chief of Combined Operations who should obtain the agreement or comments of the authorities he has already consulted when submitting the outline plan. The Chief of Combined Operations is to be responsible for launching the operation in consultation with those authorities and subject to the approval of the Naval Commander-in-Chief.

It was under this directive that C.C.O. launched the operation against Dieppe which was known as Operation "Jubilee".

Alterations to the Plan

The main changes in the plan for this new operation were that the Commandos were to carry out the neutralisation of the flanking batteries instead of the parachute troops and that the withdrawal had to take place on one tide instead of two. The Commandos were introduced because conditions were often suitable for ground troops but unsuitable for the employment of airborne troops.

Security for this operation was of an extremely high order. C.C.O. gave orders that nothing was to be put in writing and only two or three officers at C.O.H.Q. were informed. Even the First Lord and, as far as is known, the Defence Committee were never consulted. That it was one of the best guarded secrets of the war is borne out, not only by our own intelligence sources, but by captured enemy records after the war.

New Naval Force Commander

When the operation was cancelled in July, the Admiralty posted the original Naval Force Commander and his Chief of Staff to new appointments.

When the decision was taken to remount the operation, C.-in-C., Portsmouth objected to the appointment of *ad hoc* Naval Force Commanders for such complicated operations because it had a bad effect on the forces and was extremely difficult for the C.-in-C. and his staff. If this operation was to take place, he must have, in his opinion, a Force Commander and staff familiar with the plan and technique. This meant taking them from C.O.H.Q., and C.C.O., readily agreed. The Admiralty therefore appointed Captain J. Hughes-Hallett as Naval Force Commander and Commander (Acting Captain) J.D. Luce as Chief of Staff on 17th July, 1942. The Prime Minister personally approved the plan.

Planning at C.O.H.Q.

The Outline Plan for "Jubilee" was produced in C.O.H.Q., because C.C.O. was responsible for preparing the Outline Plan and for mounting raids in N.W. Europe. Facilities were available there for the staff of G.H.Q. Home Forces and the Force Commanders, when appointed, to make their detailed plans. This was a great advantage to the Force Commanders because: (1) Usually, their own headquarters were situated miles apart; (2) They had the members of the Combined Staff, who could give them first-hand information on any subject required, readily at hand; (3) The Intelligence Staff at C.O.H.Q. could provide accurate and up-to-date data on which the Commanders could base their plans without having to refer to the Service Ministries; [and] (4) Any unusual equipment required for the operation could be provided at short notice.

Lessons Learned From The Operation

From the point of view of the eventual invasion of the Continent, the lessons learnt from Operation "Jubilee" were most valuable. It is true to say that they formed the basis for the future organisation, training, technique and research for Combined Operations against a defended coast.

Frontal Assault

The main lesson learned was that a frontal assault on a defended port was not practicable and none was carried out subsequent to Dieppe.

Naval Support Fire

The Operation proved that no standard naval vessel or craft had the necessary qualities or equipment to provide sufficient close inshore support.

The staff at C.O.H.Q. at once set about producing the staff requirements for what was required and the fact that this staff was a properly integrated body of all three Services ensured that the question was tackled in the shortest possible time. Designs in blue print form were soon prepared and explained to the Service Ministries where constructive criticism and co-operation were forthcoming.

Alterations to existing craft were soon adopted, but perhaps the most revolutionary idea was that put forward by Colonel H. Langley, Deputy Director of Experiments and Staff Requirements (D.D.X.S.R.), who advocated the use of 65lb. rockets fired from rocket projectors mounted in ships and craft, and the revolutionary use of a Radar P.P.I. to obtain the exact range. In this way a beach could be drenched with high explosives just prior to the landing craft touching down and the troops could be ashore and at grips with the defenders before the latter had recovered from the initial shock. This system of fire support was used in all subsequent operations and proved most successful.

Another detail of craft was also initiated known as the Landing Craft, Gun (L.C.G.). this was an L.C.T. in which were mounted 4.7-in. naval guns

Further, all landing craft were adapted so that on the run-in, the personnel aboard could use their weapons, including the guns of the tanks when embarked.

Beach Parties

The need for well trained and efficient beach parties was again emphasised by this operation. In consequence, C.C.O. set up a special school for these units at Ardentinny in Loch Long which was commissioned as H.M.S. *Armadillo* in November, 1942. At the same time the title for the beach parties was altered to Beach Commandos.

Tanks in the Assault

At Dieppe, the tanks had found themselves in great difficulty because they had all been landed in daylight with the leading waves in the face of defences which dominated the beach and against tank obstacles which had not been breached. The lessons from this was that the tanks should not be landed until the defences had been captured and the obstacles cleared.

A school of instruction in the breaching of beach obstacles was subsequently set up and produced the technique and equipment that was required.

Arising out of this, the question of the removal of underwater obstacles which might hinder the landing craft on their way to the beach, was also investigated. Eventually the Admiralty undertook this responsibility.

Beach Recognition

The difficulty of making certain that the landing craft landed the troops in the right place was again made evident by the experience of all the forces landed. C.C.O. decided that this could only be rectified by a special course for officers who would have to guide in the leading flights. Accordingly, a Beach Pilotage School was set up at Glen Caladh, near Tighnabruaich which was commissioned as H.M.S. *James Cook* in September, 1942.

Headquarters Ship

The need for a properly fitted Headquarters Ship was again made very apparent. A destroyer, H.M.S. *Calpe*, carried out this duty at Dieppe. Although it was only a short daylight raid, her limited wireless installations were overloaded with the signal traffic. It was unfortunate that the new L.S.H., H.M.S. *Bulolo*, was not available for the operation but she had only just been completed and had not been properly worked up.

Fighter Direction

Arising out of the provision of fighter protection for the ships, the need became apparent for a ship from which the fighters could be directed and controlled. The Signal Division at C.O.H.Q. were charged with the production of the designs and, in consequence of their efforts, Fighter Direction Ships took part in all subsequent operations against the Continent and proved their worth.

Air Vice-Marshal Leigh Mallory was, at first, opposed to fighters being directed by R.A.F. officers embarked in warships, in his opinion they could be better controlled from his headquarters at Uxbridge. He did, however, foresee that there might be a need for fighter direction by destroyers in an emergency and, therefore, allowed arrangements to be made for this purpose. Nevertheless, during the operation, when it became apparent that fighters could no longer be effectively controlled from Uxbridge, he passed over all fighter direction to the destroyers on the spot.

Formation of Force "J"
Before "Jubilee" took place, it was realised that *ad hoc* arrangements for landing craft forces would not suffice. Forces must be organised well in advance. The need for discipline, morale, tactical integration and competence are not disputed in the case of war vessels, troops and air functions, therefore precisely the same should apply to ships and craft in an assault force. In addition, a Commander cannot cater for administrative needs if the administration is not one of his responsibilities.

The Naval Force Commander reported on the subject before the operation and was strongly supported by the C.-in-C. who naturally disliked the presence in his area of large forces administered by authorities extraneous to the naval chain of command. This was supported by the Admiralty but actually opposed by various administrative authorities and by many in C.O.H.Q. From this proposal Force "J" was formed which no doubt in the light of subsequent knowledge, should have been formed earlier and might have produced more raids and further success.

The Strategic Value of the Operation
Mr. Winston Churchill in his book *The Second World War* (Volume IV, pages 458 and 459) makes the following observations on the value of the operation.

> Our post-war examination of their records shows that the Germans did not receive, through leakage of information, any special warning of our intention to attack. However, their general estimate of the threat to the Dieppe sector led to an intensification of defence measures along the whole front. Special precautions were ordered for periods like that between 10th August and 19th August, when moon and tide were favourable for landings. The Division responsible for the defence of the Dieppe sector had been reinforced during July and August and was at full strength and

routine alert at the moment of a raid. The Canadian Army in Britain had long been eager and impatient for action, and the main part of the landing force was provided by them. Their story is vividly told by the official historian of the Canadian Army and in other official publications, and need not be repeated here. Although the utmost gallantry and devotion were shown by all the troops and by the British Commandos and by their landing craft and their escorts, and many splendid deeds were done, the results were disappointing and the casualties heavy. In the Canadian 2nd Division, 18 per cent of the five thousand men embarked lost their lives and nearly two thousand of them were take prisoners.

Looking back, the casualties of the memorable action may seem out of all proportion to the results. It would be wrong to judge the episode solely by such standard. Dieppe occupies a place of its own in the story of the war, and the grim casualty figures must not class it as a failure. It was a costly but not unfruitful reconnaissance in force. Tactically it was a mine of experience. It shed revealing light on many shortcomings in our outlook. It taught us to build in good time various new types of craft and appliances for later use. We learnt again the value of powerful support by naval heavy guns in an opposed landing, and our bombardment technique both marine and aerial, was thereafter improved. Above all it was shown that individual skill and gallantry without thorough organisation and combined training would not prevail, and that team work was the secret of success. This could only be provided by trained and organised amphibious formations. All those lessons were taken to heart.

Strategically, the raid served to make the Germans more conscious of the danger along the whole coast of Occupied France. This helped to hold troops and resources in the West which did something to take the weight off Russia. Honour to the brave who fell. Their sacrifice was not in vain.

Copies of the very full report on the Dieppe raid, which contained complete details and all the lessons learnt, were widely distributed, often by C.C.O. personally, at such conferences as Casablanca and to such Commanders as General Eisenhower and General Alexander.

Chapter 6

THE SWITCH TO THE MEDITERRANEAN, NORTH AFRICAN AND SICILY CAMPAIGNS

North Africa, Operation "Torch"
Early in July, 1942, General Marshal and Admiral King, Chiefs of United States Army and Navy Staffs, accompanied by Mr. Harry Hopkins, visited this country to continue the discussions begun in Washington.

The Decision to Invade North Africa
As a result of their deliberations, it was decided that a landing on the North Africa coast was to be the major operation in 1942 (Operation "Torch"). Further, it was decided that it was to take place as soon as possible and that operations on the Continent of Europe were to be confined to raids. The preparations for the re-entry into the Continent, however, were not to be abandoned but the tempo was to be slowed down because the North African operation would take such a large proportion of the available personnel, equipment and shipping.

Role of C.O.H.Q. in "Torch"
The decision on "Torch" was made on 28th July, 1942, and on that date C.C.O. appointed five planning syndicates from the planners at C.O.H.Q. to consider the five separate assaults envisaged.
On 7th August C.C.O. personally offered all his planning resources to General D.W. Eisenhower, U.S. Army, who had just been appointed

Allied Commander-in-Chief for the operation. On the same day Admiral Sir Bertram Ramsay, who had originally been appointed to the command of the naval forces for Operation "Sledgehammer" was appointed Naval Commander for this operation, mainly on the advice offered to the First Sea Lord by C.C.O.

Shortly afterwards the Allied Commander-in-Chief asked for the services of the Intelligence Staff at C.O.H.Q. and also those of the Directorate of Experiments and Staff Requirements (D.X.S.R.). This request was at once agreed to by C.C.O.

The planning of this operation entailed, not only the difficulties of such a large scale effort in what was virtually a new type of warfare, but also the complications inherent in an allied operation where the organisation, equipment, staff system and even to some extent the language of the two allies differed.

From the first, the Allied Commander-in-Chief insisted on an integrated staff; each section of the staff being composed of officers of all Services and each nationality with the senior one in each section acting as the head of that section irrespective of his nationality.

The planning officers lent by C.C.O. were distributed in the sections as the Allied Commander-in-Chief thought best and so they were associated with the plans from the beginning. There was great merit in this arrangement because the American conception of combined operations or as they called them, amphibious operations, was at this time very different from the technique evolved at C.O.H.Q. by trial and error and in the hard school of practical experience.

Transfer of American Troops from Ireland

As part of the plan, it was decided to use in the assault the American troops which were garrisoning Northern Ireland. This meant that they had to be transported from there to this country and landed as near their ports of embarkation as possible. Owing to the fact that shipping for this move was not available, C.C.O., was asked to help. By dint of using the only available L.C.T.s in U.K. waters, the troops with their vehicles and tanks were ferried across the Irish Sea and landed where required. This was done to the detriment of the training of the landing craft crews, and, to a certain extent of combined training which meant having to accept incompletely trained crews for many of the L.C.T.s.

Headquarters Ships

The Headquarters ships to be used on the operation were *Bulolo* and *Largs*. The former was ready and worked up but, as a result of exercises and discussions, certain modifications in detail were found necessary and at once carried out.

The need for a second Headquarters Ship was apparent in the planning and arose when H.M.S. *Largs* was due in the U.K. about a week later. By using *Bulolo* as a model and obtaining a large amount of equipment from all three Services, she was fitted out in Liverpool in about a month. This was only possible because of the detailed and continuous supervision and instructions provided by C.O.H.Q. working without prepared drawings or specifications.

In addition, eight ships, in which were embarked the Senior Naval Officers Landing (S.N.O.L.) were fitted as Brigade Headquarters Ships and *Keren* and *Karanga* were brought up to date. The modifications were similar to those in *Largs* and would not have been possible if suitable equipment had not been prepared and pooled at the request of C.C.O.

Special Operations

Before leaving the part played by C.O.H.Q. in the planning and mounting of Operation "Torch", mention must be made of one important exploit.

The Special Boat Section of the Special Service Brigade under Major R.J.A. Courtney carried out an operation known as "Reservist". This officer with two other Commando Officers arranged the landing of Major-General Mark Clark, U.S. Army, and his staff on the north coast of Africa; they landed from folding canoes, known as "Folbots", launched from a submarine. The conference with the French authorities which followed was successful in that French troops eventually came over to the side of the Allies.

Visit of General Patton

General George Patton, U.S. Army, was appointed to command the American assault at Casablanca. On hearing of this, he at once visited London and, during his short stay in August 1942, spent considerable time at C.O.H.Q.

He appealed to C.C.O. for advice. Accordingly, C.C.O. suggested that he should take back with him to the United States Major-General Truscott, who was the Chief of the American Army Staff at C.O.H.Q. and further, C.C.O. undertook to provide him with a team of Inter-Service Inter-Allied planners. General Patton gratefully accepted this offer which resulted in General Truscott being given command of the landing at Port Lyauty in Operation "Torch"; subsequently, in Operation "Husky", he commanded the Licata landing.

C.C.O. urged General Patton to direct the landings from a properly equipped Headquarters Ship, but the latter was of the opinion that this would not be necessary and stated that he would prefer to be in the flagship of Admiral Hewitt, U.S.N., who was commanding the naval forces. C.C.O. pointed out that, when the French Navy appeared, this flagship, a cruiser, would pursue any French ships and told General Patton that he would then be quickly removed from the scene of action and unable to control his landing. General Patton decided to accept the risk to his later consternation and regret, for just as he was on the point of going ashore to take over command on land, the cruiser (U.S.S. *Augusta*), in which he was embarked, went off at full speed after some French destroyers with General Patton as an impotent spectator.

This incident finally convinced the Americans of the need for providing properly designed and fitted Headquarters Ships on the British model.

Admiralty Remarks

The following remarks in an Admiralty report on the mounting of "Torch" are interesting:

> As soon as it became clear that our policy was switching to North Africa, control became more difficult, as the northern bases in the U.K. were involved, which had never been controlled satisfactorily by the local Naval Commander-in-Chiefs. In fact, it can be said that during this period of mounting "Torch", the Admiralty largely lost control of the situation. It should be remembered however that the speed of mounting and secrecy were the essential factors and the contributions of C.O.H.Q. to this mounting operation were immense.
>
> It was clear that "Torch" could only be a slap and not the first of a series of punches. The purpose was to get a force together of sufficient magnitude somehow and get it away secretly to date. That this force started mounting in September, 1942, and carried out the operation in November, 1942, was in itself an extraordinary piece of work, and was only achieved by the relatively independent efforts of every individual responsible. There was not time for tidy co-ordination. The result of this showed itself in considerable wastage in material and a rapid fall in the availability of craft in the U.K.

The Effect of "Torch" on the Combined Operations Organisation

It became apparent before the expedition sailed that "Torch" had put a most severe strain on all Combined Operations resources.

On 30th September, C.C.O. sent a note to the Chiefs of Staff which clearly shows the inroads that were made into his resources and the general effect of "Torch" on his organisation as a whole.

The summary of its conclusions was: (1) "Torch" had taken more landing craft than C.C.O. could produce crews, and numbers have had to be made up from other R.N. resources; (2) The standard of training of a large part of the craft crews and assault forces was not high enough for a tough or protracted assault; (3) So large a part of the Naval Combined Operations Command had been given up to "Torch" that it would not be possible to train an adequate new force before the summer of 1943; and (4) The early formation of a Naval Raiding Force was an essential prerequisite for any re-entry into the Continent, and it must be given regular fighting experience.

Manning of Landing Ships and Craft

The situation regarding the provision of crews for landing ships and craft had become critical. The planning of amphibious operations, which were proposed for 1943, was proceeding and the production programme of landing ships and craft required for these operations had been accelerated.

The intake of naval personnel had, however, been restricted by a War Cabinet decision to the extent that it was quite impossible to meet the normal Fleet commitments and at the same time provide the rapidly increasing numbers of men for the manning of combined operations ships and craft.

The only possible solution was to increase the intake into the Navy, a difficult matter in view of the War Cabinet's ruling.

Admiral Mountbatten, therefore, decided to make a direct approach to Mr. Bevin, the Minister of Labour, on the question. The Minister explained that the reason for the restriction of the naval intake was because every possible man was required for the Army for the invasion of France. However, he appreciated that if it was not possible to man the invasion fleet, the Army would be unable to reach the Continent. Under these circumstances he said he would regard crews to take the soldiers to France as part of the necessary manpower for the Army, and give directions accordingly that C.C.O. should be given all the men needed for "Overlord".

Formation of Force "J"

The ships and craft, which had taken part in Operation "Jubilee", were kept together in the Solent area under the command of Captain J. Hughes-Hallett.

The five L.S.I. (S) had to be employed ferrying landing craft required for "Torch" from the south to the north coasts. Also, the landing ships (stern chute) were likewise employed on this duty.

As recorded earlier, it was obvious that this organisation of ships and craft should be on a permanent basis. This was agreed between the Admiralty and C.C.O., and Force "J" came into being on 12th October, 1942. The Senior Naval Officer set up his headquarters in the Royal Yacht Squadron, which was commissioned as H.M.S. *Vectis*. The officers of the force occupied a block of flats on the seafront which had been originally requisitioned as Combined Headquarters for the planning and execution of Operations "Rutter" and "Jubilee".

It was intended that this force should form a prototype for other assault forces to be used in Operation "Round-up" and "Overlord". In the meantime, it was ready for further raids or operations at short notice. As it was a considerable naval force, it was fortunate in that berthing could be found in the Solent. The L.S.T.s lay off Cowes and the L.C.T.s were moored in the Beaulieu River off Exbury House, which had already been commissioned as H.M.S. *Mastodon*. The remainder berthed in the Hamble River off H.M.S. *Tormentor*. The Solent was excellent for training, as in its sheltered water it provided strong cross-tides and any form of beach that was required.

The next step taken by C.C.O. was to send a memorandum to the Chiefs of Staff, urging the formation of further similar forces. The text of the memorandum is as follows:

Need For The Formation Of Naval Assault Forces

Memorandum by the Chief of Combined Operations
(S.R. 982/42, dated 16.11.42)

(1) Of the many lessons learnt at Dieppe, the Force Commanders of that operation agree with me that the second most important lesson, next to the need for Naval Support fire, is the following:

For any amphibious campaign involving assaults on strongly defended coasts held by a determined enemy, it is essential that the landing ships and craft required for the assaults shall be organised well in advance into Naval Assault Forces. These must have a coherence and degree of permanence comparable to that of any first line fighting formations. The need for discipline, morale, tactical integration and flexibility, and professional competence, are not disputed in the case of troops, war vessels and air formations. Precisely the same applies to assault ships and craft.

(2) Against half-hearted opposition, it is, of course, possible to mount an operation like "Torch" and with very few rehearsals carry it out successfully. Against serious German opposition such as was encountered at Dieppe, a very highly trained naval force is needed.

THE SWITCH TO THE MEDITERRANEAN

(3) In fact, I postponed the operations because rehearsals showed the naval force was insufficiently trained in the assault stages, and, in all, the "Jubilee" force was kept in being and trained for a period of 13 weeks.

(4) The Admiralty have now agreed that the force should be reconstituted as a permanent Force "J" consisting initially of:
1 River gunboat,
7 L.S.I. carrying L.C.A. and L.C.S. (M),
48 L.C.T.,
6 L.C.F. (L),
72 L.C.P.,
4 M.L.,
4 70-ft. M.G.B.,
1 M.T.B.

The longer this force remains in being, the tougher the problem which it can tackle.

(5) Dieppe has shown us that against severe opposition, it is no good having a large number of craft "on paper" unless they are organised into proper fighting forces well in advance of the operation, and that force, which is to be the spearhead of the attack, should have had actual fighting experience of this kind.

(6) It is clear that in planning future assault operations, using block numbers of landing craft is unreal, and that instead the Planning Staffs must use numbers of organised forces of the type of Force "J" in exactly the same way as they plan on formed and organised military and air units.

(7) On this more rational system of reckoning, and having regard to other strategic requirements now contemplated, the possibility of obtaining a simultaneous assault lift for five British Assault Divisions in the U.K. early in 1944 as recently postulated by the Combined Commanders, is exceedingly remote.

(8) In order to enable the American authorities to obtain the first-hand experience needed for them to take part in an ultimate "Round-up" it is suggested that the American Chiefs of Staff be invited, at an appropriate moment, to form an American counterpart to Force "J" in European waters. To begin with they might send some American-manned landing craft of each type to join up with Force "J" itself.

(9) It is further suggested that suitable military formations (e.g., Brigade Groups) should be detailed to work, each with a corresponding Naval Assault Force, in order that they may get to know each other and practice and rehearse together as opportunity offers, culminating, if possible, in taking part in an actual raid before carrying out "Round-up". In the first instance, it is intended

to detail one of the Royal Marine Brigade Groups to work with Force "J".

(10) To sum up, the Chiefs of Staff Committee are asked:

(a) To invite the Admiralty to form Special Assault Forces on the lines of Force "J" as sufficient resources become available;

(b) To invite the American Chiefs of Staff to send over some American-manned landing craft of each type to join up with Force "J" and, later, to form an American counterpart to Force "J".

(c) To approve the nomination of Brigade Groups to assault forces.

(signed) Louis Mountbatten
Chief of Combined Operations,
Combined Operations Headquarters,
16th November, 1942.

Planning of Raids

When the Planning Section had been released from their duties on "Torch" with the Staff of the Supreme Commander, C.C.O. directed that they should investigate the possibilities of raids on the French coast which were within the terms of his directive. It was here that the effect of the removal of the craft for "Torch" made itself at once apparent. The greatest difficulty was over the provision of small landing craft, since those left behind in the United Kingdom were those which were not operationally fit for "Torch". Thus, we find a considerable refitting programme being put in hand; the work was mostly carried out by private yards.

As the craft became available for service, they were distributed between the Force "J" and the training establishments. This took time and its effect on the Combined Organisation has been mentioned previously.

Planning Activities

Six weeks before "Torch" sailed, the J.P.S. appreciation, and outline plan for an operation against Sardinia, was received at C.O.H.Q. from the War Cabinet. This operation was given the code name of "Brimstone".

C.C.O. at once formed a planning syndicate to consider and advise on this project. On 7th November, 1942, C.C.O. forwarded an appreciation which recommended a very drastic alteration in the outline plan. During the months of November and December, much of the planners' work was confined to the study of Operation "Brimstone" because Allied Force H.Q. and C.O.H.Q. did not see eye to eye over the scope of the prosed undertaking. By Christmas no real decision had been reached.

Another operation which came under consideration, at the Prime Minister's suggestion, was one directed against the northern part of Norway which was given the code name "Jupiter". It was then considered that if northern Norway was occupied by us, it would be of great assistance to the Russians, and would enable convoys to be sailed to Murmansk more or less without interruption. For this operation, C.O.H.Q. advocated the supply of special equipment such as "Weasels", vehicles which could be driven over snow. But beyond certain units being trained in the Cairngorm Hills in the snow, the operation was never proceeded with, owing to the claims on personnel and material made by other theatres.

Plans for raids were also studied continuously but, owing to the lack of craft and personnel due to "Torch", these operations never came to anything.

Problems after the Sailing of "Torch"

After the sailing of the convoys for "Torch", the main problems facing C.O.H.Q. were to get Force "J" trained, completed with craft and crews, and welded into a proper Naval Assault Force. In addition, the training programme had to be stepped up to compete with the greatly increased intake; and the craft for this training had to be got ready and brought up to date.

The months of November and December saw this all going ahead at high pressure.

Sicily, Operation "Husky"

In January, 1943, a conference known as "Symbol" took place at Anfa Camp near Casablanca, at which the President of the U.S.A. and the Prime Minister were present. To assist them in their deliberations were the Combined Chiefs of Staff and certain high-ranking officers of their respective staffs. C.C.O. attended in his capacity as a member of the Chiefs of Staff Committee.

The Headquarters Ship H.M.S. *Bulolo* was used as an accommodation and communications ship, and certain of the W.R.N.S., A.T.S. and W.A.A.F. personnel from C.O.H.Q. were embarked for cyphering and secretarial duties.

At this conference, the strategy[1] for 1943 was finally settled.

---

[1] The overall strategy was eventually laid down in C.C.S. 170/2 dated 23rd January, 1943.

Operation "Husky"

In his book *Crusade in Europe*, General Eisenhower writes as follows:

"At Casablanca the Sicily operation was decided upon for two reasons, the first of which was its immediate advantage in opening up the Mediterranean Sea routes. The second was that because of the relatively small size of the island, its occupation after capture would not absorb unforeseen amounts of Allied strength in the event that the enemy should undertake any large scale counteraction. This reason weighed heavily with General Marshall – moreover, this decision in January, 1943, avoided a commitment to indefinite strategic offensives in the area. Successful attack would advance our bomber bases still further, but we would not necessarily be drawn into a campaign that would continuously devour valuable resources.

Planning

In the directive issued to General Eisenhower, it was laid down that the planning for the operation was to be carried out by the staffs on the spot.

This latter proviso did not absolve C.C.O. from advising the Commanders on the Combined Operations aspects of the assault. He therefore flew straight from Casablanca to General Eisenhower's headquarters in Algiers to discuss with him and his Commanders-in-Chief the provision of the necessary additional landing ships and landing craft.

On his return from Algiers, C.C.O. directed that the planning on Operation "Brimstone" (Sardinia) was to cease as far as C.O.H.Q. was concerned; a decision which was confirmed shortly afterwards by the Chiefs of Staff. As promised to General Eisenhower, C.C.O. now sent certain of C.O.H.Q. planners to North Africa to be utilised by the Supreme Commander with the integrated planning staffs engaged on planning the operation.

Training

The training of the forces to be employed, which were already in the Mediterranean, had of necessity to be carried out on the spot and here again certain of C.O.H.Q. training staff were requested to assist.

But in addition to these forces, it was decided to send a Canadian Division from England and the American 45th Division direct from the U.S.A. The training of the Canadian Division was carried out in the Combined Training Centres in Scotland under C.C.O., and to assist in training the U.S.A. contingent, certain officers from C.O.H.Q. were sent to join the staff of the Combined Operations Liaison Officer in Washington, for attachment to the 45th Division.

Contained in the minutes of the Chiefs of Staff meetings are recorded statements by C.C.O. pointing out how the loan of both planning and training staffs was affecting the work at C.O.H.Q. at this time.

Craft

In the outline plan for "Husky" a requirement arose for a number of L.C.T. This was quite a problem in itself because L.C.T.s were originally designed for cross-Channel operations and the specification stated they would not be required to operate in a sea above Force 4. Their endurance was also limited. This problem was at once tackled and the craft were made ready, mainly at Troon, for an ocean passage. To add to the difficulty, L.C.T. (4) developed a structural weakness at the after end of the tank deck which was particularly obvious in long seas. This necessitated each one being strengthened to overcome this defect. D.N.E. (C.O.), by dint of very great effort, managed to get this fitted to the L.C.T.s required so that they were able to sail in time to take part in the operation.

In addition to L.C.T.s, a request was also received for all the available Landing Craft Flak (L.C.F.). These were accordingly prepared for the ocean passage and eventually took part in the assaults.

L.C.T. Officers

To navigate L.C.T.s for an ocean passage, the Admiralty were unable to supply from General Service the number of officers required. The training of the officers employed in L.C.T.s only comprised a course in pilotage, which did not include deep sea navigation. It was therefore necessary to institute courses for these officers in astral navigation. These courses were carried out at the Major Landing Craft Tank Headquarters (H.M.S. *Dinosaur*) at Troon and lasted three weeks, in which time the officers, through intensive studies, became sufficiently proficient and not one L.C.T. got lost on the way.

Support Fire

Amongst the many deliberations of the planners, the question of support fire in the assault was a major concern. The importance of this was fully realised at C.O.H.Q. and every means of getting the Rocket-fitted L.C.T.s (L.C.T.(R)) into commission and carrying out trials were employed. There was opposition amongst both the users and the designers who were very doubtful of the success of the project.

C.C.O., however, was most insistent and the trials of the first craft were carried out on 21st April and several L.C.T. (R) took part in the actual operation in July. These, together with the L.C.G. armed with 4.7in. guns, which were also used in "Husky", amply proved their worth.

Beach Reconnaissance

The Naval Commander-in-Chief (Admiral Sir Andrew Cunningham) for Operation "Husky" was very anxious to ascertain the gradients of the beaches selected for the landings. Here again C.O.H.Q. helped. As the result of previous operations, the Combined Operations Pilotage Parties (C.O.P.P.s) had been formed. These consisted of officers specially trained to carry out beach reconnaissance at night and included one naval navigation specialist and one Royal Engineer officer. The technique employed was for a submarine to take the party close into the beach, they would then proceed ashore in a Folbot and return on completion of their reconnaissance to the submarine.

All trained parties were placed at the dispersal of the Commander-in-Chief directly his request was received. It is interesting to record some remarks made by the Commander-in-Chief, Mediterranean (Admiral Sir Andrew Cunningham), in his report on the operation to General Eisenhower:

Collection Of Beach Intelligence

> Much credit is due to the officers and men of the C.O.P.P. beach reconnaissance parties for their arduous and hazardous efforts to obtain details of the beach gradients and sand bars.
>
> The estimation of beach conditions and gradients by air photography and study of wave velocities have now reached a fine pitch of efficiency; but where sand bars exist there is no present substitute for swimming reconnaissance so the services of these gallant parties will continue to be necessary.

Mounting for Operation "Husky"

The mounting for Operation "Husky" is covered in greater detail in Chapter 12. It is sufficient to state here that it was the responsibility of the Combined Operations Command to mount, on the Clyde, two of the major components of the assault forces. These were Force "W" and Force "V".

Force "W", which was to have a period for training in the Suez Canal area, sailed on 16th March, 1943, and was routed via the Cape of God Hope.

Force "V" carried out training at the C.T.C. Inverary and was sailed from the Clyde on 28th June. This Force was routed through the Straits of Gibraltar and took part in the assault of Sicily from the west.

The lessons learned from Operations "Torch" and "Husky"

The Commander-in-Chief, Mediterranean (Admiral Cunningham) in his report to General Eisenhower summed up the lessons learned as follows:

Lessons of the Landings

(1) The need for faster and more seaworthy craft for the landing of supporting arms.
(2) The enormous value of the L.S.T. as a means of rapid landing of reinforcements.
(3) The importance of the 'water gap' and the need for a means of crossing it. The best means so far devised is the U.S. 'side carried' pontoon; but it is only suitable in calm seas.
(4) The profound effect that D.U.K.W.s[2] have had in amphibious warfare.
(5) The importance of early hydrographical survey of the bars to find the gaps which usually exist.
(6) The need for augmentation of labour in beach groups and stevedore gangs in merchant ships to ensure rapid unloading over beaches.
(7) The importance of Senior Air Officers with executive powers and a full knowledge of the plan to accompany the Naval Commanders in the assault.
(8) The importance of A.A. fire discipline particularly in minor craft.

All these things had been given careful study by C.O.H.Q. and had been continually advocated by them.

---

[2] Production codename for wheeled amphibians which, like Tanks, has remained and become the ordinary name for them.

Chapter 7

PREPARATION AND PLANNING FOR THE INVASION OF NORTH-WEST EUROPE

During May, 1942, the Chiefs of Staff decided that, as a result of their study of the American proposals for the re-entry into the Continent, it would be advisable for C.C.O. to visit the United States to explain to the American Naval and Military authorities the British views regarding this operation. Accordingly, during the first week in June C.C.O. flew to Washington and discussed the matter with the Combined Chiefs of Staff Committee.

At a meeting held with them on 4th June, C.C.O. outlined the position in the U.K. with regard to the planning and training for the invasion of the Continent. His remarks as recorded in the minutes of this meeting were as follows:

> (a) Planning
> The present organisation in London for planning consisted of a committee composed of General Paget, Commander-in-Chief, Home Forces; Air Marshal Sholto-Douglas, Commander-in-Chief, Fighter Command; Vice-Admiral Ramsay lately Admiral Commanding at Dover; General Chaney as U.S. representative; and himself. These officers met once or twice a week and their staff officers were in daily contact.
>
> Two types of operation were envisaged for 1943. First in a condition of affairs where the Russian campaign was still in progress ('Greenback'), in which case German air forces in the West were

weak and the plan was, after landing on a wide front in Northern France and securing the port of Antwerp, to strike straight eastwards towards Berlin. Second, in a state of affairs in which relatively few forces were engaged in Russia and we should have to expect stiff opposition from both the strong German air and ground forces ('Round-up'). In this latter case two different proposals were under examination. One, favoured by the Army and Air Force, was for our forces to strike to the eastward at once and the other, favoured by the Naval Staff and the Combined Operations Staff, was first to secure the peninsular of Brittany and the French Atlantic ports to enable the follow up and maintenance to be put through them. An immediate decision on which of these two plans should be adopted was not vital, as, in any case, embarkation arrangements along the whole of the British south coast were necessary; all ports of this coast would have to be used and the preparatory disposition for both troops and ships would be the same.

(b) Assault Technique

The technique of the initial assault was under constant examination. Many exercises had been carried out, and raiding operations had been and would continue to be undertaken to test the various methods of assault which had been evolved. Raids on a larger scale than those already undertaken were planned, but it was important that these raids should not assume the appearance of an invasion. Great store was set on the value of French patriots in the final invasion, and it was important that these patriots should not rise prematurely. Arrangements were being made for adequate leadership and arming of the French population.

It had been found that during a night approach not more than 30 small craft could be relied on to move in one convoy without confusion. The maximum number of men that could be landed on any one beach from the Higgins Eureka type of craft was therefore 600. British assault landing craft, which were armoured, had a somewhat larger lift, allowing 840 to be landed in one flight and the value of the armour had been proved in operations. In either case, however, the density which we could put ashore on any one beach was insufficient particularly when vehicle landing craft for tanks, Bren carriers or guns, had to be substituted for personnel-carrying craft. For this reason the Giant R craft,[1] capable of carrying 200 men, had been proposed. Even if only 20 of these craft proceeded in company to a beach, a total of 4,000 men could be landed which greatly improved the prospects of success.

---

[1] Later L.C.P. (L).

When General Marshal visited C.O.H.Q. in April, 1942, he asked Admiral Mountbatten what he could do to help. The latter replied, 'Telegraph to-day to double every British order for landing ships and landing craft and take over the new orders yourself. Design and produce 300 L.C.I. (L), 150 for you and 150 for me,' and he sketched out the design of L.C.I. (L) there and then on a piece of paper.

With regard to infantry assault ships, only ten were at present available though many more of the cross-Channel type were being taken up and adapted. These would prove invaluable in the event of a flank attack on the western seaboard being necessary, as they could carry relays of assault landing craft.

The technical problem of getting tanks ashore at night had been solved and had been explained to certain U.S. officers. The destruction of beach defences was now being investigated.

(c) Topographical Data

Accurate information on the nature of the beaches was essential and coastal reconnaissance was being undertaken by the R.A.F. who photographed the beaches at all stages of the tides. From these photographs, charts showing the beach gradients were being prepared, and models of the whole coast and of small sections of it were being made.

(d) Supplies

In view of the unfavourable nature of the shallow beaches on the French coast and the difficulties with surf, it was essential that adequate ports, through which troops could be supplied, should be captured at the earliest possible moment. C.C.O. felt that both Calais and Boulogne, having narrow shallow entrances, would be blocked and so denied to us. It would be necessary to use such ports as Le Havre and Cherbourg and possibly certain of the Atlantic coast ports. One of the problems connected with supply was the provision of the necessary gasoline. The shortage of small tankers and the dangers which they ran from fires caused by incendiaries, had proved a difficult problem, but it was now being solved by the production of a form of Trans-Atlantic cable with a hollow core which could be laid at a speed of about 4 knots and through which 100 tons of gasoline could be pumped each day. These cables were being made in 35-mile lengths which, for the wider parts of the Channel, could be joined.[2]

---

[2] This scheme had the code name "Pluto" and was produced at a discussion between C.C.O., his D.X.S.R. (Capt. Hussey R.N.) and Mr. Geoffrey Lloyd, Minister of Petroleum Warfare.

(e) Communication

A Committee had been formed in London, consisting of communications officers of the three British Services, together with communications officers of the U.S. Army and Navy, to whom an officer of the U.S. Air Corps would shortly be added, who were evolving a common technique for use in the assault. Assault Headquarters Ships were being built which would act as Divisional Headquarters and which could be run ashore if necessary to prevent sinking by enemy action. They contained plotting rooms and map rooms and had very comprehensive wireless equipment. Each of these Headquarters Ships would contain the Commanders of the three Services responsible for a divisional front, and arrangements were being made for cables to run out to them from England as soon as they had been beached. They would be protected by special A.A. vessels and smoke clouds. A new technique had been devised, known as 'Combined Support Control' by which support from warships' guns, light or heavy support craft, bombers, fighters or smoke laying aircraft could be given at the request of Battalion Commanders.

(f) Manning of Landing Craft

The problem of provision of personnel to man the landing craft had proved a formidable one. Some 20 to 30 thousand officers and men would be required, but few active Service naval officers or petty officers were available. It was therefore necessary to train men from the very beginning, first in initial training centres where they would learn to handle their craft, then in combined training centres where they would train with the Army.

(g) Training

The problem of training personnel of the three Services to be used for the assault was one of the most important, and the U.S. staff officers now in London were helping with this difficult problem. Certain British officers had been sent over to the United States to gain experience from U.S. Amphibious Forces, and these close contacts were proving invaluable.

(h) Use of Airborne Troops

The Havre-Calais area, which was most favourable from the point of view of Air support under a British-based fighter 'umbrella', was now heavily defended by the enemy. The smaller enemy guns of from 4 to 6 inches had all been sited so that they could defend their own beaches. The coast was shallow and so honeycombed with wire and pillboxes that attack in this area was virtually impossible unless the German batteries could be mopped up by airborne troops. The Second Brigade of the British Airborne

Division was now forming and, on completion of this Division, it was hoped to form a second, but the bottleneck was troop-carrying aircraft. It was vitally important that the maximum number of trained airborne troops and aircraft should be available for the final operation.

U.S. Navy Views

The views propounded by C.C.O. at this meeting were not immediately shared by the United States Naval Chief of Staff (Admiral King, the Chief of Naval Operations). He held that the U.S. Navy was already fully occupied with operations in the Pacific and that it would severely tax his resources if he was to undertake the provision, training and manning of landing ships and craft required for the European theatre. General Marshall indicated that, if necessary, this was a task that could be undertaken by the U.S. Army, whereupon Admiral King, rather than surrender the birth right of the Navy to the Army, decided that the Navy would play its part. Consequently, he sent Vice-Admiral A. Kent Hewitt to England to work with C.C.O. in London to ensure that the technique developed by the two Navies was the same. It was Admiral Hewitt who subsequently commanded the Western Naval Task Force in Operation "Torch" and the Western Task Force in Operation "Husky".

Allied Signal Communications

From the point of view of C.O.H.Q., perhaps the most interesting decision made at the meeting is that recorded in a Combined Chiefs of Staff paper dated 10th June, 1942. It reads as follows: "The Chief of Combined Operations in London has already a small staff containing communications officers from all the British Services and also representatives of the U.S. Navy and Army. This staff is developing the special communications technique required for the proposed operations on the Continent. It is suggested that, to ensure speedy action this staff should be developed into a Combined Organisation fully representative of both American and British Services, with executive powers of decision and action."

The Committee decided that: "The Chief of Combined Operations will deal with the Commanding General, European Theatre, to ensure the co-ordination of training and technique between the forces of the two nations and to co-ordinate questions involving communications pertaining to the special combined operations."

It was also noted that:"Assault Headquarters Ships were being built which would act as Divisional Headquarters, and would be run ashore to prevent sinking by enemy action. They contained plotting rooms, map rooms and had very extensive wireless equipment. Each of these Headquarters Ships would contain the Commanders of the three Services responsible for the divisional front, and arrangements were being made for cables to be run out to them from England as soon as they had been beached."

The Combined Signal Staff under C.C.O. had prepared the layout of these ships and the Admiralty had one in hand, H.M.S. *Bulolo*, almost completed at that time. Further the Combined Signal School, H.M.S. *Dundonald II* was actually training the personnel required to man the ships when ready. Thus, it came about that, for all the landings subsequently carried out on the Continent, the Combined Operations Organisation was responsible for the signal and W/T communications, both in the provision and design of material and in the training of the personnel.

C.C.O.s Interview with the President

Before he returned to England, C.C.O. had a five-hour interview with the President of the United States. During this interview he discussed the general situation and the views held by the British Chiefs of Staff for the re-entry into the Continent.

On his return C.C.O. reported very fully to the Chiefs of Staff and the Prime Minister on what had taken place. After seeing the Prime Minister, C.C.O. sent a summary[3] of what he had said to the latter to the President as follows:

> I was very grateful to you for giving me the opportunity of such a long and interesting talk last Tuesday and I did my best to convey all that you had told me to the Prime Minister and the Chiefs of Staff. In order to make sure that I correctly conveyed your points I propose recapitulating here what I told the Prime Minister.
>
> I pointed out that you stressed the great need for American soldiers to be given an opportunity of fighting as soon as possible, and that you wished me to remind the Prime Minister of the agreement reached last time he was in Washington, that in the event of things going very badly for the Russians this summer a sacrifice landing would be carried out in France to assist them. I pointed out that no landing that we could carry out could draw off any troops, since there were some 25 German Divisions already in France and landing craft shortage prevented our putting ashore an adequate number.

---

[3] *The White House Papers of Mr. Harry L. Hopkins* by Robert E. Sherwood.

The chief German shortage lay in fighter aircraft and all our efforts were being bent towards provoking fighter battles in the West.

I said that you have asked for an assurance that we would be ready to follow up a crack in German morale by landing in France this autumn and that I had given you an assurance, that such an operation was being planned and was at present held at two months' notice.

I pointed out that you did not wish to send a million soldiers to England to find, possibly, that a complete collapse of Russia had made a frontal attack on France impossible. I said that you had asked whether we could not get a footing on the Continent sometime this year, even as late as December, in which case you would give the highest possible priority to the production and shipping of landing craft, equipment and troops. The need for securing a port for supplying the troops made it clear that we should have to capture a port such as Cherbourg and hold a suitable line such as the Cherbourg peninsula, possibly expanding across towards St. Nazaire and eventually holding the whole of Brittany.

I made a point that you were sure that, in any case, when the operation came off, we should have to secure the Atlantic ports and not go rushing off in the direction of Germany until we were firmly established, unless German morale had really cracked.

I pointed out that you did not like our sending out Divisions from England while American troops were still being sent in and that you suggested that we should leave about six Divisions in England and that the corresponding six American Divisions should be sent straight to fight in North Africa, either round the Cape to fight in Libya or straight in to Morocco with a view to joining hands with the Army of the Nile and reopening the Mediterranean. In the latter connection I told the P.M. how much you had been struck in a recent telegram by his remark: 'Do not lose sight of 'Gymnast'.'[4]

This would mean that Dakar would fall into our hands without having to fight for it and I mentioned that you considered this important because the climate was not suitable for European soldiers to fight in.

As the result of the recent losses inflicted by the U.S. Fleet on the Japanese Fleet, particularly their aircraft carriers, there was a general desire to take the offensive from Australia, using the existing U.S. Marine forces and combat shipping.

General Marshall had suggested going for Timor and General MacArthur had telegraphed on his own suggesting making for

---

[4] An operation planned for Bizerta, North Africa, in January, 1942, but which did not take place.

Rabaul. I said that you and General Marshall were anxious that two British aircraft carriers with their destroyer screen should join the American naval forces in Australia to support these operations, and that there had also been a suggestion that the amphibious force which had assaulted Madagascar should be used for operations against the Japanese.

I was so thrilled and heartened by all I saw in America, particularly by the American Army, which is forging ahead at quite an unbelievable rate.

On 17th June, 1942, the Prime Minister, accompanied by the C.I.G.S flew to America. The main objective was to reach a final decision on operations for 1942-43.

Situation at C.O.H.Q. – July 1942

It is of interest to note the situation at C.O.H.Q. during the months of June and July, 1942.

The Planning Staff was fully occupied with the planning for "Sledgehammer", "Rutter", "Jubilee" and the investigation of minor raids on the French coast. Some of these were mounted but were not executed owing to weather and other causes.

Due to the large increase in the intake of naval personnel, training was proceeding at high pressure; in addition, the military forces required for "Sledgehammer" were getting as much training as possible. In fact, all the training establishments and resources were fully extended and occupied.

The Administrative Section of C.O.H.Q. was involved, not only in the move of the craft round the British Isles to the south coast, but also in the fitting out and commissioning of new ships which were being embodied in the Combined Operations Command. In addition, the requirement for new bases in the south was now being felt and these with the organisation for the hards[5] and their necessary supplies was an undertaking of the first priority.

All sections of the staff at C.O.H.Q. were working at high pressure to make a descent on the French coast in the near future a possibility.

Planning for the Re-entry into the Continent

Contained in the report on the Casablanca Conference ("Symbol") by the Combined Chiefs of Staff as approved by the President and Prime

---

[5] Normal south coast port facilities being inadequate, embarkation and training had to be carried out over numerous specially constructed hards where craft could beach and vehicles embark unimpeded by soft sand or mud.

Minister is the following paragraph: "We have agreed to establish forthwith a Combined Staff under a British Chief of Staff until such time as a Supreme Commander with an American Deputy is appointed. A directive to govern the planning is in course of preparation."

The planning referred to was, of course, that necessary for the operation envisaged for the re-entry into the Continent.

The appointment of such an authority had been foreshadowed in an *aide mémoire* by the Secretary of C.O.S. Committee prior to a meeting of the Chiefs of Staff with the "Round-up" planners which was held on 22nd August, 1942. The relevant paragraphs read as follows:

> (6) The next and most important point is how the planning for 1943 is to be organised. No final decision has been taken by the Chiefs of Staff about this. One idea is that a Senior British Army Commander should be made responsible for directing the planning. He would presumably be the Deputy Supreme Commander. He would have under him a Combined Joint Planning Staff, the heads of which would be drawn from the three British Services and from the appropriate American Services. The top level for this Joint Staff would, it is suggested, be of Brigadier or equivalent rank. This syndicate would have at their disposal the considerable quantity of information and material which had already been collected for 'Round-up'.
>
> (7) Another suggestion, put forward by General Eisenhower, was that C.C.O. should take charge of the planning.
>
> (8) An alternative proposal is that the Executive Planning Section (E.P.S.) of the Joint Planning Staff should be augmented to deal with the planning. The principle for a co-ordinating director should remain. C.C.O.'s Staff would of course be brought in whichever method is adopted.

With regard to para. 7 of the *aide mémoire,* General Eisenhower, in his book *Crusade in Europe* referring to his visit to London in 1942, says:

> With these general ideas in mind but with no detailed studies upon which to make a firm conclusion, I went to an informal meeting with the British Chiefs of Staff. Shortly after the conference began, I was invited to present my general views concerning the nature of the projected operation. Speaking as an American planner assigned to the War Department in Washington, and with no idea that I would later be assigned to Britain, I said in substance: 'The first thing to do is to name a commander for the operation. That man must be given every bit of power that both governments can make available to him. He must be directed to plan for an invasion of Europe on the basis that it will certainly be successful, at least to the extent of establishing on the Continent a solid front capable of carrying

out effective operations against the Germans. He must be directed instantly to prepare his outlined plan and to submit to the Chiefs of Staff his requirements not only in troops of all kinds but in all types of additional equipment – land, sea and air.'

The first question asked me was: 'And who would you name as commander of this expedition?'

I replied: 'In America I have heard much of a man who has been intensively studying amphibious operations for many months. I understand that his position is Chief of Combined Operations, and I think his name is Admiral Mountbatten. Anyone will be better than none; such an operation cannot be carried out under committee command. But I have heard that Admiral Mountbatten is vigorous, intelligent and courageous, and if the operation is to be staged initially with British Forces predominating, I assume he could do the job.'

The records show that during the summer and autumn of 1942, the Combined Commanders devoted great study to the question of where the initial landing for Operation "Round-up" should be made. This study was rendered possible by two facts: (1) The dropping of "Sledgehammer" owing to the emergency of "Torch" (North Africa), [and] (2) The Prime Minister's dictum that any landing on the Continent must be one that envisaged no withdrawal.

The divergence of opinion was at first very acute, but C.C.O. stuck to his point with continued and inflexible persistence, and gradually the trend of thought veered to the C.O.H.Q. opinion, and early in 1943 a Staff Study on "The Selection of Assault Areas in a Major Operation in North-West Europe" was produced as a Principal Staff Officers Committee Draft on 5th February, 1943, the relevant paragraphs of which read as follows:

Scope of the Study

(1) The selection of assault areas in any major operation of whatever scope in North-West Europe, depends on a number of factors many of which are constant. An examination of these factors which are unlikely to change quickly, will permit certain basic deductions to be made as to the limitations and possibilities of the alternative assault areas open to selection.
(2) This study is confined to that object and is intended to form the basis on which future appreciations can be made and to which it may be attached.
(3) In Part I these constant factors are considered in general and certain important deductions are drawn. In Part II these deductions are applied to the various assault areas, and conclusions drawn as to the type of operation that might be possible in each, provided suitable resources can be made available.

Potentialities of the Sectors

The suitability of the various sectors considered may be summarised as follows:

Dutch	Not suitable.
Belgian	Suitable only for an assault by a limited force provided there were few enemy reserves and German morale is very low.
Pas de Calais	Suitable only for a feint or diversion in order to provoke an air battle under favourable conditions.
Seine	Suitable only for a secondary assault in support of a force previously landed further west.
Caen	Suitable for an assault by a large force provided the east beaches of the Cotentin peninsula are included to secure Cherbourg, and that the assaults on both Caen and Cotentin Sectors take place simultaneously or closely following each other. Subsequent operations to capture the North Seine and Breton group of port would be necessary.
Cotentin	Suitable for a limited operation provided airfields can be developed quickly. The neutralisation or capture of Alderney and possibly Guernsey will be necessary if the west beaches are required. Suitable for an unlimited operation by a small force if the scale of enemy resistance is low, but not so low as to permit operations in the Belgian Sector. Necessary if an assault is to be made in the Caen Sector.
Brittany and Biscay	Suitable only for subsidiary operations to capture large ports after a main assault has taken place elsewhere, provided the German Air Force has been reduced to an extremely low order.

The conclusions reached in this carefully drafted paper confirmed the views so persistently and strongly held by C.C.O. and the planners at C.O.H.Q. The Caen-Cotentin Sectors were those in the Baie de la Seine.

From the naval point of view, the beaches mentioned were the only ones possible. The prevailing wind from the South-West made any beaches to the eastward dead lee-shores and another disadvantage was that the greatest rise and fall of the tide in the English Channel took place on the eastern end. Also, the lift of heavy vehicles and tanks would have to be done from the south coast ports in the first instance, and so the Caen-Cotentin Sectors actually presented the shortest sea passage.

Operation "Skyscraper"

As a result of the study of the paper quoted above, we find in G.H.Q. Home Forces paper of 18th March, 1943, the following:

> Review of Certain Factors Affecting Preparations for a Return to the Continent
>
> *Introduction*
>
> (1) The object of this paper is to obtain decisions on certain major points which must govern not only planning for a return to the Continent against opposition, but more particularly the organisation, equipment and training of the Army in the United Kingdom during 1943.
>
> (2) The basis of the paper is an outline plan for operations on the Continent. This plan has not been approved by the Combined Commanders nor worked out in detail. But it is generally agreed that the original 'Round-up' plan is not a feasible one, and some other basis is therefore necessary. Whether the outline plan here discussed is subsequently generally agreed to, or whether the final plan differs from it materially, it is felt that at least it will make clear many problems.
>
> *Object*
>
> (3) Our ultimate object is at worst to establish a strong force within close bombing range of the Ruhr, i.e., somewhere north-east of the Pas de Calais. Hence: (a) The nearer to Antwerp we make our initial landing the better. (b) If we land at a distance, we must consider not only the initial landing, but the various steps until we get to the area mentioned above.
>
> *Area of Landing*
>
> (4) The study 'Selection of Assault Areas for a Major Operation in North-West Europe' (C.C. (42) 108) has left a choice of one area only – the Caen beaches, plus the east beaches of the Cotentin peninsula.

The paper then went on to the War Office to be elaborated as to what was required from the Army point of view.

The following minutes are on the War office file in which this document was circulated:

D.D.M.O. (H).
I have discussed with C.I.G.S. These plans need not be considered in detail at the moment, but they will be useful to Lt.-General Morgan.
(Intd.) D.M.O.

D.D.M.O. (H).
If you will return to me, I will pass to General Morgan.
5th April, 1943
(Intd.) D.P.

Chief of Staff to the Supreme Allied Commander

This is the first mention of Lieutenant-General Sir Frederick Morgan, so it is necessary to explain who he was.

As has been stated previously, it was decided at the Casablanca Conference that a Chief of Staff to the Supreme Allied Commander (C.O.S.S.A.C.) was to be appointed in charge of the planning pending the decision on who was to be the Commander. Lieutenant-General Morgan, who had up to now been commanding the First Corps, was nominated as the Chief of Staff and actually took up his new post on 13th April, 1943.

It is of interest to see what he says in his book[6] regarding his appointment:

Personal Background

The 'A.N.F.A.' Conference at Casablanca had meanwhile given to Western leaders the opportunity to review in company the whole strategic situation, and it was at this Conference that it was deemed that the time was approaching, even that it had already approached, for the delivery of the *coup de grâce* in the form of an invasion of Europe from the North-West. The full implications of this decision were too great even for our greatest men to swallow at one gulp, so that their decision took the form of a determination in the near future to appoint a Commander for this gigantic enterprise.

It was understandably not possible, so far in advance, now to designate the individual who should hold this position, but meanwhile the necessity was recognised to tidy up and to give point to all the many and various projects of greater or less magnitude that had been considered in connection with the frontal assault on Nazi Europe. It was decided to appoint an individual in the position of Chief of Staff to the unspecified Commander-to-be, the duty of this Chief of Staff being, in so many words, to 'give cohesion and

---

[6] *Overture to "Overlord"* – Lieut.-General Sir Frederick Morgan.

impetus' to preparations of all kinds. The authorship of this phrase it is easy to guess. It was to this post that I was nominated.

The Combined Operations Command

It is now necessary to take stock of what was happening in the Combined Operations Command with regard to personnel, ships and craft.

A Joint Planning Staff[7] paper, dated 16th May, 1943, gives the following figures concerning the total personnel available in the Combined Operations Command on 1st April, 1943.

Category	Manning	Officers	Ratings	Total
A	Landing craft crews, squadron and flotilla complement and reserve personnel to scale.	3,059	25,151	28,210
	Gun units for support craft, Royal Marines.	36	1,096	1,132
B	Beach commandos, beach signal units and beach support and reconnaissance signal units.	127	1,001	1,128
	Total of categories A and B	3,222	27,248	
C	Combined operational ships crews:			
	Naval personnel	636	1,287	
	T.124X or Merchant Navy	974	4,554	
D	Combined operational base administrative, maintenance and training personnel.	657	3,089	
	W.R.N.S.		2,177	
	Total of all categories	5,489	38,355	43,844

---

[7] A staff officer from C.O.H.Q. had by then joined the Joint Planning Staff as the Combined Operations Joint Planner (C.O.J.P.). The paper here referred to is J.P. (43) 121 (Final), dated 16th May, 1943.

With regard to the ships and craft, the figures on 6th April, 1943,[8] read as follows:

	Home	Abroad	Total
Landing ships	28	61	89
Landing craft	1,678	923	2,601
Landing barges	1,019	-	1,019

This unprecedented increase in any command, either in peace or war from a few hundred officers and men to about 50,000 with some 90 ships and 3,600 craft prompted C.C.O. to write the following letter to the Prime Minister:

> The Prime Minister
>
> The continued expansion of the Combined Operations Command has made it necessary for me to delegate, to an increasing extent, responsibility for executive action within the command.
>
> At the same time as considering internal adjustments to meet this requirement, I think it is necessary to define how my duties should be carried out on occasions of my absence, such as my recent illness.
>
> The senior members of the Staff consist of Major-General Haydon, Air Vice-Marshal Orlebar and Rear Admiral Daniel. Their present titles, in accordance with your original instructions, are respectively Vice, Deputy and Assistant Chief of Combined Operations.
>
> In addition to these I have, acting in the capacity of Chief of Staff, Major-General Wildman-Lushington, R.M. (an ex-R.N.A.S. and Fleet Air Arm pilot who held an R.A.F. commission for about six years).
>
> These four act jointly as my Executive Committee under the Chairmanship of Major-General Wildman-Lushington and individually the three Heads of Service act as Chiefs of Staff in respect of their own Services.
>
> In order to make their authority quite clear and at the same time to remove an apparent inequality status, I propose that their titles should be altered to General Officer, Combined Operations and Military Chief of Staff; Air Officer, Combined Operations and Air Chief of Staff; Flag Officer, Combined Operations and Naval Chief of Staff; and to leave Wildman-Lushington's title as Chief of Staff, Combined Operations.
>
> I propose that the Heads of Services should be empowered to deal at their own direction with all matters concerning their own Service. They will keep me informed of the more important decisions, but

---

[8] C.O.H.Q. "Green List" – a publication giving the operational states and whereabouts of these ships and craft.

need not consult me beforehand unless the matter is controversial or one on which they know me to be personally concerned.

Matters affecting more than one Service will be referred to me as necessary at the final stage through the Chief of Staff.

During periods when I am absent, I would suggest that, normally, the Chief of Staff should represent me on the Chiefs of Staff Committee or other bodies whenever any Combined Operations matter is being discussed. In the event of any complicated item dealing with only one Service, he can arrange for the appropriate member of the Executive to attend in his place.

I request your approval of the above proposals.

(Signed) Louis Mountbatten,
Chief of Combined Operations.

The Prime Minister's reply to this letter was as follows:

C.C.O.

Approved, but pray take care to maintain the position of C.C.O. and his Command intact.

I trust that the integrity of the Inter-Service Organisation of C.O.H.Q. will be preserved and that the reorganisation will not split your Staff too rigidly into separate Services.

(Initialled) W.S.C.

1.5.43.

Conference "Rattle"

With the appointment on 13th April, 1943, of the Chief of Staff to the Supreme Allied Commander (C.O.S.S.A.C.) a new authority had been given the task of planning the re-entry into the Continent. C.C.O. knew full well the difficulties which C.O.S.S.A.C. would come up against and gave every assistance which he could provide from his Command. After personal discussion with C.O.S.S.A.C., he suggested to the Chiefs of Staff that a Study Period should be organised at Largs where all the high-ranking officers engaged in the planning could study the matter in an atmosphere removed from that of Whitehall and have access to the establishments which were daily concerned with the training and development of combined operations technique. This conference was given the code name "Rattle".

This matter came up for consideration before the Chiefs of Staff and, in the minutes of their meeting on 11th June, they approved the holding of this Study Period. At this meeting, General Devers, who was now commanding the United States Forces in the European Theatre, asked if he and his staff could take part. This request was cordially accepted and thus the Study Period at once became not only an Inter-Service but an Inter-Allied meeting.

For this conference C.O.H.Q. drew up a very comprehensive agenda, which showed that every technical aspect of the re-entry into the Continent was to be reviewed and all the latest improvements were examined, together with demonstrations of new equipment. The agenda included:

(1) The German defensive system.
(2) The mounting of the operation – assembly and embarkation of forces.
(3) The naval aspect of the operation prior to the actual assault – fighting instructions – the cross-Channel voyage – navigational problems.
(4) The air aspect of the operation. Preliminary bombing – use of airborne forces – delay of enemy resources.
(5) The assault – special weapons – naval bombardment – the fire fight – day and night assault – engineer problems – allocation of craft – scale of personnel and equipment.
(6) Administrative aspects of the build-up, including movements and maintenance.
(7) The follow-up and build-up.
(8) Effect of the system of command and control of the Combined Signal Organisation.
(9) Technical developments and special equipment.
(10) Training problems.

The question of the strategy to be employed was not considered as it was felt that this would depend to a large extent on the impressions formed by the officers who would have to prepare the plans and put them into execution.

The Conference began on 28th June and lasted till 2nd July.

At all the meetings of the conference C.C.O. acted as Chairman. A list of the Senior Officers present gives a good idea of the representative nature and scope of the subjects discussed: Admiral Sir Charles Little, Commander-in-Chief, Portsmouth; General Sir Bernard Paget, Commander-in-Chief, Home Forces; Lt.-General F.E. Morgan, C.O.S.S.A.C; Air Marshal Sir Trafford Leigh Mallory, C.-in-C. Fighter Command; Lt.-General J.L. Devers, C.G., E.T.O.U.S.A.; [and] Lt.-General A.G.L. McNaughton, G.O.C. Canadian Corps.

These were accompanied by staff officers from their Commands; and representatives from the Admiralty, War Office and Air Ministry attended throughout, with of course the appropriate members of the C.O.H.Q. Staff.

The results of each day's meeting were recorded in papers prepared on the spot under the title of C.O.(R) 1 to 24 and embodied in the record of the Conference (C.O.R. (25)), dated July, 1943.

Finally, C.C.O. addressed a report of the conference to the Secretary of the Chiefs of Staff Committee which runs as follows:

Conference "Rattle"

1. The object of Conference 'Rattle' was to study the problems in Combined Operations involved in Operation 'Overlord'.

2. The subjects dealt with at this conference were discussed against the background of the German defences and dispositions as they exist to-day. The conference fully appreciated, however, that the eventual plan may have to be put into effect against a lesser degree of opposition or a lower state of morale than that which exists now, and that this may also involve an advance on the present target date. The C.-in-C Portsmouth suggests that operation 'Rankin' is for such a contingency. Commanders-in-Chief and the Chief of Staff to the Supreme Allied Commander were impressed with the necessity for ensuring that all our preparations for 'Overlord' would take into account this possibility.

3. There are three points emerging from the Conference to which I would invite the special attention of the Chiefs of Staff.

4. Firstly, the strength of the enemy defences and the limitations imposed on the degree of supporting fire, which can be brought to bear during the landing, are such that it will obviously be essential to subject the area of the assault to the most intense bombardment beforehand.

This bombardment will probably have to be carried out over a considerable period of time and it appears that it must mainly be done by the R.A.F.

5. Secondly, the most critical period will be that between the lifting of the naval and air bombardment before the first troops get ashore, and the time when the Army can get its own guns into action on land. We have not yet evolved a satisfactory solution to this vital problem; a great deal will depend on the experience we gain in 'Husky' (Sicily) and on the results we hope to achieve in forthcoming practical trials. The answer may lie in a combination of a number of measures, viz.: a carefully co-ordinated fire plan from the guns of surface ships and from a variety of weapons mounted in landing craft; the development of a highly trained force fully equipped with special weapons and machinery to enable them to overcome the obstacles they are bound to meet on the beach; the landing of the

maximum possible number of airborne troops in the rear of the enemy defences and the landing of a large number of Commandos, probably under the cloak of darkness, at difficult and therefore undefended landing points. On the other hand, there is a limit to the number of mixed groups which the Navy can hope to control off-shore. There is also a limit of the number of airborne troops we shall have at our disposal. The First Corps under the direction of the Commander-in-Chief, Home Forces, is engaged on the problem and the matter will be carried a step further at the practical trials referred to above. The Commander-in-Chief made it quite clear at the conference that a solution has got to be found.

6. Thirdly, the Army is at present inclined to the view that it will be necessary to assault in darkness, or at first light, in order to give the troops the best chance of gaining a footing. The Commander-in-Chief, Portsmouth is doubtful whether it will be possible to assemble a large number of mixed groups of craft at sea in the dark and it may be that, if the Army cannot evolve a more simple plan, naval considerations will force us to set about the landing in daylight. In these circumstances it will be all the more necessary to soften the area before the assault and for airborne troops to tackle the enemy defences from the rear.

7. With regard to training, subject to the proviso that training areas, where live ammunition can be fired and where there is suitable accommodation for troops and vehicles, are made available, the Commanders-in-Chief express satisfaction with the arrangements which were proposed at the conference. It is hoped that the Naval Assault Force at Portsmouth will be ready by the time 3 Cdn. Div. has completed basic training. 3 Div. on the other hand, will complete basic training by the middle of August and will then carry on Battalion assault training at Kilbride until the Rosyth Collective Training Area is ready in October. The dates by which the American Naval Assault Forces will be ready are not available, but it is assumed that this will soon be known. The American Divisions are receiving their preliminary basic and assault training in America and will only have to carry out collective training when they arrive in the United Kingdom towards the end of the year.

8. A number of more detailed conclusions were reached at the Conference. Among these is an important one proposing an organisation for opening up beaches and ports on the French coast. I have lodged a copy of the full proceedings of the Conference with the secretariat for purposes of record but do not propose to circulate them to the Chiefs of Staff unless they wish me to do so. I do, however, attach an annex containing certain points on which

the Chiefs of Staff may wish to issue instructions. I have suggested the authorities who might be instructed to initiate action on these various items.

9. Commanders-in-Chief, Commanding General E.T.O.U.S.A. and C.O.S.S.A.C. have seen this report and are in general agreement with it.

(Signed) Louis Mountbatten,
Chief of Combined Operations.

So much for the official report of the Conference, and here it is appropriate to quote what General Morgan (C.O.S.S.A.C.) records in his book:[9]

The Master Plan

What was wanted was a lodgement area into which we could blast ourselves against such opposition as we were likely to meet there, and from which our main bodies, having suitably concentrated themselves within it, could erupt to develop the campaign eastwards. If one analysed this definition it seemed to contain all the various desiderata. It was a question of weighing up and assessing the value of each constituent factor. The greater the opposition or the more difficult the beach conditions, then the heavier must be the air cover. This consideration drew us towards the Pas de Calais, where our air could give its maximum and where the shipping 'turn-round' would be quickest. But the Germans could read the map, too, and their defensive preparations were nicely graded along the coast to accord with their estimate of the situation which inevitably agreed pretty much with ours.

That being so, where could he find a deciding factor? In all probability this would turn out to be the matter of major parts to the requisite capacity without which it would be impossible to contemplate even prolonged occupation of a lodgement area by an army of some 25 to 30 divisions, let alone its reinforcement up to some 100 divisions to be maintained in action. Major ports are not plentiful on that section of the coast of North-West Europe to which other considerations confined our attention. Between Brest and Antwerp there exists only Cherbourg and Le Havre that are in the class for consideration as military base ports. Did we land on the Pas de Calais beaches, we should have to gain possession of either Le Havre or Antwerp before we could claim to have done that which was demanded of us.

For the port capacity of the Boulogne, Calais, Dunkirk group of minor ports, even after restoration which could take months

---

[9] *Overture to Overlord.*

probably, would be nothing like adequate to our purpose. If we went for Cherbourg, the objective of several previous projects, we should have trouble in debouching from the Cotentin peninsula. And debouch therefrom we should have to, since the capacity of Cherbourg alone, even if intact and in thorough working order, would suffice to maintain only a fraction of our projected Advanced Guard, itself but a fraction of the whole expedition. If we made for Western Normandy, we should find Le Havre unfortunately across the Seine from us and should have to turn back westwards overland to Cherbourg. And so on.

It was here in the matter of Cherbourg that we ran once more into the obstacle presented by a misunderstood or partly misunderstood catch phrase. In all the planning that had gone on in relation to the re-entry into Europe, a point had naturally been reached when all had been found to depend on 'the early capture of a port'. As I have said, past planning had been so handicapped that in any such case as had been worked in detail, 'a port' would have sufficed to carry such traffic as was envisaged. Of necessity also, thought had come to centre on Cherbourg, as the port in question. We ourselves fell into the trap for a space and it took a week or two to grasp that what was necessary for us was not a port, but some ports. Cherbourg might well be the first of these to be acquired, but our expedition was to be of a magnitude undreamed of before. I fancy it is little exaggeration to say that the sheer size of 'Overlord' was little appreciated by some of the British high-ups until very late in the day. Some, I believe, still do not appreciate how comparatively small a contribution to the whole, from the physical aspect, was the British portion. I must admit that even I, who had thought and dreamed of nothing else for years by then, was astonished at the sense of vastness conveyed by the subsequent film of the operation, previewed in company with General Eisenhower at Frankfurt in July, 1945.

To resolve the tangle, we decided to institute within the C.O.S.S.A.C. Staff a formal comparison to the two main alternatives that appeared to exist as the outcome of all previous planning. It will be remembered that the Staff was not as yet fully integrated, so that it was fortunately situated to function simultaneously on the two parallel lines. Accordingly, the United States Army members of the Army Operations Section were directed to produce an outline plan for a projected operation against Normandy and their British counterpart was ordered to do likewise for an operation against the Pas de Calais. The Naval and Air Staffs, both still weak on the United States side, were directed to participate equally in both projects. Since it was evident from the start that allotted resources in landing craft were not sufficient to admit of any subsidiary operation or diversion from the main effort, each planning group, United States and British, was told to assume that it might dispose of the whole C.O.S.S.A.C. allotment. It was to be one answer or the other.

The development of the contest, was closely watched by a small 'gallery' consisting not only of the Chief of Staff and Deputy Chief of Staff, who had been careful to exclude themselves from this phase of the affair, but also of a few privileged observers from outside, Sir Bernard Paget, then commanding British Home Forces, General Jacob Devers, Commanding General of the E.T.O.U.S.A., and, of course, the Chief of Combined Operations, Admiral Lord Louis Mountbatten. It was tough going and feeling ran high. We, the Deputy Chief of Staff and I, knew that the moment was approaching when we should have to make up our minds not only as to which of the two alternatives being worked out would prove to be the less uninviting, but, even worse, whether or not the thing was possible at all. We should, in fact, have to answer the supplementary question we had to put to ourselves in the first instance, 'If so, how, and if not, why not'?

From this appalling quandy we were rescued by the Chief of Combined Operations always a leader of progressive thought, and somewhat of an *enfant terrible* to his more elderly *confrères*. He presented us with an opportunity to uproot the whole wrangle from the arena of London, where surroundings were inimical both materially and psychologically to open-minded consideration of any bold departure from established precedent, to an entirely fresh setting. One of the routine courses in Combined Operations held periodically at the Combined Operations Scottish Headquarters at Largs, was unobtrusively altered in shape and content so as to include all the principal contestants in our C.O.S.S.A.C. scheming as well as the chief leaders of thought from outside our organisation. The congregation included men of all ranks of all Services, both American and British. The syllabus of the course was so shaped as to cover all the main points of difference between the various schools of thought. The object of the course was to give all concerned the opportunity to discuss openly with each other the whole subject of a cross-Channel operation, its feasibility in general and the practicability of all the many detailed points of execution. There were almost as many thoughts as there were men. But there was no more time for sulking, each in his own tent, and juggling with words and figures on paper. We must hear the conclusion of the whole matter argued out in comparative public. We were to discuss principles. And one principle, we, of C.O.S.S.A.C., would take care to watch was that we were now charged with responsibility for the whole business. We did not profess to be experts in any particular line.

Experts abounded, many of whom were convinced, each in his own mind, that he had in his little black bag the secret of the infallible system. The price of such an article was very often simply control, or a large part of control, of the whole operation. That belonged, all of it, by definition to our Supreme Commander-to-be, whose interests C.O.S.S.A.C. must jealously guard. We must fear all those bearing gifts of any nature.

It is very often the little things that matter, and every little thing was attended to as 'part of the Mountbatten service'. The showmanship could not have been excelled. Domestic arrangements were perfect. On guard was a Commando of such magnificent bearing as to disarm the most carping army critic. As there were suspected to be savage beasts among us, the pipe band of the local Home Guard appeared at intervals to rend the atmosphere with the indigenous substitute for music. Even the weather was apparently cajoled into giving us perfect days, and a perfect day on that Scottish coast is almost as perfect as a day can be. The only cloud in the atmosphere, favourable to our ambitions as we had gone all out to create it, was the appearance one evening in the offing of a great convoy outward-bound from the Clyde, carrying a Canadian Division to the war in Sicily, away form 'Overlord'. But even here the best was made of a bad job. General McNaughton who was one of our number, was enabled to send a valedictory message to his men by the provision, on the spur of the moment, of a highly efficient little 'Wren' signaller, complete with lamp, right there on the roof of the hotel which was the main headquarters.

At the end of our first day of discussion and study, the Chief of Combined Operations and I paced the lawns to compare our impressions. It looked hopeless from our point of view. For he and I were together from the start in our determination to see this thing through. It was, of course, my duty to obey orders. He, as distinct from most of his associates, from the start had no doubts as to the possibility of success; and this quite apart from the fact that the Chief of Combined Operations could hardly fail to advocate that which, if it came off, would stand for years, if not forever, as the apotheosis of all Combined Operations, that is of all future sailors, soldiers and airmen. But from watching 'the opposition' carefully throughout that day it looked as if there was no hope. Should we give up, here and now? He had lots of other urgent affairs that needed his attention, we decided to give it one more day. And during that day what we hoped for began to happen. A member of the opposition was seen to smile. We redoubled our efforts, and by the end of the 'course' there was not only unanimity, but enthusiasm. 'Overlord', so far as C.O.S.S.A.C. was concerned, was on.

Though naturally the Largs Course had dealt with matters of general principle and matters of method and organisation, this had been done on an hypothetical basis only. There remained with us the decision as between our two alternatives. To our way of thinking, by now the decision was easy. Western Normandy it must be. And there was no alternative if we were to keep our timetable and attack within the year.

I think it is fair to say that we had always been disposed to favour the Normandy landing, if only for the fact that so much of the groundwork already done before our time had been done in connection with projects for a variety of landings to the southward, in the Cotentin-Dieppe region rather than to the south-eastward. But there were other outstanding advantages. First, the shape of the coast. The weather records for years past were searched, and it was hard to find a case in which summer had seen heavy weather from any point of the compass other than between south and west. The Norman beaches are completely sheltered from this quarter, whereas beaches further east are not. In the event, of course, we lost that part of the bet completely when that north-easterly gale blew up just after "D" Day in 1944. But our original bet was still a good one.

Weather on the beaches brings one to the question of length of sea crossing for the considerable army, for an advanced guard of some thirty Divisions is a very considerable army, and the astronomical tonnage of all its transport and gear. Quite simply, the shorter the better. While afloat the Army is incapable of helping itself and relies upon Navy and Air for its protection, a task of immense complication and difficulty under conditions such as existed in the English Channel in this war. So very few submarines or fast torpedo boats or bomber aircraft can do such vast damage in such short a time to a slow-moving fleet of thin-skinned invasion craft. The shorter the voyage such fleets have to make, therefore, the better. Other things being equal, the Navy would hope for the Pas de Calais. But even for the Navy other things were not equal, and the voyage to Normandy was never considered to be a prohibitive length.

Then there was the vital question of beach exits, that is, ways of getting off the beaches into the country back of them. If the invasion battle takes place on the beach, one is already defeated. One hopes and plans for battle, on the other hand, as far inland from the beach as may be. There must be as little delay as possible in getting the troops and their multifarious goods off the beach and inland. This is mainly a matter of choice of beach and, as in most other things, compromise is necessary. It may be that the best beach on which to land troops from the nautical point of view is at the foot of a cliff. The best beach from the soldier's aspect may be one approached through shoals and rocks. On balance here again, Normandy was better.

Planning for "Overlord"

The Conference at Largs ("Rattle") concluded on 2nd July, 1943, and General Morgan in his capacity as C.O.S.S.A.C. forwarded his plan to the Chiefs of Staff on 15th July. His covering memorandum reads as follows:

> I have the honour now to report that, in my opinion, it is possible to undertake the operation described, on or about the target date named, with the sea, land and air forces specified, given a certain set of circumstances in existence at that time.
>
> These governing circumstances are partly within our direct control and partly without. Those within our control relate first to the problem of beach maintenance, and secondly to the supply of shipping, naval landing craft and transport aircraft. Wherever we may attempt to land, and however many ports we capture, we cannot escape the fact that we shall be forced to maintain a high proportion of our forces over the beaches for the first two or three months while port facilities are being restored; and that, in view of the variability of the weather, this will not be feasible unless we are rapidly to improvise sheltered anchorages off the beaches. New methods of overcoming this problem are now being examined. There is no reason to suppose that these methods will be ineffective, but I feel it my duty to point out that this operation is not to be contemplated unless this problem of prolonged cross-beach maintenance and the provision of artificial anchorages shall have been solved.
>
> As regards the supply of shipping, naval landing craft and transport aircraft, increased resources in these would permit the elaboration of alternative plans designed to meet more than one set of extraneous conditions, whereas the state of provision herein taken into account dictates the adoption of one course only, or none at all. In proportion as additional shipping, landing craft and transport aircraft can be made available, so the chances of success in the operation will be increased. It seems feasible to contemplate additions as a result either of stepped-up production, of strategical re-allotment, or, in the last resort, of postponement of the date of assault.
>
> I have come to the conclusion that, in view of the limitations in resources imposed by my directives, we may be assured of a reasonable chance of success on 1st May, 1944, only if we concentrate our efforts on an assault across the Norman beaches about Bayeux.
>
> As regards circumstances that we can control indirectly, it is, in my opinion, necessary to stipulate that the state of affairs existing at the time, both on land in France and in the air above it, shall be such as to render the assault as little hazardous as may be, so far as it is

humanly possible to calculate. The essential discrepancy in value between the enemy's troops, highly organised, armed and battle-trained, who await us in their much-vaunted impregnable defences, and our troops, who must of necessity launch their assault at the end of a cross-Channel voyage with all its attendant risks, must be reduced to the narrowest possible margin. Although much can be done to this end by the means available and likely to become available to us in the United Kingdom to influence these factors, we are largely dependent upon events that will take place on other war fronts, principally on the Russian front, between now and the date of the assault.

I therefore suggest to the Chiefs of Staff that it is necessary, if my plan be approved, to adopt the outlook that Operation 'Overlord' is even now in progress, and to take all possible steps to see that all agencies that can be brought to bear are, from now on, co-ordinated in their action as herein below described so as to bring about the state of affairs that we would have exist on the chosen day of assault.

Finally, I venture to draw attention to the danger of making direct comparisons between Operation 'Husky' and Operation 'Overlord'. No doubt the experience now being gained in the Mediterranean will prove invaluable when the detailed planning stage for 'Overlord' is reached, but, viewed as a whole, the two operations could hardly be more dissimilar. In 'Husky' the base of an extended continental coastline was used for a converging assault against an island, whereas in 'Overlord' it is necessary to launch an assault from an island against an extended continental mainline coastline. Furthermore, while in the Mediterranean the tidal range is negligible and weather reasonably reliable, in the English Channel the tide range is considerable and the weather capricious.

The "Quadrant" Conference, 11th-25th August, 1943
The plan proposed by General Morgan was taken by the Chiefs of Staff when they sailed for the Conference at Quebec ("Quadrant") in the *Queen Mary* on 4th August, 1943. During the voyage C.C.O. arranged for D.X.S.R. (Captain Hussey, R.N.) to give an exposition on: (1) Proposed modifications to merchant ships for launching amphibians; (2) Proposed modifications to spud pierheads for unloading L.S.T. and L.C.T.; [and] (3) On two developments for making temporary breakwaters.

The most important decision at the "Quadrant" Conference as far as C.O.H.Q. was concerned, was that taken at the Combined Chiefs of Staff meeting on 19th August, 1943, and in C.C.B. 319 the following is found: "We have approved the outline plan of General Morgan for

Operation 'Overlord' and have authorised him to proceed with the detailed planning and with full preparations."

Another matter of importance from the C.O.H.Q. point of view, which was discussed at the "Quadrant" Conference, was the employment of "Plough" Force. This force was composed of American and Canadian volunteers and was originally formed at the instigation of C.C.O. for operations in cold climates such as northern Norway. Up to date, this force although formed and trained had not been employed. The question of its future use was discussed and it was decided to keep it in being. This was a fortunate decision as it proved its worth later in South East Asia. In order to obtain battle experience, elements of the force operated in a Commando role at the Anzio landing and, also with the U.S. Forces in the Aleutian Islands.

During the Conference, the question of the setting up of a South-East Asia Command was discussed at length. It was decided to appoint a Supreme Commander to that area in the same way that General MacArthur commanded in the South-West Pacific. Careful study was given to the directive for the Supreme Commander and eventually one was approved.

Chapter 8

CHANGES AT COMBINED OPERATIONS HEADQUARTERS DURING 1943 AND THE ADMIRALTY TAKES OVER THE ASSAULT FLEET

In becoming a full member of the Chiefs of Staff Committee in March, 1942, C.C.O. found himself at a disadvantage in that he exercised little influence or control over the Joint Planning Staff, who were producing papers for the Chiefs of Staff. The effect of this was that, after being briefed at C.O.H.Q., he could alter the paper, if there was any point with which he disagreed, only when it had reached the Chiefs of Staff's level.

Institution of a Combined Operations Joint Planner
He, therefore, instituted a Combined Operations Joint Planner, of whom Brigadier M.W.M. MacLeod was the first, until his replacement after an aircraft accident on returning from the Casablanca Conference, by Brigadier A.H. Head.

C.C.O. then persuaded the Director of Plans to allow the Combined Operations Joint Planner to sit with them as a fourth member whenever they were preparing papers with a combined operations aspect. This arrangement worked well because it meant that the Combined Operations Joint Planner was able to see practically all papers destined for the Chiefs of Staff at their formative stage. The influence of C.O.H.Q. was thus greatly increased and there was a reduction of friction and disagreement at all levels. No single innovation enabled C.O.H.Q. to influence the conduct of the war so strongly as the creation of this post and with the prestige which the holders achieved for it. The Combined Operations Joint Planner accompanied C.C.O. on his visits to North Africa, Malta and Sicily and, as far as planning was concerned, became his right hand-man.

The Admiralty Takes Over the Assault Fleet

At a Chiefs of Staff meeting held on 27th November, 1942, the First Sea Lord pointed out that, as the Assault Fleet had reached such large proportions, the time had come for the Admiralty to relieve the Combined Operations Command of this commitment. He suggested that the Deputy First Sea Lord, C.C.O. and the Controller should go into this question and forward their recommendations.

Early in 1943, the Deputy First Sea Lord submitted his proposals, the main feature of which was that the Admiralty should take over the functions of Rear-Admiral Landing Craft and Bases (R.A.L.B.) by setting up various Combined Operations branches within existing Admiralty departments. These proposals were approved and the Admiralty absorbed its new responsibilities by setting up the following:

(1) The Directorate of Combined Operations Personnel (D.C.O.P.), which worked directly under the Director of Naval Personnel.
(2) The Director of Naval Equipment Combined Operations (D.N.E. (CO)) who was already established in the Admiralty, absorbed the functions of the Engineering Section under R.A.L.B.
(3) An Assistant Directorate of Operations Division (A.D.O.D. (CO)) which absorbed the Movement and Craft Section under R.A.L.B.
(4) A Deputy Directorate of Plans Division (D.D. of P. (CO) which absorbed that section of the naval staff under R.A.L.B. which had been concerned with combined operations.
(5) A Directorate of Requirements and Organisation, Combined Operations (D.R.O. (CO)), later known as the Directorate of Combined Operations Department (D.C.O.D.) Into this were absorbed certain staff functions previously carried out in C.O.H.Q.

Appointment of Rear-Admiral Commanding Combined Operations Bases, North (R.A.C.O.B. (N))

Thus, the department of R.A.L.B. became absorbed into the Admiralty, a fact that was promulgated on 13th August, 1943. However, the bases and personnel which were now occupying the coasts of Scotland had become so numerous and dispersed that it was considered necessary to have a Flag Officer in that area. Accordingly, the appointment of Rear-Admiral Commanding Combined Operations Bases, North (R.A.C.O.B. (N)) was established. Rear-Admiral Horan, who had been R.A.L.B. up to that time, was given this new appointment and hoisted his flag in H.M.S. *Warren*, the Combined Headquarters at Largs, on 1st May, 1943. This appointment existed until 15th November, 1946.

The Directorate of Training and Staff Duties, Combined Operations established in the Admiralty

The only naval functions left to C.O.H.Q., from about August 1943 onwards, were the development of tactics and the initiation of staff requirements for special assault craft and equipment. A Directorate of Training and Staff Duties, Combined Operations was set up in the Admiralty to preserve liaison with C.O.H.Q. in these matters.

The Assault Warfare Committee

In July, 1943, as a result of the "Rattle" Conference and prior to his leaving for the "Quadrant" Conference, C.C.O. had established within C.O.H.Q. the Assault Warfare Committee. Their terms of reference were as follows: (1) Study and keep under constant review all tactical problems connected with the assault phase of an amphibious operation; (2) Study tactics, technique and the developments required in ships, craft, vehicles, aircraft, weapons and equipment for amphibious warfare and associated air support, and to deduce staff requirements; [and] (3) Study requirements in the Far East.

This committee was very active and was in constant touch with the C.O.S.S.A.C. planners and assisted them in every way.

C.C.O.'s Recommendations for the Future

Just before taking up his appointment as Supreme Allied Commander South-East Asia, Admiral Mountbatten submitted a memorandum dated 20th September, 1943, on the future of C.O.H.Q. In this he described how conditions had changed since his original appointment and reviewed the need for modifications in the organisation and responsibilities of the headquarters. He pointed out that, although originally, he had been charged with the planning and mounting of raids and the build-up of an assault fleet; raiding might now devolve upon the Chief of Staff to the Supreme Allied Commander (C.O.S.S.A.C.) so that it could be related to future operations; and that the Admiralty had now assumed full responsibility for the assault fleet.

There remained to the Chief of Combined Operations the following functions:

(1) The study of tactical and technical problems of amphibious assaults and the formulation of doctrine and staff requirements.
(2) Advice on all aspects of planning and training for amphibious assaults.
(3) Co-ordination of the general training policy for amphibious assaults for all three Services and the control of Combined Training Centres in the U.K.
(4) Co-ordination of the development of communication material and inter-communication technique in amphibious warfare.
(5) Control of the Special Service Force in the U.K. prior to the whole or any part of it being handed over to a Force Commander.

Admiral Mountbatten then went on to explain how, in the light of the reduced functions of the Chief of Combined Operations and the fact that the technique and problems of combined operations were by then widely known, the study and development of the amphibious aspect of combined operations could best be carried out both in the present and post-war period. In his opinion, there were in principle two possible systems which could be adopted.

System A – Control by One Man
The retention of an independent organisation under the control of one man, who would be responsible for the functions outlined above to the Minister of Defence through the Chiefs of Staff Committee. He would have under him a reduced organisation based on the existing C.O.H.Q. and sufficient for its reduced functions. Whether he would be a member of the Chiefs of Staff Committee or not must depend on the emphasis laid on the active study and development of combined operations and the role of the latter in future strategy.

System B – Control by Committee
The establishment of a Directorate of Combined Operations within each Service Ministry. The study of technique and formulation of policy for combined operations would be the responsibility of a Combined Operations Staff formed within the Chiefs of Staff organisation and working under the directions of three Directors of Combined Operations, in a similar manner to the Joint Planning Staff. Under this system, the control of Combined Training Centres, the Combined Operations Experimental Establishment and the Special

Service Force with its inter-Service units, would devolve upon one of the Service Ministries, the Combined Operations Staff confining itself to the formulation of policy for consideration by the Chiefs of Staff Committee and for the promulgation of that policy when it had been approved.

Opinions Differ on the System to be Adopted

Admiral Mountbatten recommended System A as he considered that the advantages of having one Head, who bears ultimate responsibility for all decisions taken within the scope of his functions, outweighed the disadvantages of an establishment which had not the authority of a Service Ministry. The disadvantages of this system would be largely offset by close liaison between each Senior Service Adviser and his Ministry, it being incumbent upon each Service Adviser to represent C.C.O. the views of the Service Ministry concerned. These proposals were intended to cover the amphibious aspect of combined operations only. Should any extension of these responsibilities be contemplated, it would be necessary to re-examine the matter.

When these proposals had been studied by the Vice-Chiefs of Staff, the Vice-Chief of the Naval Staff submitted a memorandum dated 26th September, 1943, recommending that Course B should be adopted.

Both papers came before the Chiefs of Staff on 29th September, 1943, and in their minutes it is recorded that General Brooke and Air Marshal Portal disagreed with the Admiralty recommendation and expressed the view that C.O.H.Q. would work better with a single Head, who could co-ordinate and drive forward the training research and development of combined operations, and that experience had tended to show that responsibilities of this nature might not be efficiently discharged without the direction of a single Head.

The Chiefs of Staff Committee unanimously agreed that, in the new circumstances the size of C.O.H.Q. should be reduced and it was decided to appoint an impartial authority to report on the whole question without waiting for the appointment of a new Chief of Combined Operations. The Committee then sent their views to the Prime Minister and invited Air Marshal N.H. Bottomley to make the necessary investigations and report.

The Report of the Bottomley Committee

The Bottomley Committee reported to the Chiefs of Staff on 13th October, 1943, and the Air Marshal added a note to his conclusions by way of explanation.

In this note he stated that, although his terms of reference did not touch on the subject of the relations between C.C.O. and the Chiefs of Staff, that subject perforce came under review during his examination of the organisation of C.O.H.Q. opinions had been expressed on the desirability of maintaining the then existing relationship, especially as regards its effect on the status of the C.C.O.

As then constituted, C.O.H.Q. was independent of the Service Ministries, and the Prime Minister, as Minister of Defence, was its ministerial head and answerable for it in Parliament. Moreover, under the practice then obtaining, C.C.O., although acting under a directive of the Chiefs of Staff, reported on occasion direct to the Prime Minster. The Air Marshal continued, that whether the changed responsibilities called for any change in this practice was a matter on which the Chiefs of Staff could best advise.

It had been suggested that, in view of the reduced responsibilities, C.C.O. particularly in the planning and mounting of operations, might now be responsible for his functions to the Minister of Defence through the Chiefs of Staff Committee.

Air Marshal Bottomley, although offering advice only on the status of C.O.H.Q., saw nothing derogatory to the status or damaging to the present prestige of C.O.H.Q. in requiring C.C.O., as a matter of normal procedure, to report to the Minister of Defence through the Chiefs of Staff. If called upon to do so, C.C.O. would still be in a position to answer directly to the Minister of Defence and would continue to sit in committee with the Chiefs of Staff whenever matters appropriate to his responsibilities were under discussion, it was observed that this would relieve the Minister of certain matters of detail.

Following this note were the main recommendations of the Committee which were:

(1) C.O.H.Q. should be maintained as a central organisation for the study and development of the technique of combined operations. Its Chief should continue to hold the relative rank of Vice-Admiral.

(2) The principal advisers of the C.C.O., known hitherto as the Executive (also under the new proposals becoming the heads of the four main branches of C.O.H.Q.), should retain their existing ranks (Major-General Royal Marines, Major-General, Air Vice-Marshal and Rear-Admiral) the matter being reviewed after three months.

(3) The organisation of C.O.H.Q. should be remodelled, the staff being divided into four functional groups, each group

consisting of a composite staff from all three Services working under the direction of a member of the Executive.
(4) If the general recommendations were approved, the C.C.O. and his staff should evolve in detail an establishment based on the principles stated.
(5) Substantial reductions were recommended in the planning and intelligence staffs.
(6) A reorganisation of the Directorate of Combined Training was recommended.
(7) An immediate reduction of the security, public relations, records, chaplains and medical staffs was recommended, a scale reduction of the Secretariat following.

On 15th October, 1943, the Chiefs of Staff approved these recommendations, and instructed C.C.O. to submit, in consultation with the Service Ministries, a detailed establishment based on the principles set out in Air Marshal Bottomley's report.

Two days before this decision on 13th October, 1943, Admiral Mountbatten left C.O.H.Q. and took up his appointment as Supreme Allied Commander South-East Asia; the arrival of his successor was delayed until December when Major-General R.E. Laycock took up his appointment as the Chief of Combined Operations. The work of reorganisation continued during the interval under Major-General Wildman-Lushington as Chief of Staff, Combined Operations Headquarters.

New Directive issued to the Chief of Combined Operations

On 28th November, 1943, and as a result of the Bottomley Report, a new directive was issued by the Chiefs of Staff to Major-General R.E. Laycock, the incoming C.C.O.

General Laycock was charged with:

(1) Study of tactical and technical problems of amphibious operations including small scale raids and formulations on doctrine and staff requirements.
(2) Offering advice on all aspects of planning and training for amphibious operations.
(3) Co-ordination of basic training policy for amphibious operations for all three Services and control of Combined Training Centres in the United Kingdom.
(4) Direction and active progress of research and development in all forms of technical equipment including craft peculiar to combined operations.

(5) Co-ordination of the development of communication material and intercommunication technique in amphibious warfare.

(6) Control of the Special Service Group, except when the whole or any part of it is handed over to a Force Commander for operations.

In order to fulfil these responsibilities, General Laycock was to give advice to the Chiefs of Staff on the foregoing matters and was to be available to attend the Chiefs of Staff Committee when required. In addition, he had direct access to the Minister of Defence on all matters for which he was responsible.

In the planning sphere, he was to give technical advice upon all planning for combined operations at all stages; and Commanders and their staffs were directed to take advantage of the facilities he provided. In the case of North-West European operations carried out with and planned by Special Service Troops with his advice, there was the additional requirement of obtaining the general concurrence of the Supreme Allied Commander or his Chief of Staff.

In the training aspects, he was responsible for co-ordinating the teaching at Combined Schools of Instruction or Training Establishments in the United Kingdom excluding those established by Force Commanders, where his functions were only advisory. He was responsible also for the control of Combined Training Centres, for technical advice to the staffs of the Centres and advice to the Force Commanders, subsequent to their appointment for an operation, on the technical training of their forces.

It was made equally incumbent on Force Commanders to seek his advice.

The Special Service Group was placed under his control, but individual Service Ministries continued to provide, through C.O.H.Q., the necessary administrative facilities. Special Service Troops were held available for specific combined operations when they would be placed under the Commander appointed for that operation.

In addition to these responsibilities in the U.K., there was also a responsibility for the co-ordination of development in combined assault training and technique among British authorities overseas and for ensuring, so far as possible, the adoption of a common doctrine by Allied authorities both in the U.K. and overseas.

The Four Functional Groups

General Laycock's report on the reorganisation of C.O.H.Q. was submitted to the Chiefs of Staff on 22nd January, 1944.

In this report he commenced by outlining Air Marshal Bottomley's three main proposals: (1) The reorganisation of the staff of C.O.H.Q. into functional groups, each group consisting of a composite staff from all three Services working under the direction of a member of the Executive of C.O.H.Q.; (2) The drafting of a definite establishment based on the above principles; [and] (3) Reductions in certain branches of the existing organisation which were to be effected when the new establishment was drawn up.

He then commented on these proposals. The Bottomley Report had noted the existence of two types of branches in the old C.O.H.Q. organisation: the first consisting of Service staffs working under their Service Heads, and the second of inter-Service branches with a staff drawn from all three Services. The report recommended that in future the whole Headquarters should be organised on the second basis, the work of the branches being allocated on a functional basis.

It was not easy, General Laycock continued, to put this recommendation into practice as he had to make radical alterations to a machine which, for all its defects, could not be stopped whilst alterations were being made. Furthermore, the task was not made easier by the change in policy in regard to small scale raids which occurred while the investigations were being made. Nevertheless, a scheme was drawn up which conformed, broadly, to the recommendations.

The new organisation brought the whole Headquarters under the following functional groups: (1) Experiments, developments and signals; (2) Training, administration, the control of the Special Service Group and small scale raid planning; (3) Combined Operations policy, technique, plans and Intelligence; [and] (4) Combined Operations Joint Planner.

The Secretariat was provided for under a separate Head.

The Bottomley Report recognised that the allocation of duties among the functional groups must be a matter for C.C.O. and his staff to decided, but with few and minor exceptions, C.C.O. was able to follow the Bottomley recommendations, the underlying theme of which was singleness of purpose. The theme was attractive and in keeping with the basic idea of Combined Operations and it was proposed to give it a trial, but the express reservation was made that if experience showed that the new arrangement had practical defects, then such modifications as were considered necessary could be made.

Reductions in Establishment

The report contained a detailed consideration of the establishment cuts proposed, which would effect a saving of 17 per cent in officers and leave the Headquarters with 134 officers (25 per cent female), 233 other ranks (91 per cent female) and 17 civilians; a total of 384. Two Vice-Admirals, one Rear-Admiral, three Major-Generals, one Brigadier and one Air Vice-Marshal were replaced by one Major-General, one Commodore Second Class, two Brigadiers and one Air Commodore. It was agreed that a committee representing the establishment branches for all three Services should survey the new complement, but not until the new system had been in operation for at least three months.

The Security, Public Relations, Records and Chaplain Branches of C.O.H.Q., as such, were disbanded and the duties of the first three transferred to other officers as a part-time duty.

The Intelligence Branch was reduced to four and the Medical Branch to one officer. The Operational Planning Staff was abolished, but a nucleus retained for advice to Force Commanders during the planning stage, and to study the combined operational aspect of future operations.

A reorganisation of the Directorate of Combined Training was carried out as advised and this staff separated from the staff of C.O.H.Q.

In conclusion, General Laycock required a temporary staff to carry out his responsibilities, under the Supreme Allied Commander, for the planning and preparation of small scale raids until "Overlord" was mounted, and requested the Chiefs of Staff approval to his plans.

The Chiefs of Staff considered this report at a meeting at which Major-General Laycock was present.

Broadly, they were in complete agreement with General Laycock's remarks and the way in which he had carried out the recommendations of the Bottomley Report. They invited C.C.O. to investigate the possibility of amalgamating the Combined Operations Joint Planning Staff with the Plans Combined Operations Advice and to report in due course; they agreed to the review by an Inter-Services Establishment Committee after a three-month trial. The full reorganisation of C.O.H.Q. on a functional basis took shape during the Spring of 1944.

With the Admiralty assuming control of the naval side of the Command, C.O.H.Q. took over the responsibilities designated to it in the Bottomley Report and concentrated on these for the furtherance of Operation "Overlord".

Activities of C.M.S.F.

C.M.S.F. Major-General Wernher became a member of the C.O.S.S.A.C. Staff as he was mainly concerned in the provision of the artificial harbours decided upon at the Quebec Conference and the planning of "Overlord" was now in the hands of C.O.S.S.A.C. Staff.

CHANGES AT COMBINED OPERATIONS HEADQUARTERS DURING 1943

Before leaving for Quebec, C.M.S.F. had arranged with the Minister of Supply, Sir Andrew Duncan, for certain personnel employed by large firms to be available for the production of the concrete caissons and other material required for the "spud piers". Prominent among these were Mr. John Gibson and Mr. R.A. Davis. Brigadier-General H.B. Vaughan was nominated to represent the American interests. This officer had great experience in large constructional schemes and therefore possessed considerable knowledge of the problems that confronted those responsible for the construction of the artificial harbours, particularly the concrete caissons ("Phoenix"), the designs for which were presented to the contractors by the War Office in October, 1943.

The question of the labour and supplies for this large constructional job, also fell largely on C.M.S.F. and here many difficulties were encountered but, in the end, surmounted.

Some idea of the vast nature of the task can be gathered from the fact that the labour force finally numbered between 43,000 and 47,000. Material used included 105,000 tons of steel, 850,000 tons of ballast and sand and 144,000 tons of concrete. For the steel, all especially long railway wagons in various parts of the country were in use.

Finally, it is only necessary to say that the whole project was completed on time and ready in every respect for "D" Day.

Chapter 9

THE DEVELOPMENT OF THE PLAN FOR THE INVASION OF NORTH-WEST EUROPE, OPERATION "OVERLORD"

Although many changes had taken place, C.O.H.Q. was still left with the responsibility of undertaking raids. Raiding activity now more than ever had to be co-ordinated with the overall strategic concept for "Overlord".

In the autumn of 1943, C.O.S.S.A.C. asked C.O.H.Q. to undertake certain small scale reconnaissance raids on their behalf, in the Havre-Ostend area, the Cherbourg peninsula and the Channel Islands.

The aim was not only reconnaissance but also deception, in accordance with the cover plan. A small raiding syndicate was briefed by the C.O.S.S.A.C. Raid and Reconnaissance Committee and, having completed the outline plan, submitted them to G.O.C. Special Service Group for detailed planning by Force Commanders. When these plans were approved, the raids were carried out.

No detailed study of the "Overlord" beaches had been made at the time the original outline plan of "Overlord" was discussed at the Quebec Conference in August, 1943.

C.O.H.Q. suggested a further study of these beaches as a result of the examination of the Arromanches-Asnelles region from the point of view of the artificial harbours. Evidence was found, in the first place from a French Guide Book, of the existence of peat in commercial

THE DEVELOPMENT OF THE PLAN FOR THE INVASION

quantities at several places on these beaches. The presence of peat suggested difficulties for wheeled and tracked vehicles in crossing beaches. On 3rd November, 1943, Professor Bernal, the Experimental Scientific Adviser at C.O.H.Q., wrote to 21st Army Group, who were planning to assault across these beaches, suggesting that a much more detailed study should be made of the peat characteristics, and C.O.S.S.A.C. gave early approval.

From topographical, geological and biological data of the areas of the French beaches and comparison with similar beaches in England, Professor Bernal made a hypothetical reconstruction of the whole projected assault beach area, indicating places where peat and clay might be expected to occur, and where the places might be covered with deep sand.

Up to this time very little was known about the bearing power of peat or sand, with softer formations underneath. However, Brancaster in Norfolk was eventually chosen as the locality showing most nearly the characteristics of the Normandy beaches. The Combined Operations Pilotage Parties from C.O.H.Q. carried out their preliminary training at Brancaster in December, 1943, and eventually made reconnaissance of the beaches for "Overlord" in December, 1943, and January, 1944. On 1st February, 1944, C.O.H.Q., in conjunction with 21st Army Group, were able to issue a comprehensive report on the conditions of the Normandy beaches. This report was fully borne out by the conditions experienced on "D" Day.

Brancaster beach was also used for trials on the effect of bombs on the "going" for wheeled and tracked vehicles on beaches which had been attacked from the air. As a result, only 100-lb. bombs with instantaneous fuses were used against beach defences in "Overlord".

The small raids and the beach reconnaissance carried out by Combined Operations Pilotage Parties enabled the Allies to form a striking picture of the novel and formidable German beach defences.

The clearance of these beach obstacles had been made an Admiralty responsibility but C.O.H.Q. frequently gave advice. Every form of beach obstacle encountered during any reconnaissance was reconstructed at one or another of the Combined Operations Establishments and methods of destroying or neutralising it were decided upon after extensive trials. This technique helped to cut down losses from beach obstacles although they were still severe.

C.O.H.Q. Advises on Training and Planning

The evolution from outline plan to final conception of Operation "Overlord" required the greatest organisation, and the whole project became a major national undertaking to which the C.O.H.Q. contributed with advice, training, publications and other Combined Operations facilities.

At the Training Establishment, which was set up at the Headquarters of Rear-Admiral, Combined Operations Bases (North) at Largs, Ayrshire, 1,700 officers of all Services and Allied Nationalities were given short courses in the technique of the assault. These courses greatly benefited by the presence of neighbouring Combined Training Centres so that theoretical instruction could be demonstrated practically.

There were constant calls for the services of the planners at C.O.H.Q. A section of the staff known as Plans Combined Operations Advice came into being and officers from this were loaned as and when required. A complete C.O.H.Q. planning syndicate consisting of Commander Costabadie, Lieutenant-Colonel Henriques and Wing Commander Tailyour, all of whom had had much previous experience, were lent to C.O.S.S.A.C. to assist in planning "Overlord". In addition, calls came from the various commands in the U.K. for advice as to training for "D" Day; Lieutenant-Colonel Trevor and Lieutenant-Colonel Richardson of C.O.H.Q. assisted in the training of the U.S. Ranger Group, and Corporal Good and Private Blackmore of C.O.X.E. were attached to the 2nd Ranger Battalion U.S. Army and landed with that Battalion on 6th June at Pointe du Hoc, Normandy, and served with distinction in the assault.

The Combined Operations Joint Planner regularly attended the meetings of the Chiefs of Staff Joint Planners and helped in any combined operations matters that were discussed.

The requirements in South-East Asia and the Pacific produced new problems and called for new techniques, and these formed the major part of the work at the reorganised C.O.H.Q.

Fulfilment of the Plan

It is not proposed, in this history, to cover Operation "Overlord" by more than a brief reference as so much has already been written on this subject alone. The preparations for this assault absorbed a greater part of the war-making capacity of the two major powers for many months and, by the time this stage had been reached, the main contribution of C.O.H.Q. had been made.

The position was put concisely in the following signal made to Admiral Mountbatten, then Supreme Allied Commander South-East Asia, when the Prime Minister, with the U.S. Chiefs of Staff, the C.I.G.S. and Field Marshal Smuts, visited the beach area in the wake of the invading armies:

THE DEVELOPMENT OF THE PLAN FOR THE INVASION

Today we visited the British and American Armies on the soil of France. We sailed through vast fleets of ships with landing craft of many types pouring more and more men, vehicles and stores ashore. We saw clearly the manoeuvre in process of rapid development. We have shared our secrets in common and helped each other all we could. We wish to tell you at this moment in your arduous campaign that we realise that much of this remarkable technique and therefore the success of the venture has its origin in developments effected by you and your staff of Combined Operations.

(signed)
Arnold, Brooke, Churchill, King, Marshall, Smuts.

With the permission of General Eisenhower, the C.C.O. had observers at the following important points during "D" Day and subsequent operations:

Naval Officers at:
    A.N.C.X.F.'s Headquarters.
    With Admiral Tennant (Mulberry Harbours).
    With beach troops erecting causeway.
    2nd Army Headquarters.
    Navigational Leader Force "S".
    S.N.O.L. Headquarters Ship Force "J".
Air Officers at:
    Headquarters Ship Force "G".
    F.D.T. 13.
    Two American Headquarters Ships.
Army Officers attached to:
    30 Corps.
    Reserve Brigade 30 Corps.
    9 Beach Group, 30 Corps.
    Assistant Director Transportation 1 Corps.
    Beach Sub Area 1 Corps.
    Reserve Brigade 1 Corps.
Liaison Officers (Army) specially asked for by 2nd Army:
    Two officers between 1 Corps and 2nd Army.
    One officer between 30 Corps and 2nd Army.
    Two officers between 2nd Army (Tac.) and 2nd Army (Main).
    One officer between 2nd Army and C.O.B.U.
    Two officers to assist Brigadier Tarleton, liaison officer between
        2nd Army and Admiral Vian.

Fifteen Army officers from C.T.C.s were attached to units to assist during training and operations. Thus, the staff of C.O.H.Q. were able to see the operation as it developed. C.C.O. himself, accompanied by the Combined Operations Joint Planner, witnessed the opening phases of "Overlord" from the American Flagship by the invitation of Admiral Kirk.

From the C.O.H.Q. point of view, perhaps the most important problem was the organisation of the beaches and the maintenance of the supplies across them.

As soon as the reports on "Overlord" came in, C.C.O. instructed the staff at C.O.H.Q. to make an intense study of all the problems involved and promulgate them to any other theatres in which combined operations were likely to take place. This study was exhaustive and was promulgated on 8th January, 1945.

The adaption of these lessons to the conditions of the South-East Asia Command and the war against Japan necessitated sending staff officers from C.O.H.Q. to these areas. It was a C.O.H.Q. dictum that officers with first-hand knowledge were far more likely to spread knowledge quickly than any number of textbooks. Besides, time was pressing and the preparation of manuals is a lengthy business.

Just before "D" Day the Directing Staff of the Combined Training Centre at Largs became available for other duties as the courses there had ceased. Accordingly, C.C.O. arranged for these officers to be appointed as observers to the American Forces in the Pacific. These observers were present at all the important landings carried out in this area, visiting Pearl Harbour, Johnson Island, Guam, Leyte, Luzon, Palau Isles, Hollandia, Finschhafen, Townsville, Cairns, Atherton, Beac, Morotai, Palawan, Mindoro and Mindanao, covering some 30,000 miles mostly by air, and on their return to C.O.H.Q. gave the staff first-hand accounts of all operations.

Chapter 10

THE FAR EAST

The break-out from the Normandy beach head and the landing in the South of France (Operation "Dragoon") enabled C.C.O. to direct all the energies of the staff at C.O.H.Q. to the problems facing the Supreme Commanders in South-East Asia and the Pacific.

South-East Asia Command
The reports sent in by the observers in the Pacific were carefully studied and lessons co-ordinated and promulgated.

The following is an extract from the minutes of the Chiefs of Staff meeting on 13th October, 1944:

> Visit by Chief of Combined Operations to India and South-East Asia.
> Major-General Laycock said that the bulk of the work in Combined Operations Headquarters would in future be connected with amphibious operations in the Far East. He therefore proposed, subject to the approval of the Chiefs of Staff, to pay a short visit to India and the South-East Asia Command, in order to familiarise himself with the conditions on the spot.
> The Committee:
> Took note with approval of the proposed visit by the Chief of Combined Operations to the Far East and invited him to make the necessary arrangements with the C.-in-C., India and S.A.C.S.E.A.

C.C.O. accordingly visited India during the latter half of November, 1944, and returned to the United Kingdom in December.

At the end of September, 1944, the Supreme Allied Commander, South-East Asia (Admiral Mountbatten) began planning operations requiring formations trained in combined operations and set up his own Combined Operations section of S.E.A.C. staff. S.E.A.C. formations already trained in combined operations were by then committed to operations in Burma.

Directorate of Combined Operations, India

At this stage it is intended to revert to January, 1942, and trace briefly the history of the Directorate of Combined Operations, India, between 1942 and 1945 and also give some notes on the staff channels of communications and internal organisation in this theatre.

In January, 1942, the Chiefs of Staff in New Delhi approved the formation of a Combined Operations Advisory Committee to be known as Advisers Combined Operations, India (A.s C.O. (I)). They consisted of one naval member, Captain Garnons-Williams, R.N., one military member, Brigadier A.C. St. Clair-Morford and an air force member, Group Captain E.L. Tompkinson. Although the A.s C.O. (I) worked together in one office, they were each borne on the strength of their individual Service Headquarters in Delhi. The task of the committee was to advise the Commander-in-Chief (India) and all Service and Formation Commanders on matters concerning combined operations, and to maintain liaison with combined operation authorities in the U.K., Middle East or elsewhere.

In November, 1942, with the forming of Combined Operations Force Headquarters at Bombay, the Advisory Committee was discontinued and the formation of a Combined Operations Directorate on a larger establishment was authorised. The Director, known as Director of Combined Operations (India), was Captain Garnons-Williams, R.N., who was assisted by three Service advisers. The three Services continued to be borne on the strength of their respective headquarters at Delhi, and a new branch of the General Staff, General Headquarters (India), known as S.D.14, was created to hold the military establishment. The naval staff at the Naval Headquarters was known as C.O.N.

The directive issued to the Director of Combined Operations (India) by the Chiefs of Staff greatly increased his responsibilities and included advice in planning, collecting and sorting of combined operations intelligence and the supply of special combined equipment to Force Commanders, as well as assistance in the raising and equipping of the new Combined Training Centre at Madh Island. Combined Operations Force H.Q. remained responsible for training and administering the training establishments.

In January, 1943, Captain Garnons-Williams, R.N., flew to the U.K. for a short visit, stopping *en route* at Casablanca where he joined Brigadier Macleod (C.O.J.P.) who was returning from the Casablanca

Conference. Unfortunately, the aircraft crashed on reaching Wales, incapacitating both officers at a critical time for Combined Operations in India and the U.K. Group Captain E.L. Tomkinson thereupon took over as D.C.O. (I).

In October, 1943, with the formation of South-East Asia Command and the probability of increased combined operational training commitments, the Directorate was increased in strength and status and became a separate branch of G.H.Q. (I). S.D. 14 was disbanded, but the R.N. and R.A.F. Staff continued to be held on their respective headquarters. The appointment of Director was raised to Rear-Admiral, Major-General or Air Commodore with a Brigadier as Deputy Director and Chief of Staff, and an inter-Service staff.

Rear-Admiral L.E.H. Maund was appointed Director, and arrived in New Delhi at the end of October. The new directive from the C.O.S. Committee (India), invested in him the responsibility for all military combined operations training, technical advice on combined operational matters to C.-in-C. (I) and Force Commanders, and the trial and experiment of special equipment. The existing combined operational training establishments were placed under his direct control and authorisation was granted for the raising of new establishments as required in order to meet the training commitment.

In April, 1944, owing to the removal of all handing ships and craft previously allocated to S.A.C.S.E.A. and the non-arrival of the expected reinforcements of men and shipping from the U.K., combined operational training commitments in India decreased considerably. Rear-Admiral Maund was recalled to the U.K. and Brigadier A. Skeen became acting Director. Reductions in staff were made in the combined operational training establishments on orders from the Manpower Control Committee, but this did not, however, materially affect the directorate itself. Several officers were sent to the U.K. on refresher courses.

Department of Military Training – 6, War office (M.T.6)
At the end of September, the Director of Military Training (India) proposed to the C.O.S. Committee (India) that all training, including combined operations training, should come under a centralised authority. He proposed that a separate branch of D.M.T., to be known as M.T.6, should be inaugurated to take over combined operations training and the administration and organisation of the existing training establishments. This proposal was agreed and M.T.6 came into effect in early October, 1944. The D.C.O. (I) reverting once again to the role of adviser.

It will be recalled that, at about this time, the Supreme Allied Commander South-East Asia began planning operations requiring amphibious trained formations and that those divisions already trained were committed in Central Burma. The commitment was too great to be undertaken by M.T.6 and consequently the Directorate was again charged with this responsibility. Major-General A.R. Chater, Royal Marines, was appointed D.C.O. (I) and assumed his duties in New Delhi in late October, 1944. At the same time, a proposal put forward by C.C.O. to divorce the Directorate from G.H.Q. (I) and give it equal status under Defence H.Q. with Flag Officer Commanding Royal Indian Navy, G.H.Q. (I) and Air H.Q. (I), was agreed by the C.-in-C. (I) and the Supreme Allied Commander, and came into effect almost immediately.

By January, 1945, the Directorate was expanded on a new War Establishment, naval and air force personnel becoming an integral part of the Directorate. D.C.O. (I), being now empowered with direct access to the C.-in-C. (I) on matters affecting combined operations, continued to use M.T.6 as a link with G.H.Q. (I) where co-ordination of training and movement of formations were concerned.

In July, 1945, the probability arose of having to carry out combined operations training outside the sphere of India Command. As this called for the very closest liaison with S.E.A.C., it was agreed by the C.-in-C. (I) and the S.A.C., that the Directorate should owe allegiance to both Commanders and be known as D.C.O. (India and S.E.A.C.)

With the end of hostilities, the Directorate began at once to disband. General Chater was recalled in October, Brigadier C.H. Lyall-Grant was appointed Director, and plans were put in hand at once for the forming of a peace time Combined Operations Establishment in India.

Results of C.C.O.'s Visit to India and S.E.A.C.

From the outline of events in India, we return to C.O.H.Q. C.C.O. on return from his visit to India and S.E.A.C., in November and December, 1944, made the following points at a meeting of the executive of C.O.H.Q.:

(1) It had been agreed that D.C.O. (India) should come directly under C.-in-C. India in his capacity of being head of the three Services in India, but should not, however, come under G.H.Q. India.
(2) It had been agreed that D.C.O. (India) should act as Combined Operations Adviser and Staff Officer to Commander, Allied Land Forces, S.E.A.
(3) A new directive had now been issued to D.C.O. (India) by C.-in-C. India.

THE FAR EAST

(4) It had been agreed that C.O.H.Q. should deal direct with the Combined Operations Division of S.A.C.S.E.A. This latter organisation did not in any way come under D.C.O. (India) though it maintained close liaison.

(5) The technique of an assault up river mouths should be studied as a matter of urgency, as it appeared likely that most of the assaults caried out in S.E.A. would be done under these conditions.

(6) D.C.O. (India) felt the need for more information from C.O.H.Q. as to what problems were being studied in the United Kingdom, and on the type of equipment, landing ships and craft that were likely to be provided for use in S.E.A.C. At present the majority of information on amphibious warfare reaching D.C.O. (India) was from the C.C.O. Representative, Washington.

The Executive in their decisions at this meeting:

(1) Took note of C.C.O.'s statement.
(2) Instructed D.C.O. (Air) to consider the question of the provision of further information for D.C.O. (India) and to submit recommendations.
(3) Took note that the Amphibious Warfare Committee were already examining the question of the technique for assault up river mouths.

New problems were thus clearly taking shape as new conditions of ground and climate opened up under the world-wide allied forward movement across the beaches, rivers, swamps and islands of a dozen widely separated territories.

Collection of Intelligence – Europe and Far East

Amphibious operations planned for European Theatres had an advantage in that there was a mass of reliable intelligence available on all likely areas of assault. Maps were plentiful and on a large scale and, although clandestine reconnaissance was frequently employed, it was in an essential supplementary rather than, as in the East, an essential primary role.

It was at the beginning of 1944 that C.O.H.Q. developed the technique of beach reconnaissance from Midget submarines. The actual reconnaissance was made by the Combined Operations Pilotage Parties (C.O.P.P.) and it was found that the Midget submarines could undertake the role of daylight reconnaissance of the beaches. They could reconnoitre a beach without surfacing and thus obtain valuable information for the use of the planner. This technique was wanted both in the South-East Asia and Pacific Commands but, in spite of the constant efforts of C.O.H.Q., it was not found possible to send these craft overseas. In spite of the lack of Midget submarines, the Small Operations Group S.E.A.C. played a primary and vital role in operations in this theatre.

C.O.H.Q. was much concerned to maintain the same close contact with realities, and quick adaption to new requirements in the Eastern War as in the nearer European Theatres. Following C.C.O.'s visits in the new theatre at the end of 1944, his Chief of Staff, Brigadier (later Major-General) V.D. Thomas carried out a tour commencing 17th April and ending 15th May, 1945. He conferred with the D.C.O. (I) in Delhi and the Head of Combined Operations, S.A.C.S.E.A., in Kandy. His discussions covered a wide variety of subjects, some of which it is of interest to record here.

With D.C.O. (I) he discussed:

> Surf training and technique.
> Co-ordination of C.O.X.E. (U.K.) and C.O.X.E. (I).
> Development of a flying deck on L.S.T.s for light aircraft.
> Requirements for the Beach Pilotage School.
> Ships and landing craft for C.T.C.s and C.O.X.E. (I).
> Provision of staff officers and instructors from the U.K. for India and S.E.A.C.
> The new Indian Beach Organisation, Force 143.
> Training in assault amphibians and support amphibians.
> River assault technique.
> Command and control of Air Forces.

With the Head of Combined Operations, S.A.C.S.E.A., he discussed:

> Additional accommodations in L.S.T.s for assault troops.
> Organisation and training of Beach Brigades.
> Carriage of pontoons and estuary trials.
> The R.M. Assault Regiment.
> Commando requirements in S.E. Asia.
> Communications in amphibians.
> Availability of H.Q. Ships.
> Floating airfields.
> Air recognition.
> Provision of a Combined Operations Bombardment Unit.

Part II

The History And Development Of Techniques And Equipment For Combined Operations

Chapter 11

THE STORY OF SOME OPERATIONS AFFECTING DEVELOPMENT OF COMMAND AND CONTROL

Combined operations by land and sea forces have taken place throughout British history, but in modern times, the Gallipoli Campaign of World War I and the blocking of Zeebrugge, in which the young Royal Air Force was allotted a diversionary role, were the outstanding operations prior to World War II.

Between the wars some slight study of the subject was made, but it was not until 1937 that the first steps were taken to bring the matter into perspective. Although much useful constructive thought on up-to-date lines took place in 1938, very little had actually been achieved at the out-break of war, when even the small organisation which had been set up, the Inter-Services Training and Development Centre (I.S.T.D.C.), was disbanded.

The I.S.T.D.C. was re-formed in December, 1939, and a number of Independent Companies, later to form the nucleus of the Commandos, were also being formed by the War Office. During the Norway campaign, the naval and military members of the I.S.T.D.C. were called in to assist in the preparations for the Narvik operation, and six of the Independent Companies were employed between Namsos and Bodo. Two landings were made in April 1940, one at Herjangs and one on the Narvik peninsula, with the aid of the few old landing craft available; the occasion is notable for being the first in history on which tanks were landed over a beach in an operation of war.

At Dunkirk, all the available landing craft, including those newly completed, were used. Most of them were lost, but four L.C.A. survived and were finally able to return to the U.K. after evacuating 2,000 troops.

At the conclusion of the Dunkirk evacuation, the position with regard to landing craft was that, in addition to the four surviving L.C.A. and one L.C.M., there were forty-eight L.C.A., thirty L.C.M. and eight support craft building, but there were no arrangements to establish a naval organisation to man and serve these craft. The six Independent Companies raised for, but not employed in, Norway were available and ten Commandos were in the process of being formed. The I.S.T.D.C. was still in existence, but that was all.

It was from these small beginnings that Combined Operations developed, against a sombre background which began with the fall of France. Britain and the Commonwealth then stood alone, until the German invasion of Russia in mid-1941. The planned expansion of our war industries had not yet reached its full output and American aid was confined to the Lend-Lease programme and the direct orders which our limited dollar holdings permitted. Our sea and air forces were engaged in defensive battles, our land forces were recovering from the heavy losses sustained on the Continent and were being reorganised for defence against possible invasion which left few men and little material for less urgent tasks. It was not surprising that the Admiralty had stated that, owing to our urgent needs for destroyers and escorts, no priority could be given to the landing craft building programme and that no further construction could be undertaken.

As time went on, Germany became deeply committed in Russia and our war production began to approach its peak. When America entered the war in December 1941, her enormous resources became fully available and plans for re-entry into the Continent were no longer academic. From then on, the study and practice of Combined Operations had become inevitable.

It is in this context then, that we can review some of the operations which took place and some which were planned, but never executed. We shall see what effect they had on the planning, organisation and execution of operations, which finally led to the success of "Overlord", the greatest invasion of all time. Combined Operations can be divided into two categories: Raids and Assaults. Raids necessitate a short penetration followed by a withdrawal. Assaults are intended to establish a beachhead from which further operations against the enemy can be launched.

Raids

In the early days of the war, raids, rather than assaults, were the major concern, the objects of which were varied and often multiple. They were useful in sustaining the morale of the forces and the civilian population in the U.K. and their value for this purpose was frequently far in excess of the material results achieved. They were valuable, too, for training and, in almost every case, lessons were learned both in detail and principle.

In addition to these general objectives, there were the more specialised aims. The raid on Bruneval in February, 1942, was staged for the purpose of capturing parts of a new type of German radar. That on Glomfjord had the aim of destroying the hydro-electric plant.

The raid on Dieppe, in August, 1942, which was the largest raid of all, had as its primary object the containing and destruction of some of the German fighter forces which, in turn, meant a degree of relief to Russia. Without the lessons learned from this raid, a large scale rehearsal for "Overlord", the final invasion of the Continent could hardly have been so successful.

First Raid on France, June, 1940

After the appointment on 12th June, 1940, of the first Director of Combined Operations, Lieutenant-General Bourne, no time was wasted in implementing the directive to harass the enemy and cause him to disperse his forces. The first raid, which was made in the Boulogne area of France, had a threefold aim; the primary aim was reconnaissance and the subsidiary aims were to kill or capture as many Germans as possible and to destroy enemy equipment, in particular grounded aircraft and petrol supplies.

The raid was successful in so far as some useful information was obtained and two of the enemy were killed. The raiding force, which consisted of 120 men from one of the Independent Companies, was landed and withdrawn with only one minor casualty.

It was found that the steam yachts, which it was originally intended to use, were useless and had to be replaced at the last moment by eight R.A.F. high-speed launches manned by civilian crews. These craft proved to be unsuitable, partly because of their excessive draft and partly because the civilian crews lacked the necessary discipline.

Although reconnaissance was achieved and some damage was done, perhaps its greatest value was that it provided experience, taught many lessons and proved that 120 men could be landed and withdrawn without casualties.

The Raid on Guernsey, July, 1940

The next raid was carried out in mid-July, 1940 against Guernsey, but little was achieved except further emphasis on the unsuitability of R.A.F. launches for raiding. This was followed in September, 1940, by the first attempted assault, which has an important place in the story of Combined Operations.

Dakar, September, 1940

The Dakar Expedition was mounted in an effort to take advantage, after the fall of France, of what was believed to be a fluid political situation. It was hoped that the presence of the Free French Forces under General de Gaulle would encourage those elements which were anti-Vichy and make extended military operations unnecessary. The political aspects of this operation, although interesting in themselves, concern us little here, except in so far as they led to great haste in the planning and preparation. The effects of this haste were, firstly, that the various alternative plans were laid with inadequate and uncertain information, secondly, that the Joint Staff did not begin to function properly until it had set sail, and finally, that the only units and stores available at such notice had been allotted, and in some case embarked, for a totally different operation.

As a result of this *ad hoc* planning, it was realised by the Military Force Commander that an improved organisation would be required for operations where military considerations would be paramount. He therefore pointed out in his report that there was a need for a central organisation to co-ordinate combined operations and suggested that the D.C.O.'s staff should form the nucleus of such a headquarters. If for no other reason, Dakar is important since it forced, at an early stage of the war, the recognition of a need which later became more generally understood.

However, in addition to this, Dakar demonstrated the need for adequate and efficient communications whilst afloat and, by an almost perfect example, rammed home the fact that a special Headquarters Ship was essential for a Force Commander in a combined operation. This latter lesson was learned as a result of the Military Commander and his headquarters, who were embarked in the cruiser *Devonshire*, being carried away from their forces on a purely naval occasion, in an unsuccessful attempt to intercept the Vichy French Battle Squadron. The lesson, well learned by the British at Dakar, had to be re-learned by the Americans in the invasion of North Africa.

Dakar, therefore, although abortive in its main object, has left its mark on later events, and is an essential part of the story.

The Period September, 1940 – December, 1941

The next few months after Dakar are marked by apparently very little activity, but they were in fact a period of consultation and preparation for the future.

For example, a number of passenger and cargo ships were being converted to L.S.I., or L.C.M. carriers; Combined Training Centres were set up in the Middle East and at Inveraray; Lieutenant-General Bourne was succeeded as Director of Combined Operations by Admiral of the Fleet Sir Roger Keyes and the building up of a staff had begun. Various plans were being considered such as the capture of Pantellaria, the Azores, Cape Verde Island and the installation of the Free French Force in Dakar. All this was taking place against the background of a possible invasion of the U.K. and, in September, 1940, all the available Commandos and Independent Companies were placed under the Command of C.-in-C. Home Forces for anti-invasion purposes and were not released again to the D.C.O. until the end of the year.

Early 1941 saw the beginning of greater activity in matters of combined operations. In February, the first full-scale Brigade exercise was held at the C.T.C., Inveraray. In the same month, the Chiefs of Staff, on the recommendation of the D.C.O., agreed to the assembly of a striking force which was to be immediately available for amphibious operations in any theatre and, in April, the Chiefs of Staff agreed to the construction of 200 L.C.T. (3).

There was therefore a continuous build-up against many difficulties, and although during this period many operations were planned, some were not executed for various reasons. Some successful raids were made both in the Mediterranean and North-West Europe, beginning with the airborne operation against the Apulian Aqueduct in Italy in February, 1941. Other operations included Lofoten Islands, Spitzbergen, and the exploits of Layforce in the Middle East.

Some of these raids had positive value. In December, 1941 at the Lofoten Islands, besides the destruction of the fish oil factories and the sinking of over 18,000 tons of enemy shipping, 314 Norwegian volunteers were taken off, 213 enemy soldiers and civilians were taken prisoner and 14 Germans were killed in action with an armed trawler. The raid was a complete success but, while it contributed to some extent to better inter-service co-operation and much to morale, the absence of opposition and the fact that it was primarily a naval occasion prevented the operation from advancing the technique of combined operations to any great extent.

Exercise "Leapfrog", August, 1941

In March, 1941, on the recommendation of the D.C.O., the Chiefs of Staff agreed to the assembly of a Striking Force to be immediately available for combined operations in any theatre. This force would be available to land in the Canary Islands should Germany invade Spain. It was to meet this eventuality that all available ships, landing craft and raiding craft were earmarked for the use of the striking force.

The operation was to be known as "Pilgrim". The Force Commanders were appointed and the force was assembled to carry out training. In August, a full-scale rehearsal, Exercise "Leapfrog", was carried out at Scapa Flow. It was as a result of this exercise that considerable controversy arose over the question of Command and Control and agreement of future policy could not be reached between the Chiefs of Staff and D.C.O. As Admiral Keyes held strongly to his views and was unable to accept those of the Chiefs of Staff, he was relieved by Commodore Louis Mountbatten.

Command and Control Raids

The situation which now arose had no precedent and consequently had to be resolved. Drastic changes became necessary at the beginning of 1942 when it was decided, as a part of the strategy of the war, that a series of raids, becoming progressively greater in scale, should be undertaken. As a result, the system finally evolved in May, 1942, was that C.C.O. became the mounting authority for all raids in North-West Europe. His functions were as follows:

(1) To prepare an outline plan.
(2) To obtain the approval of the Chiefs of Staff.
(3) To appoint Force Commanders with the approval of the Chiefs of Staff.
(4) To allocate and assemble the requisite specialised forces.
(5) To help and advise the Force Commanders in the preparation of the detailed plan.
(6) To get any additional intelligence or equipment which the Force Commanders required.
(7) To assist and advise during the rehearsal and training stage.

On first being appointed, the Force Commanders worked at C.O.H.Q. and produced the detailed plan based on the outline plan. As soon as this was completed, they moved to the mounting area to superintend the training and rehearsals and to produce the operations orders.

With regard to the execution of a raid, C.C.O. took the view that the Naval Commander-in-Chief, in whose area the raid lay, must retain overall command of that area and of all ships, craft and escorts serving therein. Therefore, although C.C.O. was responsible for making and presenting to the Chiefs of Staff the inter-Service plan for a raid and had superintended the preparations and rehearsals, the final executive order was given by the Naval Commander-in-Chief. For really important occasions, C.C.O. always went to the Naval Commander-in-Chief's Headquarters and the decision on whether or not to sail was made jointly.

It was the responsibility of C.O.H.Q. to arrange any independent air action other than the normal air protection organised by the Combined Area Headquarters. For instance, C.O.H.Q. had to arrange for the necessary air action at Vaagso and the independent bombing of St. Nazaire when the latter port was raided.

Further, C.C.O. always insisted that members of the planning staff should accompany all raiding operations so that they would have first-hand information on the operation and gain experience.

The Raids on Vaagso, Bruneval, St. Nazaire

From the time of the appointment of Admiral Mountbatten as Adviser on Combined Operations (A.C.O.), until the climax of raiding at Dieppe, the build-up was continuous. During this period three minor raids took place which were completely successful and contributed to the confidence with which later raids were mounted.

The aims of the attack on Vaagso Island were twofold. The naval task was to capture or destroy merchant shipping found in Ulversund off the port of Vaagso. The military task was to destroy or capture enemy troops or equipment, to destroy industrial plants, to seize documents, codes and instruments, to arrest Quislings and to withdraw Norwegian volunteers for the Free Forces. A naval officer, Admiral Sir J.C. Tovey, was placed in supreme command of the operation and by 12th December, 1941, most of the forces had been assembled and training, which included a realistic landing on a small island in Scapa Flow, had begun.

The raid was executed on 28th December, and a total of 16,000 tons of shipping was destroyed and the tasks of demolition completed. Air support was successful in preventing damage to the British ships and in sinking one vessel in an enemy convoy. Vaagso, although a comparatively small operation, was significant in that it was a true combined operation in which all three Services were engaged and, although the limited but severe opposition was not able to prevent its complete success, it provided a more rigorous test of combined operations than had hitherto occurred.

After Vaagso came the Bruneval raid on 27th February, 1942. This very small operation was designed to avoid rather than to seek opposition, and had the single objective of the capture of the radar installation. This was achieved by very careful planning, close co-operation of all three Services and determined execution; it is an excellent example of its kind.

The third raid under review is that on St. Nazaire on 27th March, 1942, when the principal aim was the destruction of the lock gates and the mechanism of the large dock which was the only one on the Atlantic seaboard capable of taking the German battleship *Tirpitz*. Subsidiary objects were to destroy the smaller lock gates and any other installations that would facilitate the servicing of U-boats, and to destroy any U-boat or shipping which might be found.

In addition to achieving its main aim, that of making the dock unusable by *Tirpitz*, the success of this operation provided an uplift of morale to our forces and the country as a whole. Many Germans were killed (some by their own fire), a U-boat was probably sunk, several enemy aircraft were destroyed and valuable experience was given to planning staffs and personnel taking part. An important lesson was also learned from the Air point of view; an air raid had been planned but, since the instructions were that no bombs were to be dropped on occupied territory unless the target could be seen clearly, and in this case the visibility was bad, the effect was to alert the defences but not to occupy their attention. This may have contributed to the fact that British casualties were higher than would probably have been the case had the air attack taken place. It thus became apparent that air action over a defended area should not be used where surprise may be vital, unless its effect can be guaranteed to be decisive.

Events Leading Up to the Dieppe Raid

In October, 1941, C.-in-C. Home Forces sought approval of the Chiefs of Staff to carry out raids on the coast of Occupied France and the Low Countries, in order to provide his troops with battle experience. The Chiefs of Staff agreed to these proposals and subsequently instructed C.-in-C. Home Forces to undertake a large scale raid of some duration with a target date of spring, 1942; he was instructed to prepare plans in consultation with the A.C.O. and the appropriate Naval and Air C.s-in-C. The forces which it was estimated would be available by spring,

1942, were to be placed at his disposal. The limiting factor was ships and craft which amounted to a total of two L.S.T. (L.), ten L.S.I. (M.) and L.S.I. (H.)[1], three L.S.G., fifty L.C.T., plus minor landing craft.

Dieppe as the target for a raid of this kind was first examined by the Target Committee of C.O.H.Q. in early April, 1942, and by the middle of the month, work had begun on an outline plan under the general direction of Captain Hughes-Hallett, R.N., who was subsequently the Naval Force Commander for the event. Representatives of the General Staff Home Forces had by then already joined the planning syndicate in accordance with the procedure agreed by the Chiefs of Staff, whereby, in any raid involving forces within the Home Forces Command, a small number of selected officers from within the Command should be associated with the preparation of the plans.

Shortly afterwards, C.-in-C. Home Forces delegated his authority in the matter of this raid to Lieut.-General Montgomery, then G.O.C.-in-C., South-Eastern Command and, when Canadian troops were chosen to carry out the raid, Lieut.-General Crerar, 1st Canadian Corps, was designated to concert Canadian arrangements with C.O.H.Q.

Two plans were produced, the first, involving a frontal attack on the town, was the one eventually adopted. The frontal attack was to be supported by two inner flank attacks at Puits and Pourville and two outer flank attacks against the coast defence guns at Berneval and Varengeville-sur-Mer. In the initial plan, the outer flank attacks were to be made by airborne troops but, due to the extra weather limitation imposed if these troops were used, they were subsequently replaced by Commandos.

In the initial discussions, it was agreed that the Naval C.-in-C. of the nearest Home Port would, as a matter of convenience, be appointed the Supreme Commander of the raid. He was not, however, to be responsible for the events between the time of landing and of re-embarking. It was also agreed that there should be Joint Command. On 9th May, the outline plan for the operation known as "Rutter" was submitted to the Chiefs of Staff Committee for their approval, which was given on 13th May.

At that stage, the Military Commander (Major-General Roberts) and the Air Commander (Air Vice-Marshal Leigh-Mallory) were both appointed, but the Naval Commander (Rear-Admiral Baillie-Grohman) who was then absent in the Middle East, was not appointed until 1st June.

---

[1] Landing Ship Infantry (Hand-Hoisting).

Almost immediately, with the example of St. Nazaire fresh in the minds of the planners, a ruling was sought from the Prime Minister on the subject of the blind bombing of targets in Occupied France. The Prime Minister stated that, although the existing rule should be maintained generally, an exception could be made in the case of a coastal raid. In the event, use was not made of this concession since it was considered by the Military Commander that the destruction of large numbers of houses by bombing would probably prevent tanks from operating in the streets of the town.

A detailed and rigorous training programme was then carried out and, when the troops were deemed sufficiently trained, a full-scale exercise, "Yukon I", was held. This exercise was not a success, many of the L.C.T.s were late, some of the landings took place at the wrong time and in broad daylight, the liaison between the Royal Engineers and the Infantry was defective and the Infantry progressed inland at a very slow rate.

C.C.O. therefore decided to hold a second exercise, since known as "Yukon II", on 23rd June and it was agreed to carry out the operation at the first favourable date after 24th June. While awaiting the order to proceed, the troops remained on the Isle of Wight or on board the assault ships which were sealed.

The weather became unsuitable during the last week in June and the first week in July, and on 5th July the operation was postponed. In the discussions which followed, C.C.O. directed the Force Commanders to consider a modified plan whereby the operations would take place on one tide, whereas the original plan had involved two tides. The main advantage of the modified plan was that air support could be increased because the duration of the operation would be reduced, but, on the other hand, the compression of the timetable would limit the scope of operations ashore. The plan commended itself to the Force Commanders and was adopted, but the continued unsuitability of the weather caused the cancellation of the operation on 7th July.

On cancellation, the forces dispersed. It was difficult to assess the effects on security of sending 6,000 men, all of whom had been briefed for the operation, from the Isle of Wight where they were isolated, to the mainland where the usual leave facilities were available. There is no doubt that rumours were rife for some time after the dispersal, but when the operation finally took place, there is very little doubt that tactical surprise was achieved.

The next most favourable period for the raid would occur during August. It was accordingly decided to re-mount the operation, the code name for which was changed from "Rutter" to "Jubilee" and to adopt, with certain modifications, the revised plan for one tide instead of two. It was at this stage that Commandos were substituted for airborne troops.

It is of interest here to recall the terms of the directive under which C.C.O. launched this Operation. C.C.O. was issued with a new directive by the Chiefs of Staff Committee on 27th July. It directed that the outline plan for a raid was to be prepared by C.C.O. who, after obtaining the comments of the C.s-in-C. concerned and of the Assistant Chief of Naval Staff (Home), would submit the plan with the comments to the Chiefs of Staff Committee. If approved, Force Commanders would be appointed and made responsible under C.C.O. for the detailed planning, the operation orders, the preparation and combined training of the forces detailed to take part and for the launching of the operation. After approving the detailed plan and the orders of the Force Commanders, C.C.O. was to be responsible for the launching of the raid in consultation with the authorities mentioned above and subject to the approval of the Naval C.-in-C.

After the postponement of the operation, it was found that the Naval Force Commander originally appointed was no longer available and was therefore succeeded by Captain J. Hughes-Hallett.

Finally, after various delays due to weather or unfavourable tides, the raid was launched on the night of 18th/19th August, 1942.

The Results of the Dieppe Raid

Operation "Jubilee" succeeded in testing the German defences at a point on the French coast within the area in which fighter cover could be provided by the Royal Air Force. It also succeeded in drawing the German Air Force into battle and causing the destruction of between one-quarter and one-third of that force in the West. The raid on Dieppe taught and re-emphasised many lessons which contributed to the success of later amphibious operations, particularly "Overlord". The cost was dear but the casualties at Dieppe have been justified many times over.

Lessons Learned at Dieppe

Since so much was learned from this raid, the lessons as summarised in the official report are listed here:

(1) The need for overwhelming fire support, including close support, during the initial stages of the attack.
(2) The necessity for the formation of permanent naval assault forces with a coherence comparable to that of any other first line fighting formations. Army formations intended for

amphibious assaults must without question be trained in close co-operation with such naval assault forces.

(3) The necessity for planning a combined operation at a Combined Headquarters where the Force Commanders and their staff can work and live together.

(4) The necessity to plan a raid so as to be independent of weather conditions in the greatest possible degree. A plan based on the assumption that weather conditions will be uniform is very likely to fail; a plan, which can be carried out even when conditions are indifferent or bad, is essential.

(5) The necessity for flexibility in the military plan and its execution. To achieve this, the assault must be on the widest possible front consistent with control and the amount of naval and air support available.

(6) The allocation to the assault of the minimum forces required to achieve success and the retention of the maximum force as a reserve to exploit success.

(7) The necessity for as accurate and comprehensive a system of control and communications as it is possible to establish.

(8) The dissemination of knowledge to officers and other ranks, each of whom should know the intention of his superior, the outline of the operation and the details of the task of his own unit and those on the flanks.

(9) The value of special training, particularly in amphibious night operations. Such training must include rehearsals and the testing of inter-communication arrangements.

(10) The necessity for fire support in any operation where it is not possible to rely on the element of surprise. This fire support must be provided by heavy and medium naval bombardment, by air action, by special vessels or craft working close inshore and by using the fire power of the assaulting troops while still seaborne. Special close-support craft, which should be gunboats or some form of mobile fort, do not exist and must be designed and constructed. Support by the Royal Air Force is effective within the limits imposed by time and space.

(11) Assaults must be carefully timed. Whether to assault in darkness, at dawn or dusk or in daylight, must depend on the nature of the raid and on certain conditions such as tide and distance which will vary in every case.

(12) Tanks should not be landed until the anti-tank defences have been destroyed or cleared. L.C.T.s carrying tanks must not linger on the beaches beyond the time required to disembark their loads.

(13) Great and continuous attention must be paid to security problems and greater use made of subordinate officers who

should be partly briefed so that they can control the men under them. Only important extracts from operation orders should be taken ashore. These should be kept in manuscript form and have their official headings removed.

(14) Briefing of the troops should take place as late as possible. If airborne troops are used, arrangements must be made to increase the number of terrain models available so as to cut down the time needed for briefing. Airborne troops provide means of achieving surprise and should be used as often as possible, subject to the limitations of the weather. It should be regarded, however, as exceptional for a plan to depend for success entirely on their use.

(15) Unless means for the provision of overwhelming close support are available, assaults should be planned to develop round the flanks of a strongly defended locality rather than frontally against it.

(16) A far higher standard of aircraft recognition is essential both in the Royal Navy and the Army. This should be achieved by means of lectures, photographs and silhouettes. If possible, personnel of the Royal Observer Corps should be carried in ships.

(17) Beach Signal Parties should not land complete with the first wave, but only when the beach has been secured.

(18) The importance and necessity of using smoke cannot be over-emphasised and larger quantities of smoke must be carried in any operations of the size of the assault on Dieppe.

(19) Some form of light or self-propelled artillery must be provided once an assault has passed beyond the beach and is advancing inland.

The above list, although long, is not necessarily complete. It was clear that tactical surprise was achieved although strategic surprise was almost an impossibility; in fact, the Germans had been holding anti-invasion exercises and were maintaining advanced states of readiness at suitable stages of the tides. This ability to obtain tactical surprise was demonstrated again and again in the Mediterranean and elsewhere and finally, and to the ultimate degree, in "Overlord". It is an astonishing fact that large concentrations of shipping and other forces can be gathered together without their existence being known to every enemy agent and that it is still possible to keep their final purpose secret. Yet this was done at Dieppe, although the security arrangements for this operation did not reach the high standard achieved on later occasions.

It is stated that unless overwhelming close support is available, assault should be planned to develop round the flanks of a strongly defended locality rather than frontally. This is perhaps an understatement of one of the most important results of the raid. In the planning stage there was considerable discussion as to the relative merits of frontal and flank assaults; the naval authorities held strongly that although the Navy could put forces ashore in a frontal attack, if necessary, their success ashore was doubtful. Since the frontal attack had been made and had failed, it became clear that alternative plans would have to be adopted in an invasion of the Continent. Certain interesting speculations therefore arise. Would such intensive efforts have been made to develop and finally used so successfully the "Mulberry" harbour, if penetration beyond Dieppe had been achieved? Would the Germans not have made better preparations to resist invasion, if they had not been given false confidence by their success in throwing back our forces from the beaches at Dieppe?

Be that as it may, Dieppe was a landmark in the history of combined operations which makes a fitting climax to the story of raiding. A raid on a considerable scale had been planned, mounted and executed against severe opposition. All three Services were deployed and co-operation between them was on a high level. Planning had been done by integrated staffs from the forces to be employed and the co-ordinating headquarters, where the existing specialised knowledge was available. Command was joint and worked well. In fact, although hard lessons were yet to be learned in the execution of major operations, the general pattern of the organisation required had been set.

Operation "Torch", North Africa

After Dieppe, the next landmark is Operation "Torch", executed in November, 1942. By this time, the entry of America into the war had increased the rate of build-up. Since this operation was by far the largest so far carried out, only some of the more interesting developments will be considered.

The operation, which had been planned and mounted from the U.K., presented entirely new problems through the widespread dispersal of mounting areas, but in spite of this, it was proved possible for the Combined Anglo-American Navies to get the whole force to the right place at the right time. Further, complete surprise was again achieved thus bearing out the evidence already obtained at Dieppe.

A good deal more was learned from "Torch". The Force Commanders were worried about the nature and gradients of the beaches on which it was proposed to land. To overcome this difficulty, a small party of naval personnel were ordered to make a preliminary reconnaissance by canoe carried in a submarine to the vicinity of the beaches. At the last moment this was cancelled and a periscope reconnaissance was substituted. Similar tasks had already been carried out during the preceding 18 months by personnel of the Special Boat Section; these were the fore-runners of the Combined Operations Pilotage Parties, whose value was proved in this operation and who were later employed in every theatre of war.

On the beaches, it was shown that some form of Army beach organisation was necessary in addition to the Naval Beach Parties, since some small ports were not captured as quickly as had been hoped; stores were landed on the beaches and then loaded into lorries by Pioneers.

In addition, various new ships were employed, including the American A.P.A.'s[2] and A.K.A.'s[3]. The Americans soon realised the need for closer inter-Service co-operation, when their Army and Naval headquarters were 100 miles apart with liaison practically non-existent. Finally, the lesson of Dakar that H.Q. Ships were necessary was repeated for the Americans, when General Patton and his headquarters aboard the cruiser *Augusta*, not only found the accommodation and communication facilities quite inadequate, but were also carried away on a purely naval operation during the attack on Fedala.

Operation "Husky", Sicily

After "Torch" came "Husky". As with "Torch", planning was done by the Force planning staffs, many of whom had already been a part of the Combined Operations Organisation (Major-General Truscott, the Commander of "Joss" Force, was the head of the first detachment of American Officers to become a part of the integrated C.O.H.Q.). The operation was witnessed by C.C.O. who, immediately on his return to the U.K., submitted to the Chiefs of Staff a report stating the principal lessons learnt in the operation.

Many lessons were learned. One of the most interesting was the fact that the unexpected and adverse weather conditions, which were encountered on passage and during the assault itself, contributed to the almost complete surprise obtained, since the enemy did not believe that an assault would be attempted under such conditions.

In this operation the new American L.S.T. (2) were used for the first time in comparatively large numbers.

---

[2]   Assault ships carrying personnel mainly.
[3]   Assault ships carrying cargo mainly.

The naval bombardment proved its worth very strongly and the support craft, particularly the L.C.T. (R) which had been converted for the operation, were outstandingly successful.

Towards "Overlord", North-West Europe

After Sicily there came the assaults at Salerno and then Anzio in the Mediterranean; parallel with these were the many island-hopping operations carried out by the Americans in the Far East. These operations, important and bitterly fought as they were, taught few lessons which were applicable to assaults against larger land masses, although more specialised development occurred such as the replacement of short-range L.C.T. by its ocean-going equivalent, the L.S.M.

But these operations apart, the overall progress of the war had already begun to set the stage for "Overlord".

During discussions between C.C.O. and Lieut.-General Morgan (C.O.S.S.A.C.) on the preparations for "Overlord", it became apparent that guidance was needed on the training required, the provision of equipment and on planning. Consequently, a conference ("Rattle") was convened by C.C.O. in June, 1943, to study the various combined operations problems of "Overlord". This conference was attended by the Commanders-in-Chief Portsmouth, Home Forces and Fighter Command, C.O.S.S.A.C., Commanding General E.T.O.U.S.A., General MacNaughton of the Canadian Army, and representatives of the three Service Ministries and C.O.H.Q. As a result of this conference C.C.O. drew the Chiefs of Staff's attention to the various points which had emerged and on which immediate and authoritative decisions were required.

These included the problems of fire support in the assault, the necessity for a daylight assault owing to the vast number of mixed groups of craft involved, the need for one central co-ordinating authority for the development of artificial harbours ("Mulberry"), the need for the provision in adequate numbers of amphibians and many other problems.

Assistance with planning and training continued into 1944, but apart from this, the work of C.O.H.Q. in connection with European operations was largely finished. It is therefore appropriate to record, at this stage, that the greatest amphibious operation of all time was launched only by the mighty effort of two great nations and that almost every aspect of the nations' resources was involved at some stage or another. The preparatory part played by C.O.H.Q., however, was vital; evidence of its work was to be found in the design of ships, in the technique employed by the supporting ships and craft and in the training of officers and men.

Operations Against the Japanese

Before "Overlord", preparations had already begun for the intensification of the war against Japan, and it was possible to concentrate the activities of C.O.H.Q. with this aim in view. Two main tasks were undertaken. By agreement with the U.S. Chiefs of Staff, a team of observers proceeded, in the middle of 1944, to the Pacific where they witnessed and reported upon all major operations undertaken from then until the conclusion of the Japanese war. The second main task was an examination of the availability of suitable ships and craft for operations in the Far East and as a result, recommendations were made to the U.S.A., which in turn resulted in the peak rate of L.S.T. production being maintained.

Redeployment of forces in the Far East, however, proved difficult and slow, and although the American advances gathered momentum, only a minor British operation at Rangoon occurred in which no opposition was encountered. Had the war continued, the prepared plans and the vast amount of experience gained would have been put into practise as men and material arrived.

Conclusion

The story of Combined Operations is long and detailed, and it has only been possible to refer in this chapter to some of the landmarks in that story. There is no doubt of the value of the work of the Combined Operations Organisation, but where it begins and where it ends is hard to define. Much was gained from the system whereby planners, trained in amphibious warfare, were integrated into planning staffs, or attached as advisers or observers. Nevertheless, the recording of its shortcomings as well as its successes may contribute to that most desirable end, that the hard-won lessons do not again have to be bought unnecessarily dear.

Chapter 12

TRAINING AND TRAINING ESTABLISHMENTS

After the evacuation of the Continent in May, 1940, our main concern became the defence of the British Isles, but it was realised that the only means of offence for some time to come, except by air action, would be amphibious raids. At the same time, the foundations for an eventual return to the Continent, in force, would be laid.

The Institution of Training Establishments in the United Kingdom
The problem of training personnel for these operations had two main aspects: the training of troops; and the training of ships' and craft crews.

The troops for these raids were provided initially by the Special Service Battalions and later by Royal Marine and Army Commando units.

Ships and craft crews were at first civilians, as was the case in the Boulogne raid (Operation "Collar"), which was not successful. It was soon realised that naval personnel would have to be trained specially for the operation and maintenance of landing craft. The first training establishment was inaugurated in July, 1940, at Warsash as H.M.S. *Tormentor*, which was already being used as a base for raiding operations. At first this establishment was used for basic naval training. Advanced training with the Special Service troops was given at Archaracle (H.M.S. *Dorlin*).

At about the same time, similar training was started at H.M.S. *Northney*, a new base in Hayling Island, and a few months later, other establishments were set up at Brightlingsea and Dartmouth. These establishments, in addition to their training role, were organised as raiding bases, and Special Service troops were located near them.

There was also the Inter-Services Training and Development Centres (I.S.T.D.C.) at Eastney Barracks, Portsmouth whose primary function was the development of material, although the attendant developments in doctrine and training were, at first, also its concern. When the C.T.C. was fully operating, however, the I.S.T.D.C. dropped its training role and became the Combined Operations Development Centre (C.O.D.C.) in August, 1941 under the D.C.O.

The First Combined Training Centre, Inverary

In July, 1940, after wide reconnaissance, Inverary was selected to be the first Combined Training Centre (C.T.C.) where the landing craft flotillas could complete their training, and where it was intended to carry out Army training in amphibious warfare on a large scale.

On 1st September, 1940, Vice-Admiral T.J. Hallet assumed command of the C.T.C. as Vice-Admiral Combined Training Centre (V.A.C.T.C.) and, on 15th October, the naval wing was commissioned as H.M.S. *Quebec*.

At this time, the available ships and craft on which training largely depended, had to be divided between the various establishments mentioned above and operational requirements, to implement the policy of raiding the continental coastline. However, after the two abortive raids during the summer of 1940 and the failure of Dakar, the operational demands for the rest of the year were much reduced and full concentration could be given to building up the training establishments in personnel, both naval and military, and material.

It was at the beginning of 1941 that the first great difficulty arose in the growth of these training establishments and of the amphibious striking forces they trained. Most of the trouble was due to the lack of a central authority responsible for the various facets of the Combined Operations Command. Firstly, there was the question of administering the training establishments, opening new ones, obtaining personnel and staff and generally assembling all the necessary facilities to enable military and naval forces to train. Secondly, there was the implementation of the Chiefs of Staff raiding policy: to make the enemy disperse his forces uneconomically. There was also divergence of opinion on how the small striking force of some 5,000 trained troops should be used. The D.C.O., Admiral Sir Roger Keyes, advocated using them offensively to the greatest possible confusion of the enemy at the most vulnerable points. He used all his influence to try to gain this object, but he found these views in direct conflict with those of the Chiefs of Staff, whose policy was to use the available effort, firstly, to build up an amphibious striking force in the Mediterranean and,

TRAINING AND TRAINING ESTABLISHMENTS

secondly, as a nucleus on which to build the enormous organisation that would eventually be needed for a return to the Continent.

The C.T.C. at Inverary was gradually developed and in February, 1941, it was possible to stage the first large scale exercise involving a Guards Brigade Group.

Combined Training in the Middle East

In July, 1940, Field Marshal (then General) Wavell asked for staff to set up a combined operations training centre in the Middle East. As a result, Colonel MacLeod, who was Commandant of the I.S.T.D.C. at Portsmouth, was sent out in November and on the 15th January, 1941, the C.T.C. opened at Kabrit. Almost at once, after the first course had been completed, the C.T.C. was given the task of training the 6th Division for an attack on Rhodes (Operation "Cordite"). This Division was at first short of one Brigade and Nos 7, 8, and 11 Commandos were sent out to Kabrit from the U.K. in the three L.S.I. *Glengyle, Glenroy* and *Glenearn*. These, together with some twenty T.L.C.s, arrived in March, 1941, and training started in earnest.

Operation "Cordite" never took place, however, because Rommel, at the end of April, launched his highly successful attack in the Western Desert and the 6th Division had to be sent hurriedly into the desert to help stop the advance.

A section of the Special Boat Section was formed and trained at Kabrit during the spring of 1941, also a detachment of the Special Air Service Brigade. The tasks of the former were at first confined to landing in Folbots from submarines for beach reconnaissance and marking, and for carrying out acts of sabotage. The latter operated by means of parachutes for much the same purposes.

In April and May, 1941, the ships and craft belonging to the C.T.C. Kabrit played an important part in the evacuation of Greece and later Crete, many of them being damaged or lost.

About mid-summer the New Zealand Division was partially trained in combined operations at the C.T.C. and between then and the end of the year, the training of various engineer units, armoured units and one Brigade of the 4th Indian Division was undertaken. Courses were concurrently run for British and Allied Officers.

October, 1942, was a period of intense activity at the C.T.C as it had been decided to seize Sicily with troops from the U.K. and the Middle East. The operation was, however, later cancelled, this probably being a wise decision as the shortage of ships and craft would have made it a hazardous undertaking.

In February, 1943, C.O.H.Q. sent out by air a number of officers to the Middle East for the following purposes: (1) As a preliminary to doubling the strength of the existing C.T.C. so as to increase the tempo of training; [and] (2) To start a second C.T.C. and to form two dryshod training teams, each capable of carrying out preliminary training in Syria, Iraq and Palestine, or inland in Egypt so that brigades arrived partially trained at Kabrit and were able to devote all their time to wetshod training.

The balance of the staff available was used to train and assist in forming the Beach Groups before they came to Kabrit.

Prior to the invasion of Sicily ("Husky"), large scale exercises took place under the general direction of D.C.O. (M.E.) whilst dryshod teams were in Algeria, Damascus and Gaza. Beach Bricks were also formed and trained mainly in the light of experience gained in the Madagascar landings.

Owing to the success and speed of operations in Sicily, it became necessary to organise local training for the formations earmarked for the invasion of Italy. These were located near Tripoli and Homs. A C.T.C. was therefore set up at Tripoli (staffed by personnel withdrawn from C.T.C. Kabrit) on an *ad hoc* mobile and functional basis, and dispersed along the coast at suitable points. The system was a complete success and two Divisions and Corps troops were trained in their designated operational role in under five weeks.

In the latter part of 1943, plans were prepared for operations in the Dodecanese which required dryshod training areas at Suez and wetshod training at Kabrit.

In the spring of 1944, the training for immediate operations lapsed but the policy was accepted that combined operations training should be a normal commitment for all formations in the Middle East, a policy which kept the C.T.C. fully employed.

Training of a Striking Force in the United Kingdom
Whilst the C.T.C. in the Middle East was being established, an amphibious striking force was being built up in the U.K. and on 10th August, 1941, it was possible to stage the first full-scale combined exercise. This exercise, named "Leapfrog", was intended as a rehearsal for the projected attack on the Canary Islands. Many lessons were learned from it, chief among which was the vital need for a central authority to co-ordinate the training of amphibious forces. The responsibility for mounting this exercise was split between the Admiralty, for the assault and support ships and craft; the War Office, for a large part of

the troops taking part and administrative arrangements ashore; and the D.C.O. who, apart from his advisory capacity, was responsible for the C.T.C. at Inveraray.

In addition to this division of responsibility, the D.C.O.'s concentration on the training of his available forces for immediate operations conflicted with the long-term necessity for building up the Combined Operations Organisation for the ultimate invasion of the Continent.

System of Control of the Training of Amphibious Forces

Up to September, 1941, the training of troops and landing ships and craft crews for combined operations was the responsibility of the D.C.O., until such time as the units were handed over to the Force Commanders for a particular operation, when the intention was that the D.C.O.'s contribution should become mainly advisory. Force Commanders would necessarily be free to work up their force and be responsible that the final training, including rehearsals, was adequate for the specific operation in hand.

The difficulty arose because the D.C.O.'s desire for immediate offensive action conflicted with the Chiefs of Staff's policy, the former deeming that he should use his appointment in an executive capacity even after his forces had been allotted to Force Commanders.

When Admiral Mountbatten was appointed, his new directive made it clear that his executive powers only related to the training of combined operations forces and the mounting of small raids. Apart from these he was confined to giving technical advice for the conduct of combined operations.

Expansion of Training Facilities

From 1941 onwards, the Combined Operations Command expanded rapidly. Material was beginning to arrive in increasing quantity from America and our own building programme was bearing fruit. New training establishments were opened to train the crews for the new ships and craft, and for training the troops earmarked for amphibious operations. By the spring of 1942, the following training establishments were in existence in the U.K.:

1. Headquarters Combined Training — Largs
2. Combined Training Centre — Inveraray
3. Combined Training Centre — Auchengate, Troon
4. Combined Signal School — Auchengate, Troon
5. Combined Training Centre for R.A.C. — Castle Toward

6. Initial Training Centre for Naval Personnel and combined operations for South-East Command — Hayling Island
7. Raiding Craft Training Centre and combined operations training for Southern Command — Warsash
8. Parent Ship of Raiding Craft and combined operations training for Eastern Command — Brightlingsea
9. T.L.C. Training Base — Bo'ness
10. Special Training Establishment — Acharacle

Apart from these, with establishment of the Headquarters of the Expeditionary Force (H.Q.E.F.) at Largs, which was suggested by C.C.O. at the end of 1941, a C.T.C. had been set up in the Hollywood Hotel with a small training staff on an inter-Services basis. Courses for selected officers of all three Services were instituted at this C.T.C.

The training staff came under the Director of Combined Training, who, before he moved to C.O.H.Q. in London, had directed the training activities of the Combined Operations Command from Largs. Thus, in April, 1943, it was the custom to run courses which enunciated the principles of combined operations and, in consequence, the C.T.C. at Largs was looked upon from the Combined Operations point of view as a Staff College.

The close association of H.Q.E.F. and the staff of the Senior Officer Assault ships and Craft, which were in the same building, did much to foster co-operation and understanding. Inter-Services problems could be discussed and exercises arranged to try out new methods with the minimum expenditure of time and a conspicuous absence of paperwork and misunderstanding.

The close proximity of C.T.C.s at Inveraray and Castle Toward and the Combined Signal School at Auchengate, Troon, ensured that all establishments were in constant touch with H.Q.E.F. and thus the latter always knew what was taking place and what developments were contemplated. In fact, this grouping proved extremely effective.

The training of naval officers for combined operations was giving cause for anxiety. The facilities available at the R.N.V.R. Training Establishment at Hove (H.M.S. *King Alfred*) were not sufficient to compete with the numbers required. After much debate, it was finally decided that the Combined Operations Organisation should train their own officers.

Luckily at about this time, the Army Battle School at Lochailort, near Mallaig, became vacant. This was duly taken over and from August, 1942, until the end of the war, the naval officers required for combined operations were trained there. It is interesting to note that the officers' course lasted six weeks. Those who were successful were commissioned from raw officer candidates and probably found themselves, on their first appointment, as First Lieutenants of L.C.T.s with the probability of commanding one of these craft after about six months' such experience.

The large number of Service authorities, units, establishments and ships of, or associated with, the Combined Operations Command at about this time, is illustrated in the contents of the Combined Operations Directory of March, 1943. This lists no less than 45 establishments in the U.K., the majority of which were engaged in training, and the following eleven overseas:

North Africa	Algiers, Bougie, Djidjelli
W. Africa	Freetown
Middle East	Kabrit
India	Bombay, South India
Australia	Melbourne, Newcastle
Canada	Comax
U.S.A.	Washington

Training in Cliff Assaults

In the first annual report of the I.S.T.D.C., it was recommended that unlikely places should be chosen for landing raiding parties in preference to likely beaches. An enemy would consider a coast with cliffs an unsuitable place for a landing.

The need for special cliff-climbing equipment was stressed, including a light type of ladder, and early in 1940, it was recommended that trials should take place.

The cliff assault technique was thus introduced and training was later carried out at the Mountain Warfare Training Centre, where a large number of troops were trained.

This technique figured in several operations, an example being the raid on Dieppe where Commandos, attacking a coast defence battery, scaled the cliffs to reach their objective. An extract from an enemy document captured at a later date, records that the troops:

"Showed great skill in climbing the steep coastal cliffs. They were able to climb the cliffs at various points where small wooded rugged ravines lead down to the sea. This is terrain where observation is difficult and progress is possible only for trained climbers."

Training Organisation

With the expansion of the training organisation, the duties of the Vice-Admiral Combined Training Centre increased and in April, 1942, he became Vice-Admiral, Combined Training with his headquarters in the same building as H.Q.E.F. at Largs. In July, 1942, when he assumed the title of Director of Combined Training (D.C.T.) with the responsibility of all combined training, he moved to Montague House which was adjacent to C.O.H.Q. Here he set up a separate office with the Major-General, Combined Training and the Combined Training Staff.

Naval Training Establishments

As previously stated, the Combined Operations Base at Rosneath was transferred to the American authorities at the end of August, 1942, so that they could use it as a mounting base for Operation "Torch". This had a disastrous effect on the whole combined operations programme of expansion and training. The training activities, which were carried out at Rosneath, were transferred to Inveraray where encroachment facilities were granted in certain of the Army camps. This was a temporary measure and saw C.O.H.Q. through the difficult period of mounting "Torch".

In December, however, the American authorities gave back Rosneath and it was re-commissioned. But, this time, it was decided not to put down permanent roots there, but to use it as a British base for mounting the operations which were known to be impending in the Mediterranean. However, it was quite evident that the Combined Operations Organisation could not carry out naval training satisfactorily under the conditions existing at Inveraray. The D.C.T. stated that he could not accept the naval training being done in a Combined Training Establishment. Further, he insisted that the Navy must be trained in its own art before it met the Army for combined training.

About this time, the Admiralty decided to transfer the cadets from the Royal Naval College at Dartmouth to Eaton Hall, and the Combined Operations Naval Training to Dartmouth. In order to compete with the increased intake, a holiday camp at Brightlingsea was requisitioned. The former of these establishments was commissioned as H.M.S. *Effingham* and the latter as H.M.S. *Helder*.

Expansion was taking place elsewhere during the summer of 1942. The naval wings of the C.T.C. at Auchengate and the Combined Signal School, which had been transferred to Auchengate from Inverary, were commissioned as H.M.S. *Dundonald I* and H.M.S. *Dundonald II* respectively, on 1st April, 1942. H.M.S. *Dundonald I*, although situated on W.D. property, had no combined training commitments but, having a naval staff, was responsible purely for the initial training of ratings for major landing craft. On the other hand, H.M.S. *Dundonald II*, as the naval wing of the Combined Signal School, carried out the combined training duties of the naval wing of the C.T.C. *Dundonald I.*

The Naval Training Wing for the L.C.T. training of Royal Armoured Corps personnel was established at Castle Toward, C.T.C. in November, 1941. This naval wing was commissioned as H.M.S. *Ararat* on 1st June, 1942, and subsequently changed its name to H.M.S. *Brontosaurus* on 7th August of that year.

Training for Operation "Torch"

The assault on North Africa was mounted from the U.K. and carried out by the British First Army and the American II Corps.

At a meeting held at C.O.H.Q. on 14th August, the minutes record: "It was noted that no British Military Formations required Combined Operational Training other than rehearsals but that two Regimental Combat Teams (corresponding to Brigade Groups) of the 34th United States Division had to be trained."

As the planning progressed, it was found necessary to arrange for the training of three more Regimental Combat Teams making a total of five; this was carried out under emergency arrangement at the Combined Operations Centres on the west coast of Scotland.

In addition, the American "Shore Parties" were trained with the Beach Commandos under the Combined Operational Staff.

All this training took place in abnormal weather. In his report the Major-General, Combined Training stated:

"It is generally agreed that not for a generation has so wet a summer and autumn been experienced on the west coast of Scotland."

From the weather records at Inveraray, it appears that the rainfall averaged one inch per day during the whole period.

On the naval side, the partly-trained landing craft crews had also to complete their training and the new entries had to be given a full course. To do this the training staff had to work at full pressure. That their training was a success was well demonstrated *en route* to North Africa, when one of the American assault ships was torpedoed 150 miles from her objective. Then and there the troops were embarked in their landing craft and set off in them. They were 24 hours late at the landing place.

On the other hand, in his covering remarks on the lessons learned in Operation "Torch", Admiral Sir Andrew Cunningham, the Naval Commander-in-Chief, states:

"No officer commanding a unit will ever be satisfied that he has adequate preparation and training until his unit is trained and equipped down to the last gaiter button. There are times in history when we cannot wait for the final polish.

I suggest it should be made widely known to all units that, for, 'Torch' particularly, we could not afford to wait and that the risk of embarking on these large scale operations with inadequate training was deliberately accepted in order to strike while the time was ripe. We must now push forward our training so that such a situation cannot arise again."

Special Training

In addition to the training of the fighting formations, special training was undertaken in the following:

Fire Fighting
Some 75 officers and 680 men of the Royal and Merchant Navies received instruction, before the expedition sailed, from the Combined Operations Fire Fighting School at Rosneath. Also, officers from the School visited the Red Ensign ships and instructed their officers and men in their duties.

Damage control, Unexploded Bombs, Aircraft Recognition
Training in all these subjects was organised by C.O.H.Q. and carried out as far as time and opportunity permitted.

Communications
Much of the complex signal plan was prepared by the Combined Operations Command. The advice and resources of the Combined Operations Organisation which had gained considerable operational experience in Madagascar, Dieppe and many minor operations and exercises, were placed at the disposal of the Allied Command.

Altogether some 100 officers, and, 1,000 other ranks of all Services who took part in the operations had special signals training in the Combined Operations Command. The staff at the Combined Signal School (*Dundonald II*) was fully extended in providing, training and sorting personnel. The following were provided, trained and operationally ready:

  6 Naval Beach Sections.
  12 F.O.O. Parties.
  75 per cent of the Landing Craft Signalmen required for craft.
  2 R.A.F. Force H.Q. Sections.
  2 R.A.F. Advanced Landing Ground Sections.
  R.A.F. Light Warning Set Sections.

Effect of Operation "Torch" on Training
It was possible to mount the operation only by: (1) Stopping all combined training after 15th August, 1942; (2) Taking crews of landing

ships and craft that were not fully trained; [and] (3) Taking a large proportion of personnel from the bases and training centres and even C.O.H.Q., using the numbers so gained to supplement the men available for the force.

This meant that the long-term plan for the expansion of the Combined Operations Command to enable the large scale assault on the Continent to be made was considerably delayed.

After the sailing of the convoys for "Torch" the main problem facing C.O.H.Q. was to train the raiding force, Force "J", complete with craft and crews, and weld it into a proper naval assault force. In addition, the training programme would have to be stepped up to compete with the greatly increased intake and the craft used for this training had to be prepared and modernised.

The months of November and December saw this all going ahead reasonably smoothly.

In December, 1942, the programme of training and refitting after "Torch" was further delayed by the serious storm which damaged so many landing craft and facilities at Inverary.

Strategy for 1943, Training for Operation "Husky"

At the Casablanca Conference it was decided to proceed with the assault on Sicily. The training of the forces to be employed had, of necessity, to be carried out locally and C.O.H.Q. training staff were asked to assist.

But in addition to the forces in the Mediterranean, it was decided to send a Canadian Division from England and the American 45th Division direct from U.S.A. The training of the Canadian Division was carried out in C.T.C.s in Scotland under C.C.O. To assist in the training of U.S.A. contingent, certain officers from C.O.H.Q. were sent to join the staff of the Combined Operations Liaison Officer in Washington for loan to the 45th Division.

At Chiefs of Staff meetings, C.C.O. reported on the effect that the loan of both planning and training staffs was having on the work at C.O.H.Q. at this time.

As a result of a change in the plan for "Husky" involving the employment of an additional Division in the assault, the drain on the available ships and craft in the U.K. was increased. This resulted in a setback in the training of Force "J", which it had been hoped would be fully operational by early 1943. The reason for this was that the only available ships and craft which could be sent were those in Force "J". This at once raised the question of the L.S.I. (S) (ex-Belgian cross Channel steamers) making an ocean passage. Their endurance was limited and consequently they had to be fitted for oiling at sea. They therefore had to proceed to shipyards for the necessary modifications. Thus, for all intents and purposes, Force "J" ceased to exist as from the beginning of May. The Senior Officer and his staff were, however, kept in being and instructed to plan raids with whatever craft were left.

Combined Training for Operation "Overlord"

Once the plan for the invasion of Normandy was settled, the question of the training of the naval and military personnel was a subject which necessitated organisation and thought on a national scale. C.O.H.Q. contributed advice, training publications and facilities, and the United States Forces involved also adopted the C.O.H.Q. technique.

India, 1942-1945

In January, 1942, soon after the start of the Japanese war, a C.T.C. was set up at Kharakvasla near Poona, and, at the same, a small Inter-Services Committee, to be known as Advisers, Combined Operations, was established in New Delhi with the approval of the Chiefs of Staff. The object of this committee was to advise all Services and Force Commanders on planning and training of combined operations and to maintain liaison with Combined Operations authorities in the U.K., the Middle East and elsewhere.

A further C.T.C. opened at Madh Island, near Bombay, in December, 1942, where a Combined Operations Force Headquarters was also established.

Early in 1943, that part of the Indian Expeditionary Force concerned with combined operations moved to Bombay where five Indian Beach Groups were trained at the C.T.C.

Later in 1943, with the formation of S.E.A.C. and the crystallisation of the policy for the conduct of war against Japan, it became apparent that the overall theatre strategy would include more and more amphibious assaults against the enemy's lines of communications. The scope of Director of Combined Operations (India) (D.C.O. (I)), as the Inter-Services Committee had been re-designated, was extended to allow for the training of a large number of formations and, in December, 1943, the following additional training establishments were agreed by C.-in-C., India:

> A Mobile Combined Training Staff School.
> Two Dryshod Training Teams.

An additional C.T.C. at Cocanada. An independent Combined Operations Development Centre under direct control of D.C.O. (I).
A Combined Signal School.
A Combined Operations Bombardment Unit, as well as a number of co-ordinating teams and groups.

At the same time, the complementary naval training organisation was extended and came under command of a Rear-Admiral, designated Senior Officer, Royal Naval Establishments (India) (SORNE (I.)), at Bombay.

The main factors which influenced combined operational training policy in India at this time were as follows:

Weather
Wetshod training could not be undertaken on the west coast during the south-west monsoons and similarly on the east coast during the north-east monsoons. Since the commitment of D.C.O. (I) made continuous training essential, C.T.C.s at both Madh Island and Cocanada were authorised.

Distances and Communications
Divisions coming from the U.K. at the conclusion of the German war would require both combined operations and jungle training. Unless Jungle Training Centres could be located nearer to C.T.C.s much time would be lost during transit periods with the result that the overall training target might not be reached.

Provision of Craft for Training
C.O.H.Q.'s appreciation of the availability of training craft showed that the prospects of a greatly increased allotment to India was unlikely until the end of 1944.

Early in 1944, 33 Indian Corps was rushed to Imphal and Kohima, and later manpower shortages resulted in the reduction of training establishments. In the autumn, training teams were sent to Burma to assist in the preparation of the amphibious assault on Rangoon from the sea and the recapture of Malaya. The latter operation also involved the training of General Transport Companies, R.A.S.C. and an Amphibious Support Regiment R.M. in the use of L.V.T.s. On the cessation of hostilities, all commitments for combined operations training and experiment ceased and by the end of 1945, only the new Combined Operations Establishment with a link to New Delhi remained.

East Africa, 1943-46

In December, 1943, the question arose of reconnoitring Combined Training Areas for the use of troops destined for S.E.A.C. The Chief of Staff tabled a memorandum to the Chiefs of Staff suggesting the despatch of a team from the Service Ministries and C.O.H.Q. to reconnoitre suitable areas for jungle and combined training. The Chiefs of Staff decided at their meeting on 1st December, 1943, to defer the despatch of this inter-Services team until a decision on the strategy of S.E.A.C. had been made. Eventually, this paper was overtaken by events and, in fact, no reconnaissance was ever made.

Subsequently, the subject was reopened in 1946 at the time of the Anglo-Egyptian negotiations, when the Joint Planning Staff were instructed by the Chiefs of Staff to examine the practicability of stationing in East Africa the whole or part of our Strategic Reserve. The Joint Planning Staff were of the opinion that the area as a whole offered excellent training facilities. The coastal belt, however, had the characteristics of being hot and malarial; airborne and combined operations training had of necessity to be carried out on the coast owing to the altitude of the interior.

C.O.H.Q. was represented by two officers, Colonel Hobbs and Lieutenant-Commander Adams, on the Inter-Services Committee, 501 Mission, which carried out this reconnaissance. The "Report on Combined Operations Training Areas in East Africa" recommended the selection of Kilifi as a Combined Training Establishment in the event of the development of East Africa as a base.

Post-War Training

In May, 1945, C.O.H.Q. recommended to the three Service Ministries that a post-war Combined Training Centre should be formed in the U.K. This subsequently led to the establishment of the School of Combined Operations at Fremington.

Chapter 13

THE LANDING CRAFT AND BASES ORGANISATION

In 1940 the activities of the Combined Operations forces were confined to a few small raids on the enemy coastline. As the available craft were so few, the existing facilities available at naval and civilian shipyards for maintenance and repairs were sufficient.

Administration of Ships and Craft, 1940
At first, the fitting out and manning of ships and craft was done in a somewhat haphazard way, using the Admiralty organisation supplemented by the various training establishments such as Inveraray, where on 12th September, 1940, a Senior Naval Officer Landings (S.N.O.L.) and Senior Naval Officer Transports were established to administer the ships and craft assembled in the Clyde for the projected operations against the Atlantic Islands. This establishment was commissioned as H.M.S. *Quebec*.

The organisation did not work satisfactorily at first because there were so few ships and craft that there was conflict between the short term requirement in the form of the forces allotted to Force Commanders and administered by the S.N.O.L., and the long-term necessity for the building up of Combined Operations forces, for which the Vice-Admiral Combined Training Centre under the D.C.O. was responsible.

Personnel Organisation, 1941
The year 1941 saw a big increase in the number of personnel being absorbed into Combined Operations and a need was felt for a separate

Personnel Organisation. The Personnel Records Office for Combined Operations personnel was therefore established in H.M.S. *Quebec* on 8th May, 1941. At the same time the Pay Section was also established in H.M.S. *Quebec* where all accounts and records for major and minor landing craft personnel were held. This arrangement existed until the transfer of Captain, Landing Craft Tank (Captain L.C.T.) to Troon on 3rd March, 1942, when he took with him, from *Quebec*, the Personnel Records and Pay Accounts of all officers and ratings of major landing craft. The Personnel Records and Accounts of officers and ratings of minor landing craft and of units such as Royal Naval Beach Parties remined in H.M.S. *Quebec*. Captain L.C.T. (afterwards Captain, Major Landing Craft) commissioned H.M.S. *Dinosaur* at Troon on 1st April, 1942, as his Administrative Headquarters.

Throughout 1941 the commitments of H.M.S. *Quebec* increased and, between October and the end of the year, the Combined Signal School and Navigational Aids Unit were established there. In November the drafting pool of ratings was transferred to H.M.S. *Quebec* from H.M.S. *Northney*.

At the end of 1941, the functions of Commodore, *Quebec II* were absorbed by the new appointment of Senior Officer Assault Ships and Craft (S.O.A.S.C.) who established his headquarters at Largs to which H.M.S. *Quebec II* was transferred. Most of the ships in S.O.A.S.C.'s command moved to Greenock and, although the staff offices were at Largs, the Accountant Officer opened his offices and stores at Campbell Street, Greenock. This, in view of subsequent developments, turned out to be a far-sighted move.

Rear-Admiral Landing Craft and Bases Appointed

As the building programme got under way in 1941, and the ships and craft ordered from America began to arrive, it became clear that there was to be a very rapid expansion in the number of crews required to man them. Consequently, on 3rd December, Commodore Mountbatten submitted the following proposals for an effective organisation to control them:

> The Admiralty wish me to take over the command and administration of all landing craft and crews, which will amount to 500-700 L.C.T.s (250 tons each) and 2,000 smaller craft, involving 2,000 officers and 20,000 men joining my command within the next 16 months. They also wish me to organise and administer suitable bases. For this purpose, a small administrative staff will have to be created, which may subsequently require expansion. It is proposed that this should be under a Rear-Admiral Landing Craft and Bases

(R.A.L.B.) and I should like to propose Rear-Admiral H.E. Horan for this appointment. Assault shipping and their associated landing craft would be under a Commodore in company with them to be known as Senior Officer Assault Ships and Craft (S.O.A.S.C.). For this appointment I propose Commodore G.L. Warren.

This proposal was approved by the Chiefs of Staff on 9th December.

The Landing Craft and Bases Organisation, 1941

During December, 1941, the transfer of ships and bases to C.C.O. took place. This meant that under the R.A.L.B. a naval administrative staff came into being whose duty it was to carry out the day-to-day naval administration of the Combined Operations Command. It was divided into Personnel, Material, and Ships and Craft Sections.

For the first three months, the most important role played by the Administration was that of providing the necessary base and accommodation facilities for the personnel of the command.

By the beginning of 1942, however, the best sites for both bases and accommodation facilities had been filled by other Services and Ministries and there was very little left from which to choose.

Administration of Bases

All the Northern Combined Operations bases (except those occupied by the S.O.A.S.C.) were administered under R.A.L.B. by the Senior Officer Combined Operations Northern Bases (S.N.O.C.O. (N.)), who was the Commodore, H.M.S. *Louisburg* at Rosneath.

S.N.O.C.O. (N.) dealt with the Admiralty on matters of routine administration, or with the local naval authorities in matters of their concern, but in all questions of policy and in those affairs directly affecting the Combined Operations Organisation, he dealt direct with R.A.L.B.

Administration of Ships and Craft

Ships allocated for combined operational purposes in the British Isles, together with their associated landing and raiding craft, were organised into groups by the Admiralty. All home-based ships and their attached craft in the Combined Operations Command were under the command of the S.O.A.S.C., who received his orders from C.C.O. Ships or craft required for an operation were, however, placed under the orders of Force Commanders. The administration of these ships was carried out through the normal channels, until they reverted to S.O.A.S.C. after the operation.

The Development of Bases, 1942

Early in 1942, it was known that the personnel of Combined Operations would be increased to the target figures required for the invasion planned for the Spring of 1943. With these increased numbers in view, the R.A.L.B. wrote to the Combined Operations Section of the Admiralty stating that it was becoming a matter of urgency to establish a base in the Clyde area as a Combined Operations Depot. He suggested establishing such a depot at Rosneath by 1st May, 1942. It appeared from earlier enquiries that Rosneath, which was being given up by the American authorities, would be suitable for these purposes. As a result of a meeting held on 3rd March, the base at Rosneath was commissioned as H.M.S. *Louisburg* on 15th April, 1942.

Other developments were also afoot at this time and on 23rd January, 1942, a few days before R.A.L.B. raised the question of a depot in the Clyde area, S.O.A.S.C. recommended to the Admiralty the opening of a Landing Craft Maintenance Base at Port Glasgow. Maintenance work had up to that date been carried out by personnel embarked in S.S. *Machada*. This recommendation was followed by a visit from R.A.L.B. after it was decided to requisition and open a base of this description. On the same day, 14th April, 1942, that the completion of the requisition was reported by the Chief Surveyor of Lands, the base was started up by the party landed from S.S. *Machada*. At this time there was no accommodation available for officers or ratings in the area and all personnel had to be billeted in the vicinity. This situation lasted for some time and was most unsatisfactory.

Expansion of Bases

The base at Rosneath soon began to prove its usefulness. Here was a reasonably equipped hutted camp with a deep-water quay, adjoining which were workshops with machine tools installed. It formed the holding camp for the naval ratings who had completed their training at the small schools in the south of England. Training areas were good, and it was well situated for mounting any overseas operations which sailed from the Clyde. The rapidly increasing size of the Command on the west coast of Scotland made it necessary to appoint a Senior Officer to have general charge of the bases in this area. Accordingly, the Commodore, Rosneath (Commodore I.M. Palmer) was appointed Senior Naval Officer Combined Operations (S.N.O.C.O. (N.)) and assumed that office on 28th June, 1942.

Acting on the advice of C.C.O., the Admiralty had increased the intake of naval personnel embarked for duty with the landing craft, so that in two years it would have increased by 500 per cent. (This was later increased to 600 per cent, in one year.) This was then thought to be the figure required for operations in the spring of 1943, when the re-entry into the Continent was planned to take place.

Work on the facilities on the south coast was also proceeding with this target date in mind and necessitated the constant requisitioning of property for the accommodation of the personnel.

The question of the pay, records and accounts of all Combined Operations personnel was also causing anxiety so a central office for this most important part of the Administration was set up under C.C.O. in London in June, 1942.

In fact, during this period, the command was expanding at a rate never before dreamed in the annals of the Services. This rapid expansion introduced many difficulties which necessitated very quick decisions. Often new methods were essential and naturally these met with much criticism from many quarters but, in the end, they stood the strain of war.

Craft Concentration in the South

During the period April to June, 1942, the main problems were the concentration of the landing craft required in the south for "Sledgehammer" and, also, the move of the Thames barges to their assembly area. The latter was treated as an operation and given the code name "Consular". A most carefully prepared plan was made for this because it was necessary to tow the barges from the Thames to as far west as Poole; this not only meant the provision of tugs but also of air and surface escorts.

Towards the end of July, the assembly of landing craft was nearly completed and the movement of the barges was well under way.

Reversal of Strategy

In August, 1942, the decision was made to invade North Africa ("Torch"). As this was to be mounted from the north and west coasts, all available ships and craft had to be moved north again in the shortest possible time. In a C.O.H.Q. docket dated 18th August, 1942, the following minute appears, signed by R.A.L.B.:

"The Admiralty are making operation 'Torch' a 'clear lower deck operation'.

I am sure that, to meet the craft and crew requirements, it will be necessary to use not only the ships and craft asked for by C.-in-C. X.F. (Commander in Chief Naval Expeditionary Force). But L.S.I.s (S), at present in the South, as carriers. It is therefore recommended that until

C.-in-C. XF's requirements are met, no raiding operations necessitating the use of crews, craft or ships be undertaken.

When casualties in 'Jubilee' are known and C.-in-C. X.F.'s requirements are stabilised approximate dates on which the L.S.I.s. (S) and L.S.I.s. (H) are available will be stated."

Manning of Craft for Operation "Torch"

The craft crews were a responsibility of C.C.O. With regard to the personnel, the large expansion approved by the Admiralty was just beginning to take shape but, owing to the disappointments in the delivery of craft, both the basic and advanced training of the crews had lagged behind. The quota of craft for raids had been kept up to gain operational experience and provide incentive, but at a cost. Shortage of accommodation accentuated by the departure of ships, craft and key personnel for Operation "Ironclad" (Madagascar), meant restricting the intake of naval Combined Operations personnel for a time. Thus, not only were the craft crews not fully ready to man the craft required for the operation, but also more crews had to be trained and trained quickly. There was also always a difficulty in getting skilled ratings for maintenance parties, a most important part of the flotilla organisation.

All these matters were at once put in hand but a severe setback occurred when, on 12th August, orders were received to turn the main Combined Operations base at Rosneath over to the American Forces. It was on the use of this base that all programmes of training were founded. The base was actually turned over to the United States authorities on 25th August, by which time British personnel had been found other accommodation, a complete and difficult operation in itself. In addition to the complementing of craft, there were also Beach Parties to be manned; Beach Commandos and Beach Signal Parties to be trained; and, above all, personnel of the three Services to be specially trained for manning the communications of the two Headquarters Ships.

Fitting of Ships for Operation "Torch"

The ships to be used on the operation were, at the beginning of August, for the most part carrying out their normal trading activities. As they became available for the necessary alterations and additions to fit them for their assigned roes, S.O.A.S.C., under C.C.O. who was the only authority who knew what was required, had to arrange all the details and see that each ship was capable of carrying out her duties. As these ships were allocated to yards round the coast from the Clyde to Southampton, the work undertaken by his staff is worthy of record.

THE LANDING CRAFT AND BASES ORGANISATION

The following table shows the ships and craft requirements when first made known in August and the final form the expedition took when it sailed in October.

Notified	Ships	Sailed
1	H.Q. Ship	2
15	L.S.L. (L.)	25
3	L.S.G.	3
3	L.S.T	3
15	M.T. Ships with craft	34
37	Totals	67
	Craft	
91	L.C.A.	140
13	L.C.S. (M.)	12
93	L.C.P.	120
43	L.C.M. (Mk I)	49
42	L.C.M. (Mk III)	87
282	Totals	408

In appreciation of the work done, the following letter was sent to S.O.A.S.C. by Admiral Ramsay on 10th November, 1942:

> I would like to pay tribute to the manner in which you and your staff successfully handled the immense task of equipping and preparing for sea the large number of vessels concerned in Operation 'Torch', and to thank you and those with you for this great work.
>
> It was a task for which your organisation was scarcely equipped, and the departmental and physical difficulties in the way were very great; but thanks to your energy, initiative and disregard for red tape, all obstacles were overcome, resulting in the sailing of the expedition according to programme.
>
> The part played by you and your organisation had mostly been behind the scenes and is unlikely to receive the publicity which is its due, but its importance cannot be over-estimated, and the successful launching of the operation may in no small measure be attributed to you and your staff.

Maintenance of Landing Craft for Operation "Torch"

The staff of C.O.H.Q. had carefully drawn up a schedule of all spare gear required for the maintenance and repair of landing craft when used in operations. The raiding forces were fully equipped, and the requirements envisaged for Operation "Sledgehammer" had also been met. Now, however, a much larger operation ("Torch") was being mounted and the demands for spares increased as the planning progressed. Further, the operation was taking place overseas and so the resources in the U.K. would not be on hand for maintenance.

Added to all this, no spares were coming forward for the craft being supplied from the United States. To get these flotillas properly fitted out meant the craft in the U.K. must be sacrificed. In this way craft were "cannibalised" and so put out of action; an expensive form of improvisation which had the most severe repercussions of the training programme for the ensuing year. But it may be recorded that the schedule of craft and flotilla spares was correct when the expedition sailed.

As the result of previous exercises, it was found necessary to form Beach Recovery Units whose role was to recover craft which had become casualties during the operations. These had to be improvised for the operation and were embarked, but the equipment such as mobile cranes could not be provided in time. This was unfortunate as, after "D" Day, the swell on the beaches caused many casualties among craft and, in consequence, a large number of landing craft were lost which might have been recovered had the necessary lifting gear been available. This was rectified in all future operations. This put a severe strain upon the Landing Craft and Bases Organisation.

Formation of Force "J"

After the return of the ships and craft which had taken part in Operation "Jubilee" (Dieppe), they were kept under the command of Captain J. Hughes-Hallett, R.N. in the Solent area, where they were ready for any further raids.

The small L.S.I.s and the landing ships (stern chute) had to be employed ferrying landing craft required for "Torch" from the south to the north coasts.

It was clear to C.C.O. that this force must remain in being and kept on the alert for any further operations. He therefore suggested to the Admiralty that the ships and craft should be organised as a permanent force and given the title of Force "J". The idea that this force should form the prototype for the other assault forces, which were to be used in Operation "Overlord", was agreed by the Admiralty.

Force "J" came into being on 12th October, 1942, and the Senior Naval Officer set up his headquarters in the Royal Yacht Squadron at Cowes which was commissioned as H.M.S. *Vectis*. The offices of the Force occupied a block of flats on the sea-front which was originally requisitioned as a combined headquarters for the planning and execution of operations "Rutter" and "Jubilee".

The next step taken by C.C.O. was to send a memorandum to the Chiefs of Staff urging the formation of similar forces. The text of the memorandum is quoted in full in Chapter 6.

It will be seen from this memorandum that Force "J" was of considerable size and it was fortunate that berthing for the ships and craft could be found in the Solent. From the point of view of training, the Solent was excellent, as in sheltered water it provided strong cross-tides and any form of beach that was required.

The formation of this force, whose duty it was to keep in training for an operation at short notice, laid the foundations for the assault forces which were eventually used on "D" Day of Operation "Overlord".

Mounting of Forces for Operation "Husky"

The middle of February, 1943, found the base at Rosneath once again a going concern in the hands of C.C.O. It had been decided that this establishment was not to be considered as a Training Base but was to be used for mounting overseas operations. The facilities provided were a deep-water jetty, large storage space, facilities for fitting out craft, accommodation for personnel and excellent workshops.

Another and most important part of this establishment was a small engineering school, fitted out by the Americans at the instigation of C.C.O., where all engine room and maintenance ratings could be given courses in the engines that they were likely to find on service, most of which were of American manufacture.

Every facility that the base at Rosneath possessed was used to the full during 1943. In fact, without it, the mounting of the forces, which were required for overseas operations, could not have been carried out as quickly and economically as they were.

The plan for "Husky" entailed the mounting of two Assault Forces on the Clyde, Force "W"[1] and Force "V". The composition of these two Forces was as follows:

	Force "W"	Force "V"
L.S.H.	1	1
L.S.I.	11	8
M.T. Ships	18	18

---

[1] Force "W" sailed from the U.K. as such but it later became Force "G" and at "Husky" was Force "A".

Force "W" sailed from the Clyde on 16th March, 1943, via the Cape of Good Hope to the Suez Canal area, where training was carried out prior to the operation. To assist in the training, additional landing craft had been embarked prior to sailing from the U.K.

Embarked in the ships of Force "W" were 240 landing craft of various types, Beach Commandos, Beach Signal Sections, Beach Recovery Units and others.

The embarkation of the equipment, spares and stores was accomplished in the short time available because they were issued from the S.O.A.S.C. store on the pier at Greenock and the Landing Maintenance Base at Glasgow, both of which were easily accessible by sea and rail.

Force "V", which was also mounted by Combined Operations Command on the Clyde, was sailed on 28th June, 1943, via the Straits of Gibraltar. This Force, which contained the 1st Canadian Division, took part in the assault on Sicily from the west.

In order to provide Force "V" with a H.Q. Ship, a third ship, S.S. *Hilary*, was taken over by the Admiralty in March, the other two H.Q. Ships, *Bulolo* and *Largs*, already being committed. The *Hilary* was fitted out with the necessary communications equipment under the supervision of the C.O.H.Q. Signal Section; and S.O.A.S.C. ensured that the ship was fitted for her duties in time for her to sail with the convoy.

In addition to Force "W" and Force "V", there was a third force which was mounted in the Mediterranean on a hastily extemporised basis and was to carry out a shore-to-shore assault on Sicily from Tunisia.

An Admiralty report on the mounting of "Husky" remarks:

The complexity of the problems involved was so great that they cannot be covered in this report; accordingly, we will only say here that the job was done and achieved success.

A division of labour between C.O.H.Q. and the Combined Operations Section of the Naval Staff was drawn, and the former must take full credit for the assembly and launching of these forces. The Combined Operations Section concentrated entirely during this period on the build-up of the logistics to support these forces.

In the meanwhile, the build-up of close support craft as a result of experience at Dieppe was being pushed forward by C.O.H.Q., Beach Group Organisations were coming into existence as the result of experience from 'Torch'. D.U.K.W.s were beginning to make their appearance and the problem of bridging the water-gap between L.S.T.

and the shore was solved by the introduction of N.L. pontoons. In all these matters C.O.H.Q. played a leading part.

Manning the Assault Fleet for Operation "Husky"

The problem of finding the manpower for the assault fleet, including the craft and the various special parties required, came under very close study during the first quarter of 1943. At this time, the manpower situation was critical. The difficulties in the provision of personnel are well described in a report written by the Combined Operations Section of the Naval Staff at the end of the war. Although it is not quoted in full, it clearly shows the steps that had to be taken to achieve the target required by "D" Day:

> Personnel
> (1) As a result of the personnel computations contained in J.P. (42) 983 and the serious manning problem thereby presented, the First Sea Lord held a series of meetings on this subject, the first being held on Sunday, 3rd January, 1943. These meetings resulted in the presentation of his note of 5th January, 1943, to the Chiefs of Staff. Some interesting points concerning the personnel difficulties at that time are brought out by the first draft of this note which was prepared in the form of minutes of the meeting held on 3rd January, 1943.
> (2) Broadly speaking, this investigation set a limit to our abilities to man landing craft, and stated that if operations were required against the Continent above a certain scale, it would be essential that America should provide the balance. Furthermore, the suggestion was first mooted that personnel should be transferred from other Services to the Navy to assist in this manning problem, thus producing an optimum effective offensive effort by a redistribution of Service manpower.
> (3) The First Sea Lord's note was written prior to the Casablanca Conference (January, 1943), and it should be borne in mind, at this juncture, that this programme of personnel intake to Combined Operations, which was then proceeding at a rate approaching 3,000 per month, was due to cease on 31st May, 1943. Then followed a period when, perhaps due to the essential concentration of all the Staff on the acute problem of mounting 'Husky', no decision was made with regard to continuing this manpower intake.
> (4) In due course, an inter-Services committee was set up under the Deputy First Sea Lord to investigate the manning requirements of the forces shown in a paper, dated 16th May, 1943, which was prepared in advance of the 'Trident' Conference.

(5) On 9th June, 1943, the Deputy First Sea Lord's Committee reported that some further 31,000 officers and ratings would be required, and put forward certain proposals as to how this shortage could be met. These are complicated and should be examined.

(6) Briefly, it was proposed that the load must be divided between the three Services, the Army and the Air Force making a certain contribution to assist the Navy, and the Navy reorganising the Royal Marines Division in order to provide Marines to man minor landing craft. This proposal required a further intake of recruits into all three Services, which in turn required Cabinet approval.

(7) On 10th June, 1943, a further report was submitted by the Deputy First Sea Lord, stating that he had examined and found satisfactory the basis upon which manpower calculations had been prepared.

(8) C.O.S. meeting of 24th June, 1943, further discussed this problem of manpower for the ultimate invasion ('Overlord'), and decided that 'Overlord' should receive priority in the Service Departments in the allocation of available manpower, and agreed in general to the report of the Deputy First Sea Lord, subject to certain modifications.

(9) This started the introduction of Royal Marines into the manning of minor landing craft; previously they had only manned the guns of support craft. Although this decision was inevitable, it introduced further considerable complications in the already extremely difficult problems involved in the build-up of forces, in that a re-training programme was now necessary. The Royal Marines required to be trained as minor landing craft crews and the existing trained minor landing craft crews and flotilla crews had to be broken down and re-trained for major landing craft. This programme was commenced and proceeded satisfactorily, except that we were faced in the end, some three months before 'Overlord', with the necessity to stop this shuffling process as the Force Commanders were not prepared to accept it any longer.

As the disbandment of the Royal Marine Division was then a fact, it was found on 'D' Day that we had accumulated a considerable surplus of Marines, who were awaiting draft to flotillas which had been formed and trained for the operation and which the Force Commanders were not prepared to recommission with Marines.

(10) It is interesting to note that the total manpower requirements for Combined Operations had now reached over 80,000.

(11) It should be noted in the conclusions of the C.O.S. Meeting on 24th June, 1943, that the gap in training activity introduced by

the delay in arriving at manpower decisions was now causing anxiety.

(12) Consequently, with the long-term problems discussed above, we were faced with the immediate problem of meeting 'Husky's' manpower requirements. These were dealt with by devious means and entailed manpower movement problems of considerable complexity, since bases had to be built up and training flotillas manned at each end of the Mediterranean, with an indeterminate date as to when passage through the Mediterranean would be possible; this depending on the progress of the Tunisian campaign. These problems required detailed forecasting of dates of arrival via the Cape and by the first transport through the Mediterranean. Shortages of manpower occurred due to these complexities, both in the Eastern and Western Mediterranean, and the shortage fell particularly on base administrative staffs.

(13) At this time the strengthening of 'Hostilities Only' personnel was called for by the Force Commanders and brought out the necessity for extreme care and tact in the infiltration of Active Service personnel into a force which, although composed almost entirely of R.N.V.R. and 'Hostilities Only' personnel, had had considerable experience, some of it operational. As was to be expected, considerable criticism with regard to the discipline and bearing of the combined operational craft crews then existed, but the fact remains they did carry out successfully hazardous and difficult operations, and, in many cases, crews which had never been out of sight of land before brought major landing craft of a new type across the Atlantic without mishap or incident. It is suggested that much of the criticism, which had been levelled at the Combined Operations personnel, has not taken into account adequately the other side of the balance sheet.

The Landing Craft and Bases Organisation Becomes too Large for the Combined Operations Command

In October, 1942, the problem of manning the large number of L.S.T.s became increasingly serious and an Admiralty memorandum was discussed by the Cabinet in which it was pointed out that the manning of our portion of the Amphibious Fleet would have a drastic effect on the Eastern and Home Fleets, the convoy system and the drafts to foreign stations. In effect, the Director of Plans stated that the commitment until 31st March, 1943, amounted to approximately 44,500 officers and men. This state of affairs was presented to the First Sea Lord on 10th

October; later a revised estimate gave the figures as 61,000 officers and ratings to be incorporated by 1st August, 1943.

This statement became the basis of considerable enquiry by the First Sea Lord and in the minutes of the Chiefs of Staff Committee Meeting held on 27th November, 1942, is found the following entry:

> The First Sea Lord considered that the Assault Fleet and the personnel to man it had reached too large proportions to be dealt with by the Combined Operations Organisations and it would appear that the Admiralty should assume responsibility for this commitment. He suggested that the Deputy First Sea Lord should go into the whole question with the Chief of Combined Operations and the Controller, and make recommendations as to what organisation, as between the Admiralty and Combined Operations Headquarters, was necessary to deal with the Assault Fleet and its attendant problems.

At the same meeting C.C.O. stated that:

> Although some help was being received from the United States, very great difficulties were being encountered in obtaining the personnel and equipment for the maintenance and repair of landing craft now coming into service both at home and overseas. The stranding and damaging of a great many landing craft in 'Torch' would accentuate these difficulties. He considered that the time had come when he must press for the provision of the necessary resources in full, both at home and overseas, otherwise it might be impossible to implement our plans for 1943.

> The Committee:
> (a) Invited the Deputy First Sea Lord, in consultation with the Chief of Combined Operations and the Controller, to investigate the organisation, as between the Admiralty and Combined Operations Headquarters, required to deal with the very great increase in the Assault Fleet.
> (b) Invited the Admiralty to accord the highest priority to the immediate needs of the Chief of Combined Operations for engine room and maintenance personnel.

As a result of this, the Deputy First Sea Lord made his recommendations as to the future administration of the Assault Fleet. These recommendations are contained in Chapter 8.

Chapter 14

COMMANDOS IN COMBINED OPERATIONS

The history of Commandos during the Second World War is one of gradual expansion from a small makeshift beginning to a large organisation fighting in all the British Theatres of operations.

The Need for a Raiding Force
Initially raised from existing Army volunteers, they developed through subsequent reorganisations into an inter-Service force almost equally composed of soldiers and Royal Marines. In point of time, their origin preceded the formation of C.O.H.Q., but for most of the war they were closely linked and the Commandos were one of the main components of the Combined Operations team.

In June, 1940, the whole of the northern coast of Europe was held by the enemy, and to the threat of imminent invasion at home was added the task of defending the sea link through the Mediterranean and the Suez Canal. The Army had been driven out of Europe and was fully committed in defence, but in order to maintain offensive morale as well as to hamper the enemy's preparations for the expected invasion, it was essential that a method be found for carrying the war into the enemy's camp, if only in a minor way. This was the problem to be solved and it was against this background that the idea of Commandos was conceived.

Lt.-Col Dudley Clark, on the staff of the C.I.G.S. was thinking over this problem while walking home on the evening of 4th June, 1940; the day of Mr Churchill's famous "fight to the end" speech. Remembering the occasions in history when small, highly mobile forces, particularly in the Boer War, had succeeded in harassing a very much larger enemy, he felt that similar results might now be achieved by means of amphibious Commandos which, as we still had command of the sea, could carry out mobile hit and run raids across the Channel. In addition to being good for morale at home, these might provide valuable intelligence, and must also force the Germans to devote at least some of their attention and troops to coastal defence over a wide area. The next morning, he was told by the C.I.G.S. (General Dill) that an immediate means of fostering the offensive spirit of the Army was needed and he forthwith explained his ideas. General Dill was impressed, submitted the idea to the Prime Minister, and the next morning the scheme was approved. The inspiration and the name for these new forces had come from our enemies in a previous war.

Formation of Commando Units

Traditionally, this type of amphibious warfare belonged to the Royal Marines and, earlier in 1940, landing parties of that Corps had, on occasions, been employed. In the summer of the same year, however, they too were very short of men and the Royal Marine Brigade was one of the few trained formations left in the U.K. which could be used in a counter-invasion role. Apart from this, the requirement at this time was for small, detached independent units capable of being moved rapidly from point to point to carry out lightening raids on the enemy coastline. It was therefore decided to disband the Army Independent Companies that had been raised for the Norwegian campaign and to form Commando units in accordance with a War Office letter (dated 24th October, 1940) and thus, although the first Commander of Raiding Operations was a Royal Marine Officer (Lieutenant-General Sir Alan Bourne), the Army found and continued to find all the personnel until the formation of the first two Royal Marine Commandos in 1942. The administration of the Army personnel also remained a War Office responsibility.

> No. 1 Commando was formed from the disbanded Independent Companies.
> No. 2 Parachute Commando was the original airborne unit of the British Army. It was eventually disbanded.
> Nos. 3 and 4 Commandos were formed from Southern Command.
> Nos. 5 and 6 from Western Command.
> No. 7 From Eastern Command.
> No. 8 Commando from London District and Household Brigade (it is interesting to note that Lt.-Col. Laycock (later C.C.O.) who

formed it, managed to get one officer and 12 other ranks Royal Marines from the Adjutant-General Royal Marines).
No.8 Commando also contained the original Special Boat Section.
Nos. 9 and 11 Commandos were formed from Scottish Command.
No. 10 Commando should have been formed originally by Northern Command but as they could not produce the personnel it was later formed as an inter-allied Commando, consisting of French, Dutch, Belgian, Polish and Norwegian soldiers, together with a troop of pro-British Germans and Austrians.

All Commando personnel were volunteers for mobile raiding operations.

During 1940, while resources were still very small, the Commandos were only used for raids from Great Britain, but, in succeeding years, they were used further and further afield. In 1941 Nos. 7, 8 and 11 Commandos were sent to the Middle East where they joined up with two locally raised Commandos. In 1942, No. 5 Commando took part in the Madagascar landings. By 1944 there were four Commando Brigades, two at home, one in Italy and one in S.E.A.C.

The First Commando Raid

The first Commando raid of the war was made on 24th June, 1940, only twelve days after the appointment of the Commander of Raiding Operations and the night before the France-German armistice came into operation. It was only a small raid and of necessity was not elaborately planned with so little time available. It was, however, fairly successful; a reconnaissance of German defences in the Boulogne area was made, two Germans were killed and the party returned safely though somewhat disorganised to England. The only casualty was Colonel Dudley Clark who accompanied the raid as an observer and was slightly wounded.

Control and Development

As mentioned above, a Commander of Raiding Operations had been appointed on 12th June but he was succeeded in July by Admiral of the Fleet Sir Roger Keyes as Director of Combined Operations responsible for both training and the initiation of raids. It was under him that the original organisation of the Commandos took shape.

Initially the Commandos were raised from the men who had volunteered for independent mobile operations in the Independent Companies, and further recruits were also obtained from volunteers. Each Commanding Officer chose his own officers who, in turn, chose their own men, and a Commanding Officer could return any officer or man to regimental duty without warning at any time. For this purpose, the pick of the Home Forces was available at first, but later were allowed to recruit from Young Soldiers Battalions. This was not, however, a great handicap as it avoided "milking" units; and recruits, with no preconceived ideas to forget, did very well after further Commando Training.

The requirements for a Commando were self-reliance, imagination, fitness and tactical ability, and the rigorous training was designed to foster these. Normal barrack life was avoided, the men worked in small parties and usually found their own accommodation in billets. They received a special lodging allowance for this, but otherwise received no extra pay.

In November, 1940, all these irregular forces were reorganised into a Special Services Brigade of five Special Service Battalions. Each Battalion consisted of a headquarters and two Commandos with a total strength of over a thousand. This was soon found to be too cumbersome for efficient control and, in 1941, these units were again reorganised into Commandos of about 450 men, sub-divided into a headquarters and five troops, all the Commandos coming under the one Special Service Brigade.

Commando Raids, 1940-1941

The first raid in June, 1940, was followed by many more which, as time went on, became more daring and went further afield. Small parties were constantly landing on enemy territory bringing back information and prisoners, and thus helping Intelligence in England to keep in touch with changes in German defences and preparations on the northwest coast of Europe. Under the direction of Combined Operations, the scope and range of the raids was also expanded and, in addition to these reconnaissance raids, 1941 saw destruction raids carried out further north against Vaagso, the Lofoten Islands and Spitzbergen.

These operations were all successful in damaging German controlled installations and in hampering their supply of raw materials, and they undoubtedly had a beneficial effect on morale at home. Whether or not they were regarded so favourably by the Norwegians is open to question. The troops were warmly welcomed when they first arrived, but the Norwegians' attitude often cooled when they found the raiders were not staying. This was understandable as their means of livelihood was destroyed, and the Germans were apt to inflict vicious reprisals on the innocent inhabitants after the raid was over.

Commandos in the Middle East

As mentioned above, Commandos had been sent out to the Middle East early in 1941, where they fought under the operational control of G.H.Q. In April of that year, No. 7 Commando carried out a raid on Bardia and later, together with the two locally raised Commandos, was used in the defence of Crete, where all units suffered very severe causalities. No. 8 Commando was part of the garrison of Tobruk; No. 11, having forced the crossing of the Litani River in the Syrian campaign, carried out the famous, but abortive, raid on Field-Marshal Rommel's Headquarters, for which Lieutenant-Colonel Keyes was awarded a posthumous V.C. By the end of 1941, these operations had so depleted the original three Commandos sent overseas that they had to be disbanded, but many of their survivors carried on the combined operations traditions in the Long Range Desert Group, the Special Raiding Section, the Special Air Service and Special Boat Service.

The Raids on St. Nazaire and Dieppe

In October, 1941, Admiral of the Fleet Sir Roger Keyes was succeeded by Commodore Lord Louis Mountbatten with the title of Adviser on Combined Operations (changed to Chief of Combined Operations in March, 1942), and for a time the scale of operations, planned at C.O.H.Q. and carried out by the Commandos, was increased still further.

In March, 1942, No. 2 Commando and specially trained demolition parties detailed from other Commando units, took part in the famous raid at St. Nazaire, which succeeded in destroying harbour installations and in blocking the main dock by blowing up H.M.S. *Campbeltown* against the outer dock gate.

In August of the same year came the raid on Dieppe, in which Nos. 3 and 4 Commandos silenced the coast defence batteries overlooking the landing beaches, and a Royal Marine Commando, No. 40, took part for the first time.

After Dieppe, small scale raiding on the north coast of Europe and in Norway continued uninterruptedly, but there were no further large-scale amphibious operations in this theatre until the actual invasion of Europe in 1944. For the most part, these raids were pin-pricks against the German defences, with reconnaissance as their main objective, but nevertheless they were sufficient to cause the Germans to divert more troops and considerably increase their coastal defences. The degree of annoyance caused can be judged from the severe reprisals taken against captured Commandos, culminating, at the end of 1942, in Hitler ordering that all those captured should be shot.

Commandos in Major Operations

Combined Operations Command also provided Commando troops for special tasks in other major operations about this time. No. 5 Commando was used in the Madagascar landings; later in 1942, Nos. 1 and 6 Commandos took part in the Anglo-American landings in North Africa.

After North Africa came the invasion of Sicily where No. 3 Army Commando, Nos. 40 and 41 R.M. Commandos and also the Special Raiding Section were in the initial landings. They were later joined by No. 2 Commando and all four took part in subsequent operations. No. 3, in a particularly spectacular operation, captured a bridge over the Lentini River, and, although the operation was not a success due to the main advance being held up, the bridge, when finally captured intact, was renamed Commando Bridge.

In September they all landed in Italy, where No. 2 Commando and No. 41 R.M. Commando took part in the battle for Salerno, protecting the left flank of the bridgehead by holding La Molina pass.

Reorganisation, Special Service Group formed in November, 1943

In November, 1943, a major reorganisation of the Commando Forces took place, for which there were two main reasons; one operational and one to simplify command. From the operational point of view, the conduct of war, as far as the Allies were concerned, was entering an offensive stage and the requirement for raids on the enemy coast was giving place to larger scale and more sustained operations, such as those in Italy mentioned above. This made it necessary to modify the training, organisation and reinforcement procedure of the Commandos, and provide longer range supporting weapons such as 3-in Mortars and some regimental transport which had hitherto been lacking.

On the Command side, the number of Commando units was now large and they were widely dispersed. At the time there were nine Army, two Royal Marine and three special purpose Commandos in the S.S. Brigade; of these, the Royal Marine and two of the Army Commandos were in Italy. Apart from the S.S. Brigade, there was the Royal Marine Division that had grown out of the Royal Marine Brigade of 1940. It was now planned to break up this formation and turn the six infantry units into Commandos under C.O.H.Q.

It was obvious that the Special Service Brigade H.Q., already overloaded, was inadequate to control this very large force and considerable thought was given to the establishment of a larger organisation to do this and to implement the new training and reinforcement requirements. As a result, in November, 1943, a Special Service Group, commanded by Major-General Sturges, Royal Marines was set up to replace the old S.S. Brigade. Under it, eight Army and eight Royal Marine Commandos were grouped into four Special Service Brigades, each having both Army and Royal Marine units. In addition, there was also a Holding Commando, Commando Depot, Special Boat Section and a Mountain and Snow Warfare School all under the S.S. Group Headquarters. This organisation remained virtually unchanged until the end of the war, except that the names of the headquarters were later changed to Commando Group and Commando Brigade.

Functions of the Holding Commando

The Holding Commando was formed to meet the training and reinforcement requirements involved in the new sustained operations now being undertaken. While the role of Commandos had been raiding only, it had been possible to send them partially trained reinforcements who completed their training with the Commando while it was training itself for the next operation.

In sustained operations, however, this was impracticable and the Holding Commando's function was to receive the intake from the Commando Depot, complete their specialist training in heavy weapons, demolitions, signals, etc., and draft them to individual Commandos as required. Battle and other casualties were also passed to the Holding Commando for drafting back to their original units. The only alternative would have been considerable drafting from one Commando to another which would have been bad for the *esprit de corps*. Commandos proceeding overseas took with them a pool of 15 to 20 per cent reinforcements to make up casualties occurring before normal reinforcements could arrive.

Disposition of the Four Special Service Brigades

Of the four Special Service Brigades, No. 2 was formed in Italy where four individual Commandos were already operating. This formation remained in the Mediterranean for the rest of the war under the theatre commander. They played a distinguished part in the fighting in Italy, Albania, Greece and in Yugoslavia where they co-operated with Marshal Tito's partisans.

The other Brigades were formed in England, where Nos. 1 and 4 remained under the control of C.C.O. until they were required for "Overlord". No. 3, however, was sent immediately to India.

No. 3 Special Service Brigade

No. 3 Brigade in S.E.A.C. spent much of its time in an ordinary infantry role and at one time, filled a defensive position at Silchar. They had rather a discouraging start which resulted in gloomy reports being sent back to the S.S. Group and C.O.H.Q. This was largely due to their having to acclimatise themselves to a new theatre and its methods as well as to the tropical climate. These difficulties were overcome, however, and later they carried out a number of amphibious operations. In March, 1944, two of the Commandos (Nos. 5 and 44) landed behind the Japanese lines near Teknaf, which resulted in a general advance in the area, and towards the end of the year, the Brigade made a number of reconnaissance raids. Early in 1945, three landings were planned, at Akyab, Myebon and Kangaw, to hasten the Japanese withdrawal and disorganise it by cutting off as many of his troops as possible. These went well, particularly the last which involved most bitter fighting. At the end of the war No. 3 Brigade was sent to Hong Kong as part of the re-occupation forces.

Nos. 1 and 4 Special Service Brigades

The reorganisation in the autumn of 1943 still left C.O.H.Q. with the responsibility for raiding operations and the two remaining Special Service Brigades were available to it for this purpose until they were required for "Overlord". All the emphasis, however, was by now on the plans and preparations for this invasion and the work of C.O.H.Q. in planning operations for the Commandos was closely co-ordinated with the requirements of C.O.S.S.A.C. Numbers of small raids were carried out on the north-east coast of Europe and also in the Channel Islands with the object, not only of reconnaissance, but also of supporting the cover plan. These raids and beach reconnaissances enabled the Allies to form a very clear picture of the Normandy beaches and their defences. In particular they furnished detailed information of the German beach obstacles and thus enabled the Combined Operations Training Establishments to reconstruct them and devise methods for removing or destroying them.

For "Overlord", in the planning of which C.O.H.Q. had been fully represented, the command of the Brigades was transferred to the Force Commanders. Both formations were landed in Normandy on "D" Day and took their full share of the fighting to secure the bridgehead. No. 1 Brigade, on the left, pushed ahead to link up with the 6th Airborne Division and then took up a defensive position near Le Plein. Each Commando of No. 4 Brigade had its own individual task at the landing but, when these were completed, they concentrated and moved over to assist No. 1 Brigade in the Le Plein area. The two Brigades continued to hold the left flank of the beach-head for forty days without adequate rest or relief and can truly be said to have performed a most vital part in the operation as a whole.

In October, 4 Brigade joined the Canadians in Holland for the attack on Walcheren, the capture of which was to clear the mouth of the Scheldt and enable Allied shipping to reach Antwerp. The Canadians had already captured Breskens and were clearing South Beveland of the enemy and, having completed this, they were to attack Walcheren across the causeway from Beveland while the Commandos carried out two landings near Flushing and Westkapelle. These landings were made, as planned, on 1st November and both towns were captured in spite of severe opposition from the enemy. The success of the Commandos in this operation was very creditable in view of the strength of the defences which had to be overcome by such a light force.

No. 1 Brigade, having fought for a time with the 7th Armoured Division, was employed in the clearing of the Rhine-Mass triangle and then prepared for its part in the crossing of the Rhine. The Commandos crossed the Rhine west of Wesel and, having infiltrated through the enemy defences on the banks, entered Wesel itself from the north-west. The next day, having cleared the town, they turned back towards the river and linked up with the main bridgehead. The Brigade continued to be employed with the Army during the advance into Germany and was used to force the crossings of the Weser, Aller and Elbe Rivers, and, during these operations, they developed a technique of infiltrating behind the enemy's lines and attacking their objective from an unexpected quarter, which seems to have been largely responsible for the remarkable successes they achieved.

Post-war Proposals for the Retention of Commandos

With the end of the war, the problem of the future of the Commandos immediately arose. It had to be decided whether they were to be retained in peace time and, on the assumption that they were, there were far more difficult problems of organisation, size and composition. C.O.H.Q. was most anxious to retain both Commandos and also their inter-Service nature. The proposals were for a Commando Group of two Brigades made up of both Army and Royal Marine Commandos. Brigadier Churchill, commanding No. 2 Brigade, went so far as to propose that the individual Commandos themselves be made up of both Services. A Territorial Army Commando, based in London, was also suggested.

The Army's manpower difficulties, however, led to opposition to the C.O.H.Q. proposals and the Chiefs of Staff eventually decided that all Army Commandos were to be disbanded. One Royal Marine Commando Brigade was, however, to be retained.

This decision left C.O.H.Q. and the Commando Group Headquarters, which was soon to be disbanded, with the difficult problem of carrying out the reorganisation when various existing Commandos were actively employed both in the Far East and in Germany. The Army personnel were returned to their own units or depots. The Royal Marines units in Germany were brought back to England and contributed to the formation of the new peace time Brigade. This brigade was thus left alone to carry on the tradition and the training for possible future amphibious Commando operations. Their versatility and offensive spirit have been since proved both in Korea and Malaya.

Chapter 15

ROYAL MARINES IN COMBINED OPERATIONS

At the outbreak of war in 1939 the functions of the Royal Marines were as follows: To provide detachments which, whilst fully capable of manning their share of the gun armament of ships, are specially trained to provide a striking force drawn either from the Royal Marine Divisions[1] or the Fleet. This force to be immediately available for use under the direction of the Naval Commander-in-Chief for such amphibious operations as raids on the enemy coast and bases, or the seizure and defence of temporary bases for use by the Fleet.

These functions envisaged the Army waging a continental war with the Royal Navy holding the seas and conducting, as a subsidiary to naval strategy, such amphibious operations as were necessary with its Royal Marine forces. It was under these conditions that the Corps carried out its initial amphibious operations of the war, notably in Norway, France and the Low Countries in 1940. To this end, too, the original Royal Marine Brigade was formed, expanding later to the Royal Marine Division.

When the Army was driven from Europe, a totally different state of affairs arose, in which combined operations assumed a major role in the grand strategy. In particular, raids on certain parts of the enemy coasts became the province of the Director of Combined Operations and not of the Admiralty, to whom, strictly speaking, the Royal Marine formations belonged. The course of events proved,

---

[1] This refers to the Headquarter Establishments at Chatham, Portsmouth and Plymouth which were, at that time, called Divisions.

moreover, that an amphibious operation for the seizure of a naval base had assumed proportions far beyond the strength of any force of which the Corps could dispose. At the same time large Army formations were being trained in the technique of landing operations; such operations had become part of Allied grand strategy rather than the responsibility of the Naval C.-in-C. alone. In actual fact, Royal Marine formations found themselves operating under Army rather than Naval Command. The old definition of the Corps' function was, in practice, obsolete.

The functions of the Royal Marines were therefore re-defined as follows:

> To provide:
> (1) Detachments for service in H.M. Ships which, whilst fully capable of manning their share of the gun armament, are specially trained to undertake such landing operations as the Naval Commander-in-Chief may find it necessary to order.
> (2) Units to undertake, in co-operation with other Services, special amphibious operations.
> (3) Units for the rapid establishment and temporary defence of Naval and Fleet Air Arm Bases.

Although this definition was not laid down until 1943, it should be realised that it was made, in fact, after the event. From 1940 onwards, the Corps had swiftly developed and adapted itself to meet the changed amphibious conditions of the times. During the process, the work of C.O.H.Q. became linked more and more with that of the Royal Marines. It is the purpose of this chapter to outline briefly the major amphibious commitments which were undertaken by the Corps.

These may conveniently be grouped as follows: (1) Commando forces; (2) Support; (3) Minor Landing Craft; (4) Beach Maintenance; (5) Raiding; [and] (6) Miscellaneous.

The part played by the Royal Marine Commandos has been included in Chapter 14, and details of the Royal Marines in the support role, both afloat and ashore, are given in Chapter 16.

Landing Craft

Prior to 1943, minor landing craft had been manned by sailors. During the first quarter of 1943, the problem of finding the manpower for the assault fleet and, at the same time, to provide the various and multitudinous special parties required, came under very close study. Possible solutions including the provision of American landing craft crews and the transfer of personnel to the Navy from the other Services.

In the event, it was agreed that the load should be divided between the three Services, the Army and the Air Force making a certain contribution to assist the Navy. It was at this time that the Royal Marines Division was disbanded and its units reorganised to meet the requirements of the new situation: its Headquarters, under Major-General Sturges, provided the main element of the new Commando Group Headquarters, its infantry battalions were re-formed as Commandos, and the large number of officers and other ranks from the other units of the Division were used to man landing craft. Thus, the Royal Marines assumed what was to become one of their permanent war and post-war commitments. Previously they had only manned the guns of support craft.

The acceptance of this landing craft commitment involved a considerable change of policy for the Corps. In particular, the admission of Royal Marine Officers to the command of commissioned ships of the Royal Navy in itself a marked departure from tradition and a development of importance. A.F.O. 3795/43 is of interest in this connection:

Royal Marines Command in Certain Classes of Vessel

(C.W. 24996/43 – 19 Aug. 1943)

In the following classes of vessels, officers of the Royal Marines are to be employed as Executive Officers. For the purpose of assessing their relative executive rank, Article 224, Clause 2, of K.R. and A.I. is to be followed. The order of command of such officers amongst themselves and in relation to Executive Officers of the Royal Navy, Royal Naval Reserve and Royal Naval Volunteer Reserve, will then be governed by the rules in Article 175-181 and elsewhere.

They will be entitled to command money, entertainment allowance and First Lieutenant's allowance at the same rates and under the same rules as for executive officers.

Royal Marine Officers appointed in command will exercise all the powers of Commanding Officers of H.M. Ships.

All Royal Marine Officers appointed to these vessels will previously have been given a suitable course of navigation.

Classes of Vessels affected:
    Landing Craft, assault   (L.C.A.)
    Landing Craft, flak   (L.C.F.)
    Landing Craft, gun   (L.C.G.)
    Landing Craft, infantry   (L.C.I.)

Landing Craft, mechanised	(L.C.M.)
Landing Craft, personnel	(L.C.P.)
Landing Craft, support	(L.C.S)
Landing Craft, tank	(L.C.T.)
Landing Craft, vehicle	(L.C.V.)
Landing Barges	(L.B.)

Nine months after the decision that the Corps should man British minor landing craft, two thirds of the British craft in the "Overlord" landing were manned by Royal Marines. This is ample evidence both of the adaptability of the Corps and of the excellence of the training organisation which was set up to meet the commitment. From then onwards Royal Marine-manned landing craft took part in amphibious operations in all theatres, notably at Walcheren, in the Mediterranean and the Arakan. One advantage of having soldier/sailor crews for such craft was brought out during operations against the island of Brac in the Adriatic in 1944. L.C.A.s had landed about 50 men of 2 Commando, who held a small perimeter after the main force had withdrawn. The craft were lying in a cove when the Commandos ashore were heavily engaged by the Germans. Headed by their officer, the crew of the L.C.A. left their craft in charge of one man and went ashore as a military organisation to extricate the Commandos. They carried Brens and carbines, and their arrival tipped the scales enabling the Commandos to withdraw, bringing with them a seriously wounded officer who could not otherwise have been evacuated.

Beach Maintenance

The development and employment of the Beach Organisation is fully dealt with in Chapter 18. The chapter shows how the Army itself became responsible for its own beach maintenance and the provision of the organisation to carry out the task. But mention will be made here of the R.M. Beach Unit, which was formed in 1941 for use in support of the R.M. Brigade, and the part played by the Royal Marines in the formation and operation of Beach Bricks for operations in Sicily and Italy in 1943.

The 7th Battalion Royal Marines, which left U.K. for South Africa in late 1942, was ordered to the Middle East in December, 1942. On arrival, the Commanding Officer was required to draw up a draft organisation for a Beach Brick within five days.

This was done. The Battalion remained at Kabrit from 1st January, 1943, until embarking for Sicily in July, 1943. During this time, in conjunction with the C.T.C., Kabrit and G.H.Q. Middle East, in Cairo, the Beach Brick Organisation was evolved and Bricks were formed and trained. Briefly the Bricks consisted of a nucleus battalion, to which specialised units (an A.A. Regiment, Signals, R.E., R.A.S.C., R.O.A.C., R.A.M.C., a R.N. Beach Commando) were added, making up a total strength of about 2,600. A defence company with carrier-borne mortars was provided by the nucleus battalion, but the essence of the idea was that all Brick personnel were prepared to fight, the rifle companies of the nucleus battalion provided the hard core of this defensive potential.

7 R.M. trained itself and its attached units for this role, and produced teams of instructors to assist in the training, in Egypt and Palestine, of the four infantry battalions chosen to fulfil a similar role (1st Bn. Welch Regiment, 1st Bn. Highland Light Infantry, 2nd Bn. Argyll and Sutherland Highlanders and 18th Bn. Durham Light Infantry) and their attached units. All five Bricks were employed in the landings in Sicily.

Mobile Landing Craft Advanced Bases

Some mention must be made of the M.O.L.C.A.B.s These were bases possessing facilities which could rapidly be established on a selected site for the accommodation of personnel and the maintenance of first aid repairs of hulls, machinery and armament of landing craft. The total strength of a M.O.L.C.A.B. was 36 officers and 374 other ranks, of which the major proportion were Royal Marines, under a Royal Marine Commanding Officer. The functions of the M.O.L.C.A.B. were as follows:

(1) As a temporary advanced base at which the short range portion of the assault force (the Build-up Group) could assemble in preparation for an assault.
(2) As an advanced base set up in captured territory directly after an assault to support the build-up phase of an operation.
(3) As an advanced base at which a Build-up Group could re-form, recuperate and refit, after an assault, in preparation for a new operation.
(4) As a temporary addition to a static rear base in order to provide increased facilities during a peak load period.

These units were designed primarily for use in South-East Asia and the Far East and, in the event, owing to the collapse of Japan, the five units which had been planned were not all found necessary. However, half of one M.O.L.C.A.B. was sailed across the Channel, transported by road to the Rhine and used to assist in the Rhine crossing. Subsequently two M.O.L.C.A.B.s were located in the Far East.

Raiding

The Commando role of the Royal Marines, with its embodied responsibility for amphibious raiding, was by no means a new departure for the Corps. Operations by various ships' detachments early in the war (notably by that of H.M.S. *Ramillies* at Diego Suarez, Madagascar) can reasonably be considered as falling within its scope. Other purely amphibious raiding operations by units other than Commandos were also undertaken; details of operations by three such units are narrated briefly here.

11th Battalion Royal Marines

This unit was the infantry battalion of 1st Group of the Mobile Naval Base Defence Organisation (M.N.B.D.O.), which was organised to establish and defend an advanced naval base. After the withdrawal from Greece, this unit was located in the Middle East and carried out a small raid on the island of Kuphonisi to destroy a radio location station. Later it attempted a much larger scale raid to destroy harbour installations at Tobruk. This operation, undertaken when Rommel had driven the 8th Army back to El Alamein, did not succeed owing to bad weather and the preparedness of the defenders.

Royal Marine Boom Patrol Detachment

This unit, under the cover name of the Royal Marine Boom Patrol Detachment, had been formed, in July, 1942, from selected officers and other ranks of the Royal Marines. They had been specially trained in the use of canoes with the object of carrying out operations, either of reconnaissance or attack, against targets which could not be dealt with by other means.

The detachment underwent very severe endurance tests, and were expert in the use of "limpet" mines.[2] This form of attack was specially useful against ships in harbours where it was not desired to employ aircraft in bombing, owing to the presence of neutral or friendly inhabitants. This force from its inception was under the command of C.C.O.

On 30th October, 1942, the following letter was sent by C.C.O. to the Secretary to the Chiefs of Staff Committee:

---

[2] Small explosive charges which could be secured to the hulls of ships by electric magnets and which were fitted with fuses.

Operation 'Frankton' has been planned to meet Lord Selbourne's requirement, that steps should be taken to attack Axis ships which are known to be running the blockade between France and the Far East.

Both seaborne and airborne methods of attacking the ships have been carefully examined, and the plan now proposed is the only one which offers a good chance of success.

On an average, between six and ten blockade runners are usually found alongside the quays at Bordeaux, in addition to other shipping. It is hoped to deal with at least six blockade runners.

Briefly, the plan is for one officer and five other ranks of the Royal Marine Boom Patrol Detachment to paddle up the River Gironde in 'cockles,'[3] moving during the hours of darkness only, and to place 'Limpets' on the water-line of the ships they find at Bordeaux. The 'Cockles' will be carried to within nine miles of the mouth of the river in a submarine which will be on passage to normal patrol duty and thus will not require to be specially detailed.

At their meeting on 3rd November, the Chiefs of Staff "approved the plan for Operation 'Frankton.'"

No 1 section R.M. Boom Patrol Detachment under Major H.G. Hasler, Royal Marines, was selected to train for this operation. The following programme was carried out:

31st October-7th November	In H.M.S. *Forth*, with six cockles Mark II, developing the technique of hoisting a boat fully loaded (480-lb. load including crew) by means of tackle and an extension girder 4 ft. long on the muzzle of the gun of a 'T' Class submarine. Training included dummy limpet attacks and 24 hours' training in P. 339.
10th-14th November	Carry out exercise "Blanket" (attack on Deptford from Margate, via River Swale).
19th-20th November	In H.M.S. *Forth* preparing and packing stores, testing hoisting gear under full load, swinging compasses, field training ashore, fusing limpets, etc.

---

[3] A semi-folding canoe, quick to erect and capable of carrying two men and 200 lb. of stores. Designed by Mr. Goatley to the specifications of C.O.H.Q.

30th November-5th December   On passage in H.M.S. *Tuna*, briefing crews, study of air photographs and reconnaissance reports.

The cockles embarked in H.M.S. *Tuna* were launched off the mouth of the Gironde River at about 8 p.m. on the night of 7th December. In his report on the operation to the Secretary of the Admiralty, dated 29th April, C.C.O. reported as follows:

I forward herewith the report of the Force Commander (Major H.G. Hasler, R.M.) on Operation 'Frankton'.

Of the six canoes, each manned by two Royal Marines, which were launched from H.M.S. *Tuna* off the mouth of the Gironde River, one was damaged in launching and never left the submarine, two were capsized in tidal races and one lost touch at the mouth of the Gironde.

The remaining two canoes manned respectively by Major Hasler and Marine Sparks and by Corporal Laver and Marine Mills, successfully reached their objective 50 miles up the Gironde River and attached the limpets to six ships.

There is good reason to believe that at least three and probably five ships were holed, of which at least three are believed to have been blockade runners.

Of the personnel engaged, Major Hasler and Marine Sparks have successfully regained this country. Lt. MacKinnon is believed to be a prisoner of war. Marine Moffat is known to have been found drowned by the Germans at the entrance of the Gironde River. Nothing is known of the fate of the remainder.

This brilliant operation carried through with great determination and courage is a good example of the successful use of the 'limpeteers'.

From documents captured at the end of the war, it is now clear that the following ships sustained damage: *Alabama*, five limpets exploded; *Tannenfels*, two limpets exploded; *Dresdan*, two limpets exploded; [and] *Portland*, one limpet exploded.

A further explosion occurred on the seaward side of *Sperrbrecher 5*. No damage was caused and it was presumed that the explosive charge had dropped off the ship's side and exploded on the river bed.

R.M. Detachment 385

This detachment was specially formed early in 1944. It was composed of ranks who were highly trained canoeists and trained, to a moderately good standard, as swimmers. It formed the general-purpose part of the Small Operations Group, whose task in S.E.A.C. was to provide small parties of uniformed troops trained and equipped to operate against targets on enemy-occupied coasts or in river and lake areas. Other units in the Group were Combined Operations Pilotage Parties, a Special Boat Section and a Sea Reconnaissance Unit. It is of interest that the setting up of this Group was the first attempt made to co-ordinate the activities of various units with similar roles which had previously operated as "Private Armies". It is also of interest that the Small Operations Group was commanded by a Royal Marine officer, Colonel H.T. Tollemache.

Miscellaneous Tasks

In addition to the major roles which the Corps was called upon to fulfil in Combined Operations, there were many others, smaller and, maybe, of more temporary or *ad hoc* nature. This is particularly true in the case of north-west Europe where:

(1) R.M. Port Parties fulfilled a multitude of roles during and after "Overlord" in France and Belgium.
(2) R.M. Signallers (800 personnel) played a large part in naval communications ashore.
(3) A R.M. Provost Company landed with Forces "G", "J" and "S" in the initial assault on the Normandy coast and was wholly engaged in operational duties on the beaches for the first fourteen days.
(4) R.M. Engineers, from the earliest days of the operation, performed a variety of tasks in France.
(5) The R.M. Engineer Commando provided Landing Craft Obstruction Clearance Units during the assault and afterwards took part in operations inshore as demolition teams with 1st and 4th Commando Brigades
(6) R.M. Armoured Support Group. Originally it was intended that this Group should man Centaur tanks mounting a 95-mm gun, which would act as a ready-made turret in L.C.T. (A.). The craft would beach and the unit (then known as the R.M. Support Craft Regiment) would operate as Field Artillery from their beached craft. The role in which the Group finally operated added a third task, which was to strengthen the fire of the divisional artillery and, with this end in view, the tanks went ashore and operated up to ten miles inland.

This chapter would not be complete without reference to the part played by Royal Marine Officers within C.O.H.Q. Officers of the Corps were to be found in all branches of the staff and were concerned in all its various activities. In particular, the first Director (later Deputy Director of Combined Operations) from 21st July, 1940, until 13th November,

1940, was General Bourne; Brigadier Wildman-Lushington was R.M. Advisor to C.C.O. and later Chief of Staff from 19th December, 1941 until 20th December, 1943; and Brigadier V.D. Thomas, R.M., was Chief of Staff from 21st December, 1943 until 22nd September, 1946.

Conclusion

The part played by the Royal Marines in Combined Operations in World War II has been summarised in this chapter under its main headings. To give a final picture of the part played by the Corps, it is of interest to enumerate the main roles performed by them in the Normandy invasion. Some 17,000 Royal Marines were in action, by far the largest Royal Marine effort of the war. The following were the main activities:

> Five R.M. Commandos and 4 S.S. Brigade H.Q. with tasks ashore.
> R.M. Landing Craft; more than two-thirds of the L.C.A. and most of the minor craft in the Build-up Force were manned by Marines.
> R.M. Armoured Support Group.
> Guns crews of L.C.G. and L.C.F.
> About half the Landing Craft Obstruction Clearance Units were Royal Marines.
> R.M. Signals were largely employed in the organisation of the Flag Officer, British Assault Area.
> Detachments in H.M. Ships in the Bombardment Force, several detachments were in greater than normal strength.
> Naval Camp Staffs on both sides of the Channel.
> R.M. Provost employed on beaches in naval ports and attached to Commandos.
> R.M. Port Parties in three ports on the Normandy side.
> R.M. Hard Parties loading craft on the U.K. side.

Oil burning on the surface of the sea at Stamsund, which was attacked by No.3 Commando during Operation *Claymore*, the Lofoten Raid, on 4 March 1941. The men who landed at Stamsund successfully destroyed the Lofoten Cod Boiling Plant located there. (Historic Military Press)

Burning oil tanks photographed from HMS *Legion* during the Lofoten Raid. (Historic Military Press)

Commandos in action during Operation *Archery*, the Combined Operations raid on Vågsøy and Måløy undertaken on 27 December 1941. (Danish National Museum)

One of the wounded raiders is assisted back to a landing craft during Operation *Archery*, the Combined Operations raid on Vågsøy and Måløy, 27 December 1941. (Danish National Museum)

The Würzburg radar station at Bruneval on the French coast. It was reconnaissance photographs of this site, taken in January 1941, which led to plans for Operation *Biting* being drawn up. This raid was carried out on the night of 27/28 February 1942. (Historic Military Press)

German prisoners, captured during the attack on Bruneval during Operation *Biting*, being searched by some of the raiders. (Historic Military Press)

A final training exercise is underway prior to the assault on Dieppe on 19 August 1942. Here Canadian infantrymen are embarking on landing craft. (Library and Archives Canada)

Landing craft approach the beaches at Dieppe during Operation *Jubilee*, on 19 August 1942. Fires are burning in the hinterland as a result of the naval and aerial bombardment. (Historic Military Press)

The bloody aftermath of Operation *Jubilee* – a still from a wartime newsreel showing some of the casualties and their equipment, as well as abandoned Churchill tanks and landing craft, on the beach at Dieppe. (Historic Military Press)

Troops crouch inside a LCVP bound for Omaha Beach on D-Day, 6 June 1944. Ernest Hemingway, who was in one of the LCVPs that day, later wrote about the men: 'Under their steel helmets they looked like pikemen of the Middle Ages to whose aid in battle had suddenly come some strange and unbelievable monster.' (NARA)

A cameraman peers between men crowded in a landing craft to obtain this shot of the first wave going ashore as his own LCVP nears the smoke-shrouded Omaha Beach. The LCVP on the far left has been identified as being from the Arthur Middleton-class attack transport USS *Samuel Chase*. (USNHHC)

Commandos of 47 (RM) Commando coming ashore from LCAs on Jig Green Beach, Gold area, on 6 June 1944. A number of LCTs can be seen in the background unloading the priority vehicles of 231st Brigade, 50th Division. (© MoD/Crown Copyright 2019)

At exactly 08.32 hours on 6 June 1944, Sergeant Jim Mapham of No.5 Army Film and Photographic Unit photographed this scene on Queen Red sector in the centre-left of Sword Beach. The shutter clicked just as the beach came under heavy artillery and mortar fire from German positions inland. (Historic Military Press)

Troops of the 9th Canadian Infantry Brigade, more specifically men of the Highland Light Infantry of Canada, disembarking with bicycles from LCI(L)s (Landing Craft Infantry Large) onto Nan White Beach at Bernières-sur-Mer, shortly before midday on 6 June 1944. (Conseil Régional de Basse-Normandie/Canadian National Archives)

A view not dissimilar to those seen during the Dieppe Raid. Here, medics attend to wounded in the shelter of a Churchill AVRE from 5th Assault Regiment, Royal Engineers on Sword Beach, 6 June 1944. (Historic Military Press)

The view from the eastern end of Nan Green sector of Juno Beach, looking towards Courseulles-sur-Mer, on the afternoon of 6 June 1944. A Sherman tank of the 2nd Canadian Armoured Brigade and support troops of 7th Canadian Brigade Group are pictured coming ashore. In the foreground, Royal Canadian Engineers are working to improve the beach exit with the aid of an armoured bulldozer. (Conseil Régional de Basse-Normandie/Canadian National Archives)

Landing craft on the beach at Akyab Island during the Arakan Campaign, on 4 January 1945. (Historic Military Press)

The first wave of assault troops land at Ramree Island, Burma, on 21 January 1945. These men were from the 25th or 26th Indian Divisions. The Battle of Ramree Island was fought for six weeks during January and February 1945, as part of the Indian XV Corps' 1944/45 offensive on the Southern Front of the Burma Campaign. (Historic Military Press)

Chapter 16

CLOSE SUPPORT AND COMBINED OPERATIONS BOMBARDMENT UNITS

The question of air support is not considered in detail in this chapter as to a very large extent it is either strategical in its conception or conforms to the systems employed in the normal land battle.

Close Support

The problem of close support of an assault was one of many considered by the I.S.T.D.C. in its early days. Their initial efforts were concentrated on the question of providing the assault troops with covering fire during the vulnerable period of the approach to, and the crossing of the beaches. The first practical achievement towards the solution of this problem was the production of a few small and lightly armoured support craft, which could be carried to the scene of operations and could accompany the leading flights of landing craft to the beach. When combined training first started at the C.T.C. Inveraray, support landing craft armed with a naval 4-in. smoke mortar and two 0.5-in. machine guns were the only form of close support craft available for assault, but it was not long before C.C.O. asked the War Office for Daimler armoured car turrets with 2-pdr. guns to be provided for a new, heavier support craft.

The pre-war manuals on Combined Operations envisaged that heavier support would be provided by warships whose fire was to be controlled by Forward Observation Officers (F.O.O.s) landed with the assaulting troops. The details concerning provision and training of these F.O.O.s early in 1941 is dealt with in the second section of this chapter, but suffice to say here, that in the summer of that year, the first specially trained F.O.O.s were sent to the C.T.C. to join assault formations already under training.

The Force Commanders of the Royal Marine Division and later 110 Force were directly concerned with this problem and sought advice from C.O.H.Q.

In January 1942, C.C.O. convened a meeting to consider the control of bombarding ships allotted for support of an assault landing; representatives of the three Service Ministries, 110 Force and the Senior F.O.O. were present. The meeting decided on the principle of a central control for all types of support and that warships, although initially allotted in support of specific units, should remain under a central control which could re-deploy them as the situation demanded.

Once these principles were established, the necessary communications and codes were drawn up to put them into effect. The staff of C.O.H.Q. worked very closely with the Service Ministries in the preparation of procedure manuals and signal books, which were issued by C.O.H.Q. in the summer of that year.

At Dieppe, the theory of control stood the test of action, but the fact that the fire power available was inadequate to the extreme stood out with distressing force. The support landing craft had not sufficient fire power nor were they heavily enough armoured, the *Hunt* Class destroyers also were inadequate for their role as they could not stand up to the fire from coast defence batteries that had not been previously neutralised.

It was not until after Dieppe that really serious thought was given to the problem by the three Service Ministries, C.C.O. and S.O. Force "J". It was brought home to all that heavily armed support craft were required to provide effective neutralising fire on the beaches, and that the provision of the right type of support for the Army, once they were ashore, was a problem needing further special study.

The Study of Fire Support for the Assault

C.C.O. set up an Assault Committee under the chairmanship of Chief of Staff with representatives from the Admiralty and War Office to study all aspects of the problem of the assault against well-defended beaches and, at its first meeting on 11th November, 1942, three sub-committees were formed:

> No. 1 Sub-Committee (Chairman M.G.C.T.) to decide the scale of maximum opposition that is considered reasonable to engage when planning an assault.

No. 2 Sub-Committee (Chairman M.G.C.T.) to make recommendations as to the support required in an assault against the type of opposition indicated by No. 1 Sub-Committee.

No. 3 Sub-Committee (Chairman D.X.O.R.) to report on how recommendations of No. 2 Sub-Committee could be met.

The War Office staff, under the orders of the C.I.G.S., were at that time preparing a paper on "Fire Power required under an Assault".

C.C.O. wrote a memorandum to the Chiefs of Staff Committee on 16th November, pointing out that the overriding lesson learned from Dieppe was the need for overwhelming fire support in the initial stages of an assault and that no standard naval craft had the necessary qualities or equipment to provide such support. He asked the Chief of Staff Committee to invite the Admiralty to: (1) State what the cost to the naval building programme would be if heavy and small monitors were included in the programme about to be considered; (2) Consider as a matter of urgent necessity, a programme of shallow-draught protected gunboats of fair speed for close inshore support fire for the initial assaults.

This memorandum was discussed at a Chiefs of Staff meeting on 2nd December, 1942, and it was decided, on the recommendation of the First Sea Lord, to form a Technical Sub-Committee to consider and report on: (1) Whether the requirements of fire support in assaults could be met by bombing, gunfire from ships, or a combination of both; [and] (2) What special measures were to be taken to meet this requirement.

This Committee was formed under the Chairmanship of the Assistant Chief of Naval Staff (Weapons) (A.C.N.S. (W)), Rear-Admiral P.R. McGrigor, the other members being the A.C.I.G.S., the Director of Bomber Operations and V.C.C.O. (Major-General J.C. Haydon).

Recommendations of the Assault Committee

Before the Technical Sub-Committee held its first meeting, C.C.O.'s Assault Committee produced a paper – "Summary of recommendations of C.O.H.Q. Assault Committee on Fire Support for the Assault on Defended Beaches", and this was used by the V.C.C.O. as a basis of C.C.O.'s views.

In the production of this paper, technical advice was given by the Admiralty, the War Office, G.H.Q. Home Forces, Canadian Military H.Q., and the Ministry of Supply. It detailed the type and weight of fire required and proposed which Service should provide it during the various phases of the assault. The conclusions of this paper were as follows:

To summarise, in order to ensure that the assaulting troops can get ashore and can maintain their attack beyond the beach, it is considered, that in addition to whatever naval and air bombardment can be included in the plan (and this should obviously be the maximum possible), the following additional methods of producing fire support are essential:

(a) Support of the initial waves by direct close range fire, and by indirect fire when required.

Some form of gun comparable to the 25-pdr. gun now carried in special craft. This is fundamentally a military problem so far as the provision of the weapons, their manning and their employment is concerned. The craft would, however, have to be provided by the Navy.

(b) The support of the assault beyond the beach.

This is fundamentally a military problem though again the provision of the craft in which the guns are carried would be a naval responsibility. The requirement could be met by:

(i) Some form of gun comparable to the 25-pdr. gun now mounted in self-propelled armoured tracked carriers.

(ii) H.E. firing rocket projectors mounted in L.C.T.s provided trials proved satisfactory.

(c) The neutralising of enemy battery positions.

Fundamentally a naval and air problem. Guns of 4-in.-6-in. calibre mounted in monitors or 'Mobile Support Towers' in addition to any 15-in. gun support can be made available.

(d) Air support.

In all stages of the action, all forms of air support would be an urgent requirement.

Recommendations of the Technical Sub-Committee

The Technical Sub-Committee produced a paper which was taken by the Chiefs of Staff on 15th December. The conclusions of this paper were:

(a) Unless we are prepared to use old battleships and cruisers, we must build a number of 6-in. 15-knot monitors and self-propelled Maunsell towers. We recommend that the practicability of the latter should be examined at high priority.

(b) In close support, 52 special armoured craft mounting army type guns or howitzers are required for each assaulting Brigade.

(c) For immediate support of the Infantry as they advance we need 48 self-propelled guns for each assaulting Brigade.

(d) We note that there may be a requirement for Canal Defence Lights in special small craft, but this has not yet been fully examined.

C.C.O., who was present at the Chiefs of Staff meeting, in referring to the conclusions pointed out that some 100 guns would be required to support a Brigade Group, half in armoured craft and half in landing craft. This latter factor would result either in displacing a corresponding number of vehicles or in increasing the total number of landing craft required, or in reducing the number of brigades which could take part in an assault; if Maunsell towers proved feasible, the effect on the shortage of landing craft would be most beneficial.

The decisions of this meeting were that "R" Class battleships would not be used to support a landing, but that design and experiment for special gun craft should proceed at once. It was also decided that the construction of two pilot models of Maunsell towers should be accorded high priority.

As a result of these decisions, a meeting was held on 21st December, 1942, to discuss the armament of "Mobile Support Towers" and it was agreed that two towers would be designed, each mounting two 6-in. howitzers with ammunition on the scale of 200 rounds per gun. The question of fire control and communications was also investigated. In the event, other projects of a higher priority prevented production being completed in time for Normandy and the work on the prototype ceased in the spring of 1944 before firing trials had been conducted.

The First Designs of Landing Craft Gun (L.C.G.)

On 22nd December, 1942, a meeting was held at C.O.H.Q. to consider in detail the requirements for close support gun craft. The General Officer Combined Operations was in the chair and G.O.C.-in-C., 1st Canadian Army and the Director Royal Artillery were present, together with representatives from the Admiralty, War Office, G.H.Q. Home Forces and the Ministry of Supply. It was agreed that D.N.C. should produce two designs for this craft, one to have a speed of 15 knots and the other 10 knots. D.C.N.'s designs were discussed at a further meeting on 4th February, 1943, with C.C.O. in the chair, and he stated that agreement had been reached with U.S. authorities that the title of support craft should be L.C.G., and that there was little prospect of these craft being built in the U.S.A. for use by British Forces. At the Casablanca Conference he had emphasised the importance of this type of support and had given General Marshall a letter on this subject.

Conclusions of the meeting were: (1) That the speed of 15 knots was essential; (2) That the craft should mount two 25-pdrs., 17-pdrs. or 95-mm. guns; (3) That the quantitative demand for craft for 1944 should be based on 26 x 2-gun craft per Brigade, with a provision that, if Rocket craft were successful, this number may be reduced to 12.

The Conversion of Landing Craft Tank into Support Craft

It soon became apparent that it would not be possible to produce these L.C.G. (M), as they were to be called, before 1944, and that improvised support craft would have to fill the gap meanwhile. C.C.O. therefore made available an L.C.T. for experimental conversion to a provisional gun craft mounting two 4.7-in. naval guns in turrets. At the same time, an idea of mounting rockets in L.C.T.s put forward by Combined Operations Development Centre (C.O.D.C.), was given every encouragement by C.C.O., who saw in it a method of providing a great weight of concentrated fire on beach defences.

Rocket craft were discussed at a meeting held at C.O.H.Q. on 26th February, and it was decided, if experiments made with a prototype showed promise, to convert six L.C.T. (2) and equip each of them with 792 Rocket Projectors by 1st May.

Both these experiments proved successful and work was put in hand in March, 1943 for the conversion of further L.C.T.s. As a result, nine L.C.G. (L) (manned by Royal Marines) and three L.C.T. (R) were constructed in time to take part in Operation "Husky". The L.C.G. (L) were able to stand close inshore and engage pillboxes and bunkers with direct fire and cover the approach of the leading waves. Once Forward Observers were landed, these craft, grouped in threes and under the control of a Bombardment Liaison Officer, were able to provide indirect fire, when stopped, on target areas.

The L.C.T. (R), mounting 1,000 5-in. rockets in fixed mountings with a set range of 3,500 yards, fired onto the beaches some 10 minutes before touch-down, with devastating effect on the enemy, and at the same time gave enormous encouragement to the assault troops.

Self-Propelled Artillery

On 15th March there was a meeting to discuss the requirement of S.P. artillery. This was attended by representatives of the Director Royal Artillery, the Director of Artillery, and G.H.Q. Home Forces.

The conclusions reached were: (1) That there was a definite requirement for S.P. 25-pdrs. in assault; (2) On the basis of 8 Assault Brigades, each supported by 48 S.P. 25-pdrs, this would amount to the provision of 384 equipments, not including reserves; (3) Investigations should be made as to whether S.P. artillery could be waterproofed during manufacture.

Trials were therefore carried out under the direction of S.O. Force "J", firing S.P. 25-pdr. field guns from L.C.T.s approaching the beaches; a technique was evolved enabling the Field Regiments of Assault

Brigades to provide covering fire on the beach area during the run in of the leading waves.

Support in the Assault against a Heavily Defended Coast
C.C.O. had at this time been considering the establishment of a permanent Support Committee in C.O.H.Q. to prepare Fighting Instructions covering the use of fire power in the assault, but, at an executive meeting on 6th April, it was decided that the work of the Committee should be restricted to the preparation of a technical pamphlet, as Fighting Instructions must be written by Force Commanders. The Committee was established under the Chairmanship of D.D.X.S.R.

This Committee, in consultation with the Service Ministries, produced a paper: "Considerations governing the support of a seaborne assault against a heavily defended coast." This was submitted by C.C.O. to the Chiefs of Staff, as a result of which the First Sea Lord proposed that a Committee of all three Services should be set up to study the problem of the provision of close support of troops on a heavily defended coast. At their 190th Meeting on 17th August, the Chiefs of Staff agreed to this proposal and directed that an Inter-Services Committee should be set up as a matter of urgency with the following composition and terms of reference:

Composition:	Chairman to be nominated by C.C.O.
Members:	To include A.C.N.S. (W) and an officer to be nominated by the War Office and by the Air Ministry.
	The Committee to have power to extend its membership to include, *inter alia*, the Chief Scientific Advisors and to consult any of the authorities concerned.
Terms of Reference:	To consider all existing means of providing fire support when landing forces on a heavily defended coast, and to make recommendations, as a matter of urgency, for improving the degree of support.

The Inter-Service Committee first met at C.O.H.Q. on 4th September, under the Chairmanship of Air Vice-Marshal R. Graham (A.O.C.O.), the members being Rear-Admiral W. Patterson, Major-General J.A.C. Whitaker, Major-General W.J. Eldridge, Air Vice-Marshal W.A. Coryton and Air Vice-Marshal Breakey. The Scientific Advisers to the three Service Ministries attended all meetings, and representatives of the three Services Ministries, C.O.S.S.A.C., C-in-C. Portsmouth, C-in-C Fighter Command, C-in-C Bomber Command, VIII and IX U.S. Army Air Force, 21st Army Group, the Air Liaison Officer (Tactical Air Force) and C.O.H.Q. were present at the majority of the meetings.

Among the papers considered were all those submitted previously to the Chiefs of Staff by C.C.O. All existing means of support and those under development by C.C.O. were considered at subsequent meetings.

The Graham Report

The final report of this Committee was taken by the Chiefs of Staff on 23rd December, 1943, together with a seven-page covering note summarising the scope of the investigations, the conclusion and recommendations. As far as C.O.H.Q. was concerned, it was recommended that action should continue to: (1) Augment the fire support from landing craft and special craft in any way possible; (2) Investigate further the explosive head and/or fusing of 5-in. rockets; (3) Improve the arrangements for aircraft recognition and control of A.A. Fire.

The Chiefs of Staff agreed that the proposals submitted for improving the degree of fire support should receive attention of the highest priority and, when promising, should be developed.

The report became known as the Graham Report and was finally published as a Cabinet paper on 7th January, 1944. This paper had a wide distribution to planning staffs and, on request of C.C.O. copies were sent to D.C.O. (I), D.C.O. (M.E.), C.T.C. Largs and Combined Operations Staff S.E.A.C. It consisted in the main of statistical data governing weight of support required to neutralise or destroy various types of target under various conditions and was therefore a guide for planning, but it put forward no new methods or suggestions as to how close support might be provided in future operations.

About this time the paper produced by the Assault Warfare Committee for the Inter-Services Committee was published as a Combined Operations pamphlet entitled "Support of the Assault", with the object of presenting the problem of support in a seaborne assault against a defended coast after a short sea voyage; and depicting the combined resources of the three Services available for its solution through all its phases. The pamphlet included signal diagrams for the control of all types of seaborne and airborne support. C.O.H.Q. shortly after this, published the first pamphlet on the technique of firing S.P. artillery from L.C.T.s.

CLOSE SUPPORT AND COMBINED OPERATIONS BOMBARDMENT UNITS

The responsibility of keeping the Graham Report under review, and revising it in the light of operational experience, was delegated by the Joint Technical Warfare Committee to one of its sub-committees, on which C.O.H.Q. was represented by Professor Bernal and Commander Unwin.

This sub-committee studied the recent American operations in the Pacific and drew comparisons between the weight of fire support put down by U.S. Forces and the theoretical scales recommended in the Graham Report. It was found that only one-third of the theoretical scale was used and it appeared that there was no scientific analysis of the effects. C.C.O. put forward to the Technical Warfare Committee a proposal that a scientist who had experience on this subject should be sent to America to make a detailed study to the effect of fire support in the Pacific. This proposal was agreed by the Chiefs of Staff, so the Senior Scientific Advisor to the War Office, who was due to visit the B.J.S.M., was briefed to study this aspect of the war.

The most difficult problem still remained; the provision of close support between "H" hour and the deployment of the divisional field artillery. The L.C.G. (M.) had been designed to fill this gap, but, as stated previously, production fell far short of the requirement which was now assessed by the C.O.S.S.A.C. planners as 36 craft for each Assault Division. Two-thirds of these craft were required for H.E. support and one-third for dealing with concrete emplacements.

The L.C.G. (L.) had proved itself effective in dealing with concrete and adequate numbers were able to be produced. As an alternative to 25-pdr. L.C.G. (M.), C-in-C Home Forces put forward a proposal to C-in-C. Portsmouth, whom the Admiralty had made responsible for co-ordinating the demands for all support craft, to consider the possibility of mounting two Centaur tanks, armed with 95-mm. guns, on a platform in an armoured L.C.T. This proposal was readily accepted and C.-in-C. Portsmouth asked the Admiralty to make L.C.T.s available for this purpose. C.C.O. provided Bombardment Liaison Officers to assist in their training which took place at Studland Bay, where the L.C.G. (L.) were working up. The Admiralty agreed that the tanks, which had been made available by the War Office, should be manned by Royal Marines, and the Royal Marine Armoured Support Group (R.M.A.S.G.) was vested with its primary role, that of providing close support for the assault battalions. In "Overlord", the leading elements of the R.M.S.S.G. landed at "H" hour, only a few moments behind the D.D. tanks. Owing to the fact that only 60 per cent of their guns made the passage and that there was no F.O.O. within the R.M.A.S.G., their effectiveness was limited.

Recommendations for the Far East

During the autumn of 1944, C.O.H.Q. devoted much time to the study of the system of control of bombardment in "Overlord", with a view to improving it for the war in the Far East. A paper was sent to the three Service Ministries on 17th November, 1944, recommending certain increases in Liaison Officers and Control Staff as well as additional means of communications, with the object of reducing delays and ensuring that the guns and the various forms of observation were used to the best advantage and where most needed by the Army.

These recommendations were examined in detail at an inter-Services meeting at C.O.H.Q. on 8th February, 1945, and, as a result, a new organisation was submitted to the three Service Ministries. On request from C.C.O., this organisation was promulgated through inter-Service channels as well as in Combined Operations pamphlet No. 7C.

The new organisation reinforced the principle of centralised control and made provision for the control organisation being established ashore once Corps H.Q. was landed. This new organisation was shortly put into force and had its one and only trial in Operation "Zipper" (Malaya).

As can be seen from the previous paragraphs, thought was being given to the requirements for support in the Far East and, in accordance with the policy laid down by the Chiefs of Staff, it was the responsibility of the Army to state their requirements in terms of weight of fire. At the instigation of C.O.H.Q., the War Office held a meeting on 26th May, 1945, at which representatives from C.O.H.Q. were present. The scale of support craft required for each Assault Brigade was decided as being: 12 L.C.S. (R.), 12 L.C.G. (M.), 25-pdr., 4 L.C.G. (M.), 17-pdr.

The Admiralty were then asked to plan production on the basis of six Assault Brigades, but it was fully realised that owing to the production limitations, this quantity might not be produced initially but that the ratio of the three types should be maintained. It soon became apparent that the shortage of support craft would in fact be serious and that reliance would have to be made on some alternative and complementary means.

C.C.O. put forward proposals to the Admiralty and the War office on how this should be done and, at an inter-Services meeting on 13th December, 1944, it was decided that the deficiency in L.C.G. (M.), which was the most serious shortcoming, would have to be made good by mounting S.P. 25-pdrs. in L.C.T.s, and that C.O.H.Q. would promulgate a technique for this as well as investigating means of mounting 25-pdrs. in D.U.K.W. and L.V.T. However, the situation was somewhat eased by the retarding of the dates by which the three Assault Forces were to arrive in the Far East; the final War Office requirement was for one

Army Field Regiment (S.P.) to be mounted in L.C.T.s for each Assault Division. The Admiralty were able to make available the following craft for Force "W": 12 L.C.T. (R.), 8 L.C.G. (L.), 24 L.C.G. (M.).

In the event, the war came to an end before the assault on Malaya had taken place and, when Force "W" made their landing, no fire support was required.

It can be seen that the problem of close support was never mastered, principally due to the fact that it was never possible to produce in sufficient quantities the right type of specialist craft and weapons. C.O.H.Q., throughout all the stages of the war, was the main instigator in the development of technique and equipment.

Combined Operations Bombardment Units

On 15th June, 1941, the Commander of the Royal Marines Division wrote to the Adjutant-General Royal Marines, on the question of the provision of Forward Observation Officers (F.O.O.) for naval gunfire.

Training of Forward Observation Officers and Army Liaison Officers
He drew attention to the disparity between the "Manual of Combined Operation" and a D.C.O. Memorandum on "Opposed Landings". The former stating that bombarding ships will supply Naval F.O.O.s while the latter decreed that F.O.O.s would be Army officers and have Naval signals personnel. The Commander of the Royal Marines Division favoured Naval F.O.O.s.

The matter was referred to the D.C.O. who reaffirmed that F.O.O.s were to be Army officers, principally because of their value on the tactical side. Courses in naval gunnery at H.M.S. *Excellent* for Royal Artillery Officers had already started and C.s.R.A. of all the divisions of Home Forces had recently carried out indoor exercises in conjunction with Naval officers from the Gunnery School.

The following month, eleven selected officers who had already attended the course at Whale Island were sent to the C.T.C. at Inveraray for training as Forward Observers, or as Army Liaison Officers (A.L.O.) for duty on board the bombarding ships. Naval Telegraphists were provided for the communications and the first F.O.O. parties were formed. These parties subsequently trained with the Royal Marine Division which was, at that time, earmarked for the occupation of the Canaries (Operation "Pilgrim").

In July, 1941, the F.O.O. parties took part, with the Royal Marine Division, in Exercise "Leapfrog", and at once made their mark in the secondary role of providing the H.Q. Ship with tactical information on the situation ashore, much to everyone's surprise.

In August, 1941, the Admiralty drew attention to the fact that twelve courses had been run at H.M.S. *Excellent* and 179 Royal Artillery Officers had been trained there, but none of these had actually observed the fire of H.M. ships due to the lack of a bombardment range. D.C.O. replied that no further courses were necessary at the moment, but he was unable to get the Admiralty to provide a warship for bombardment training or a suitable range. Meanwhile, most of the officers who had been trained at Whale Island were attached to the newly-formed Force 110 for F.O.O. duties.

On 8th September, 1941, the Joint Commanders, Lieutenant-General Alexander and Rear-Admiral Hamilton, wrote to the Admiralty, the War Office and D.C.O., expressing their anxiety about the holding and further training of the twenty-three Royal Artillery Officers with their twenty naval and ten army signallers. The proposal submitted by the Joint Commanders was that D.C.O. should continue to assume responsibility for the training of F.O.O. parties, an operational school should be formed under his aegis, with the object of the initial training of F.O.O. parties and A.L.O.s as well as refresher courses of those attached to Force 110. This would necessitate the provision of suitable facilities, in particular a Naval Gunnery Officer Instructor, and they proposed that accommodation for the school of twenty-five officers and thirty naval ratings should be provided in a naval establishment.

The War Office agreed with the Joint Commanders' recommendations for the training of F.O.O.s and A.L.O.s, and promised to consider them in the plans, which were being drawn up, concerning the whole question of training for combined operations. A meeting was held in the D.C.O.'s office on 6th October, 1941, under the Chairmanship of Lieutenant-Colonel T.H. Ely, with representatives of the three Service Ministries, and the Senior F.O.O., Major A.T. Edgington, R.A., to discuss the further training of F.O.O.s and A.L.O.s.

As a result of this meeting, D.C.O. made V.A.C.T.C. responsible for the tactical training of F.O.O. parties and arranged with the Admiralty that a Naval Gunnery Officer would be added to his staff. V.A.C.T.C. was also made responsible for assisting the Force Commander in the further training of his bombardment teams. V.A.C.T.C. was asked to find a bombardment range and instructed to form a Bombardment School. It was also proposed that gunnery training should be undertaken with H.M.S. *Cardiff* which was then based at Lamlash. A range was eventually found on the Kintyre peninsula by the Captain of H.M.S. *Cardiff*; the Bombardment School was opened at Inverary in

October, 1941, under Captain F.K.R. Long, R.A., and the War Office agreed to provide officers to meet the D.C.O.'s requirements.

Madagascar, Operation "Ironclad", May 1942

During the autumn, F.O.O. parties trained with 29th Independent Brigade and ten officers and nine ratings, under the command of Captain R.L. Spiller, R.A., embarked in March, 1942, with Force 121 for the Madagascar operation. Three F.O.O. parties landed with the assault and the six bombarding ships were each provided with an A.L.O. During this operation there was little opportunity for naval support, but the principles evolved in training at the C.T.C. were found to be satisfactory, as was shown by the following extracts from the report of the Flag Officer Commanding Force "F":

"F.O.O.s carried out their bombardment duties in a very able manner and there were no cases of confusion between them and the firing ships. B.L.O.s (formerly A.L.O.s) were most useful. The organisation and training of these officers had been very efficiently carried out and their presence made it quite unnecessary to have a Naval F.O.O. or Directing Officer ashore."

The F.O.O. parties remained with 29 Independent Brigade and, other than one officer who returned to U.K., moved with it to India where they established a Bombardment Section.

Formation of No. 1 Bombardment Unit

The next and most important step taken was the proposal to form the individual F.O.O. parties, which were at the time attached to H.Q.R.A. Force 110, into a Unit. The idea was first put forward to the War Office by the Commander Force 110 in February, 1942, and was at once supported by C.C.O.

The term Bombardment Liaison Officer (B.L.O.) was adopted about the same time in place of A.L.O.

On 26th April, 1942, No. 1 Forward Observation and Bombardment Unit was formed at the C.T.C. Dundonald under the command of Lieutenant-Colonel L.S. Seccombe, R.A. Major Long continued as the Chief Instructor of the Bombardment School, which had moved to Dundonald in March, and which had now become an integral part of the Unit. Courses of three weeks' duration started in May and were held monthly; from the twelve students who attended each course, selected officers were posted to the Unit. C.C.O. retained operational control of the Unit and V.A.C.T.C. were made responsible for its training. The administration remained an Expeditionary Force responsibility, but all matters of policy and selection, with regard to appointments and promotions were referred to C.C.O.

The War Establishment strength of the Unit was forty-nine officers, fifteen gunners (Observation Post Assistants) and two clerks. It was sub-divided into three Sections each designed to support one Assault Division, each commanded by a Major and consisting of five F.O.O. parties and ten B.L.O.s. Unit Headquarters comprised the Lieutenant-Colonel, his Adjutant and two clerks. The Unit was not designed to be self-supporting and had therefore to be attached to another formation, the same applies to the sections. The naval ratings, who made up the communication personnel of the F.O.O. parties (two telegraphists and one signalman), were borne on the books of H.M.S. *Dundonald II* as part of a Beach Support Unit.

After their initial training at the C.T.C., F.O.O.s were attached to infantry and artillery units of the Expeditionary Force; and some carried out training with the Special Boat Section of Brigadier Laycock's Commandos.

In June, 1942, C.C.O. moved one section of the Unit down to the Isle of Wight for training with the 2nd Canadian Division and Force "J"; this section, under the command of Major G.F. Sinclair, R.A., took part later in the Dieppe operation.

Also in June, 1942, C.C.O obtained approval from the War Office to the change of title to No.1 Bombardment Unit as the old title was unnecessarily unwieldy.

The Dieppe Raid, Operation "Jubilee", August 1942

In the assault on Dieppe, three British F.O.O. parties were landed, together with three Canadian officers who had been trained at the Bombardment School. Major C.F. Sinclair, R.A., embarked in H.M.S. *Calpe* as the Senior B.L.O. and Major F.K.R. Long as his deputy was in the standby H.Q. Ship, H.M.S. *Fernie*. B.L.O.s were embarked in the five *Hunt* Class destroyers, one in the gunboat *Locust* and one in the Polish destroyer *Slazak*. The F.O.O.s suffered heavy casualties, two were killed and two were taken prisoner; one, a Canadian, subsequently escaped through Spain and was awarded the D.S.O. Four of the B.L.O.s were wounded.

The Section remained with Force "J" expanding to a Unit in January, 1944. The third Section of the Unit was formed shortly after Dieppe in order to provide the requisite number of F.O.O.s and B.L.O.s for Operation "Torch".

Formation of Bombardment Troops authorised by the War Office

The demand for F.O.O.s was constantly increasing as more and more combined operations were being planned and more forces raised.

C.C.O. submitted a proposal to the War Office in October, 1942, for the formation of a Bombardment Training Pool which would hold and train F.O.O. parties and B.L.O.s at Dundonald in readiness for allotment to formations earmarked for an assault. These proposals involved a non-operational headquarters of five officers and an unspecified number of operational bombardment troops, each of sixteen officers.

However, this plan met with a certain amount of opposition, particularly from the War Establishment Committee, and was finally withdrawn in December when C.C.O. put forward a proposal to form Headquarters Bombardment Unit, Bombardment Wing, Combined Training Centre, consisting of three officers and eight other ranks at Dundonald, which would be under the command of the Commandant and administered by the staff of the C.T.C. At the same time an establishment for a standard Bombardment Troop consisting of a Major, fifteen Captains and five Artillery N.C.O.s was submitted. These proposals were agreed by the War Office War Establishment Committee at the end of the year and, on 9th January, 1943, C.C.O. asked the War Office to mobilise four Bombardment Troops to meet the following requirements:

(1) One Troop in the Western Mediterranean to exploit any opportunities for naval bombardment in support of land operations that may continue to occur.
(2) One Troop with Force 125. (For capture of Canary Islands but the Force was never mounted.)
(3) One Troop with Force "J".
(4) One Troop to be trained for attachment to Force "K". (A naval striking force based on Malta.)

The War Office approved and authorised the raising of a fifth Troop when required. This Troop organisation remained throughout the war in Europe, except that early in 1944 when more Troops were required, further Bombardment Units, each of three Troops, were raised, and the Troops then comprised seven F.O.B. parties each.

North Africa, Operation "Torch"

In 1942 "Torch" involved five F.O.O. parties with the U.S. 2nd Corps at Oran and five B.L.O.s in the supporting British warships. Major F.K.R. Long, R.A., was the Senior B.L.O. on Admiral Troubridge's staff in the H.Q. Ship *Largs*.

At Algiers, seven F.O.O. parties were landed, including two with No. 6 Commando and one with No. 1 Commando. Colonel L.S. Seccombe R.A., was released by C.C.O. to be Senior B.L.O. in the Force H.Q. Ship

Largs on the proviso that he would be returned immediately after the operation. The main shore bombardments took place at Oran where H.M.S. *Rodney*, on call from an F.O.O., bombarded the fort of Djebel Santon intermittently for two days before its final surrender.

The F.O.O.s again proved their worth, not only in directing ships' fire but also in providing communication between H.Q. Ships and units ashore. The final attack on Oran by two American Regimental Combat Teams was ordered by the Corps Commander in the H.Q. Ship through an F.O.O. In the middle of the battle of Oran, the Squadron Signals Officer, Lieutenant-Commander Phillimore, R.N., decided to allot a special communications wave for bombardment traffic between ships. This was found to be so successful in speeding up the reallocation of ships to F.O.O.s and the receipt of shore information on board the H.Q. Ship that it became thereafter standard practice. On more than one occasion a F.O.O., through his attached bombarding ship, called for and was given air support, the combination of air strikes and naval gunfire proved most effective in reducing the main resistance from the French forts.

After the completion of Operation "Torch" all the F.O.O.s and B.L.O.s were recalled by C.C.O. to their parent unit at the C.T.C. for re-equipping and refresher training.

F.O.O.s in Support of Airborne Forces.

Early in 1943, C.C.O. foresaw the possibility for the employment of F.O.O.s in support of the rapidly expanding airborne forces. Major-General Haydon made arrangements with Major-General Hopkinson, commanding the Airborne Division, for F.O.O. parties to be trained as parachutists at Ringway. By the time Operation "Husky" started to be planned in earnest, there was in existence a small pool of parachute-trained F.O.O. parties, for whom C.C.O. had obtained the additional qualification pay granted to the parachutists of the Airborne Division.

C.C.O. on request of the Commander-in-Chief, Mediterranean, sent out, in March, 1943, the first contingent of F.O.O.s consisting of twelve parties, under Major F.K.R. Long, R.A., who were destined to remain in that theatre for the rest of the war. Seven parachute trained F.O.O. parties followed in May and joined the 1st Airborne Division. By August the strength of the F.O.O.s in the Mediterranean had grown to seventy officers and one hundred naval telegraphists and other ranks; and with the agreement of C.C.O., a headquarters and training base for them was established at the C.T.C. Djidjelli which had a good bombardment range in the neighbourhood. This detachment thereafter became the responsibility of the Commander-in-Chief, Mediterranean, but C.C.O. remained responsible for the provision of trained reinforcements and replacements.

Sicily, Operation "Husky"

Planning at home also was proceeding for Operation "Husky", and C.C.O. allotted one Bombardment Troop to Force "V" early in 1943.

The Sicilian operation offered the first opportunity of testing the command-and-control organisation for naval gunfire support, to which so much time and thought had been applied by C.O.H.Q. since the North African landings. Thirty-one F.O.O. parties were employed in the assault and were controlled by three Senior B.L.O.s in the Divisional H.Q. Ships, *Keren*, *Largs* and *Hilary*. The effectiveness of the naval support given throughout the campaign brought Admiral MacGrigor a personal signal of appreciation from General Dempsey, the G.O.C. 13th Corps.

The main lesson learned in Sicily was the essential need for F.O.O. parties to be provided with their own transport as it was impossible for them to keep up with fast-moving infantry battalions and, at the same time, engage targets and report the battle situation to the H.Q. Ship. In spite of every effort by C.O.H.Q. it was not until shortly before Normandy that the establishment of a Bombardment Troop was amended to include vehicles for the F.O.O.s parties. Sicily was shortly followed by the invasion of Italy, where the F.O.O.s, under Commander-in-Chief, Mediterranean, were deployed to meet the requirements of the Assault Force Commanders. No new principles were evolved, but strides were made towards combining Air O.P.s and F.O.O.s.

At Salerno, fifteen F.O.O. parties were deployed with 10th Corps, the Commandos and U.S. Rangers, and between them over 270 targets were engaged. F.O.O.s were subsequently redeployed for the Anzio landings.

Reorganisation and Expansion. Change of Title to Combined Operations Bombardment Unit (C.O.B.U.)

Meanwhile in the U.K., more Bombardment Troops were raised to meet the commitment of "Overlord". C.C.O. obtained, from the War Office on 1st January, 1944, approval to change the Bombardment Unit Organisation of a headquarters and up to six Troops to three Headquarters Bombardment Units each with three Troops. But it was not until after much correspondence that a provisional reorganised establishment for the new type Units and Troops, each with their own vehicles, was authorised on 28th March, 1944. The title Combined

Operations Bombardment Unit (C.O.B.U.) came into force at the end of April.

At the same time as this reorganisation was taking place, the Admiralty had under consideration the organisation, administration and status of the Beach Support Units of which the F.O.B.s telegraphists were a part. The question of the number required for future operations was also being considered.

C.C.O. proposed that the title, Beach Support Unit, should be dropped and that a naval equivalent of a Bombardment Troop should be introduced. With the Admiralty's agreement, the naval element of the Bombardment Troop eventually became a Naval Section Bombardment Troop (N.S.B.T.). The N.S.B.T. consisted of one Petty Officer Telegraphist, two Leading Telegraphists and twenty Telegraphists, and was commanded by a Combined Operations Signals Officer. Seven provisional N.S.B.T.s were, however, formed and the officers appointed in time for Normandy. They were numbered to coincide with their equivalent Combined Operations Bombardment Troops, for example No. 3A N.S.B.T. operated with "A" Troop of No. 3 C.O.B.U. This was the first time the naval organisation became parallel and directly connected with the army organisation and establishment.

A change in the nomenclature was finally brought about on 29th January, 1944, when the three Service Ministries eventually agreed to C.C.O.'s recommendation, instigated in November, 1943, that F.O.O.s controlling naval gunfire should be known as F.O.B.s (Forward Observers Bombardment) to avoid confusion with the F.O.O.s of the Army controlling land artillery.

While this expansion of Bombardment Units was proceeding, C.C.O. had been discussing with the War Office the question of control of the three Units (which shortly was increased to four on request of 21 Army Group) and proposals were submitted for a Headquarters Combined Operations Bombardment Unit.

Commander Bombardment Units Appointed

A meeting was held in the War Office on 21st March, at which the D.C.O. Military put forward the case for a Colonel with a G.S.O. 3 and two clerks to compose the H.Q.C.O.B.U. The necessity for this Unit was agreed and it was subsequently sponsored by the R.A. Directorate. The establishment was authorised on 5th May, and the appointment of Commander Bombardment Units was filled by Colonel L.S. Seccombe, R.A. who set up his headquarters at C.O.H.Q., with the functions of: (1) Adviser to C.C.O. on the development and policy affecting the Bombardment Units and their equipment; (2) Chief Bombardment

Officer (C.B.O.) on the Staff of A.N.C.X.F., responsible for the provision of troops to implement their planning and to advise on planning; [and] (3) Training of approximately 200 officers, 100 N.C.O.s and 275 naval ratings of the four Combined Operations Bombardment Units.

Employment of Combined Operations Bombardment Units in Operation "Overlord"

The Combined Operations Bombardment Units were deployed for "Overlord" as follows:

>C.B.O. with Allied Naval Commander Expeditionary Force.
>Chief B.L.O. with Naval Commander Eastern Task Force.
>Chief B.L.O. with Naval Commander Western Task Force.
>11 F.O.B.s with 50th Division.
>10 F.O.B.s with 3rd Canadian Division.
>8 F.O.B.s with 3rd British Division.
>6 F.O.B.s with 6th Airborne Division.
>7 F.O.B.s with Commandos.

Staff Officers Bombardment (S.O.B.) were attached to U.S. 5 and 7 Corps and British 1 and 30 Corps, as well as to H.Q.R.A. of each British Division. Seventy-eight B.L.O.s were embarked in supporting ships and craft.

In the assault, the initial shoots were observed and controlled by fighter aircraft according to a prearranged plan; the pilots had been trained in "Airspot" procedure by the Bombardment Wing at the C.T.C. and had worked up with warships firing on the Kintyre range. The F.O.B. parties which landed with the Assault Brigades, met considerable opposition and several parties were completely knocked out very early on "D" Day, while the majority of those with the Airborne Division were so widely scattered that they were unable to operate satisfactorily for at least 24 hours.

The close nature of the countryside made observation difficult unless an O.P. was established in some obvious point of vantage such as a church tower or factory chimney. However, many targets were engaged effectively without observation as a result of information obtained from patrols. These "blind" shoots were a novel feature of the first few days of the assault.

On each divisional front, the control of bombardment was exercised by the Combined Support Control in the H.Q. Ship. F.O.B.s were re-allocated to ships to meet the changing requirements of the military situation ashore.

Once H.Q.R.A. was established ashore together with its S.O.B. party, Naval Bombardment was co-ordinated with the Divisional Artillery's day to day fire plans and included at night in harassing fire tasks. By the time 1st Corps Headquarters was established ashore, the majority of warships were concentrated in support of the left of the Eastern Sector and the S.O.B., in conjunction with the C.R.A.'s Staff, co-ordinated the support from the Bombarding Force. A considerable amount of counter-battery fire was undertaken by warships, details of targets being supplied through the S.O.B. from the Corps counter-battery staff. Air O.P.s observed for the supporting warships, relaying through F.O.B.s situated on their landing strips.

Naval gunfire was used to the extreme limits of the heavier ships' maximum range in support of the final attack on Caen and the subsequent advance eastward by the 6 Airborne Division. By this time, the H.Q. Ships had been withdrawn and Bombardment Control Headquarters was set up ashore at Courseulles, the Headquarters of the Flag Officer British Assault Area. As the advance eastwards was continued, a Mobile Bombardment Headquarters moved along the coast and co-ordinated the requirements for warships' fire with the Flag Officer Commanding the Bombarding Force.

Naval support was required less and less as the artillery built up its strength ashore and, by 20th July, only "B" Troop of No. 3 C.O.B.U. was left in France. This Troop moved to Ostend for the Walcheren assault.

The Far East

As mentioned earlier, the majority of the officers employed as F.O.B.s and B.L.O.s in Madagascar moved with 29 Independent Infantry Brigade to India where a Bombardment Section was formed. The decision to form a Unit coincided with the arrival, in the autumn of 1943, of Rear-Admiral L.E.H. Maund, to be Director of Combined Operations, India.

Initially the Unit consisted of a Headquarters and two Troops, each Troop being designed to support an Assault Division, and consisting of five F.O.B. parties, ten B.L.O.s and one Senior B.L.O. (Major). The Unit was raised at the C.T.C. Madh Island and shortly afterwards, in November 1943, a revised establishment for No. 5 C.O.B.U. was approved by the Support Bombardment and Reconnaissance Committee of the Directorate of Combined Operations, India. It had a Lieutenant-Colonel in command and introduced, as a result of experience gained in Europe, a second officer (Subaltern R.A.) into each F.O.B. party and a jeep with trailer for its transport. Lieutenant-Colonel E. McEwen-Window, R.A., was appointed Commanding Officer and his duties included Chief Bombardment Liaison Officer to the Commander-in-Chief, Eastern Fleet.

The Commanding Officer was responsible to the Commander-in-Chief, Eastern Fleet for the general efficiency and training of the Unit and also for liaison with the Navy. He had direct access to M.G.R.A. (India) on artillery matters and to the D.C.O. (I) on operational matters. The initial training of the F.O.B. parties and B.L.O.s took place at the C.T.C. and, as no combined operations were mounted in 1944, the personnel of the Unit were sent to gain battle experience with the XIVth Army in Assam. One of the main lessons that emerged from this was that a proportion of the ratings should be R.I.N. and, as a result, two R.I.N. ratings were included in each F.O.B. party. These ratings were trained at the Combined Signals School, H.M.S. *Braganza III*. Gunnery training took place at the R.I.N. Gunnery School near Karachi and, a little later, F.O.B. parties were trained as parachutists at Chaklala.

Early in 1944, with the expansion of the C.T.C., the Unit moved to Juhu where its Headquarters remained until the end of the war. A bombardment range was established on Manori Island (north of Madh) where R.I.N. sloops and gunboats carried out practice firings.

In December, 1944, the Unit took part in its first operation in the Arakan and, from then on, was continually deployed with one Troop in support of 15 Corps at Akyab and subsequently at Myebon and Kangaw, the second Troop at Ramree, Cheduba and Rangoon.

Early in 1945, the requirements of bombardment personnel for the war against Japan were reviewed in S.E.A.C. and it was envisaged that one Unit of three Troops would be required, together with a Training Wing. The Commander Bombardment Units (C.B.U.) flew to India in April and discussed the proposals for a new and increased C.O.B.U. War Establishment which was being prepared by the War Office and C.C.O. The result of this visit was the formation of the Combined Operations Bombardment Unit (Light). This Unit consisted of a H.Q. and three Troops with a total of 79 officers and 146 O.R.s. A new Unit, No. 6 C.O.B.U., was formed in the U.K. on this establishment at the end of June and moved out to India in August. The remaining personnel of No. 5 C.O.B.U. were absorbed into the new Unit; Lieutenant-Colonel W. Hewitt, R.A., who had commanded No. 5 C.O.B.U., was flown out from the U.K. to the Staff of Force "W", who were then completing, in Bombay, their plans for the invasion of Malaya.

Revised Responsibilities of the Commander Bombardment Units

In March, 1945, C.C.O. drafted for the approval of the three Service Ministries, a directive for the Commander Combined Operations Bombardment Units, which detailed the Control of Bombardment Units and gave the C.B.U. the command of all units in the theatre in which he, with his Headquarters was situated. He was made responsible for giving technical advice on policy and training, initiating changes in organisation and equipment and advising Force Commanders on the sub-allotment of his Units. The channel of communications was also detailed. These instructions were approved by the Service Ministries and distributed to Supreme Commanders and Commanders-in-Chief on 24th April, 1945.

Formation of a Naval Section Bombardment Unit (N.S.B.U.)

Meanwhile as a result of lessons learned in Normandy, C.C.O. had forwarded proposals, submitted by H.M.S. *Dundonald II*, to the Admiralty on the reconstitution of the naval element of the C.O.B.U. It had been found during "Overlord" that when the Headquarters of a Bombardment Unit landed and established itself at Corps Headquarters, it was frequently necessary to remove the Combined Operations Communication Officer of the N.S.B.T. from Division to Corps Headquarters to assist in the control of the N.S.B.T.s and bombardment communications. The final naval organisation that was eventually agreed and promulgated on 21st June, 1945, was a Naval Section Bombardment Unit consisting of three communication officers and eighty-five ratings. This N.S.B.U. was designed to dovetail in with the C.O.B.U. and divide into a headquarters and three Sections. This organisation became effective in time for Operation "Zipper" and a N.S.B.U. was deployed with 6 C.O.B.U. in support of 34 Corps.

In the event, peace was declared just before the assault, but the F.O.B.s remained with the infantry battalions and, for the first 24 hours of "Zipper", provided H.Q. 34th Corps afloat with their only wireless link to their formations ashore. The Unit's last operations ended on the same note as the first exercise in 1942, by proving so convincingly that F.O.B. communications can play not only a vital part by calling for ships' fire, but also by providing an invaluable link between the H.Q. Ship and formations ashore.

Chapter 17

COMBINED OPERATIONS SIGNALS ORGANISATION

In October, 1941, when Commodore Lord Mountbatten was appointed Adviser on Combined Operations, there was no signal department at Combined Operations Headquarters. There was at this time an Inter-Services Committee sitting at the War Cabinet Office, whose directive was to investigate and report to the Chiefs of Staff Committee on "Communications in Combined Operations".

The Inter-Service Communications Committee
This subject had in the past received little attention and, in view of the likely course of the war, was obviously one of great importance. This Committee was under the Chairmanship of a Captain R.N. with naval, military and air force members and was then at work on its first report. The naval member had, incidentally, been involved in the abortive Dakar operation and was acutely aware of the lack of up-to-date doctrine on this subject, and the absence of the necessary specialised ships, equipment and trained personnel.

With the arrival of the new Advisor on Combined Operations, a naval signal officer was appointed to C.O.H.Q. as Signal Officer Combined Operations for inter-Service signal duties, and almost immediately, took over the Chairmanship of the above-mentioned Committee in addition to his duties at C.O.H.Q. It was soon realised, however, that the scope of the signal work at C.O.H.Q., both in connection with the signals of the growing Combined Operations Organisation and the development of combined operations communications technique, then practically non-existent, was far too great for one officer. It was therefore decided, in agreement with the Chiefs of Staff Committee and the Service Ministries, that the Committee should move to C.O.H.Q. to complete its work, and that the naval, military and air force members of it should join C.C.O.'s staff under the Chairman who, as a Captain R.N., became Chief Signal Officer Combined Operations.

In the course of their deliberations on the subject of "communications in combined operations", the Inter-Services Communications Committee submitted six reports during the period from December, 1941 to May, 1942. The subject of these reports were as follows:

(1) W/T equipment.
(2) Support Control. This included the H.Q. Ship requirement.
(3) Cyphers, codes and code names.
(4) Line communications.
(5) Radar.
(6) Anglo-American signals co-operation.

The succeeding paragraphs cover these reports in greater detail.

W/T Equipment required for Combined Operations
By December, 1941, the report on W/T equipment had been passed by the Combined Operations Committee and was forwarded to the Chiefs of Staff and Service Ministries for early action in view of the unsatisfactory state of affairs. All Services stressed the urgent need for specialist equipment, particularly:

(1) Light, portable and waterproofed equipment for beach operation. Some of that recommended for combined operations purposes eventually passed into much wider use (e.g., Nos. 22 and 46 sets).
(2) Additional equipment, especially R/T sets and VH/F sets, for rapid installation in ships of all kinds in order to increase their communications facilities at short notice.
(3) Provision of transportable or mobile R/T equipment and warning radar for ground-air use.

The Headquarters Ship
The Committee then continued its work at C.O.H.Q. and produced, in January, 1942, its second report which dealt with "Support Control in Combined Operations", an aspect of amphibious communications which had, in the past, been far from satisfactory. It was during the preparation of this report that the idea of the H.Q. Ship was resurrected

as a matter of urgency, and practical recommendations were made for its fulfilment; earlier concepts were rejected as too limited and slow of execution, and the Committee's opinion was that the signal communications in an amphibious operation could not reach the required standard of efficiency without the use of such ships. In their opinion, also, the special amphibious ships and craft then being built, the army formations then undergoing or about to undergo amphibious training and the air force units which would eventually be used, could not be employed to the best advantage unless H.Q. Ships were provided, from which combined control and communications could be exercised.

The Chiefs of Staff Committee noted the report and decided that this matter should be pursued, but this course was not without difficulties since various disadvantages were apparent to the Ministries concerned. There was the acute shortage of shipping which caused the Ministry of War Transport to be averse to providing any ships for the purpose. Further, whilst it was agreed that it was desirable for the naval, military and air commanders to be together during an operation, the naval commander had in the past always been in a man-of-war, the military commander was in the habit of landing at a very early stage with his troops, and the air commander preferred remaining at a shore headquarters where very full communication facilities were available.

It was realised that the full air communications and radar requirements could not be fitted in the H.Q. Ship and that the ideal would be one with an associated fighter direction (or perhaps air control) ship, but, with the shortage of shipping, this ideal was agreed to be unattainable at the time.

After various meetings between the three Services to decide on communication requirements for such a ship, an armed merchant cruiser, H.M.S. *Bulolo*, was made available and was taken in hand in April, 1942, at Messrs. Green and Silley Weir, Royal Albert Docks, London, for conversion to a specification produced by C.O.H.Q.

The communication requirements were briefly: V/S – standard of cruiser flagship; W/T and R/T – approximately 19 transmitting sets, 23 receiving sets; D/F – navigational only (H/F D/F was not a requirement); [and] L/T – line terminals for both speech and telegraph circuits.

The conversion of H.M.S. *Bulolo* was completed in mid-June, 1942, Later H.M.S. *Largs* was converted and she, with H.M.S. *Bulolo*, took part with success in the North African operation. It was by then recognised that the H.Q. Ship was an essential feature of an assault force and further ships were converted. There was still, however, great difficulty in obtaining suitable ships owing to the grave shortage of shipping and constant opposition was met from officers who disliked "putting all the eggs in one basket."

The counter-argument that the eggs could not otherwise be carried, however, won the day and was justified by events. The American authorities had by now adopted the idea and produced several excellent H.Q. Ships built to a much more ambitious specification, which was, nevertheless, based directly on that of H.M.S. *Bulolo*. In the invasion of the Continent, a large number of H.Q. Ships, both British and American, took part, including a new smaller type of H.Q. Ship and the Landing Craft Headquarters, both of which were built according to C.O.H.Q. specification.

Cyphers, Codes and Code Names in Combined Operations

In February, 1942, the Inter-Services Committee sent in its third report dealing with the signal books required in a combined operation, which must be common to all Services taking part.

Most of these requirements were covered by the programme for common communications systems which were then in hand for the three Services and later included the U.S. Army and Navy, but several special Combined Operations pamphlets were required and these were compiled at C.O.H.Q. They included the Combined Operations Signal Book, the Combined Operations Code and Landing Craft Signal Pamphlet.

Line Communications in Combined Operations

The fourth report, which was also sent in by the Inter-Services Committee in February, 1942, dealt with land-line requirements in an amphibious operation, with particular reference to a continental operation. Firstly, the question of cross-Channel telephone and teleprinter requirements were discussed and, secondly, the line requirements to serve the shore headquarters.

Meetings were held with the G.P.O. and the earmarking of cable ships, the manufacture of submarine cable and the building of static and mobile terminals were put in hand. At a later date, after the range of V.H/F communication had been further investigated by C.O.H.Q. and tested in the Dieppe operation, a plan was initiated known as the "south coast radio scheme". This enabled V.H/F radio links to be used as soon as our invasion forces had landed. Static terminals were built on high ground at such places as Beachy Head and Ventnor (Isle of Wight), and were connected to the normal telephone system on the south coast;

for landing on the far side, mobile equipment was constructed. In the event, very good communication was established, in the early stages of the invasion, between H.Q. Ships off the Normandy coast and any required locality in England.

Meetings were also held to warn the G.P.O. of the very heavy line requirements of the Combined Headquarters which were being built on the south coast. These requirements appeared to be astronomical, but were finally met by the efforts of the G.P.O. and proved to be by no means excessive.

Radar in Combined Operations

The fifth report sent in by the Committee dealt with radar requirements in combined operations and included, *inter alia*, the recommendation for fighter direction ships. Again, the shortage of shipping prevented implementation for some time, but L.S.T.s were fitted as fighter direction tenders before the Sicily operation, one with a R.A.F. mobile G.C.I. unit temporarily embarked and operating on board. This requirement had been recognised when shipping had been sunk by night bombers at captured ports during the North African operation, and the G.C.I. did much to prevent repetition of this off the coast of Sicily. Later, more ships were permanently fitted and naval fighter direction ships, which had not been fitted for an amphibious role, were reconverted. In the invasion of the Continent, a large number of fighter direction ships and tenders took part, and subsequently the L.S.T. (1) class were put in hand for conversion.

It is pertinent, at this juncture, to mention that at C.O.H.Q. a study was made of the radio warfare problems that would arise in a major Channel operation, including both the implementation of cover plans and radio countermeasures against enemy radar. The plan that eventually came into operation in the Normandy invasion, especially in the latter field where conspicuous success was achieved, owed much to these studies.

Anglo-American Co-operation in Combined Operations

The sixth and final report was completed in May. This dealt with the problem of Anglo-American co-operation in combined operations.

In brief the report recommended that strenuous efforts be made to achieve the maximum standardisation of methods between the various Services of both countries.

Later in the year, the Chief Signal Officer Combined Operations went on a short visit to Washington to discuss combined amphibious communication technique with the Combined Communications Board (C.C.B.) in Washington, with a view to the production of a combined publication on the subject. As a result of this visit, the C.C.B. sent a group of officers to London and a series of meetings with the Signal Staff of C.O.H.Q. took place. A draft was produced at C.O.H.Q. and after it was agreed by the U.S. authorities, was published as C.C.B.P. 01.

The Formation of the Combined Operations Communication Committee

After the reports mentioned above had been forwarded, the Inter-Services Committee on Communication in Combined Operations ceased to function as such, but the members continued their work at C.O.H.Q., which included the follow up and implementation of the recommendations in the reports. They then formed the "Combined Operations Communications Committee", which C.C.O. in his directive had been ordered to set up.

In order to cope with the additional work at C.O.H.Q. which was brought about by the rapidly growing Combined Operations Organisation, it had become necessary to increase the staff of the signal department so small naval, army and air force sections were formed under their respective senior staff officers.

Signal Personnel and Training

During 1940, it became apparent that a combined organisation was required for training signal personnel of the three Services and for co-ordinating their activities in any combined exercise in which they might be taking part prior to operations.

With this end in view, in the autumn of 1940, when Vice-Admiral Combined Training hoisted his flag at Inveraray, a Lieutenant R.N., a Major Royal Signals and a Squadron Leader R.A.F. were appointed. These three formed a Combined Signal Board to establish a Combined Signal School and to plan and train for future communication requirements for amphibious operations.

The Combined Signal School at Inveraray, under the command of a Commander R.N., commenced to function as such on 1st November, 1941. The school consisted of forty-five Nissen huts, thirty used for accommodation and fifteen for lecture rooms, with a further nine huts in the course of erection for additional classrooms. The instructional staff totalled eight officers and fourteen ratings from the Royal Navy and Army. The only R.A.F. Officer was the member of the Combined Signal Board.

Early in 1942, it became apparent that more co-operation with the R.A.F. was needed and that a landing strip was essential. This was not available at Inveraray. It was therefore decided to move the Combined Signal School from Inveraray to Dundonald, about 2½ miles north of Troon, Ayrshire. The school was commissioned on 1st April, 1942, as H.M.S. *Dundonald II*, the name of the ancient Royal Stuart stronghold close by.

Training of officers and ratings of all Services proceeded with ever-increasing tempo. Personnel concerned included navy and army beach signal parties (trained together), forward observation parties (comprising army and navy personnel), air force parties for forward air control and H.Q. Ship detachments which included naval, army and air force personnel. Special Naval Combined Operations Signal Officers were also trained. This school held up to 400 personnel and the necessary landing craft; signal equipment and a mock-up H.Q. Ship were provided. In addition, a school for landing craft signalmen was later established at H.M.S. *Pasco* on the Clyde. This became necessary when it was finally agreed that landing craft needed signalmen and that the only way to provide the necessary numbers was to give Combined Operations seamen a short signal course confined only to those aspects of signals required in landing craft. There was also a Navigational Aids school at Northney, on Hayling Island, where the necessary personnel were trained in the use of wireless, radar and infra-red navigation aids.

Beach Signal Sections

The necessity for specially trained naval and army beach signal personnel was recognised in 1940 and, by the beginning of 1941, the first Beach Signal Section was formed and trained. A further three sections had been formed by the end of 1941 and, by the time of the invasion of Normandy, as many as eighteen Naval Beach Signal Sections had been formed and trained at the Combined Signal School.

A naval section consisted of twenty-eight communications ratings under the command of a Sub-Lieutenant R.N.V.R. who had been specially trained as a Beach Signal Officer. Once formed a section carried out intensive working up as a team. A physical hardening course was carried out during which wet and dry landings from minor landing craft on to rocks and quays, up rope-ladders and through surf were practised. Instruction was also given in the care and use of arms, first aid, map reading and assault course, and battle training was undertaken in realistic conditions.

At a certain stage in its training, the Naval Beach Signal Section was joined to an Army Beach Signal Section and the two sections became a unit which was then allotted to a Beach Group. Advance training then proceeded.

Combined Headquarters

Very close touch was kept with the signal departments of the three Service Ministries and the senior signal officers of each Service at C.O.H.Q. paid almost daily visits to the Directors of Signals and their staff at Admiralty, War Office and Air Ministry. In this way much time was saved, misunderstandings avoided and paper work reduced to a minimum.

With the growing Combined Operations Organisation and constant dealing with various Service authorities, a comprehensive signal office organisation was required at C.O.H.Q. The existing communications system of the three Services were utilised for this purpose, C.O.H.Q. being connected as necessary to various Service telephone and teleprinter switchboards. The Signal Officer at C.O.H.Q. was manned entirely by personnel of the Women's Services and formed a separate section under a W.R.N.S. Officer. The Duty Signal Officers were W.R.N.S., A.T.S. or W.A.A.F in rotation and the remainder of the staff came from the same three Services. A local combined method of message handling was used inside C.O.H.Q. and all personnel were trained to use the necessary different procedures when dealing with the various Services.

One of the tasks given to the signal department of C.O.H.Q. was organising the layout and planning the communications of the underground Combined Headquarters which might be required for the invasion.

The Portsmouth Headquarters, the excavation of which had already begun, was the first of these and was finally the most important in the invasion. It was realised that this, although large, would not be big enough for the final invasion requirements but, as it had a fixed completion date for an operation which did not finally take place, there was no time to have manufactured the necessary steel rings required for wider tunnels or to have additional excavations made.

During the Normandy invasion, the Headquarters of the Allied Army and Naval C.s-in-C. were placed near this Combined Headquarters, thereby increasing its scope after building up its resources as a communications centre; this could not have been done but for the permanent arrangement already established.

The next Combined Headquarters to be constructed was at Dover. After considerable discussion as to its location, it was decided to excavate under the existing tunnels of the Castle where the staff of Vice-Admiral, Dover, was already housed. Plenty of time was available and a very good headquarters was constructed which, however, was never fully used since the objectives finally chosen for the invasion operation did not call for an assault headquarters at Dover. This headquarters was, however, exploited as a key point in the cover plan, in the furtherance of which the work put into it and the W/T facilities provided were most important factors.

The third Headquarters, originally considered as the least important, was at Plymouth. On this occasion discussion as to its location was even more protracted, but a decision was finally reached to excavate an extension to the existing Area Combined Headquarters. Various delays were experienced and it was only completed shortly before the invasion, in which it was of major importance to the Western (American) Task Force.

Signal Maintenance Depot, Ashford

To cope with all the special equipment now required for combined operations, a signal maintenance depot was established at Ashford, near Staines. Here was stored and maintained the necessary equipment that might be wanted in an operation, and this could be issued at very short notice when required, complete with the requisite ancillary gear such as batteries and crystals. This was a requirement not formerly met under normal conditions because ships were self-supporting in this respect. On completion of operations, this equipment was returned and repaired or reconditioned as necessary.

Modifications to existing equipment to meet special requirements could be quickly carried out at this depot, whereas it could not be done elsewhere without upsetting the normal work of other Service establishments. Mobile wireless maintenance units mounted in lorries were evolved and fitted at Ashford. Many were later sent abroad and still more were used for the invasion. A mobile crystal grinding unit was also designed and a small number were used both abroad and at home. This organisation was later expanded with sub-depots added and was of great value in operation "Overlord".

The Dieppe Raid, August, 1942

During 1942, various small raids culminating in Dieppe took place. In addition, many more raids were mounted, and even more planned.

For these the signal department of C.O.H.Q. prepared the outline signal plan, obtained or improvised the special equipment to be used, made arrangements for the specialised personnel and supervised their training. Each operation had its own special requirements and special equipment was invariably needed. The various types of special radio equipment required are too numerous to mention but were mainly concerned with the problem of getting to the right place.

This problem came to a head during the preparations for the Dieppe raid when, in a rehearsal, various elements of the force failed to make landfalls with anything like the necessary accuracy, due to the difficult tide conditions in the Channel. The R.A.F. "Gee" apparatus had, a year or two previously, been discarded for naval purposes owing to the lack of range which it was thought to possess when working in ships. Initial trials carried out by C.O.H.Q. had shown that the signal could be held to good distances, but neither had the range nor the accuracy been definitely established. It was, however, decided to rely on this apparatus as being the only aid likely to achieve the necessary results; additional ships and craft were hurriedly fitted and the necessary personnel trained in its use.

In the operation, this method proved a success and a big programme of fitting in Combined Operations ships and craft was begun. This was later extended to nearly all naval ships and craft operating in areas covered by the R.A.F. "Gee" chains. The similar Decca system, which gave more precise results for minesweepers in the invasion of Normandy and which was under strenuous development for other purposes, was also adapted and sponsored by the Admiralty on the advice of C.O.H.Q.

The above is a good example, but only one of many, of the equipment of one Service being of very great value to another Service, and for this purpose C.O.H.Q. kept in very close touch not only with the Service Ministries, but also with the experimental and research establishments of all three Services. Another example is given by the later developed rocket craft which called for a very high degree of accuracy in positioning and ranging if the desired effect was to be achieved. This problem was overcome by the use of the R.A.F. H2S equipment, used in bombers, being slightly modified for the purpose.

Another feature of the Dieppe operation was the use of H.Q. Ships specially fitted for Channel operations. No fully equipped L.S.H. was by that time ready, nor would one have been suitable for this type of operation. It was decided to use *Hunt* Class destroyers, but one alone was found to be too small to carry all the requisite communications. The Joint Headquarters was therefore split between H.M.S. *Calpe* and H.M.S. *Fernie*, who were closely linked by V.H/F and H/F R/T; some measure of duplication to allow for casualties was also provided by this device. Embarked in the *Calpe* were the naval and military Force Commanders with a senior representative of the Air Force Commander; the Air Commander himself remaining at his headquarters at Uxbridge. It had been intended originally that all aircraft taking part should be controlled from Uxbridge, but permission had been obtained to fit the necessary V.H/F sets in the H.Q. Ship for communication with fighters should this be desired. In the event all direction of fighter aircraft in the assault area was carried by the H.Q. Ship with extremely successful results.

Command and Control

The evolution of technique, ships and headquarters during all this period was governed by a developing pattern of command and control. In any modern force, the Commander's methods are to some extent restricted by the available means of communication. In the complicated circumstances of an amphibious force, there is particular need for him to do so; the interlocking of three Service Commands in conditions, which are nearly always unfamiliar and are generally most exacting as regards the use of radio, calls for a signal system which is closely matched to that of command and control. It follows that the signal planners must combine close study of tactical progress with something of a gift for prophecy and must frequently suggest lines of operational development which are opened up or, in some cases, enforced by available technique. The Signal Staff of C.O.H.Q. made this study their special concern and provided a strong measure of continuity between successive operations including those planned by other authorities.

The signal communications provided for the control of amphibious operations developed from the Madagascar landing onwards. The larger number of signal personnel required for the North African landings and subsequent operations, and the limited time available for training, meant that a lower standard of operational efficiency had to be accepted. This disadvantage was to some extent offset by the provision of specially equipped Headquarters ships.

When the time came to plan the communication facilities for the Normandy landing, the communication procedures developed by Force "J" in the Channel were incorporated in the system which had been developed in the larger operations in the Mediterranean.

India, 1942-1943

Signals entered the Combined Operations sphere in this theatre in July, 1942, when British 2 Division were ordered to raise the first Beach Signal Section in India in anticipation of future operations. A small Combined Training Centre was in existence at Kharakvasla, but there was no signals wing and no signals staff to formulate the theory and practice of signals in the assault.

A second Beach Signal Section was formed by 2 Division in October and, at the same time, a small instructional staff was appointed to the C.T.C. exclusively for the training of assaulting formations in landing technique as applied to signals.

With the arrival of 36 Division from Madagascar, a major reorganisation took place. This Division took over specialist training from 2 Division but the C.T.C. continued to give basic instruction. At 36 Division Headquarters Combined Operations Signals were organised on an inter-Services basis, there being army, navy and air force signal officers on the staff.

A Combined Signal School was formed at Bandra, the task of which was to give initial training to newly-formed beach sections of the three Services; refresher training to sections on return from operations; training to brigade and divisional Signal Sections of formations undergoing basic training at the C.T.C.; and to act as a landing depot for all Combined Operations Sections in India, irrespective of Service. Help on the naval side arrived in December when No. 3 R.N.B.S.S. (Royal Naval Beach Signal Section) joined the Combined Signals School.

Until January, 1943, when the Chief Signals Officer established liaison with Combined Operations Signals in the U.K., Combined Signal Policy in the two theatres was not co-ordinated. From then onwards, equipment, views and policy were exchanged regularly, supplemented by exchange of visits. Home ideas, however, were not always suitable for the Far East and generally had to be modified.

Lack of craft and equipment prevented the first wetshod signals exercise being held in India until February, 1943, when the craft used in the Madagascar operations became available. A brigade wetshod exercise ("Viking") was then instituted.

Normal assault training and developments continued until another major change in organisation took place in July, 1943. The Indian Expeditionary Force, formed from 10th Army, took over control of Combined Operations Policy in India from 36 Division, which was then mobilised as a normal Infantry Division. The Indian Expeditionary Force carried out the planning and training from Bombay and a new unit, 218 H.Q. Signals, was formed in July, 1943, to train and administer all Army Combined Operations Signals Sections.

The lack of proper H.Q. Ships was severely felt in training but 218 H.Q. Signals were given the task of supervising the conversion of existing ships. A start was made by building a mock-up H.Q. Ship at the C.T.C. Madh Island, which eventually became a model H.Q. Ship complete with fighter direction communications.

The difficulty of running dryshod exercises without craft and H.Q. Ships was overcome by the construction of three mobile H.Q. Ships. Each ship consisted of two units, one housing six receivers and the other six transmitters with separated aerials carried on 48-ft. masts, so that the layout was as near that of a real ship as possible.

These ships enabled a full-scale divisional signals dryshod exercise to be run in August, 1943, the first in India. It was carried out in the Poona-Ahmednagar area utilising two Beach Signal Sections and two Ship Signal Sections from 2 Division.

Towards the middle of October, a full-scale wetshod exercise ("Otter") was arranged for 36 Division, in which *Bulolo* took part as Corps H.Q. Ship. This was the first time a properly fitted H.Q. Ship had appeared in India.

A further change took place when the Indian Expeditionary Force faded out of the picture and 33 Indian Corps took over combined operations work.

India, 1944

1944 brought a rapid growth in the whole Combined Operations Organisation in India. Plans which had been awaiting sanction, either because of finance or policy, were put into effect and the Signals branch expanded to meet expected training and operational requirements.

One of the most important changes was that Bandra ceased to be an army establishment in January. Instead of remaining under 218 H.Q. Signals, it became a naval establishment named H.M.S. *Braganza III* and was commanded by a Commander R.N. This brought the Signal School into line with H.M.S. *Dundonald II*.

Early in 1944, all Signal Sections were allocated to Brigades or Beach Groups and were carrying out dryshod exercises under their respective formations.

During the summer of 1944, 2 and 36 Divisions, followed by 15 and 25 Divisions carried out training and exercises in combined operations. All but two Beach Groups were disbanded. As a result of these exercises, it was decided to reorganise the two existing Beach Signal Sections and form the Beach Maintenance Area Signals Sections. Beach Signal Sections were to provide tactical communications for the assaulting formations, and Beach Maintenance Area Sections were to provide administrative communications for the Beach group.

In August 1944, 218 Indian Combined Operations Signals took the place of 218 H.Q. Signals. The establishment on which 218 H.Q. Signals was raised was sufficient to control a unit, the strength of which fluctuated between 500 and 800 personnel, with equipment which surpassed that held by a normal divisional signals.

At this time, combined operations were being planned to take place on the Burma coast. As no H.Q. Ships were available, H.M.S. *Haitan* was converted at Colombo and completed by *Braganza III* at Bombay.

Operations in S.E.A.C.

After the Arakan operations in early 1945, in which a Beach Signal Section was placed under command of 26 Indian Division, planning for the recapture of Rangoon began in April and the assault was launched on 2nd May. By this time the long-awaited H.Q. Ships had arrived from England. Only one, however, H.M.S. *Largs* could be used in its proper role. H.M.S. *Nith* and *Waveney* could not be used as Brigade H.Q. Ships as they could not proceed up the Rangoon River until it had been cleared of mines and any shoals located, therefore an L.C.H. had to be used for Brigade headquarters.

A novelty was introduced in the shape of an L.C.I.(L) which was converted in 24 hours into a "step-up" W/T ship. There was a 30-mile gap between the divisional H.Q. Ship anchorage and the assault beaches and a relay link was necessary. As it happened, this craft was vital to communications and a serious breakdown would have occurred without it.

The fall of Rangoon in May, followed closely by the fall of Germany, meant an all-out effort for Malaya at the end of the monsoon. This was the real climax for Combined Operations work in India and, for the first time, there was an abundance of everything, assault signals, ship signals, H.Q. Ships and assault equipment.

When the Divisions embarked, they were superbly equipped and trained. Full-scale exercises could not be held owing to the unavailability of shipping and the monsoon, but the Division held signal exercises before they set off.

For Operation "Zipper", the assault on Malaya, all the signal resources of Combined Operations were needed. Two Assault Sections, two Beach Group Signal Sections and seven Ship Signal Sections took

COMBINED OPERATIONS SIGNALS ORGANISATION

part, in addition to one Ship Signal Section which took part in the landing at Hong Kong.

With the conclusion of these operations individual sections were gradually disbanded and, as there was no longer the need for 218 Indian Combined Operations Signals, the unit was broken up.

Chapter 18

THE BEACH ORGANISATION

The aim of this chapter is to trace the part played by the Combined Operations Command both directly and indirectly, in the development of Beach Organisation during the war.

The task is complicated by the fact that development proceeded independently in different theatres at the same time, and involved the intimate welding together of all three Services within one Organisation. Thus, in order to produce a connected history of the development of the beach organisation, it has been necessary to follow progress chronologically in the different theatres, and to take the problems of all three Services together as a whole rather than deal with each separately.

To avoid clouding the main issue, which is already sufficiently complex, the problems of seaward and air defence have not been included. But it will, of course, be realised that these are complimentary problems, and that no operation involving the beach organisation could be under-taken without due consideration being paid to them.

For a similar reason, no attempt has been made to describe in detail the part played by beach organisations in the many operations in which they took part during the war. However, as far as possible, where operations produced lessons which influenced development or technique, reference has been made to them in the text.

The Background to Development
Before the war, the responsibility for the development of material, technique and tactics for all inter-Services operations had been vested in the Inter-Services Training and Development Centre at Portsmouth,

the Centre being responsible to the Inter-Services Training Sub-Committee of the Deputy Chiefs of Staff Committee. However, in June, 1940, when the Directorate of Combined Operations was set up in the Admiralty, the Directorate assumed responsibility for the activities of the Inter-Services Training and Development Centre, this responsibility being taken over in turn by C.O.H.Q. when it was set up a month later.

From this time, therefore, the responsibility for the development of a suitable Beach Organisation together with the responsibility for stating requirements for special equipment arising from it, was that of the Combined Operations Command.

The Position at the Beginning of the War

At the outbreak of war, the system of beach organisation laid down in Chapter 23 of the "Manual of Combined Operations, 1938" was in force. No formed beach units, as such, existed. It was intended that personnel needed to work on the beaches following an amphibious assault, should be drawn from base or Service units of the landing force to meet the requirements of a particular operation, being returned to their parent units as soon as normal maintenance could be resumed. The early capture of a port was considered at the time to be essential in any combined operation, beach maintenance being regarded as an interim measure of short duration only. However, an inter-Services system for the command and control of beaches was laid down, and this was the nucleus around which subsequent development was to take place. The system was as follows:

A naval officer was appointed Principal Beach Master. He was responsible to the Senior Naval Officer Landing, and controlled all landing craft and personnel within the naval area. His main task was to ensure the most rapid discharge and turn-round of landing craft, consistent with meeting military requirements ashore. He exercised control over the beaches, which were sub-divided into sections and landing points, through Beach Masters, Assistant Beach Masters and Beach Lieutenants R.N. respectively. He worked in close conjunction with his Army equivalent, who was known as the Principal Military Landing Officer.

The Principal Military Landing Officer was a "Q" Staff Officer. He was responsible to the Force Commander for clearing the dumps and supervising the arrangements for guiding troops forward into assembly areas. He, in turn, was assisted by a Military Landing Officer on each beach, and by an Assistant Military Landing Officer on each section of each beach.

The Early Development of Beach Organisation

At a meeting of the Future Operations Planning Section on 21st September, 1940, it was agreed amongst other matters that the D.C.O. should be responsible for: (1) The working out in detail of beach organisation, and (2) The technical development of beach piers, cranes, etc., for landing stores on the Continent.

Following this decision, the D.C.O. forwarded to the Admiralty and the War Office, a memorandum on Beach Organisation prepared by the Commandant, Inter-Services Training and Development Centre. He proposed that Vice-Admiral Combined Training at the C.T.C., Inveraray, which had opened recently, should have his staff representatives of the transportation staff, to assist in beach organisation training; and raised the question of maintaining a nucleus beach party instead of forming *ad hoc* units with ordinary regimental personnel for operations as they were planned, as was the existing practice.

There followed a period of discussion between the D.C.O., the War Office (Directors of Movements and Transportation), the Inter-Services Training and Development Centre and the Air Ministry. A number of meetings were held at C.O.H.Q., the results of which can be summarised as follows:

(1) The D.C.O. assumed responsibility for co-ordinating work on the beach organisation and for technical development.
(2) The War Office undertook the provision and storage of specialised equipment to meet requirements stated by the D.C.O.
(3) The scope of the Beach Organisation was to be extended beyond that of maintaining a small force, and developed so as to cater for the maintenance via the beaches of a larger force for a considerable period.
(4) Training at the C.T.C., Inveraray, was to cover the period from the initial landing up to the capture of a port.
(5) The basic organisation for the control of beaches laid down in Chapter 23 of the Manual of Combined Operations was to remain in force.
(6) The War Office were to provide selected Docks Operating Companies and Field Companies, Royal Engineers, for training at the C.T.C.
(7) Labour on the beaches was to be undertaken by pioneers.

No further development took place in 1941. During this time, C.O.H.Q. was largely engaged in estimating and stating requirements for special equipment, the evolution of a standardised beach organisation and formulating plans for training.

THE BEACH ORGANISATION

The Formation and Training of Naval Beach Parties

A meeting was held at C.O.H.Q. in December, 1941, which was attended by representatives of 110 Force, Vice-Admiral Combined Training and various Admiralty Branches at which it was decided that eight Brigade Front Naval Beach Parties would be required by the end of 1942. Each party would be required to handle the boats required to land a brigade.

It was agreed that a Brigade Front Beach Party should consist of: 1 Lieutenant R.N., Principal Beach Master; 3 Lieutenants or sub-Lieutenants, Beach Masters; 3 Lieutenants or sub-Lieutenants, Assistant Beach Masters; [and] 48 Ratings.

Each Brigade Front Beach Party was to be known by the letter, A, B, C, etc., and consisted of three sub-units numbered A1, A2, A3, etc., each sub-unit being designed to operate on a Battalion Front.

It was also decided at the same meeting that the training of naval beach parties would be carried out in close conjunction with Army Beach Groups whose training was to start shortly. The training of naval beach parties started at Inverkip in April 1942, on the basis of one naval sub-unit to an Army Beach Group. A record was maintained showing which sub-unit trained with which Beach Group, so that both could be called together again when wanted for an exercise or an operation. On completion of training, personnel of naval beach parties were retained within the Combined Operations Organisation.

Responsibility for Training Beach Groups in the United Kingdom

Early in 1942, the Army Council announced the formation of a permanent organisation to undertake overseas operations, to be known as the Expeditionary Force. Headquarters Expeditionary Force was located at Largs, together with Headquarters Combined Training, the latter remaining under command of the Commodore Combined Operations. Expeditionary Force responsibilities, which were laid down at the time, included assisting the Commodore Combined Operations in the supervision of the training of Expeditionary Force units and formations at C.T.C.s.

Although the ultimate responsibility for training Expeditionary Force units rested with the Commander Expeditionary Force, it will be noted that considerable assistance in their training was given by C.T.C.s. The gradual development of a beach organisation was worked out between Headquarters Expeditionary Force and C.O.H.Q. New techniques, after inter-Services agreement, were published under the direction of the Chief of Combined Operations, who became the central authority around which development took place, and who was responsible for co-ordinating the requirements of all three Services in these matters.

Beach Group Training in the United Kingdom

In February, 1942, a meeting was held in C.O.H.Q. at which the Commodore Combined Operations presided. Vice-Admiral Combined Training, Director of Transportation and Director of Supplies and Transport from the War Office, Commander Mobile Naval Base Defence Organisation II and others attended this meeting at which it was decided:

(1) That beach training should be carried out at the Combined Training Centre, Dundonald. A programme drawn up by the Commodore Combined Operations was agreed in principle.
(2) That the Expeditionary Force Beach Training Centres should operate in conjunction with the C.T.C., Dundonald.
(3) That personnel of the three Services should live together at Dundonald to foster the team spirit required by the Beach Organisation.
(4) That R.M. and R.E. units to be employed in similar work should receive the same training and work to the same standards.
(5) That beach parties trained in combined operations should be reserved for that purpose.
(6) That the R.A.F. should be invited to include in their Servicing Commandos a Beach Liaison Officer to supervise the handling of R.A.F. stores and undergo training with beach parties.

In April the same year, Headquarters Expeditionary Force started the training of Beach Groups in conjunction with the Combined Training Organisation. By this time a standardised Army Beach Group had evolved, which was designed to support the landing of a Battalion Group. Beach Groups were formed from detachments from Expeditionary Force units or reserve units. Each Beach Group carried out three weeks' training at C.T.C., Ardgowan, followed by ten days at Dundonald. Beach Groups were numbered consecutively 1, 2, etc., on formation. On completion of training, personnel were returned to their parent units, but were earmarked for return to the Beach Group, with which they had trained, when required. This cycle of training was designed to complete the training of one Beach Group every ten days. These Beach Groups were made up as follows:

	Officers	Ratings/O.R.s
Movement Control Group	2	15
Det. Army Transportation Coy. R.E.		2 (N.C.O.s)
Det Docks Operating Coy. R.E.		10 (1 Offr. per 3 dets.)
Mechanical Equipment Sec.		10

	Officers	Ratings/O.R.s
Three secs. Pioneers	1	75
Total Army Personnel	3	112
R.N. Beach Party sub-unit	2	16
R.A.F. Beach Party	1	3
Total	6	131

The organisation was first tried out in Operation "Ironclad" in May, 1942, the assault on Madagascar.

Referring to the beach organisation, the G.O.C. Force 121 said in his report: "Judging by results, the administrative arrangements of Operation 'Ironclad' may be said to have worked in the manner intended." It must be noted, however, that on Operation "Ironclad", complete air superiority allowed work to continue unhampered on the beach, beach conditions were perfect and night work was made possible by a good moon. Nevertheless, a start had been made and an organisation which worked had been produced.

Combined Operations Pamphlet No. 2, Beach Organisation and Maintenance

In the autumn of 1942, a pamphlet on Beach Organisation and Maintenance was issued under the Direction of C.C.O. The term Beach Organisation was defined as including all arrangements made by beach parties for the movement of personnel and vehicles across the beaches to assembly areas and dumps respectively; and for their reception at those areas and dumps by the formation and Services concerned. It also included the provision and operation of all necessary facilities for this purpose.

The respective naval and army responsibilities were laid down, together with the method of development of the beach organisation in the order of landing of its various components from first touch-down to the setting up of a ferry service and a beach maintenance area.

For the first time a standard beach party for one brigade at assault scales, known as a Brigade Brick, was laid down.

Naval Beach Commandos

In October, 1942, Admiral Mountbatten wrote to the Admiralty expressing concern at the poor quality of officers and ratings selected for beach parties and requested that the matter should be reconsidered.

The word "Party" gave the wrong impression, being sometimes regarded as a working party, and in order to indicate that beach parties were in fact fighting units that go ashore in khaki battledress with the soldiers, he had arranged for them to be known in future as Naval Beach Commandos.

The Inter-Services System of Command

In April, 1943, a Combined Operations pamphlet dealing with the duties of Naval Commandos was published under the direction of C.C.O. This pamphlet dealt in great detail with the composition, training and employment of Naval Beach Commandos. An agreed naval/military chain of Command was laid down as follows:

Naval	Military
Senior Naval Officer Landing	Brigade Commander
	Principle Military Landing Officer (in development stage only)
Principle Beachmaster	Beach Group Commander
Deputy Principle Beachmaster	Military Landing Officer
Beachmaster	Beach Company Commander
Assistant Beachmaster	2 i/c Beach Company, Unit Landing Officer

One Senior Naval Officer Landing was appointed per assault brigade. He shared joint responsibility with the Brigade Commander for the section of enemy coast allocated to the brigade. The Senior Naval Officer Landing was responsible for the organisation and control of the anchorage and waters in his section of the coast. He exercised control over the beaches through the Principle Beachmaster. The disembarkation of R.A.F. personnel and stores was the Army's responsibility. When necessary, R.A.F. Liaison Officers were appointed to assist in the landing and clearance of R.A.F. personnel and material.

Development in the Middle East

Owing to the circumstances surrounding the development of the beach organisation, in particular the availability of personnel and material, the majority of training had been carried out initially in the U.K., the development of new technique being centralised in C.O.H.Q.

Nevertheless, in October, 1940, the C.-in-C. Middle East had proposed the setting up of a Combined Operations School with an Inter-Services Staff in the Middle East, as a wing of the Middle East Staff School. The War Office, after consultation with the other Service Ministries and the D.C.O., agreed to this proposal. Colonel MacLeod, who was the Commandant of the Inter-Service Training and Development Centre at the time, was appointed G.S.O.1 of the new school on the advice of the D.C.O., so that his experience with the Inter-Service Training and Development Centre could be used to the best advantage and to ensure that training and instruction in the Middle East was carried out on similar lines to the U.K.

The school was opened early in 1941 as a C.T.C. at Kabrit, at the southern end of the Great Bitter Lake, taking the C.T.C. at Inverary as a pattern. A naval establishment, H.M.S. *Saunders*, was set up nearby to accommodate naval personnel and crews of minor landing craft. By September, 1941, although suffering considerably from shortages of equipment and having to depend largely upon local resources, beach organisation training had been started in addition to running normal combined operations courses. Experimental work on pier construction, the clearing of beaches, demolition of underwater obstacles, etc., was also carried out at the C.T.C., periodic progress reports being sent to C.O.H.Q. at home. The technique taught at Home and in the Middle East was the same, and development in the theatre progressed along very similar lines subject to local operational necessity and limitations of equipment.

The Landings in North Africa, Operation "Torch"

The training of early Beach Groups, which had started at the C.T.C., Dundonald, early in 1942, continued and provided a number of trained units drawn from Headquarters Expeditionary Force which were employed on Operation "Torch" in November of that year. Unfortunately, from the records now available, it is not possible to state, by number, the Beach Groups which took part in the operation, as the various sub-units and detachments comprising them were shown as such and not as formed Beach Groups. However, it can be said that the organisation used on Operation "Torch" was basically the same as that used at Madagascar (Operation "Ironclad") earlier in the year.

A great many reports covering experiences gained on the operations were received by C.O.H.Q. These were evaluated and produced in pamphlet form under the direction of C.C.O. in June, 1943. Reports on the working of the Beach Organisation during the operation showed that the organisation was too rigid. There was a general lack of training and discipline, and esprit de corps was poor. Lack of organisation and bad planning led to the complete exhaustion of docks operating personnel after 24 hours. So far, the Beach Organisation had been subjected to a minimum of operational difficulties and, had it not been possible to capture a port in the early stages of the operation, it is doubtful if the organisation could have continued to maintain the forces ashore.

Field Marshal Alexander in his Despatch (The Conquest of Sicily), referred to Operation "Torch" as follows:

"It is still an essential element of the doctrine of amphibious warfare that sufficient major ports must be captured within a very short time of the initial landings to maintain all the forces required for the maintenance of the objective; beach maintenance could only be relied upon as a very temporary measure."

Technical Training Wing of the Combined Training Centre, Dundonald

As a result of experience gained in training Nos. 1 and 2 Beach Groups and as the technique of beach organisation became more apparent, C.C.O. decided that a proper staff should be formed with the sole responsibility for training Beach Groups. Accordingly, a special wing was formed at the C.T.C., Dundonald, in November, 1942, for training Beach Groups, which was known as the Technical Training Wing. This wing completed the training of Nos. 3 and 4 Beach Groups and 103 Beach Sub-Area Headquarters which had formed recently and were under training at the C.T.C. for Operation "Husky". As a result of experiences gained on Operation "Torch", the question of using pioneer labour in Beach Groups was re-examined.

There were two very definite schools of thought regarding the use of infantry or pioneers as the nucleus of a Beach Group. Those who favoured an infantry nucleus did so because full advantage could be taken, within the Beach Group, of the well-proved channels of command of the infantry battalion and because improved esprit de corps and morale resulted. The fact that infantry could fight on the beaches, if required, was also a valuable asset.

The arguments in favour of a pioneer nucleus were: that the use of infantry in a beach maintenance role was improper and uneconomical; that, if infantry were used to do pioneers' work, their morale suffered; that infantry were more likely than pioneers to become involved in the land battle, resulting in a vacuum on the beach; that pioneers, providing they were carefully selected and kept together after an operation, worked well and their morale was good. However, largely because of the difficulty of keeping Beach Group personnel together after an operation, it was decided that subsequent Beach Groups to form, should do so around the nucleus of an infantry battalion.

The Training of R.A.F. Beach Units

At the same time (1942), it was decided that R.A.F. Beach Units should be formed in parallel with Army Beach Sub-Areas and that they should train and be despatched overseas with the Beach Group to which they belonged. Nos. 68 and 69 R.A.F. Beach Units accordingly started to train with 3 and 4 Beach Groups at the C.T.C. The R.A.F. Beach Unit consisted of one Beach Unit Headquarters, attached to the Sub-Area Headquarters; and two Beach Flights (one Flight per Beach Group).

R.A.F. Beach Units were designed to supply the technical knowledge, not possessed by the Army, concerning R.A.F. equipment and stores; and to safeguard the sorting, assembly and forwarding of equipment, stores and vehicles peculiar to the R.A.F. The formation of R.A.F. Beach Units completed the inter-Services representation within the Beach Organisation.

The Birth of the "Overlord" Beach Organisation

It was by now quite clear that, if a re-entry into Europe was to be made in the future, there would be an increased need for the formation and training of Beach Units.

The decision to form a Technical Training Wing for the training of Beach Groups was therefore followed by a letter from C.C.O. to the War Office in which he pointed out the paramount need for a properly constituted unit to undertake the various duties included under the heading of "Beach Organisation". In this letter he proposed:

(1) That approval in principle be given immediately to the establishment of Beach Groups, the preparation of a War Establishment for the Group Headquarters and the appointment of Group Commanders and their staffs.
(2) That detailed consideration be given to the preparation of a suitable War Establishment; this to be undertaken by the War office, assisted as necessary by representatives of G.H.Q. Home Forces and C.O.H.Q.
(3) That one Beach group should be formed immediately in each Command in the U.K.
(4) The formation of such further Beach Groups as may then be considered necessary as a result of projected future operations.

Thus, was born the "Overlord" Beach Organisation, and the Technical Training Wing of the C.T.C. at Dundonald started to operate in its primary role, the training of Beach Groups for "Overlord".

The Formation of Middle East Beach Bricks

It will be appreciated that although the question of re-entry into Europe remained uppermost in mind, the change of strategy following "Torch" and leading up to the projected landings in Sicily and subsequent operations in the Mediterranean, caused attention to be focused on the Middle East for a time. It is necessary, therefore, at this stage, to examine what progress had been made in that theatre.

In October, 1941, the C.-in-C. Middle East had set up a Directorate of Combined Operations with a small Inter-Services Staff at G.H.Q. This Directorate was responsible to the C.-in-C. Middle East for the direction of the C.T.C. Middle East, which had been established at Kabrit. It was not in any way responsible to C.C.O. and liaison between the Directorate and C.O.H.Q. might well have been better.

The idea that some organisation was required to control activities on the beach during an assault landing arose as a result of interviews with officers who had taken part in Operation "Ironclad", the Madagascar landings. The Directorate of Combined Operations Middle East, was instructed by G.H.Q. to prepare outline establishments and to consider what training was necessary. Whilst this was being done, a little information came through from C.O.H.Q. by means of liaison officers, Monthly Information Summaries and pamphlets. On 6th April, 1943, G.H.Q. Middle East published an establishment for a Beach Brick. Five Bricks, Nos. 31 to 35, were formed round a standard existing major unit, usually an infantry battalion, supplemented by a Brick increment with naval and R.A.F. elements attached. A Brick was designed to control all activities on a beach on which part of an assault force was landed and through which it was subsequently to be maintained for a certain period. Its stores handling capacity was laid down as being 500 tons a day, discharged from a maximum of six landing craft simultaneously.

In fact, there were no great differences in principle between the U.K. Beach Group Organisation evolved by C.O.H.Q. and the Middle East Beach Brick Organisation. There were, of course, many differences in detail due to differing staff problems in the two theatres. This was inevitable.

The North Africa Beach Groups

To complete the story in the Mediterranean, it is necessary to state briefly what had been taking place in North Africa.

In April, 1943, Allied Force Headquarters North Arica set up a C.T.C. at Djidjelli, the instructional staff being largely provided from the U.K. by C.C.O. In addition to training assault formations, the training of Nos. 20 and 21 Beach Groups was undertaken in May and June, 1943. These Beach Groups were the original Nos. 1 and 2 Beach Groups (U.K. pattern) which had taken part in Operation "Torch". After the operation they were re-formed, their basic element being provided from 1/4 Hampshire Regiment. Further details of this organisation are not now available, but it would seem that the current practice at the time had been followed in that these Beach Groups had been hastily re-formed after Operation "Torch" for the subsequent invasion of Sicily. Each consisted of some twenty-four different units which was unsatisfactory both for command and training.

The Landings in Sicily, Operation "Husky"
Many important lessons affecting beach organisation were learned on Operation "Husky" and new equipment was tested which revolutionised thought on the scope of beach maintenance. In addition, the operation enabled a comparison to be made between the three different types of organisation which were used, the United Kingdom Beach Group, the Middle East Beach Brick and the North Africa Beach Group.

The following British Beach Formations took part in Operation "Husky": Nos. 3 and 4 Beach Groups (United Kingdom pattern); Nos. 20 and 21 Beach Groups (North Africa); Nos. 31-35 Beach Bricks (Middle East).

The value of the Naval Lighter (N.L.) Pontoon and the D.U.K.W. was established. On 19th July, 1943, Admiral Mountbatten forwarded to the Chiefs of Staff Committee his remarks on Operation "Husky". This paper was subsequently issued as a Chief of Staff paper and promulgated to Commanders-in-Chief abroad. It was based upon C.C.O.'s personal experience of the operation; upon conversations he had had with the various Commanders-in-Chief and other Commanders concerned; and upon the experience of members of his staff who had been lent to assist in various parts of the operation. C.C.O. made the following points in his report:

(1) An efficient beach organisation, during both the initial landing and subsequent maintenance period, has an enormous influence on both the military operations ashore and the duration of risk suffered by large ships lying off-shore. There were two main defects in our beach organisation. Firstly, the

procedure must be simplified and standardised, and become a drill in which all personnel including landing craft crews are carefully trained. Secondly, key positions in the control of this very important function must be filled by first class naval and military officers.

(2) The training and provision of Principal Military Landing Officers and Military Landing Officers should be C.C.O.'s responsibility.

(3) Specially trained personnel who form part of Beach Groups must not be broken up after an operation, but retained to continue training for their next task.

(4) Three different types of beach organisation were in use during the operation. The organisation of Beach Groups should be standardised, even though particular operations may involve special reorganisation of Beach Groups.

(5) Weather conditions at the time of "Husky" were ideal for beach maintenance. As developed at the time, it was essentially a fair-weather method of maintenance and the object should be to get such tonnages shore on good days as to allow work to be suspended when the sea is not sufficiently calm.

In addition, reports on "Husky" from many other sources were received by C.O.H.Q. These were collated and published as a digest in October, 1943. In addition to stressing the points mentioned by C.C.O. in his report referred to above, the digest included the following matters of interest affecting beach organisation:

(1) Maintenance over the beaches was well and speedily carried out. Conditions for the build-up were good, with little enemy interference and calm seas. Both 7th and 8th Armies proved that, under these conditions and with adequate small craft and D.U.K.W.s maintenance of large forces over captured beaches is not only possible but, under conditions pertaining in the Mediterranean, easier than expected.

(2) The Beach Brick and Beach Group Organisations were sound, but should be standardised. The organisation should not be broken up after an operation, unless circumstances fully justified it.

(3) The same naval parties should work with the same beach parties.

(4) A battalion of infantry should form the nucleus of a Beach Group.

(5) Still further examination of the problem of crossing the water-gap is needed, in spite of the very efficient part played by the American naval pontoon and the D.U.K.W.s.

(6) Ships should anchor as close to the beaches as possible once coast defences have been overcome. This renders them less likely to sink when bombed and more immune from submarine attack. It also brings them closer protection of the beach anti-aircraft defences and has the overwhelming advantage of shortening the turn-round.
(7) The maintenance area must be sited only a short distance inland of the beaches to reduce the turn-round as much as possible.
(8) British Beach Groups averaged a daily tonnage of about 500 tons.

The Formation of Headquarters Sub-Area (Beach) and Beach Groups

On 10th July, 1943, the War office announced that the Army Council had decided to set up for operations likely to involve a sea-borne assault, tactical and administrative headquarters and formations known as Headquarters Sub-Area (Beach) and Beach Groups. The principles of beach organisation were laid down as follows:

(1) General Organisation.

The Beach Organisation would be based on a Beach Group which was a composite formation containing a number of standard or specialised sub-units together with a labour element. Beach Groups were to be allotted on the basis of one to each assault brigade front and would be responsible for the movement of personnel, vehicles and stores from landing ships, craft, etc., across the beaches to transit areas, dumps and assembly areas.

The Beach Group was to be commanded by the Officer Commanding the Infantry Battalion; the Infantry Battalion would find the bulk of the labour required.

Included in the Beach Group were signal elements, a Royal Engineer unit for preparing tracks and exits from the beaches, stores holding and issuing units for all main commodities and a recovery and emergency repair unit.

Anti-aircraft units would be attached to groups to meet operational needs.

Operational requirements might necessitate variation in the composition of the standard Beach group.

(2) The Beach Sub-Area.

Command of two or more Beach Groups would be vested in a Commander, Headquarters Sub-Area (Beach) who was responsible for the layout and operation of the beach maintenance area.

The Beach Organisation was responsible for the issue of stores from the various dumps. In certain circumstances there might be a pool of transport, controlled by a Sub-Area (Beach) Commander, for delivery forward.

In order that beaches and the beach area could be properly controlled, all movement, whether of stores or of personnel, of all Services in the beach area would be under the control of the Commander Sub-Area (Beach).

(3) Subsequent Development.
Every unit of the Beach Group would be found by taking a unit which had a place in the ultimate rearward organisation of a force, or by forming a special unit, men of which would be later absorbed into units of the Lines of Communication Organisation.

(4) Liaison with other Services.
Naval and Air Force elements would be attached to the Army Beach Organisation. These were normally:

(a) One R.N. Beach Commando.

(b) One R.A.F. Beach Unit consisting of:

(i) Beach Unit Headquarters which will be attached to the Headquarters Sub-Area (Beach), and

(ii) Two Beach Flights which will be attached to the two Beach Groups normally operating under each Headquarters Sub-Area (Beach).

The Position in India

In order to establish the background against which development in India was to take place, it is necessary briefly to summarise the progress which had been made at Home and in the Middle East at that time.

In the U.K., the training of Headquarters Sub-Area (Beach) and Beach Groups, started in 1942, was continuing at the Technical Training Wing, Dundonald, with a view to preparing for a re-entry into Europe. In the Middle East, Beach Bricks Nos. 31 to 35 had been formed and trained at C.T.C.s controlled by the Directorate of Combined Operations at G.H.Q. The general principles and technique taught in Middle East was similar to that taught by C.T.C.s in the U.K. The interchange of information between the U.K. and the Middle East had much improved.

The development of beach organisation in India had started at the beginning of 1943 when the C.-in-C., India, sanctioned the formation of five Indian Beach Groups. Prior to this, between January and October, 1942, an Inter-Services Committee known as Advisers on

Combined Operations (India) had been set up at G.H.Q. (India). This Committee was responsible for keeping in touch with combined operations policy emanating from C.O.H.Q., London, and assisting planners and formation Commanders in difficulties arising from an inter-Services operation. The Committee was later re-designated the Directorate of Combined Operations (India), new directives being issued from time to time, as war strategy changed. This has been fully dealt with elsewhere in this History, but it can truly be said, as far as the development of beach organisation is concerned, that the development in India was invariably based upon doctrine and techniques disseminated by C.O.H.Q in London or the Directorate of Combined Operations, Middle East. In all, five Indian Beach Groups were formed and trained in India, numbered 1 to 5 and later re-numbered 41 to 45.

The organisation of the Indian Beach Groups followed closely on the lines of the U.K. pattern, such differences as existed being due to differences in war establishments and Equipment Tables of the Indian Army organisation. They were designed to support the landing of an assault Brigade Group and to handle 600 tons of stores and 300 vehicles a day.

The War Office Committee on Beach Organisation, 1943

On 9th October, 1943, the Quartermaster-General appointed a Committee on which C.C.O. was represented, to make recommendations on the establishment, organisation and working of Beach Groups and Headquarters Beach Sub-Areas: (1) in view of early use in a continental operation; and (2) to consider what changes in respect of existing beach organisation were desirable for more distant tasks, especially for operations in South-East Asia.

At the same time, a C.O.H.Q. Committee on Beach Organisation was formed to enable C.C.O.'s representative on the War Office Committee to put forward the agreed policy of C.O.H.Q. on matters under discussion.

The report of the War Office Committee was circulated by C.C.O., at the request of the War Office, on a world-wide distribution. It took the form of a memorandum on Beach Organisation and established a basis for training, it being made clear that its contents were not to be regarded as a directive by C.C.O., but as a firm policy agreed and endorsed by all three Services for adoption at home. The following is a summary of the more important items on which agreement was reached from the point of view of a re-entry into the Continent:

(1) The importance of deciding, by the end of November, 1943, at the latest, the beach organisation to be used.
(2) The adequate provision of D.U.K.W.s and other equipment for training.
(3) That no part of a Beach Group should be set aside permanently for defence.
(4) That the Royal Navy should be responsible for the control of a ferry service between ship and shore in accordance with the wishes of the Army (except in respect of purely naval considerations such as weather, etc.).
(5) That the Infantry Battalion should be retained as the "hard core" of a Beach Group.
(6) That the Infantry Battalion Commander should command the Beach Group, retaining the rank of Lieutenant-Colonel.
(7) That the existing organisation of Royal Air Force Beach Units was satisfactory.
(8) Certain additional staff officers were recommended for a Headquarters Sub-Area (Beach) consistent with keeping it as small as possible.
(9) The responsibilities of the Principal Military Landing Officer to the Beach Sub-Area Commander were re-defined.

The Training of Beach Formations for "Overlord"

When the training of 103 Beach Sub-Area with its associated Beach Groups, Naval Beach Commandos and R.A.F. Beach Flights had been completed in 1942, the Technical Training Wing of the C.T.C., Dundonald, continued with the training of Beach Units. By the end of 1943, a further three Beach Sub-Areas and five Beach Groups, together with their associated Royal Naval Beach Commandos and R.A.F. Beach Units, had completed training at Combined Training Establishments.

Operation "Overlord", 6th June, 1944, Beach Order of Battle

To deal in detail with Operation "Overlord" is beyond the scope of this chapter, nor is it necessary in view of the many and comprehensive reports which have already been written. The lessons learned on the operation were studied in great detail by a C.O.H.Q. Committee set up shortly after the operation for the purpose of making recommendations on a suitable beach organisation for operations in the Far East. On the whole, it can be said that the beach organisation stood the test of Operation "Overlord" very well. The Beach Groups proved efficient machines with a good performance. The beach order of battle for the operation was as follows:

THE BEACH ORGANISATION

	Left	Centre	Right
(a) Navy	Force "S" N.O.I.C Sword R.N. Beach Commandos F.R	Force "J" N.O.I.C. Juno R.N. Beach Commandos L.P.S.	Force "G" N.O.I.C. Gold R.N. Beach Commandos J.Q.T.
(b) Army	3rd (Brit.) Inf. Div. 101st Beach Sub-Area 5th and 6th Beach Groups	3rd (Cdn.) Inf. Div. 102nd Beach Sub-Area 4th, 7th and 8th Beach Groups	50th (Northumbrian) Inf. Div. 104th Beach Sub-Area 9th and 10th Beach Groups and 36th Beach Brick
(c) R.A.F.	1st R.A.F. Beach Unit 101st and 102nd R.A.F. Beach Sections	2nd R.A.F. Beach Unit 103rd and 104th R.A.F. Beach Sections	4th R.A.F. Beach Unit 107th and 108th R.A.F. Beach Sections

The Combined Operations Headquarters Committee on Beach Organisations for the War against Japan

In July, 1944, the Directors of Administrative Plans instructed the Administrative Planning Section to review the "Overlord" system of beach organisation with special reference to the war against Japan; and to prepare, in conjunction with C.O.H.Q., a short report containing a concise series of principles for the guidance of Commanders and Staffs.

Accordingly, C.C.O. set up a Committee whose terms of reference were to recommend changes in the system of beach organisation and maintenance for the war against Japan, in the light of Operation "Overlord". A report was subsequently forwarded to the Joint Administrative Planning Staff by C.C.O. This report took into account the main tasks that the beach organisation would have to carry out, the main defects in the existing organisation, factors peculiar to the Far East likely to affect the organisation and made the following recommendations:

(1) Four Beach Brigades would be required, each capable of landing with an assault division to develop the beaches and to carry out long-term beach maintenance.
(2) Each brigade should consist of Beach Brigade Headquarters, two Beach Groups and Beach Brigade Troops.

(3) A Beach Organisation Holding and Reinforcement Unit on the normal Army reinforcement scale would also be required.
(4) Three Commanders Beach Organisation corresponding roughly in status with Commanders Royal Artillery, together with the necessary staff should be appointed.
(5) The naval chain of command during the build-up and maintenance period should be standardised.
(6) Certain extra officers to strengthen the naval and military links during planning, training and execution of operations were required.
(7) The Beach Signal Organisation needed reorganising.
(8) Naval basic Beach Training Centres should be placed under the direction of C.C.O., so that both Services would be taught the same doctrine in beach organisation.

The Beach Brigade Establishment

As a result of C.C.O.'s recommendations based upon C.O.H.Q. Committee's examination of the beach organisation required for the Far East, the War Office announced that the existing Beach Sub-Area and Beach Group Organisation would be superseded by an organisation known as a Beach Brigade. The organisation was designed to handle 1,000 tons of stores rising to 1,500 tons of stores per day over the beaches; and it was intended that one Beach Brigade should be allotted per assault division.

It is interesting to note that the Infantry Battalion round which the old Beach Group was built was to be replaced by working companies, organised on Pioneer Company establishments.

In addition, brigade troops were shown for the first time as "basic" and "non-basic," the former being those regarded as essentially an integral part of the organisation for training and operations, and necessary to foster team spirit and esprit de corps within the brigade.

Beach Organisation and Maintenance for the Long Range Assault in the Far East

In June, 1945, a Combined Operations Pamphlet was published which dealt with; the division of responsibility between the three Services; the Command and functions of the new Beach Brigade Organisation; the organisation and handling of Beach Brigades and Beach Groups; the operation of the ferry control organisation; and the development of beach maintenance. In fact, it can be said that it summarised the development of beach organisation as at the end of the war.

The Formation of 22nd Beach Brigade for Operations in the Far East

In May, 1945, the War Office gave authority for the formation of 22nd Beach Brigade at the C.T.C. Dundonald. The brigade consisted of 100th and 101st Beach Groups and was organised on the new establishments which had been recommended by the C.O.H.Q. Committee and agreed by the three Services Ministries. Training started at the C.T.C., Dundonald, but was discontinued at the termination of hostilities with Japan, when orders for the disbandment of the brigade were issued.

Conclusion

It has been the purpose of this chapter to follow the gradual evolution of the beach organisation throughout the war and, in particular, to trace the part played by the Combined Operations Organisation both at home, where it can be said to have been largely responsible for training and development, and abroad, where development, although independent, was influenced to a great extent by information summaries and pamphlets published in London and by visits of liaison officers.

The fact remains that, from a system of control of beaches laid down in the 1938 Manual of Combined Operations which was all that existed at the beginning of the war, the Beach Brigade Organisation containing elements of all three Services was evolved by the end of the war. The Beach Brigade Organisation was never tested operationally as the collapse of Japan took place before the training of 22nd Beach Brigade at Dundonald had been completed. It was, however, developed almost entirely by C.O.H.Q. as a cumulative result of operational and training experiences of the war. It will undoubtedly form the framework of any beach organisation which may be required in the future.

Post-War Development

In March, 1946, proposals were put up to the War Office for the establishment of a Territorial Beach Brigade as a permanent peacetime formation. Arising out of this, 264 Scottish Beach Brigade was formed in October, 1946.

Chapter 19

COMBINED OPERATIONS ORGANISATION FOR EXPERIMENTS, TRIALS AND DEVELOPMENT

This chapter traces the history of the development and experimental establishments together with the organisation of their controlling authorities in Combined Operations Headquarters.

The detailed story of the many trials and experiments is dealt with in other chapters of this history. The evolution of the Combined Operations Organisation for experiments, trials and development is traced from 1935 through the years prior to the war, to the first two years of the war, through the period required for the preparation of the Invasion of Europe, thence to the preparation of the Far East and so to the end of the war and the reorganisation required for peace.

Together with the phases mentioned above, the growth of the experimental side is intimately linked with the changes made in directives issued to successive Directors or Chiefs of Combined Operations on appointment concerning their responsibilities for development of equipment required for combined operations.

The Inter-Services Training and Development Centre (I.S.T.D.C.) up to April, 1942

In 1935 the Imperial Defence College, all three Staff Colleges and the Directorate of Sea Transport recommended the establishment of an Inter-Services Committee to investigate the problems connected with opposed landing and the institution of a Combined Services Training and Development Centre charged with the duty of developing the material required for opposed landings. These proposals were not approved by the Chiefs of Staff at their 178th meeting on 16th June, 1936. In 1936 and 1937 there was general dissatisfaction concerning the readiness for action of British Amphibious Forces. The Military Staff College particularly had protested on the inadequacy of knowledge and development in combined operations. As a result of this, the Chiefs of Staff agreed to set up a Sub-Committee of the Deputy Chiefs of Staff Committee with the following terms of reference:

(1) To study Inter-Services exercise and present collated and agreed reports on the lessons learned.
(2) To make recommendations for the study of problems of Inter-Services operations.
(3) To make recommendations for the development of equipment for Inter-Services operations.
(4) To keep under review the Manual of Combined Operations (previously the responsibility of the three Staff Colleges).

The Committee known as the "Inter-Services Training Sub-Committee of the Deputy Chiefs of Staff" (D.C.O.S.(I.T.)), consisted of the Assistant Chief of Naval Staff, the Director of Military Operations and Intelligence and the Deputy Chief of Air Staff or their representatives.

The Deputy Chiefs of Staff instructed D.C.O.S. (I.T.) to consider the question of establishing an Inter-Services Training and Development Centre (I.S.T.D.C.). Recommendations for its organisation and terms of reference were submitted to the Chiefs of Staff and agreed, in July, 1938. The centre was set up at Eastney, Portsmouth, where its proximity to the R.M. barracks was an advantage, as the latter were always willing to help in experiments and the provision of personnel and equipment. The I.S.T.D.C. consisted of a Captain R.N., (Commandant), a Major, a Wing Commander and a Captain R.M. (Adjutant). Its terms of reference were to study the development of material, technique and tactics for all inter-Services operations it is important to notice that these terms of reference included the study of all forms of inter-Services operations and were not confined to opposed landings.

In August, 1938, the I.S.T.D.C. submitted an interim report in which the main recommendations concerned with combined operations were: (1) That a landing craft carrier should be provided by the Admiralty; (2) That designs should be prepared for a self-propelled assault landing craft to carry a platoon of infantry at 8-10 knots and to have a low silhouette so as to attain some surprise. (The forerunner of the L.C.A.);

[and] (3) That experiments should be carried out with beach piers over which to discharge stores.

D.C.O.S. (I.T.) disagreed with (1) and suggested converted merchant ships instead. It gave orders for on self-propelled landing craft to be constructed. It recommended that the I.S.T.D.C. should investigate the use of infra-red rays for beach finding; the problems of naval gunfire in support of the Army; and of the beach piers for the discharge of stores.

In September, 1938, at the time of the Munich crisis, the I.S.T.D.C. was disbanded, but started work again in 1939. Activities were nevertheless restricted and a few L.C.A. and L.C.M. and one L.C.S. only were constructed.

This relatively insignificant development of amphibious ships and craft in readiness for a war which was clearly imminent, may be explained by the reluctance of the Admiralty to provide adequate sums for amphibious materials out of Navy votes. The minutes of the meetings of the Chiefs of Staff in December, 1938, reveal the trend of thought at that time:

General Ismay – "We should be making poor use of our strong suit, command of the sea, if we relegated Combined Operations to the background of our war plans."

"War Office – felt strongly that the time was long overdue for provision of modern amphibious material and they were prepared to take their share, provided that the principle of the Admiralty responsibility remained unchanged."

"Air Ministry – did not think the landing of troops against opposition was a likely form of operation for British troops in the near future."

"Admiralty – could not visualise any particular combined operation taking place, and were not, therefore, prepared to devote any considerable sum of money to equipment for combined training. In any case, only a limited amount of expenditure could be justified in peace time."

Nevertheless, it was agreed that the cost of providing the small quantity of material for the I.S.T.D.C. should be shared equally between the three Services.

A list of the more important subjects being studied at I.S.T.D.C. in early 1939 gives some idea of the work of the centre:

> Dropping troops by parachute.
> Landing water and petrol in amphibious operations.
> Landing tanks.
> Use of amphibian tanks.
> Methods of crossing underwater obstacles.

Maintenance and supply from the air.
Use of ships as headquarters for amphibious operations.
Production of a floating pier.
Provision of landing punts for coastal raids.

From this list it will be seen that amphibious operations played a large part in the work of I.S.T.D.C., although their terms of reference were the study of all inter-Services operations. In addition, the officers of the centre did much; they lectured at the Staff Colleges and elsewhere; they spread their knowledge of amphibious operations and the experimental work being done, but the précis of these lectures show that technique and tactics were more heavily stressed than development and experiment. Experiment, nevertheless, went on and in June, 1939, in addition to problems already being studied, the following more interesting points were added:

Design of a tank landing craft.
Beach organisation.
Beach roadways.
Floating piers.
Transport of troops be air.

The Work of the I.S.T.D.C. during the period September, 1939-July, 1940

In September, 1939, on the outbreak of war, the I.S.T.D.C. was again closed. The naval and air force members received new appointments, but the army member remained and in November, 1939, the I.S.T.D.C. was re-formed. Its work was very similar to the earlier centre but three points should be noted: (1) Its work was related to certain operations under consideration (e.g. capture of the Dodecanese); (2) It was much more than a development and experimental centre. Its members continued to lecture at the Staff Colleges and other establishments and, in these lectures, tactics and technique still took a more important part than development; and in April, 1940, the naval and military members assisted in the preparation for the Narvik operation; [and] (3) Control was still exercised by D.C.O.S. (I.T.). Combined operations, as they are known today, were not under consideration and large scale work at the centre was not contemplated.

A letter dated 13th November, 1939, gives a list of I.S.T.D.C. activities at the time; the more interesting points are given below:

1) Watching brief in the production of the first L.C.A., which was constructed as a result of I.S.T.D.C.'s recommendations.
(2) Trials of proposed armament of support landing craft.
(3) Trials of new L.C.M. to be held in the near future.
(4) Use of L.N.E.R. train ferry as landing craft carrier.
(5) Tests of gravity type davits to carry L.C.A. and L.C.S.
(6) Modifications to the newly tested pontoon pier.
(7) Trials of ropeways and scaling ladders.
(8) Water supply by distillation of sea-water.

Work at the I.S.T.D.C. continued along these lines through the early part of 1940. In June, after Dunkirk, when it was clear that combined operations would be a necessary prelude to the defeat of Germany, a small Directorate of Combined Operations was set up in the Admiralty under Lieutenant-General Bourne (until then Adjutant-General Royal Marines). His title was Commander, Raiding Operations and Adviser to the Chiefs of Staff on Combined Operations. Raiding operations were considered his primary role; as a second role the directive, stated: "Your second role will be to take over command of the Inter-Services Training and Development Centres and to act as our (i.e. Chiefs of Staff) adviser on the organisation required for opposed landings. In addition, we wish you to press on the development and production of special landing craft and equipment and to advise us, when the occasion arises, as to its allotment."

The I.S.T.D.C. therefore came under the command of Lt.-General Bourne. There appears to have been a certain lack of central direction and poor liaison with the planners with the result that the new system perhaps gave the I.S.T.D.C. less direction than the old D.C.O.S. (I.T.). The new Directorate seemed more concerned with its primary role, the planning and organising of raiding operations using already existing material, and in consequence, experimental work lacked the very necessary central control.

The Work of the I.S.T.D.C. when Admiral of the Fleet Sir Roger Keyes was Director of Combined Operations, July, 1940-October, 1941

In July, 1940, Admiral of the Fleet Sir Roger Keyes was appointed Director of Combined Operations (D.C.O.) with General Bourne temporarily as his D.D.C.O., and the Headquarters was moved from the Admiralty to Richmond Terrace. The I.S.T.D.C. remained under the D.C.O.'s command. Although no directive was issued to the D.C.O., in a memorandum, dated 6th September, 1940, entitled "Director of

Combined Operations – Organisation of Departments and Bases", it is stated:

> D.C.O. will be responsible to the Chiefs of Staff for the following:
> (a) Assistance in the tactical planning of landing operations and the assistance to Commanders appointed for such operations in the preparation of their plans and orders.
> (b) The planning and necessary co-ordination of raiding attacks on coasts occupied by the enemy.
> (c) The training of naval, military and air forces for landing operations.
> (d) The development of material that may be needed for all kinds of landing operations.

In the same memorandum the functions of I.S.T.D.C. were given as follows: "Development of material and training is undertaken by the Commandant, I.S.T.D.C., at Fort Cumberland (Portsmouth) with his staff of a Commander, an Adjutant R.M., and the help of the Wing Commander on the staff of D.C.O. When the base has been established at Inverary, development in training will become the responsibility of the Admiral Commanding at that base."

Two points are apparent from this memorandum: (1) I.S.T.D.C. has become concerned with amphibious operations; the study of all inter-Services operations has been dropped; [and] (2) On the opening of the Combined Training Centre (C.T.C.) at Inverary problems of training, and therefore very largely problems of tactics, would be transferred from the I.S.T.D.C. to the C.T.C.

C.T.C., Inverary, opened in August, 1940, but it was some months before it was fully organised. A close link between the I.S.T.D.C. and Inverary was established and officers of the two centres visited each other regularly. At the same time there still appeared to be a lack of definite directions for the work at the I.S.T.D.C. The D.C.O. was far more concerned with planning, organising and training the Special Service Troops, leaving the I.S.T.D.C. to fend for itself.

For some time, the work at the I.S.T.D.C. continued under its old terms of reference, although their studies were now amphibious; training and tactical responsibility was moving to C.T.C., Inverary. On the development side, the officers were particularly concerned with new landing ships and craft necessary for large scale combined operations. The officers of a centre, whose terms of reference had included the study of technique, tactics and training, were in a very favourable position to judge the types of ships and craft best suited to varying needs; the original ideas for these new ships and craft were usually put up to the

D.C.O. by the I.S.T.D.C., or the Admiralty Division concerned, and not because of a requirement expressed by the planners in London. D.C.O. then stated the requirement to the Admiralty who was responsible for design. Among the ships and craft thus originated were the Landing Assault Craft; Landing Tank Craft, L.C.T. (1), (2) and (3); Landing Ships Tank, L.S.T. (1) and (2) and later the L.S.D.; also the Glen Ships and the Maracaibos (oilers converted for carrying landing craft as well as oil); and the conversion of train ferries into L.C.M. carriers.

In February, 1941, the following were some of the problems under consideration at the I.S.T.D.C.:

(1) The fitting of directional control equipment for the control of landing craft into *Glen* class merchant ships.
(2) The first designs of L.S.T.s (Winettes) and Maracaibos (shallow draft oil tankers).
(3) The design for a more heavily armed and armoured Landing Craft Support (L.C.S.).
(4) Illumination for landing tanks at night. Under consideration were: (a) Star Shell fired from Mortars mounted in L.C.S.; (b) 1 lb. rocket releasing magnesium stars.
(5) The landing of vehicles from L.C.T.s. The following were under consideration: (a) Waterproofing of vehicles by covering certain parts in bags and towing ashore by winch, lorry or tractor; (b) A catamaran floated into position ahead of an L.C.T. and which would sink when the weight of a vehicle came on it; (c) Bridging the water gap by means of a form of gangway lifted by a crane fitted with a grab; (d) A specially designed ramp to be built at the side of a pier so that an L.C.T. could go alongside the pier and then be warped up to the ramp to discharge vehicles.

The I.S.T.D.C. was therefore keeping abreast of Combined Operations needs; and the problems with which the centre was already concerned were those which were to arise again and again in later years.

In March, 1941, a directive was issued to the D.C.O., the following extracts from which are relevant:

2. The Director of Combined Operations is responsible, under the general direction of the Minister of Defence and the Chiefs of Staff, for: (b) The development, including experiment, research and trial, of all forms of special equipment and craft required for opposed landings; (e) The provision of advice to the Chiefs of Staff on technical aspect of opposed landing operations.

4. The Director of Combined Operations will have under his command and direction the Inter-Services Training and Development Centre.

These points do not differ very much from the instructions given to his Command by the D.C.O. in his memorandum of September, 1940, nor from the more general directive issued to Lt.-Gen. Bourne in June, 1940. It did, however, clearly make him responsible for the development, including experiments, research and trial of craft and material required in combined operations. From the last part of the directive quoted, it is seen that the I.S.T.D.C., remained under the command of the D.C.O. Thus, with the opening and growth of the C.T.C., Inverary, and other training bases from August, 1940, onwards, the centre became more concerned with development and experiment and less with training and tactics.

At the same time, it would be wrong to pretend that the issuing of the directive immediately solved all the problems of guidance for the I.S.T.D.C. There was still a lack of co-operation between the planners and experimenters; the former did not know exactly what the latter had to offer, nor were the experimenters given an intimation of the ideas and requirements in the planners' minds. Nevertheless, an Inter-Services Organisation, independent of the three Service Ministries, had come into being and, even if the authorities at the London Headquarters were more concerned with training and planning, the I.S.T.D.C. could at least function, unfettered by the troubles of dealing with three separate ministries.

In spite of the fact that this Inter-Services Organisation had been specially set up to deal with the problems of assault operations in which all three Services were involved, it met with a certain amount of opposition, particularly in the Admiralty. In the autumn of 1940, a paper had been circulated recommending the abolition of the Directorate of Combined Operations and suggesting that training should be the concern of the Admiralty and War Office, and that all development of ships and craft should come under the control of the Admiralty, with the Commandant I.S.T.D.C. acting as the link between the Admiralty and development. This proposal came to nothing but it shows some of the difficulties under which the new Directorate was working.

Throughout the summer of 1941 and until the appointment of Commodore Mountbatten, the I.S.T.D.C. continued with development and trials at Portsmouth.

The Chiefs of Staff Directive to Commodore Mountbatten, December, 1941

In October, 1941, Commodore Mountbatten was appointed in place of Admiral Keyes and took the title of Adviser on Combined Operations (A.O.C.); and Commodore Combined Operations (C.C.O.), when acting in an executive capacity for units under his command. In December, 1941, a new directive was issued from which the following extracts are taken:

> 2. Under the general direction of the Chiefs of Staff you will: (a) Act as technical adviser on aspects of, and at all stages in, the planning and training for combined operations; (b) Be responsible for co-ordinating the general training policy for combined operations for the three Services; (c) Study, in conjunction with the Chiefs of Staff Organisation, tactical and technical developments in all forms of combined operations varying from small raids to a full scale invasion of the Continent; (d) Direct and press forward research and development in all forms of technical equipment and special craft peculiar to Combined Operations.

From the above extracts it will be seen that the A.C.O. had more limited powers than the late D.C.O., although these were later increased so that he took on, in effect, all the functions previously exercised by the D.C.O. Nevertheless, his primary role, besides the active prosecution of training for combined operations, was largely advisory. His responsibility for experimental work was covered by the words "Direct and press forward research and development" compared with the responsibility for the "development including experimental, research and trial, and of all forms of special equipment and craft required for opposed landings", which was laid down in Admiral Keyes' directive of March, 1941.

Development of Ships and Craft: Mission to the U.S.A. (December, 1941)

Following Commodore Mountbatten's appointment, the I.S.T.D.C. remained at Portsmouth. In December, 1941, the Commandant and representatives of D.N.C. and D.N.E. Admiralty, visited the U.S.A. to see what assistance could be gained from American production of landing ships and craft. The designs and specifications of the L.S.D., L.S.T (2), L.C.T. (5) were taken to the U.S.A. to be produced in their shipyards; during the war these were produced as U.S. ships and craft, but the fact that they were British in conception and design must not be overlooked, which reflects great credit on the close co-operation between the I.S.T.D.C. and D.N.C. The U.S. L.C.M. (3) was also inspected and certain modifications suggested and accepted; and the craft was put into production soon afterwards.

The Experimental Section of C.O.H.Q and the Combined Operations Development Centre, April, 1942-August, 1942

Formation of the Combined Operations Development Centre and an Experimental Section within C.O.H.Q.

In April, 1942, a reorganisation to co-ordinate and control experiments and developments in combined operations took place. The Chief of Combined Operations (as Admiral Mountbatten had become) divided the I.S.T.D.C. into two parts: one part moved to London and joined the staff of C.O.H.Q.; the other section remained at Portsmouth now known as the Combined Operations Development Centre (C.O.D.C.).[1]

This division was of considerable importance as, to all intents and purposes, it marked the beginning of the slowly strengthening link between the planners and the experimenters. The Commandant of the I.S.T.D.C. took charge of the section in C.O.H.Q. and was known as "Co-ordinator of Experiments and Developments in Combined Operations (C.X.D.)". As his staff he had the following officers:

Experiments and Development:
    Army G.S.O. 2.
    Naval Staff Officer.
    Army G.S.O. 3.
    Naval Assistant Staff Officer.

In addition C.X.D. had the help of the following:
    Naval Camouflage Officer.
    Senior Engineer Officer and Senior Constructor Officer of the Staff of Rear-Admiral Landing Barges.
    An officer belonging to the Air Staff.

The Signals Section were also available to give advice to the C.X.D. In this connection it should be noted that the Signals Section always worked independently of the main experimental section throughout the war, but close liaison was constantly maintained.

---

[1] The change of title from I.T.S.D.C. to C.O.D.C. became effective in August, 1941, when the training responsibility of the I.S.T.D.C. was taken over by the C.T.C. Inverary.

The directive to C.X.D. was as follows:

C.X.D. is directly responsible to C.C.O. for the following duties:
(1) He will co-ordinate all experiments carried out by formations, ships and establishments under the command of C.C.O.
(2) He will be responsible for the development of all special craft and equipment required for use in combined operations.
(3) He will ensure that development is kept in step with staff requirements.
(4) He will maintain close liaison with naval, army and air force experimental establishments and will be responsible for presenting to them the combined operations aspect of development which they are carrying out.
(5) He will be responsible for advising all combined operations Force Commanders and planning staffs on the following subjects: (a) Capabilities of existing combined operations equipment; (b) The probable capabilities of equipment under development; (c) The possibilities of improving or developing equipment to deal with special problems which may arise in the course of a particular operation.

Procedure for Furthering Projects

C.C.O. laid down the procedure for experimental and development work. Decisions on staff requirements regarding quantity, nature and function of combined operations material, and for research and development were made, after due consideration, by the appropriate Member or Members of the Council. That is to say that for a purely naval requirement the decision (for C.C.O.) was given by the Assistant Chief of Combined Operations, or if it was a combined military and air requirement, the decision would be given by the Vice-Chief of Combined Operations and the Deputy Chief of Combined Operations in consultation.

For developments there was C.X.D. on the staff of C.C.O. in C.O.H.Q. Under him worked the staff officers of the three Services engaged in development. The C.X.D. was empowered to decide for C.C.O. all questions of development for all three Services, in respect of their technical aspects.

The normal cases to be considered fell into one of three categories, as follows:

Case 1 – Requirement originating with the Operational Staff.

If a requirement originated with the operational staff as a result of experience in a raid or at one of the training establishments, it was to be put up by the staff concerned through V.C.C.O., D.C.C.O., or A.C.C.O., as the case may be, who, after deciding that it was a genuine requirement, would refer it to the C.X.D. for development action. C.X.D. would then decide whether it was, on the face of it, practicable, and if it was, would set the necessary machinery in motion. If it was not practicable, he would refer the question back to the Member of the Council concerned for further discussion or cancellation of the requirement.

Case 2 – Proposal for requirement arising out of an actual development. This was the most common case. If, in the course of development, it was seen that a promising line had been opened up for a particular piece of material, the question of what use should be made of it and the reactions of this upon the further stages of development would be referred by the originator to the C.X.D. The latter would decide whether it was worth putting to the Council and, if it was, would do so with the object of getting the Member or Members of the Council concerned to state whether an operational use of this material already existed or could be foreseen and, if so, exactly what. If possible, the Council would then draw up an outline staff requirements for guidance of further development and refer these back with the original paper to the C.C.D. for action.

Case 3 – Development and Definition of function occurring together. There were cases where the development of a piece of material and its use would go hand in hand, because the requirement preceded the development (or vice versa) in the course of exercises or training. In such cases, the man on the spot generally took the development and the idea to quite an advanced stage before he put it up to the higher authority. These cases, though generally comparatively minor, often gave rise to technique and material of the greatest practical value. Papers from ships and establishments containing reports of such ideas or developments would go, in the first instance, to the C.X.D. who would decide, according to their nature, whether they should first be seen by his staff or by the operational staff. Thereafter they would be handled as Case 2 or Case 1 above, whichever was applicable.

It was essential that the closest liaison and co-operation was maintained between the officers on the operational staff and those concerned with development, as this was the only way possible way to deal with two aspects of the same problem. The new organisation facilitated this and often enabled a definite proposal to be put up for decision to the C.X.D. or the Member of the Council as the case may be, by the staff officer, who first saw the paper, having discussed it with his opposite number, thus saving a lot of minutes and time. Any modifications affecting existing craft were referred to Rear-Admiral Landing Craft and Bases (R.A.L.B.) and trials were arranged by R.A.L.B. or A.A.Q.M.G. Unfortunately, this personal liaison link, so necessary between the planners and the development side, was not always evident; for example, no one in the Experimental Section knew of the Dieppe raid until it was over. The outcome of this was that the C.X.D. was immediately authorised to attend all planners' meetings.

The Directorate of Experiments and Staff Requirements (D.X.S.R.), later becoming the Directorate of Experiments and Operational Requirements (D.X.O.R.), August, 1942-October, 1943

The enlargement of the Experimental Section at C.O.H.Q. by the absorption of part of the C.O.D.C. together with the formation of Combined Operations Experimental Establishment[2] (C.O.X.E.) was an important step forward. In August, 1942, C.C.O. issued a memorandum setting up the Directorate of Experiments and Staff Requirements (D.X.S.R.) as a branch of C.O.H.Q. The memorandum briefly defined the duties of D.X.S.R. as the formulation of qualitative requirements and gave instructions on the manner in which he was to work with other branches of the Headquarters. The memorandum also transferred the Technical Data Section, which had been started in C.O.H.Q., from the Directorate of Combined Training to D.X.S.R.

The directive issued to D.X.S.R. included the following:

(1) The D.X.S.R. was to be a member of the Combined Operations Council and Operations Committee and was entitled to attend Chief Planners' Committee Meetings whenever necessary.

(2) The primary function of D.X.S.R. was that of formulating qualitative staff requirements. The secondary function was that of arranging with the appropriate technical departments of the Service such experiments as are necessary to facilitate the formulation of staff requirements and to establish the correct method of using equipment. He did not undertake development but, when necessary, arranged for it to be undertaken by the appropriate Service Department.

(3) He was to co-ordinate all experiments and trials, other than naval service trials and tactical trials, carried out by ships craft, formations and establishments under the command of C.C.O. and for this purpose was to maintain close liaison with the

---

[2] This Establishment was evolved from the I.S.T.D.C., part of which remained in Portsmouth and became the C.O.D.C. in August 1941. In August 1942, it expanded and moved to Westward Ho, North Devon, where it was known as C.O.X.E.

staff of the Director of Combined Training, with the G.O.C. Royal Marine Division, the Commander S.S. Brigade and with formations to which the C.C.O. acted in an advisory capacity. In the case of naval equipment, for type trials requiring more than the resources permanently allocated to the C.O.X.E., he was to apply through the Naval Q Planner (N.Q.P.) staff, for any additional resources needed. For service and tactical trials of naval equipment he was to transfer the matter formally to the N.Q.P. staff to propose the necessary programme.

(4) When, as a result of trials with a prototype, D.X.S.R. had put forward a recommendation for production, he was to hand the matter over formally to the Q Planners concerned who, thereupon, were to take over responsibility for initiating the necessary action and for arranging all consequential matters of manning, training and maintenance.

(5) D.X.S.R. was to direct, on behalf of C.C.O., the work of the C.O.X.E., Westward Ho, instructions being passed through the Commandant and N.O. i/c Appledore.

In this directive two points should be noted: (1) The definite instructions that D.X.S.R. was to have access to the planners; (2) That his primary function was that of formulating qualitative staff requirements; secondly, he was the co-ordinator of trials and experiments but he did not undertake development which he arranged, when necessary, with the appropriate Service Department.

The Technical Data Section, which had previously worked under the Director of Combined Training, was brought under D.X.S.R., partially because of the fact that D.X.S.R. officers were constantly in need of information from this section, but mainly because the section needed to work closely with the division responsible for developments, in order that the information in the Technical Data Section could be kept up to date. The section was, of course, available to all within C.O.H.Q. and outside authorities.

With the enormous increase of work and with the growth of many committees required for the spade work for Operation "Overlord", difficulties arose in D.X.S.R. owing to the staff work involved. Individual experimental officers were a satisfactory link between the C.O.H.Q., the appropriate branches of Service Ministries, C.O.X.E., etc., but the immense task of correlating reports and distributing them to outside authorities necessitated the increase in the strength of the Staff Duties Section.

Throughout 1942, a great deal of the preparatory work for "Overlord" was carried out by the various committees on which the

C.C.O. was represented; on many, his representative was D.X.S.R. From the beginning of the year, there had been regular meetings at C.O.H.Q. to discuss development and experimental work, and the small experimental section at C.O.H.Q. had done much to circulate information on the results of trials and development within C.O.H.Q. and to Commands in this country and overseas.

Experimental Sections of the "Round-up" Administrative Planning Committee (R.A.P. Committee)

Of the Committees started in 1942, the most important was perhaps the "Round-up" Administrative Planning (R.A.P.) Committee. This administrative committee studied the problems of the invasion of Europe; it was advisory only, but the results of its deliberations did much to make the assault on North-West Europe possible. The Committee itself was divided into a number of sections, each responsible for the study of some particular problem or series of problems. The two sections of most concern to D.X.S.R. were that dealing with the Experimental Aspect, Combined Operations Technique (Section FF) and the section dealing with Beach Equipment (Section O). D.X.S.R. himself was convener of the former. Other sections on which D.X.S.R. was represented were:

> R.E. Works and stores, including bridging. (Section F.)
> Water supply. (Section J.)
> Petrol, oil and lubricants. (Section K.)
> Ammunition, including R.A.F. bombs (Section L.)
> Co-Ordination of policy regarding maintenance and supply. (Sections M and N.)
> Provision of transportation plant, equipment and stores for overseas. (Section BB.)

From this list can be seen the type of problems which were under review. To the section dealing with the experimental aspect came many requests from other sections for assistance. Terms of reference for Section FF were: (1) Co-ordination of all experimental work and development in connection with the combined operations aspect of "Round-up" (original code word for "Overlord"); (2) Initiation of experimental work and development of technique in the use of equipment as requested by other sections of the R.A.P. Committee.

But both (1) and (2) were to be limited to the embarkation and disembarkation, including the beach maintenance area and the port maintenance area, until normal port working commences.

This section of the R.A.P. Committee met at fortnightly intervals throughout the later months of 1942 and a list published in October, 1942, of experiments and trials either in progress or recently completed shows the magnitude and complexity of the problems on which the section was engaged:

(1) In progress:
Special boats for bridging water-gap from beached coasters.
Tank flotation.
Bren carrier flotation.
Tank wading.
Waterproofing and wading of wheeled vehicles, including vehicle maintenance after sea water immersion.
Amphibians.
Vehicle barges.
Hamilton mat pier.
Medium coasters to carry vehicles.
Landing of vehicles from Schuyts.
Petrol bulk landing.
Petrol cable.
Flextella roadway.
Manhandling aids.
Destruction of beach minefields.
Destruction of underwater obstacles.
Piers for use on flat beaches.
Extension ramp for L.S.T. (2).

(2) Completed:
Tractor and trailer.
Jones super crane (for fitting into barges and capable of a 1-ton lift).
Simplex spacing truss (to facilitate rapid erection of 3-in. tubular piers).
Blasting channel through sandbars.

At each meeting of Section FF, a full review was given of developments, trials and experiments, including a detailed report by the Commandant of the work being carried out at C.O.X.E. Experimental work for other sections of the R.A.P. Committee was discussed and initiated.

A very important sub-committee of this Section was formed to deal with the subject of petrol supply, the complexity of which warranted special and detailed study. This Petrol Sub-Committee dealt with the experimental work necessary for the landing of petrol in combined operations and, of necessity, brought this Section into very close touch with the section dealing with petrol, oil and lubricants. This Sub-Committee did much useful work, among which can fairly be credited the development of the idea and the early trials of Operation "Pluto" (Pipeline under the Ocean). Another sub-committee organised experiments and developments for the destruction of beach obstacles, the start of a very important branch of work for opposed landings which continued with varying urgency up to the time of "Overlord" and later, when the Japanese obstacles became the primary consideration.

Other committees were formed, as the sections of the R.A.P. Committee finished work in early 1943, mainly to deal with problems which had become pressing as the result of the Committee deliberations. D.X.S.R. was actively concerned with many of these. Perhaps the most important was the Beach Recovery Committee, which was formed in February, 1943. This was an executive committee, convened and presided over by D.X.S.R. and working in close conjunction with the War Office, G.H.Q. Home Forces and later with U.S. authorities. The Committee dealt with the experimental work of a special R.E.M.E. detachment which was studying the problem of beach recovery of wheeled and tracked vehicles. This detachment was under the command of the Commandant C.O.X.E. and requests for experimental work to be done were sent through C.O.H.Q. to the Commandant C.O.X.E.; and reports were submitted through C.O.H.Q. for the consideration of the Beach Recovery Committee. The Committee met regularly and considerable progress was made in problems under the following headings: (1) Trials of recovery equipment on all types of beaches; (2) Investigation of the recovery of vehicles from the water, the beaches and the beach maintenance area, to ascertain what special equipment was required in addition to recovery vehicles.

In July, 1943, this Committee issued a report on the progress made in beach recovery problems which served as a guide for future experimental and development work and assisted materially in the final experiments for "Overlord". The Committee continued to meet in order to correlate and co-ordinate new projects until early in 1944.

Change of title, D.X.S.R. becomes D.X.O.R.

Experimental work continued and, in May, 1943, the title of D.X.S.R. was changed to the Directorate of Experiments for Operational Requirements (D.X.O.R.) as more appropriate to his duties. It had become clear during the first half of 1943 that, unless some definite conclusions were reached speedily on which the provision of equipment for the assault on Europe could be based, experimenters would find it exceedingly difficult, if not impossible, to assess priorities; and planners would have little knowledge of the availability or the potentialities of new types of equipment. The headquarters of the Chief of Staff to the Supreme Allied Commander (C.O.S.S.A.C.) had been formed in November, 1942, and had appointed a special liaison officer to C.O.H.Q. As this officer had considerable previous experience of combined operations (he was in fact from C.O.X.E.), there was a strong link with D.X.S.R. At the same time, it was necessary to clarify the situation and in order to come to definite conclusions on which the provision of equipment and future training and planning could be based, the "Rattle" Conference was held in H.M.S. *Warren* at Largs in June, 1943.

The "Rattle" Conference was of great importance, but, as was to be expected, not all the decisions hoped for were reached. However, a great deal of ground was covered and the air was cleared of many of the difficulties which attended an assault on North-West Europe. But at this conference, details of equipment, craft, ships and so on, which had been designed, developed and tried by D.X.O.R. or his predecessors, were put clearly before the naval, military and air Commanders. D.X.O.R. himself and D.D.X.O.R. gave lectures to the conference and among the developments put before the conference, where production decisions were often taken, were:

Hedgerow.
L.C.G. (M.).
L.C.T. (R.).
Flame-throwing craft.
Bogus bombs.
Rocket projectile weapons.
Construction of artificial harbours.
Waterproofing vehicles.
Load-carrying amphibians.
Supply of P.O.L. by pipeline.
Temporary breakwaters for artificial harbours.
Engineer problems in the assault, including the breaching of beach obstacles above and below high water mark.
Bridging the water-gap by pontoons and vehicle landing ramps, etc.

The above list shows the various problems with which C.O.H.Q. and, in part, D.X.S.R. were occupied during 1942-43. Other branches had been concerned with working out tactics and techniques, but to D.X.S.R.

had fallen the task of testing and experimenting with new ideas, most of which arose in the minds of members of the Directorate. From this, staff requirements eventually emerged and, after consultation with the planning and training branches, the requirements were passed to the Service Ministries.

But the original idea was usually found within D.X.S.R., where the officers in their day-to-day work were more in touch with the particular problems involved and the possible methods of overcoming them. In addition, the appointment of a Chief Engineer to C.O.H.Q. was of real assistance to D.X.S.R. in advising on R.E. activities at C.O.X.E. and elsewhere. In later months he became far more closely concerned with D.X.S.R. as Deputy Director of the Experimental Branch. His work on R.E. matters concerning opposed landing and his close liaison with engineer authorities in other headquarters, contributed to the successes achieved in "Overlord".

The "Rattle" Conference made it very clear that there was still a lack of co-ordination of tactics, technique, equipment and development within C.O.H.Q., the Service Ministries and other headquarters. The position was obviously better than in the early years of Combined Operations, but there was still no means whereby all interested parties within C.O.H.Q. could meet together and, in conference, solve the problems of tactics, technique and development and thus keep all branches of the Headquarters working along similar lines of thought and development. Also, it was clear that officers concerned with planning, training or experiments had not time to consider, in addition to their normal tasks, the more general problems of warfare; nor had they sufficient time to assimilate the many lessons which could be learned from reports of Allied operations and exercises and ensure that these lessons were dealt with either through amended training instructions or new developments. It was therefore undesirable that D.X.O.R. should be entirely responsible, as laid down in his directive, for formulating qualitative staff requirements; too many other authorities and factors had to be taken into consideration. In order to clarify and assist in these difficulties, two important changes in internal affairs were made within C.O.H.Q.

The Assault Warfare Committee and Changes Within D.X.O.R.
First, in June, 1943, the Assault Warfare Committee and Assault Sub-Committee were formed. These Committees studied the recognised problems of warfare in a combined assault and made recommendations to the Executive on any measures, tactics, weapons or equipment likely

to help in solving them. In other words, the Committees studied warfare and considered qualitative requirements. D.X.O.R. was represented on both committees, which was necessary because the Committees were given powers to initiate action with the appropriate section of C.O.H.Q. for the carrying out of any experiments and trials needed. It should be noted that the planners were not represented as members of these committees, but a weekly briefing on plans by a planner kept both sides fully in the picture.

These Committees supplied a long-felt want in C.O.H.Q. and continued until after the war. From time to time their directives were slightly changed and membership varied, but throughout, D.X.O.R. was represented on both. The policy of C.O.H.Q. was clearly laid down through these committees, and development and experiment was kept in line with tactics and technique by the insistence that all major development and experiments must receive the approval of the Assault Warfare Committee. Small trials and experiments however, remained within the powers of D.X.O.R.

These Committees also emphasised the need for a division within C.O.H.Q., whose primary task was the study of warfare from a combined operations aspect and the recommendation of tactics, weapons and equipment and were likely to be of value; this necessarily implied a very close liaison with outside authorities and the initial examination of all reports, particularly operational reports. The Naval Staff Duties and Training Section of C.O.H.Q. already covered this from a naval point of view, but on the military side there was no section to undertake this task, except the military Staff Duties Section of D.X.O.R. The R.A.F. interests in this matter were necessarily small at the time.

In D.X.O.R.'s department, the need for a separate section to study these problems was fully realised and it was largely due to the advice of D.X.O.R. that such a section was set up. This was the second important change in the summer of 1943, and in July the military Staff Duties section of D.X.O.R. split off to form this new warfare section and the whole of D.X.O.R. was reorganised. The new section eventually became part of the Assault Warfare Committee or, as it was known at the time, the Amphibious Warfare Committee.

A new directive to D.X.O.R. was also issued to confirm the changes; the relevant extracts are as follows:

(1) The Director of Experiments for Operational Requirements is the head of an Inter-Services Department responsible for arranging experiments and trials (but not user and tactical trials) for the purpose of defining operational requirements for combined assault warfare.

(2) He is a member of the Assault Warfare Committee. As such he is responsible with them for the study of the technique of combined assault warfare and for making recommendations to the Executive as to any measures, tactics, weapons or equipment likely to prove of value.
(3) He is to direct on the behalf of C.C.O. the work of the C.O.X.E., Westward Ho, instructions being passed through the Commandant and the Naval Officer-in-Charge Appledore.
(4) He is to supervise the C.O.H.Q. Technical Data Centre which is to keep a library of technical statistics and other information on combined operations craft and equipment for the use of all three Services.
(5) He is to arrange trials and experiments only in connection with material considered by the Assault Warfare Committee to be of potential value in the combined assault. This applies also to inventions and suggestions concerning craft and equipment received from the Directors of Scientific Research, Admiralty, War Office, Air Ministry and elsewhere. The results of such trials and experiments are to be submitted in the first instance to the Assault Warfare Committee for consideration of further action.

It is of interest to compare these extracts with those of the directive issued in 1942. The department's main responsibility was now the arrangement of experiments and trials to define the operational requirements for Combined Operations; and large scale trials and developments were not to be arranged without the consent of the Assault Warfare Committee. D.X.O.R. was not now primarily responsible for formulating qualitative staff requirements, although he and the department were naturally consulted in the matter through the Assault Warfare Committee. The Technical Data Section remained administratively under D.X.O.R. but, as before, was available to any branch of C.O.H.Q., the Service Ministries and other headquarters. Until "Overlord", it was kept very busy by people seeking information on combined operations ships and craft and all types of army equipment and vehicles, for planning, experimental or development purposes.

Within the Directorate itself, various organisational changes took place and the Chief Engineer Combined Operations became D.D.X.O.R. in addition, which was an indication of the importance now being attached to sapper problems of the assault. Problems of beach and underwater obstacles, breaching concrete walls, etc., were of extreme importance and urgency, and the Chief Engineer and C.O.X.E. were concerned with these problems, often in conjunction with other authorities. In addition, beach roadways came within the R.E. province, as did the many and urgent transportation problems. To help the Chief Engineer in his dual function, a Military Trials Section was set up; in addition to this work, the section assisted in the co-ordination of the military side of D.X.O.R.'s experimental work, which was, very extensive.

The position of A.D.X.O.R. should also be noted; the Experimental Section worked under his direct supervision and he, being in touch with all development and experiment which was in progress, represented D.X.O.R. on the Assault Warfare Sub-Committee. The position of a Constructor Captain on the staff lapsed, but day to day problems on craft could be dealt with in the Technical Data Section where a qualified Admiralty draughtsman was attached from D.N.C.

Towards the end of 1943, most of the major experimental work for the assault on Europe had been completed and the equipment, which had been tested, was in production, but there were also many projects still under investigation which were directly and indirectly related to the operation. On the naval side, this problem was tackled by a committee which was formed to ensure that the responsibilities for any technical development in combined operations were clearly defined, that any necessary action was initiated and that co-ordination was organised and adequate. The committee ensured that, from a naval point of view, the following functions were adequately carried out:

(1) Advising from a technical point of view on the best use of existing and future equipment.
(2) Bringing designers of equipment then under development into close contact with the user (in particular with regard to forthcoming operations).
(3) Searching for new or unfulfilled staff requirements for which research and development facilities should be given.

The Combined Operations Experimental Establishment (C.O.X.E.). August, 1942-October, 1943

In 1942, two shortcomings were apparent in the Experimental and Development Section of C.O.H.Q. First, the very small staff at C.O.H.Q. found it difficult to cope with the steadily increasing work and, at the same time, maintain the very necessary liaison with the Service Ministries. In addition, the development centre (C.O.D.C.) took its orders and directions from this Section. Secondly, the C.O.D.C. (Portsmouth) was not ideal for the work which had to be done. The magnitude of the task of preparing for the re-entry into Europe was being realised more clearly and the existing organisation for development and experimental work was not yet in a position to cope with it.

During summer 1942, action was taken to overcome these two shortcomings. Reconnaissance was made to find a suitable locality for a Combined Operations Experimental Establishment (C.O.X.E.) in place of the existing C.O.D.C.; the amended war establishment was studied and was finally approved in July, 1942; and the officers of C.O.D.C. most of whom had considerable experience in combined operations matters, were moved to C.O.H.Q. to reinforce C.X.D.'s section or sent to help in the start of the new experimental establishment at Westward Ho.

C.O.X.E. was formed on 2nd August, 1942. The site was chosen in the Westward Ho-Appledore-Instow-Bideford area because tidal and beach conditions most nearly approximated those expected in the forthcoming assault on North-West Europe. There were, in addition, advantages in having both open and sheltered beaches, so that work could continue when severe weather conditions made use of the open beaches impracticable. This establishment was under the direct control of the Experimental Section of C.O.H.Q.; C.O.X.E. carried out trials and rendered reports, but initiation of projects and dissemination of the results of trials (as given in the C.O.X.E. reports) were the responsibility of C.O.H.Q. Experimental Section. Although a certain amount of minor development work was inevitably carried out by C.O.X.E., it must be emphasised that, by its terms of reference, it was essentially a trials centre. Development work was carried out by other authorities at C.O.H.Q.'s request and C.O.X.E. merely carried out the trials of equipment as ordered.

On 6th August, Admiral Mountbatten signed his first directive for the Commandant of the C.O.X.E. The opening paragraphs of this directive include the following:

> The object of the Combined Operations Experiment Establishment is the investigation of all problems of assault landings including those arising from flat beaches with a large rise and fall of tide, particularly with regard to the following matters:
>
> The handling of stores and conveying these stores across the beaches; the wading of tanks, tracked vehicles, armoured cars and wheeled vehicles; the landing of petrol in bulk.
>
> Your investigations should lead, not only to the development of special equipment, but also to the development in the technique of its use.
>
> The authority for initiating the development of a particular type of equipment or for holding trials, will come from me.

There was already operating in the area the experimental wing of the Department of Tank Design of the Ministry of Supply, which was primarily concerned with the modifications to tanks to enable them to wade ashore. This wing was attached immediately to C.O.X.E. for administration and discipline. The new establishment also absorbed a small Royal Engineers Transportation Experimental Depot which had been operating for a short time in the area. This depot was engaged on problems connected with the discharge of stores in assault landings.

As many of the problems concerned Field Engineers, a Royal Engineer Field Wing was immediately started for work on beach roadways and the demolition of both above and below water beach obstacles. It became apparent, after three months, that the original war establishment was not sufficient to cope with the multitude of projects, which were rapidly mounting up, and it was found necessary to include, as an integral part of the establishment, a Navy Wing, a Royal Army Service Corps Wing and later a Royal Artillery Wing.

As the majority of trials involved the use of landing craft, two composite flotillas, one consisting of all types of major landing craft and the other of minor craft, were based at Appledore for use by the establishment. These were administered by the Naval Officer-in-Charge who was also designated Co-ordinator of Combined Operations Establishments in the area and was responsible to C.C.O. that the establishment followed the general experimental policy laid down.

The workshops, tank hangars and stores were situated at Westward Ho, because, although a great deal of work took place on the beaches in the estuary, it was necessary for the workshops to be positioned as close as possible to the open beaches where most of the trials were carried out.

The establishment was a military one, consisting of some 30 officers and 500 other ranks but, since nearly all the trials carried out had, to some extent, a naval aspect, the Commandant had on his staff a Commander, R.N., as adviser on combined problems where craft were employed and who personally conducted naval trials.

The establishment was primarily engaged in investigating the practicability of equipment for the assault, or for the defence against seaborne landings; these investigations, by their special nature, required the ability to understand the technicalities of the equipment and to make on the spot modifications. In the course of these investigations, it was frequently found necessary to produce special equipment to meet some last-minute requirement and to develop a technique for its use.

The original directive only covered a bare outline of the work which ultimately devolved upon the establishment and space does not permit anything but a brief reference to some of the types of projects and problems which were studied; it is indeed difficult to name any problem or piece of equipment used in amphibious landings which did not, at some time, undergo examination by this establishment.

Some Examples of the Experimental Work of C.O.X.E.

The naval wing of C.O.X.E. was responsible in the U.K. for the initial operational trials of landing ships and both major and minor landing craft, to ensure that they met the joint naval and military requirements. In these trials, particular attention had to be given to such items as the handling and manoeuvrability of the craft on and off flat beaches and loading hards; the draughts and the depths of water at the bow of the craft for troops or vehicle disembarkation; the ability of the craft to withdraw through surf and the efficiency of the anchors and winches.

Many modifications to craft were carried out locally with the approval of the Admiralty whilst other craft were converted to meet special needs. Other trials covered the discharge of vehicles from ships and craft by pontoons and causeways, the swimming off of amphibians and D.D. tanks and the mounting and firing of guns and self-propelled artillery from the tank deck of landing craft.

Associated with these trials were problems relating to the discharge of stores from cargo ships and coasters by aerial ropeways, conveyers, amphibians and pontoon barges under every condition likely to be encountered in an assault landing and during the build-up phase. All types of mobile cranes, tractors and stores handling equipment were tested and reported upon. Methods for the recovery of stranded major and minor landing craft and for the salvage of sunken vehicles were also developed.

Extensive work was also done on the problem of the clearance of beach obstacles, which were known to exist in Normandy, by the use of landing craft equipped with special devices and also the clearance of beach minefields by the Royal Engineers. These obstacles had been secretly examined on the Normandy beaches by C.O.X.E. officers during a night reconnaissance raid.

One of the many interesting war-time projects, which required the full resources of the establishment, was the laying of an experimental undersea petrol pipeline, in association with the Petroleum Warfare Department, across the Bristol Channel from Wales to North Devon, a distance of 34 miles. From this, much valuable information was obtained and later incorporated in "Pluto" for the supply of petrol by pipeline to the Normandy beach-head. C.O.X.E. was responsible for laying, by landing craft, the pipeline from the pumping station in Wales to the Cable Ship Holdfast; and the landing of the terminal delivery end from the Holdfast to the petrol storage installation on the North Devon coast. The capacity of this pipeline was 120 tons per day and, for many weeks, petrol was supplied to south-west England through this experimental pipeline. A fuller account of this operation is given in Chapter 21.

C.O.X.E. was also responsible for the service trials of all amphibians in the U.K. in order to evaluate their surf performance; their ability to traverse mud, shingle, and sand dunes; and their troop and cargo carrying capacity. Considerable work was done to confirm the best means of evacuating casualties from amphibians to ships. All minor landing craft underwent comparative trials with particular attention to their performance in high surf and the discharge of troops, stores and guns under all conditions.

Waterproofing of vehicles was another problem on which a great deal of work was done. On flat beaches there is always a water-gap between the landing ship or craft and dry land, through which vehicles will have to pass. The maximum depth through which an untreated vehicle could wade was about 18 inches but, when it was known that the landings would be on the flat beaches of Normandy, C.O.X.E. was called upon to produce a solution which would enable vehicles to safely negotiate much greater depths. It was gradually increased, first to 3 ft. 6 in. and, by June, 1944, all vehicles, guns and equipment could wade ashore in depths of up to 4 ft. 6 in. As the size of craft grew larger so these wading capabilities again had to be increased.

During the course of the wading trials carried out in 1943, it became evident that many problems were likely to occur in embarking vehicles, guns and equipment in all types of landing ships and craft and even more so on disembarking them operationally on to a beach. It was clear that the principal consideration was the gradient of the landing beaches selected for the assault operation. The main difficulty encountered was that vehicles with low ground clearance, or long overhanging sections such as guns and tank transporters, were unable to negotiate the steep angle of the ramps. It was decided that there were two potential lines of enquiry which should be pursued. First, how could landing craft be modified to enable the vehicles to be landed on the flatter beach gradients, and, secondly, what modifications could be carried out to the vehicles which would enable them to be landed without difficulty?

It was at first thought that only certain vehicles would be affected, but it was soon found that the problem applied to the majority of vehicles, and could only be overcome by the modification of either the vehicle or the craft, or in some cases, both. This was an extremely serious matter for it meant that, in the short time remaining before "Overlord" every type of vehicle, gun and equipment destined to take part in that operation had to be subjected to trials by the establishment. This involved the examination of some 260 different types of equipment, most of which had been subjected to actual disembarkation trials on the beaches in the area.

Reorganisation to Prepare for the War in the Far East October, 1943 to the end of the War

On completion of most of the experimental work on equipment required for the assault on Europe, the thoughts of C.O.H.Q as a whole were turning to the Far Eastern War. It was clear that this would involve a series of combined operations, and problems not associated with the invasion of Europe would have to be tackled. With the major European tasks done or in hand Admiral Mountbatten was, in August, 1943, appointed S.A.C.S.E.A. and, after a short interval Major-General Laycock was appointed C.C.O.

On 27th November, 1943, C.C.O., General Laycock, was issued a new directive by the Chiefs of Staff in which the following points were of importance to the Experimental Branch:

> Under the general direction of the Chiefs of Staff you will:
>
> (a) Study tactical and technical problems of amphibious operations, including small scale raids, and formulate doctrine and staff requirements.
> (b) Direct and press forward research and development in all forms of technical equipment including craft peculiar to combined operations.
>
> In addition to your responsibilities in the U.K. you will also be responsible for the co-ordination of development in combined assault training and technique among British authorities overseas, and for ensuring, so far as possible, the adoption of a common doctrine by Allied authorities both in the U.K. and overseas.

In spite of the changed wording of the directive as far as experiments and trials were concerned, there was little change in the character of the work of D.X.O.R. Of the four functional groups set up within C.O.H.Q. as a result of the Bottomley Report, the Directorate came under that of the Director of Combined Operations (Naval) (D.C.O.(N.)) whereas previously D.X.O.R. had dealt with C.C.O. direct. The work, including that of D.C.O.(N.)'s group, was as follows:

(1) All developments regarding ships, craft, weapons and equipment.
(2) Experiments and trials other than user trials.
(3) Co-ordination and development of all Inter-Services Signals and C.O.H.Q. Signals Organisation.
(4) Technical information and data; the preparation of technical pamphlets and information.
(5) Control of C.O.X.E.'s work.
(6) Proposals for user and tactical trials related to the above functions.
(7) Study of technical reports from outside sources and circulation within C.O.H.Q.

From this, the functions of D.X.O.R. can be clearly seen as, in effect, all the above with the exception of sub-paragraph (3) were his concern; the Directorate was slightly reorganised to conform to the general reduction in staff throughout C.O.H.Q. It is interesting to note in the list given above that the promulgation of information was now in the form of technical pamphlets. This was in accordance with the new scheme working throughout C.O.H.Q. of publishing information in the form of the Monthly Information Summary, or, for individual subjects, in the form of a bulletin. Information received as the result of trials, was sent out at once to the authorities most intimately concerned and later published for all outside authorities in the form of a bulletin or article in the Monthly Summary.

Preparation of these for the Press necessitated a great deal of work and, although the Training Branch were responsible for issue, a special officer was necessary in D.X.O.R. to handle the vast quantity of material as, in fact, the subject matter of most bulletins and the Monthly Summaries was provided by D.X.O.R. officers. This officer became part of the Technical Data Section. In addition, the Technical Data Section had the services of an official photographer; and, a little later, a Dark Room was set up to cope with the enormous demand for photographs both from within C.O.H.Q. and from outside authorities.

In 1944, therefore, C.O.H.Q. was working under the functional group system and D.X.O.R. had settled down as a part of the D.C.O.(N.) group. The Amphibious Warfare Committee[3] and Sub-Committee continued to function as before and a new directive was issued in March, 1944.

---

[3] Formerly the Assault Warfare Committee. The change of the title became effective in January 1944.

The terms of reference were similar to the earlier directive, namely: the study and review of all tactical and technical problems connected with amphibious operations throughout the world and making recommendations to the Executive.

D.X.O.R. and A.D.X.O.R. represented the branch on the main Sub-Committee and the work was classified under three main headings: (1) Initiation of the study of new problems or new aspects of old ones; (2) Investigation of problems passed to them for consideration; [and] (3) The study, with a view to making recommendations, of the technique and tactical developments of Allied and enemy nations.

From this it can be seen that a lot of the work of D.X.O.R. had necessarily to pass through the Committee. D.X.O.R., with thoughts of the Far East War and long-term developments, would not recommend the development of any major items unless Amphibious Warfare Committee's and the Executive's authority were obtained. As the directive stated:

> The Committee is not to initiate action for carrying out experiments and trials, involving major expenditure or effort by outside authorities, without the prior authority of the Executive.
>
> D.X.O.R. is responsible for carrying out such experiments and trials as may effect his department in connection with the requirements of the Committee, and for following matters up with the appropriate Service Ministries as may be requisite.

D.X.O.R. officers, therefore, besides forming the necessary link with the outside authority responsible for the development of any particular project and being responsible for the arrangement of the many trials needed, had also, to prepare many papers for the consideration of the Amphibious Warfare Committee and render reports on progress made. In addition, dissemination of information immediately the trials were completed and the writing of articles for the Monthly Information Summary or complete bulletins on varying subjects took up a considerable amount of time.

The Effect of the Invasion of Europe on Trials and Experiments

After the assault on North-West Europe, a small committee was set up to study all reports and make recommendations for future action, particularly with regard to the war in the Far East. A considerable amount of the work undertaken by D.X.O.R. during the following months arose from this committee's recommendations.

For the remainder of the year 1944, D.X.O.R. was fully occupied in assimilating the lessons learned in "Overlord", and C.O.X.E. was conducting trials and experiments which were necessary as a result of the operation. Knowledge of conditions in the Far East was somewhat slight in British circles, but realising this, C.O.H.Q. obtained permission for a party of observers to be attached to the U.S. Forces in the Pacific during their island-hopping campaigns. Armed with a formidable questionnaire from C.O.H.Q., observers took part in all the major U.S. amphibious operations in the S.W. Pacific and a great deal of useful information was collected from their reports which guided all branches of C.O.H.Q. in planning technique, tactics and developments for the Far Eastern War. There was also close liaison with S.E.A.C., copies of projects and reports were sent to the Combined Operations Division and conversely the Combined Operations Division sent to D.X.O.R. many requirements which needed development and trial. Liaison visits by D.X.O.R., D.D.X.O.R. and D.D.C.O.(Mil.) helped considerably to put the problems in the correct perspective, both in C.O.H.Q. and in S.E.A.C. Later in the year, a Director of Combined Operations was appointed to represent C.C.O. in India and the relationship between this Directorate and C.O.H.Q. was always very close.

In September, 1944, following the successful invasion of Europe, a new directive was issued to C.C.O. In this directive, the sections of importance to D.X.O.R. were:

> (2) Under the general direction of the Chiefs of Staff you will: (a) Study tactical and technical problems of amphibious operations, including small scale raids, and formulate doctrine and prepare staff requirements; (b) Initiate demands for research and stimulate action for the development of all forms of technical equipment, including ships, craft and vehicles.
>
> In overseas theatres you will be represented by Directors of Combined Operations, who will be under orders of local Commanders-in-Chief. Such Directors of Combined Operations will be responsible for technical advice in accordance with the doctrine for amphibious operations approved by you.

Minor changes should be noted in this directive, particularly the paragraph stating that C.C.O. will "initiate demands for research and stimulate action for development". This illustrates the task of the D.X.O.R. who did not carry out developments or research although he had a considerable watching brief on many developments and put out the demands for research to the appropriate authorities.

Organisation Overseas

As work continued for the Far East, it became clear that authorities in this country could not wholly and satisfactorily carry out all the developments and trials necessary owing to the very different conditions found in that theatre of war. Much useful and rapid work could be done in this country because of the advantages of the long-established experimental centres and facilities for manufacture and modification, but these did not supply the whole solution. The Directorate of Combined Operations (India) and the Combined Operations Division at S.E.A.C. had been set up; and C.O.H.Q. and D.X.O.R. were very closely linked with them and exchanges of needs and information were regular, but the necessity for some experimental establishment in the Far East to test various equipment in appropriate local conditions became more and more apparent. As a result, C.O.X.E. (India) was formed under the control of D.C.O.(I.).

This establishment was similar to the C.O.X.E. in the U.K. Projects were sent to it from D.C.O.(I.) and it was essentially a trials and not a development establishment. A close liaison was maintained with C.O.H.Q. and copies of all projects which were sent to C.O.X.E.(I.) were forwarded to D.X.O.R. in order to keep him informed and prevent duplication of the work at C.O.X.E.(U.K.); similarly, copies of all C.O.X.E.(U.K.) projects were sent to D.C.O.(I.). Reports were dealt with in the same way so that there was a complete interchange of information, supplemented by the Monthly Information Summaries and bulletins, and the monthly bulletin which D.C.O.(I.) started. The work done in India consisted of confirmatory trials in local conditions. Sometimes both C.O.X.E.(U.K.) and C.O.X.E.(I.) carried out similar trials in order to correlate results; of these, the trials of equipment in mud, swamp, fast-flowing rivers and undergrowth became of great importance to both centres.

Work continued for the Far East through the early part of 1945; in addition, important trials were arranged at C.O.X.E. preparatory to the Rhine crossing. These trials were carried out as emergency trials done on the highest priority and covered such points as:

> Carriage of minor landing craft on tank transporters.
> Launching of minor landing craft from tank transporters without the use of a crane.
> Overloading minor landing craft with carriers or vehicles for a river crossing.
> Handling of amphibians in fast-flowing river.
> Amphibians and minor craft towing rafts in rivers.

The handling of these trials possibly showed D.X.O.R. and C.O.X.E. working at their best; the value of an inter-Services team, which had all the necessary contacts with the operational forces, the Service and

Supply Ministries was very clearly emphasised and the trials were carried out expeditiously and well.

Reorganisation of D.X.O.R.

With the establishment of D.C.O.(I.) and the opening of C.O.X.E.(I.), a certain amount of work, which normally would have been carried out by D.X.O.R., was done in India. It was therefore possible to make a reduction and reallocation of the officers in D.X.O.R. In the previous organisation, a division had been made between the Trials Section and the Experimental Section; this was a somewhat invidious division as it was not at all clear where a line could be drawn between trials and experiments. While tasks carried out were fairly well understood within C.O.H.Q., the instructions covering the new organisation made this quite clear:

> The Experimental Section will be responsible for the initiation and conduct of all trials and experiments, naval, military and air.
>
> The Direction and Data Section will be responsible for the co-ordination of all experimental work of the Branch, and also for any subsequent action considered necessary such as, for example, the promulgation of reports to outside authorities. This section will also be responsible for collation and maintenance of data and records.

With minor modifications, mainly reductions in staff, this arrangement remained in force until the end of the war, when the Department was slowly reorganised on to a peace-time basis.

The Amphibious Warfare Committee continued to function within C.O.H.Q. and as before D.X.O.R. and G1 (Experiments) (late A.D.X.O.R.) were representatives of the Directorate on the main and sub-committee respectively. As before, the work in D.X.O.R.'s branch was largely concerned with these committees and in the arranging of trials and promulgation of information.

With the end of the war in Europe, the needs of the Far Eastern War were the main concern of D.X.O.R. but, with the easing of tension, longer term policy came more to the fore and consideration was given to many post-war problems. Certain reductions of staff took place within the Directorate. In May, 1945, the division of responsibilities between the Admiralty and C.O.H.Q. was finally decided, and the technical matters, in which D.X.O.R. was primarily interested, were agreed; these were in conformity with the directive issued to C.C.O. in September, 1944.

In July, the method of initiating experiments, trial and development projects was again defined; D.X.O.R. had for some time been working according to these instructions, but their issue clarified the position defining more exactly his duties and function.

At the same time as the issue of this Acquaint, D.X.O.R. took over the responsibility for the development of equipment for small scale amphibious operations which had previously been the responsibility of the A/Q division of C.O.H.Q. By this action D.X.O.R. became responsible for all experimental, trial and development work.

Until the end of the war, experiment and development for the Far East continued. In D.X.O.R. the necessary knowledge and experience was gathered; the difficulties and problems in design, development and trial of combined operations equipment were only too well known. The manner in which work should be handled and completed had been learned in the experience and evolution of the Directorate through the years of war.

End of the War and Reorganisation for Peace

In August, 1945, with the end of the Japanese war, C.O.H.Q. and, with it D.X.O.R., began to reorganise on to a peace-time basis. The Department was firmly established and working smoothly and efficiently. In peacetime with a reduced establishment, it continued to work on long-term projects.

The road from the I.S.T.D.C. had been long and changing; and D.X.O.R. had grown to a vastly different and more important organisation than was visualised by the small group of men who gathered at Eastney in 1938 to study the problems of combined operations.

Since the end of the War, two Boards have been brought into being. First the formation of the Amphibian Requirement and Development Board. Second, the formation of the Correlation of Development Board.

As early as January, 1944, a meeting had been called to correlate the development of landing craft and ships, and Army and R.A.F. vehicles and equipment; it was hoped, thereby, to ensure that the Admiralty did not construct ships and craft unsuited to new and proposed Army and R.A.F. equipment, and that the War Office and Air Ministry did not build equipment which was unsuited to naval craft and ships. It was agreed that, when new landing craft were planned, an inter-Services meeting should be called for correlation; also, that any problems which might arise with existing craft and new or modified Army and R.A.F. equipment should be dealt with by an ad hoc meeting. In fact, this suggestion did not work out, under war conditions. However, with the end of the war, C.C.O. called a meeting to discuss the best methods of ensuring correlation in the development of vehicles, equipment and craft, including amphibians, and to study the carriage of these items in merchant ships. This meeting decided to set up a Standing Committee for this purpose, under the Chairmanship of C.C.O.

In spite of the urgent need for economy and reorganisation, it was decided that the C.O.X.E. should continue in peace-time. Experience had shown that the organising and execution of trials demanded highly specialised and skilled work requiring considerable appreciation of what to look for and how to look for it and, unless personnel employed in this work were continually fulfilling their function, valuable data would be lost through inexperience. The necessity for continuity in such trials was considered to be of paramount importance for there was an obvious need for the evaluation of equipment, produced for one Service and which might be of use to the others, being examined by one establishment who was able to carry out trials bearing in mind the difficulties and problems of each Service.

Chapter 20

THE DEVELOPMENT OF SHIPS AND CRAFT

Before describing the history of the development of ships and craft, it is necessary to understand the Admiralty definitions of staff targets and staff requirements. They are as follows:

Staff Targets:
Are intended to provide points of aim for research and development. They are stated in general terms and look ahead as much as possible. They take no account of the technical promise of their being met and are therefore purely a Staff Appreciation of what they would like to have. They also take no account of whether two targets are in practice mutually interfering and whether therefore compromise may be necessary.

Staff Requirements:
Aimed research having shown that a staff target is a practical possibility, staff requirements can be stated. These are designed to guide development of the staff target along the desired channels and are broad statements of the main features of the equipment, and the function it is required to perform. Staff requirements are liable to be, and should be, amended at intervals to keep them up to date.

It will be seen that the Staff, when formulating requirements, must keep within the bounds of possibility. If the assault technique requires a performance from a ship which cannot be met by existing equipment, and invention or development is necessary before it can be evolved, then it is termed a "staff target". It was no use requiring a speed of 20 knots when the only engine available could give 10 knots.

In all amphibious operations, a certain number of ships and craft are required to "beach". They must, therefore, have shallow draught, but this requirement conflicts with seaworthiness. Again, the requirements of carrying capacity, armament, speed (which means heavy engines) and seaworthiness conflict with shallow draught. Designs were therefore difficult and every means had to be adopted to reduce weight without loss of speed or strength.

The Americans overcame this by the extensive use of acetylene welding, as opposed to our riveting, and by using diesel engines instead of steam in their L.S.T.s. We were handicapped by not having these facilities. This largely explains the good performance of the L.S.T. (2) vis-à-vis the British later type of L.S.T., although the British got out the basic design of both.

From the beginning of the war up to and including the first L.C.T. and L.S.T., there were no "staff requirements" formally stated, as we know them. The ships were designed by the Director of Naval Construction (D.N.C.) and Thornycrofts at the instigation of a few naval officers who had a knowledge of the existing technique of assault landings and also of existing army equipment. These officers were either members or recent members of the staff of C.O.H.Q. The "staff requirements" of these vessels were written out subsequently for record purposes.

Later, when the staff of C.O.H.Q. had settled down, gained experience and evolved a modus operandi with the Admiralty, the procedure became regularised. "Staff requirements" were considered and stated by the combined staff in C.O.H.Q., in consultation with Admiralty staff divisions and technical departments, before designs were begun.

The Development of Ships and Craft up to 1940

During World War I, the only ship especially adapted for landing operations was the *River Clyde*, an ex-collier. The troops were to disembark through sally ports cut in her sides on to staging and then cross a hopper which formed a bridge to the shore and which was reinforced, if necessary, by lighters. This ship was used in the Gallipoli Campaign but, in the event, it proved a task of the utmost difficulty to secure the hopper and lighters in the appropriate position; and, despite great heroism and determination, nearly all, who attempted the assault, became casualties of one sort or another. The lesson derived from this operation appeared to be that it was unwise to assault land from a vessel without the means of very rapid disembarkation and without some degree of dispersal.

After the failure of the Gallipoli campaign, little further thought was given to amphibious warfare until the end of the war, when lighters were produced for use in Mesopotamia. These self-propelled lighters carried horses or troops in the hold, disembarking them over the bows by means of portable ramps.

In Britain, the period between the two great wars produced no revolutionary thought and little in practice with regard to the development of special ships and craft for amphibious warfare. It was left to the Japanese to design, in secret, a stern launching landing craft carrier, a landing ship fitted with bow doors and which carried vehicles and some small ramped landing craft; these they used with success in operations in the Hai-Ho River in 1937.

Generally speaking, British effort was confined mainly to academic studies conducted by Staff Colleges. However, one small water jet-propelled landing craft capable of carrying vehicles was produced in 1922, and three more were produced between 1928 and 1930. The Italy-Abyssinian war brought about the further construction of six similar craft. These were the fore-runners of the present L.C.M.

The Small Craft Situation during the first year of World War II
When war broke out in 1939 the amphibious fleet consisted only of the following special vessels:

> 12 Assault Landing Craft (L.C.A.).
> 10 Mechanised Landing Craft (L.C.M.) old jet-propelled type.
> 1 New L.C.M.
> 1 Support Landing Craft (L.C.S.).

All these vessels were lost on amphibious operations at Narvik during the second quarter of 1940, and the activities of the Inter-Services Training and Development Centre had ceased as regards practical work except that, at the end of 1939, two prototype new design L.C.A. were completed to meet the requirements laid down by them.

By May, 1940, nine new L.C.A. and two new L.C.M. had been built. They took part in the evacuation of Dunkirk during which six craft were lost. Although forty-eight L.C.A. and thirty L.C.M. were ordered after Dunkirk, no priority could be given for their construction due to the urgent needs of the Navy for all other classes of warship.

In June, 1940, the Prime Minister appointed a Director of Combined Operations, with instructions to prepare for and carry out offensive raids. As a result, C.O.H.Q. increased the order to 93 L.C.A., 106 L.C.M.,

25 L.C.T., 13 L.C.S. and 3 infantry landing ships. Nevertheless, at that time, the Navy was fully extended and, with the threat of invasion, the possibility of launching an amphibious operation on any scale seemed remote. Therefore, the construction of the larger special vessels came to a standstill.

Long Term Plans for Invasion
It was not until September, 1941, that the British planners were ordered to put up a paper on the possibility of a return to the Continent. The result caused food for thought, as the Staff solution recommended the assault being made by three armoured divisions and thirteen infantry divisions with a consequent demand among other things for a very large number of landing craft of different types. The concept of an invasion of Europe mounted from Great Britain therefore influenced the design of all or nearly all special amphibious equipment.

The Development of Landing Ships and Major Landing Craft
In September, 1940, the first expedition against Dakar was launched and failed. At a meeting of the Directors of Plans summoned by the Prime Minister after the event, it was made clear that no such operation could succeed without supporting armour and that no vessels capable of carrying tanks and transporting them over a long sea journey were in existence.

Tank Landing Ships "Winettes" and "Maracaibos"
After some discussion the Prime Minister stated that this was a problem that would constantly recur and no offensive would be possible until it was solved. He stated the need for a ship capable of carrying large numbers of tanks across the oceans of the world and landing them directly on the enemy shore. The Admiralty were directed to produce these ships as a matter of urgency.

As a result of the Prime Minister's directive, the D.N.C. put in hand the design of new type tank landing ships, the first batch being known as "Winettes". These vessels and their successors of various designs were to influence future amphibious warfare in a similar way to which the armoured tank had already changed many aspects of land warfare.

However, in order to cover the long period required for the design and production of entirely new ships, it was decided to convert certain light draught tankers which had been specially built to cross the bar of the Maracaibo River in South America. Three "Maracaibos" completed conversion by June, 1941, whereas, due to production difficulties, the first of the "Winettes" was not completed until early 1943.

Neither of these tank carrying craft proved satisfactory in practice. The "Maracaibos" with a fault in their bow doors, were unseaworthy in bad weather; and there was an excessive water-gap for vehicles to cross when landing direct on to any but the steepest beaches. The "Winettes" had too deep a draught and an unsatisfactory ramping system. Nevertheless, they were important as being the first ships ever used for landing tanks direct on to a beach and their early completion enabled many problems to be studied.

The Landing Ship Tank, Mark II (L.S.T. 2)

In October, 1941, when plans for the invasion of Europe began to receive serious attention, the Joint Planning Staff reported that about 2,000 tank landing vessels would be required to carry the invading force contemplated. Thus, with all ship building capacity in the U.K. stretched to the full, help was sought from the U.S.A. However, at that time, the Americans had no Combined Operations Organisation or experience and were reluctant to build for us any ships other than those of conventional design.

It was not until the President personally intervened in the matter and gave instructions that the ships should be produced at the highest priority, that a start was made. Once started, production of this new type vessel, suitable for an Atlantic crossing and embodying British experience, was quick and the first L.S.T. (2) was completed in November, 1942. Altogether over 1,000 were built in two years, of which 115 were taken over by the British.

The L.S.T. (2) design proved very successful and only a few modifications were subsequently found necessary. However, after the ships had been in service, the need for their use on flat beaches was realised. It was then found that, like the "Winettes" although not to the same extent, their draught was too great for direct beaching on the flat shores of North-West Europe. The difficulty was solved in four ways: (1) By drying out as in Normandy, where the rise and fall of the tide was large; (2) By using pontoons as in Sicily and Italy, and in the Pacific theatre; (3) By the use of special pier heads as erected in the artificial harbours in Normandy; [and] (4) By the construction of suitable hards in captured ports.

The Landing Ship Tank, Mark III (L.S.T. 3)

In October, 1943, plans for the overthrow of Japan made it necessary for a proportion of L.S.T.s to be built in the U.K. The Staff required a larger ship than the L.S.T. (2) with the same beaching characteristics, but with greatly increased endurance and speed and with slightly larger bow doors. However, material limitations prevented the staff requirement being fully met at the time.

This was due partly to the fact that the Admiralty could only make available steam reciprocating engines (originally earmarked for frigates but now not required due to the cancellation of part of the frigate programme); and partly because the British and Canadian shipyards were only equipped to produce craft with riveted plates which result in a heavier and higher craft than the American diesel-driven all-welded ships. The additional draught was a great disadvantage, as it involved the need for a means of bridging the water-gap on all but steep beaches. However, there was no other alternative and the design was approved, staff requirements being modified accordingly as follows:

> To land 500 tons of vehicles on a beach slope 1 in 50 with draught not exceeding 4 ft. 7 in. forward and 11 ft. 6 in. aft.
> Accommodation for all vehicle crews.
> Speed 13 knots, endurance 8,000 miles at 11 knots.
> Power operated bow door.
> To be capable of carrying L.C.T. on deck.
> Ramp from upper deck to tank deck to carry 10 tons.
> Provision for carrying N.L. pontoon equipment.
> Six L.C.A. to be carried, two in davits, four under derricks.
> The height between decks and the width of the bow door to be increased so as to facilitate the carrying of amphibians.

Landing Ship Dock (L.S.D.)

At a meeting held in the Admiralty on 19th September, 1941, to discuss the problem of producing an L.S.T. with suitable beaching characteristics, Captain Hussey produced a picture of a "Popper" barge transporter. This transporter had been built for use on the Danube and was designed to be flooded down and to "float" on Danube River barges, one on either side of the superstructure; subsequently by pumping out, the "Popper" barge lifted the two Danube barges out of the water. Captain Hussey suggested that a number of similar ships should be built for landing operations and from his idea was evolved the conception of a landing craft carrier, later L.S.D. The fact that this ship could carry L.C.T.s gave it the following advantages over the L.S.T.:

(1) Tanks could land in shallower water from L.C.T.s than from L.S.T.s.
(2) Dispersal of the tank unit on disembarkation.
(3) The smaller target presented by an L.C.T. compared with an L.S.T.
(4) Greater speed of disembarkation of tanks.
(5) The L.C.T.s could be made available for alternative duties during an operation.

The above presupposes that the L.S.D. can discharge her L.C.T.s in water not subject to fire from enemy shore defences.

At a meeting held on 30th September, 1941, it was agreed that there was a need for this type of vessel to meet the following staff requirements:

>Endurance 5,000 miles at 14 knots.
>To carry two L.C.T. (3) or (4).
>Accommodation for the crews of twenty-four tanks and administrative staff, and for L.C.T. crews and maintenance personnel.
>Derrick and winches for hoisting out vehicles up to 10 ton in weight, carried on the upper deck.
>Armament, close range A.A. weapons only.
>Not required to beach.

D.N.C. was at first opposed to the idea of these ships on the grounds of their extravagance, but the design he prepared was subsequently accepted by the Americans without modification.

Bearing in mind the above points and in view of the fact that three ships were then considered to form a tactical unit, it was agreed by the Admiralty to recommend that of the seven "Winettes" ordered in America, the first three should proceed without modifications and the last four should be replaced by L.S.D.

On arrival of the Combined Operations Mission in America in December, 1941, the U.S. authorities after investigation, reported that it would be easier to substitute L.S.D. for all seven "Winettes" as construction had not yet been started. Although doubtful as to the value of these ships initially, the U.S. authorities eventually came to the conclusion that the L.S.D. were likely to be of the utmost value; the order for seven was increased to fifteen and subsequently to twenty-two, of which four only were assigned to the British.

These ships were entirely successful from their inception and were of the utmost value. They ferried major and minor landing craft, amphibians and vehicles to all parts of the world. To increase the carrying capacity for amphibians, the Americans devised a second deck that could be erected by a dock yard in 48 hours and which doubled the carrying capacity for amphibians and vehicles.

They were also used to a minor extent for docking landing craft for repairs, but their use in this connection was limited by the fact that, when flooded down, the maximum depth of water over the deck was only 9 ft., whereas a damaged major landing craft probably drew more.

Their ability to operate was restricted to reasonably calm sea conditions owing to the surge of the water in the dock if any appreciable sea was running.

The vessel assigned to the British were returned to the U.S.A. after the war.

The Landing Craft Tank (L.C.T)

In parallel with the development of large landing ships to carry armour over long ocean passages, smaller tank landing vessels with a reduced radius of action and less carrying capacity were also a requirement. In particular it was necessary to have shallow draught craft with good beaching characteristics so that armour could be landed direct, even onto fairly flat beaches. As early as June, 1940, the Prime Minister directed that the production of such craft was to be pushed forward.

No staff requirements as such were laid down for the earlier L.C.T., the first of which was completed in November, 1940. It was a ramped, flat bottom craft designed to carry three or four tanks in the hold and to have a speed of 10 knots; its manoeuvrability and sea-keeping qualities left a good deal to be desired. A number of these craft were shipped to Alexandria in sections and proved invaluable for primary training in amphibious warfare, for the ferrying of vehicles and stores and in the supply of Tobruk. In the latter event, they also carried tanks which helped the garrison to break out and join up with the relieving forces in December, 1941.

In general, the L.C.T. development did not keep pace with the production of heavier tanks. Various improved types of L.C.T. were built, but the trend of design of these craft was towards a larger vessel with better sea-keeping qualities, improved arrangements for the accommodation of tank crews and increased endurance. All these qualities were ultimately achieved without loss of good beaching characteristics even on flat beaches.

Intermediate types, L.C.T. (3) and (4), made primarily for a cross-Channel invasion, were used operationally by the British in North Africa, Sicily, Italy and Normandy. The L.C.T. (3) proved a very good general-purpose craft, but it was the L.C.T. (4) for which one finds the first recorded staff requirements. (They were in fact the first staff requirements laid down for any type of landing craft). These were:

> Speed 8 knots.
> Beaching draft – tanks 3ft. vehicles 1ft. 6ins., on a 1 in 150 beach.
> Protection on very limited scale to wheelhouse, etc.
> Utmost simplicity so as to facilitate production.
> No armament.
> Low silhouette.
> Seaworthy up to sea force 4.
> Twin screw, endurance 500 miles.
> To carry six Churchill or nine Sherman tanks.

However, as a result of estimating that 2,150 L.C.T. of existing types would be required for "Overlord" and in view of the fact that this number could be neither produced nor manned, a smaller type of L.C.T., the L.C.T. (5) was produced. This smaller L.C.T. was capable of being carried on deck in a merchant ship and had the advantage that it could be manufactured in large quantities in the U.S.A. and shipped across the Atlantic without difficulty. Their disadvantage was that, unless the sea passage involved was short, they had to be transported to the scene of operations in an L.S.T. and could not be used in an initial assault. However, as Vehicle Ferry Craft (which was their original name), they were used with every success in all theatres of war. This L.C.T. and parallel U.S. types constructed between 1942 and 1944 were adequate for the purposes for which they were designed, but lacked the qualities necessary for long sea voyages and therefore, in view of operations in the Pacific, new large L.C.T. were developed, culminating in the L.S.M. of U.S. design and British L.C.T. (8). The former proved successful in the later part of the Pacific war, but the latter were not built in time to take part in active service.

Although Tank Landing craft were intended primarily for the carriage of armour and vehicles, these vessels were adapted to a variety of uses. They were used as salvage vessels, mobile repair units, fire support craft, rocket support craft, casualty stations and for the anti-torpedo net defence of the Fleet.

However, none of these functions were other than a matter of convenience, no other available vessels having the requisite size, stability and beaching qualities.

Landing Ships Infantry (L.S.I.)

As far back as 1938, it was agreed that it would be necessary to convert special ships to carry Assault Landing Craft to the scene of operations.

Warships were unsuitable because the lowest weight of the proposed L.C.A. was 10 tons. Thus, the main staff requirements were laid down as follows:

> Speed 17 knots.
> To carry an infantry battalion (less its transport) and to land them in waves in about 15 L.C.A.
> Range, minimum 1,000 miles.
> Troops to be embarked for not longer than 7 days.

To meet these requirements, Glen Line's merchant ships were nominated for conversion on the outbreak of war, but an alternative plan to convert them to Fleet auxiliaries for a projected operation in the Baltic ("Catherine") prevented their use as infantry landing ships until early 1940, when the course of the war had altered.

L.S.I.s, 1940

Glengyle, Glenearn and *Glenroy* were put in hand as L.S.I. (L) (troop capacity 36 officers and 500 men) during the summer of 1940 and were despatched in February, 1941, to the Mediterranean theatre. Particular stress had been laid on the necessity for each ship to be able to land all her assault troops in one flight of landing craft; this was possible at that time due to the relatively small number of assaulting troops in a Commando.

In addition, two Dutch cross-Channel Steamers *Queen Emma* and *Princess Beatrix* (troop capacity 30 officers and 350 men) were taken over and made into what were later known as Landing Ship Infantry, Medium (L.S.I. (M.)).

Finally, five small Belgian Dover-Ostend ships, *Prince Charles, Prince Leopold, Princess Astrid, Princess Josephine Charlotte* and *Prince Phillippe* (troop capacity 16 officers and 250 men), were converted for short cross-Channel operations and became Landing Ships Infantry, Small (L.S.I. (S.)).

As well as the Infantry Assault Ships, three R.F.A. oilers, *Dewdale, Derwentdale* and *Ennerdale*, were specially fitted to take a deck cargo of L.C.M. To hoist these out, special gantries had to be constructed on the upper deck. Hence it was that these ships came to be known later as Landing Ship Gantry (L.S.G.).

Probably as the result of what had been seen of Japanese operations during their campaign in China, two Harwich-Zeebrugge train-ferries were fitted to carry landing craft, which could be launched over the stern on rails. These were slow ships of short endurance and, although they did not take part in any overseas operations, they were invaluable for ferrying landing craft round the coasts of the British Isles and were employed in the Normandy landings.

Late in 1940, the Royal Scotsman and the Ulster Monarch were converted. Their troop capacities, for short passage only, were 30 officers and 450 men, and 60 officers and 520 men respectively, but having cabins where other ships had promenade decks, were unsuitable for fitting gravity davits and were fitted with spurs to hoist the landing craft which were then secured outboard.

L.S.I.s, 1941

Meanwhile, the British India Company's ships *Karanja* and *Kenya* (renamed *Keren*), which were still under the Red Ensign, had been used as landing craft carriers at Dakar. Late in 1941 they were commissioned as H.M. ships and, together with a number of large Red Ensign ships also acting as landing craft carriers, joined a force being mounted and trained for long-range operations.

The capacity of these two L.S.I. (L.) was 80 officers and 1,200 men and in addition they could carry in the holds thirty 15-cwt. trucks or the equivalent. Their davits did not allow L.C.A.s to be hoisted fully loaded, nor did their spacing allow the craft to be stowed inboard. Eight L.C.A. were carried at davits; and two L.C.P. and two additional L.C.A. could be hoisted out by derrick.

Constant exercise with troops embarked, a better supply of landing craft and the prospect of an operation in tropical conditions spurred the S.N.O.L. of the Force and his naval staff to attain improvements in the internal communications, workshop accommodation and other ships' administrative requirements, which the developing assault technique showed to be needed.

L.S.I.s, 1942

By the spring of 1942, the Madagascar Operation ("Ironclad") was mounted. The minor improvements had been fitted in the Red Ensign L.S.I. (L.) and the *Keren* and the *Karanja* had been fitted with the additional communications, operations rooms and staff offices that the S.N.O.L. had found necessary.

Close attention was now being given to the problems of the re-entry into Europe which it was hoped could be mounted in 1943. Channel conditions would allow the use of smaller ships, which were available and which were unsuitable for long voyages, and thus the larger ships could be released to ocean trooping for which they were urgently required. The requirement, therefore, was for ships able to carry a

THE DEVELOPMENT OF SHIPS AND CRAFT

comparatively large number of troops who would be embarked for short periods only.

These requirements were met by the L.S.I. (H.) (Hand-hoisting) which carried six landing craft at spur davits; the craft had to be hoisted by hand but the ships were later fitted with portable electric motors giving power assistance. Ships were converted into L.S.I. (H.) both for White and Red Ensign service, the former capable of embarking for 96 hours and the latter for 48 hours. They carried about 30 officers and 400 men each. After the assault, the landing craft would be left in the operational area and the ships used as short passage troopers. Twenty-seven were originally ordered, but nineteen only could be found from the available shipping. Seven were converted to White Ensign: *Brigadier, Duke of Wellington, Invicta, St. Helier*, the *Royal Scotsman* and the *Ulster Monarch* previously mentioned, and the *Royal Ulsterman* which had been converted on a similar basis to the *Royal Scotsman* after having taken part in Operation "Ironclad".

Twelve were converted for service under the Red Ensign. These L.S.I. (H.) were mostly British railway company Cross-Channel ships of low endurance, some of them coal-fired. They were all quite unsuitable for service outside the Channel, but they fulfilled their limited function for "Overlord" satisfactorily.

General Somerville (Chief of Service and Supply in the U.S.A) suggested, in the early autumn of 1942, that the shortage of L.S.I. (H.) should be made up by the employment of shallow draught U.S. river steamers as L.S.I. and fourteen were selected, of which only four arrived in this country. In the event it was not found possible to use them, except as accommodation ships at Combined Training Centres.

In November, 1942, the Canadian authorities offered two ships for conversion into L.S.I.s (M.) and the crews to man them. This offer was accepted and H.M.C.S. *Prince Henry* and *Prince David* were converted in Canada under Canadian supervision. They were larger ships than the *Queen Emma* (gross tonnage 6,983 as against 4,135) and were given an increased armament of two director-controlled twin 4-in. mountings, two hand-worked single Bofors all on the centreline, and eight Oerlikons. Communications to the existing S.N.O.L. or Brigade Headquarters' standard were fitted. This was more comprehensive than previous installations in S.N.O.L. ships.

The existing Asdic was retained and sic L.C.A. and two L.C.M. (3) were carried at davits. Their troop capacity was 30 officers and 500 other ranks. By the time the ships came into service, the requirement for carrying L.C.M. had lapsed to some extent, owing to the difficulty of having L.C.M.s, converted for additional hoisting, readily available.

Though the ships were converted generally to the British staff requirements, inexperience in the type of work in Canada led to a number of minor alterations having to be carried out while the ships were in the European theatre.

After serving with a R.C.N. compliment, both in the Mediterranean and Home theatres of war, they were due to be taken in hand in 1945 for further conversion for service in the Far East, which include transfer over to the R.N., as Brigade H.Q. Ships for a Commando Brigade. This work was abandoned on the collapse of Japan. Had further time been available, their 4-in. armament would have been replaced by twin Bofors mountings which would have complied with the current staff requirements and would have reduced the overloaded condition of the hulls.

Need for closer control during the early stages of an assault, which had been experienced in Operation "Ironclad" and on many exercises, had firmly established the requirement for a S.N.O.L. for each Brigade front. This required one L.S.I. (L) in three to be fitted as a S.N.O.L. or Brigade Headquarters Ship.

For "Torch" (North Africa) only three White Ensign L.S.I. (L.) for S.N.O.L. were available but the two extra required were provided from Red Ensign Ships. The entire balance of L.S.I. (L.) in this operation was Red Ensign.

L.S.I. (M.) and (S.) were established as special duty or Commando carrying ships, working to a flank or special objective.

Madagascar experience had shown the need for spare landing craft crews and bigger and better-organised beach parties. All these extras, together with their equipment, had to be carried in the L.S.I. (L.) with an increased bulk of landing craft spares and stores, all unfortunately at the expense of the lift of fighting troops.

L.S.I.s, 1943

Experience had shown that, while it was desirable for all L.S.I. to be White Ensign, it was essential for the L.S.I. (L.) in which the S.N.O.L. was embarked and from which he exercised control. The importance of getting the assaulting infantry and the naval beach personnel ashore quickly necessitated a larger number of assault craft per ship, spur or gallows davits being reluctantly accepted.

Naval experience in the Mediterranean generally, and "Torch" in particular, had shown the grave risk of air attack to large ships and called for much improved H.A. protection. A new set of staff requirements covered these points with special modifications for L.S.I. (L.,) carrying S.N.O.L.

The *Glenearn* and the *Glenroy* had been severely damaged in the Middle East in 1941. Near misses and direct hits by small and medium bombs, serious fires, damage from torpedo bombers and serious stranding had in turn ravaged one or the other. But the ships were still afloat and it was clearly more economical to repair and refit them than to replace. To some extent the peace-time policy of the Alfred Holt Companies in setting a higher standard of construction and a greater margin of safety for their ships in their original form must take credit for this. These two damaged Glens were taken in hand and, after about six months in dockyard hands, emerged with three director-controlled twin 4-in. mountings, generous batteries of Oerlikons, vastly increased troop accommodation, twenty-four L.C.A. at davits or spurs and the increased S.N.O.L. requirements.

The losses of the large L.S.I. (L.) employed in "Torch" were causing the Minister of War Transport some concern. A paper of 24th May, 1943 drew attention to the position and pointed out that the present L.S.I.s (L.) in use included nine liners of 15-23,000 tons. Their use as assault ships exposed them to exceptional risk and their retention for operational use, usually in the U.K. meant that they could not be used for trooping at any time. The shortage of troopers was acute and these ships could undoubtedly be most economically employed as troopers. The Minister of War Transport reported that no further suitable British ships of 15 knots or upwards were available. The nearest existing ships to meet the ideal requirements were certain of the Dutch Jays [and] American combat loaders.

Both types were operated by the American Army and Navy; several of the Jays were then trooping and the American programme still included a number of combat loaders under construction. The Minister of War Transport recommended that nine ships from American production should be converted to British L.S.I. (L.) and should replace large liners, and, further, that another four ships should be provided to cover estimated 1943 operational casualties. Neither of these types could, however, be provided, so it was decided that thirteen American C.I.B.[1] cargo hulls should be converted to enable the big troopers to be withdrawn. The C.I.B.s were converted specially for the "Overlord" cross-Channel operation; they were to carry eighteen L.C.A., accommodate a maximum number of troops and be fitted with the best available close-range H.A. armament. They were to serve under the Red Ensign and, for the first time, British L.S.I.s incorporated cafeteria

---

[1] C.I.B. More generally known as the Empire Weapons class.

messing for the troops. These C.I.B.s started to arrive in Home Waters at the end of 1943, and proved to be sound austerity L.S.I. (L.) for use in the Channel.

L.S.I.s, 1944

During 1944, every available landing ship was required for operations and exceptional sacrifices had to be made to refit landing ships, particularly the L.S.I.s in time for "Overlord". Except for the few employed in the Mediterranean, every L.S.I. took part in this operation after a gruelling period of training and, in some cases, directly following Mediterranean operations.

When ports were available, the L.S.I.s continued to work as troopers. Two of the Weapon class and the L.S.I. (S.) *Prince Leopold* were sunk in the Channel and several, including the *Glenearn*, were damaged by mines.

L.S.I.s were only acceptable as White Ensign ships because more administrative and ancillary personnel were required; and accommodation and the provision of fresh water had to be improved.

The successful L.S.I. (M.) was still wanted for Commando and raiding work but was suspect for the arduous Far Eastern conditions. Built to light scantlings they were now, by the addition of armament and considerable constructional weight, overloaded and there was little spare room for improvements. They had, nevertheless, served magnificently in the Mediterranean and as far afield as the Artic Circle, Madagascar, the Equatorial West Coast of Africa and India. The best of them, *Queen Emma*, *Princess Beatrix*, *Prince Henry* and *Prince David*, were sent East, their small range, endurance and limited sea-keeping qualities being accepted. The two most successful of the L.S.I.s (S.), the *Prince Albert* and the *Prince Baudouin*, were included, but the remaining three steam Belgians were ruled out as wholly unsuitable for employment in the Far East.

In July, 1944, the U.S.N. asked for some L.S.I.s (L.) for special employment in the Pacific. As an emergency and at short notice, two L.S.I. (L.) fitted for S.N.O.L. duties, four Empire Weapons and the H.Q. ship *Lothian* were mounted as Force "X" and sailed west-about. The L.S.I. (L.) of this Force entirely failed to satisfy the Americans, partly on account of the living conditions not meeting the higher and more particular American standards, partly on account of their inadequacy for prolonged work in tropical conditions, but chiefly because five of them had been turned over from Red to White Ensign and had sailed without an opportunity of working up. Besides, this, the American technique of the assault landing was different to the British technique and their A.P.A. was designed to carry few landing craft, fewer troops, but an addition of the troops' motor transport and 400 tons of immediate operational stores. Consequently, none of the ships of Force "X" were used operationally by the Americans. In the meantime, other L.S.I. (L.) both C.I.B. and others, had been prepared for Far Eastern service which included improvements in living conditions.

The S.N.O.L. had originally existed as a solitary figure generally controlling naval activities on a Divisional front and was borne in an L.S.I. (L.). His duties in "Overlord" had expanded still further and for the Far East he was transformed into Senior Officer Assault Group (S.O.A.G.), his staff was necessarily larger and L.S.I. (L.) fitted as S.O.A.G. ships had to be further modified to provide officers and accommodation suitable for prolonged occupation. Each Assault Group contained three L.S.I. (L.) one fitted for S.O.A.G. duties, the second was specially fitted with facilities for evacuating military assault casualties and treating them on passage.

This was achieved with a minimum assault lift loss, giving accommodation for nine Medical Officers, eight Nursing Sisters and fifty-two R.A.M.C. personnel, with a preparation room, operating theatre, resuscitation ward and plaster room all easily accessible on the upper deck with a cot case ward immediately below. The third L.S.I. (L.) of the group was required to act as a parent ship to the crews of the major and minor landing craft of the Assault Group in the beach area and was fitted accordingly. Between the three ships the personnel, plant and stores of the Landing Craft Recovery and Clearance Units were carried, in addition to the Beach Commandos, Beach Signalling Parties, etc.

L.S.I.s, 1945

Five years have thus seen the development of the early Infantry Assault Ship into a highly specialised L.S.I. (L.). The three L.S.I. (L.) of each Assault Group were together able to land a complete team, not only to fight but also to control the landing; to clear obstacles; to develop the beach organisation; to remove and treat casualties and to repair and maintain minor landing craft. In addition, they included facilities for the preparation of the naval and brigade assault plan, and accommodation and amenities for the otherwise homeless Combined Operations personnel in the assault area.

After the end of the war, financial stringency made it impossible to retain any of the existing L.S.I.s, which were all returned to trade. In order to replace this type of landing ship in the peace-time Assault Training Force in the most economical way it was proposed to convert some of the existing L.S.T. (3) to L.S.T. (Assault) and in November, 1946, the staff requirements for the L.S.T. (A.) were produced.

These requirements allowed for six L.C.A. and two L.C.P. to be davit-carried and additional accommodation for 26 officers and 329 other ranks was provided. Five L.S.T. (A.) are required to lift one assault battalion and its appropriate ancillary units. While L.S.T. (A.) may be suitable for cold war requirements, they would be unsatisfactory for L.S.I.s in a major war on account of their slow speed.

Landing Craft Infantry (L.C.I.)

Early in the war, with limited resources, raids continued and produced valuable lessons, but it was realised that raids must be small operations and the danger of allowing L.S.I.s to linger off a hostile coast was fully appreciated. Accordingly Landing Craft Infantry (Large) were built to the designs produced by C.O.H.Q. to provide a landing craft capable of transporting some 200 troops in reasonable comfort and landing them dryshod on an enemy shore. As the shipbuilding resources in Great Britain were fully occupied, these craft were constructed in the U.S.A. The trials were not at first satisfactory owing to the design of the ramps which had to be modified.

These craft were of a very novel design and were originally known as "Giant R Boats". They had accommodation for sleeping and feeding all the troops embarked and, as they had to make the passage of the Atlantic under their own power, had good endurance and excellent sea-keeping qualities. It is of interest to note that all those used in the continental operations made the sea passage without incident and were used in many major operations. The majority of the officers and men who manned them came from the Combined Operations Command.

The main disadvantage of such a craft was that, unless tactical surprise was achieved, it presented a good target to the enemy.

The Close Support Problem

Preparations for bigger operations continued and the Dieppe raid in August, 1942, provided experience in the use of new equipment. Experience here showed that a frontal attack on a well defended port was impracticable without the means for providing intimate close support after the infantry have got ashore and before the artillery were deployed. Close support has been covered in Chapter 16, it is sufficient to state here that the need for it was met by the provision of Landing Craft Rocket and Landing Craft Gun.

THE DEVELOPMENT OF SHIPS AND CRAFT

The Landing Craft Rocket (L.C.T.(R.))

It was recommended by C.O.H.Q. in September, 1942: "That trials should be carried out to see whether it is possible to mount in a suitable craft, a number of Rocket Projectors, firing rocket 5-in. 'U' fitted H.E., with a proportion of smoke. This weapon will enable a crash area shoot to be called down or planned on any battery interfering with the landing, which cannot be seen from the beaches, and should go a considerable way towards ensuring the neutralisation of such batteries."

The next step was taken by the Admiralty who, on 27th November, 1942, approved the fitting of 5-in. rockets in L.C.T. 161. Nevertheless, the Gunnery Division at the Admiralty as late as January, 1943, remarked that they had never been particularly enthusiastic over this project, and the more they saw of it, the less they liked it. The Gunnery Division's main interest was that these craft, if successful, would replace, in some measure, vessel carrying guns. However, in February, 1943 C.C.O. again pressed for the fitting out of these craft in time to take part in Operation "Husky" when they were, in fact, used with great success.

The following paragraph from the report of this operation by Admiral Sir Bertram Ramsay, the Commander Naval Assault Forces, is of interest: "Both the enemy and our own troops have spoken of the very great moral and physical effect of such a volume of fire and it is considered that L.C.T. (R.) should be employed in the assault in future whenever possible."

Lieutenant-General Leese, Commander of 30 Corps also reported favourably: "The Rocket Ship did excellent work; with further opportunity for training, a greater number of craft and with greater understanding of the use of the Radar instruments for checking the position, they will be first class in an assault. They should be used in large numbers."

The Commander of the 8th Army (General Sir Bernard Montgomery) agreed with the above remarks.

Actually on "D" Day of "Overlord", from six to ten L.C.T. (R.) were used on each Assault Brigade Group front.

The Landing Craft Gun (L.C.G.)

Another type of craft developed as a result of the Dieppe operation was the Landing Craft (Gun). These were L.C.T. modified to take two 4·7-in. naval guns. Their role in the assault was to proceed close inshore, which was rendered practicable by their shallow draught, and engage targets which were interfering with the advance of the assaulting troops.

In fact, they carried out the role that destroyers would normally perform in combined operations.

Thus, at comparatively small expense, a very efficient form of close support craft was evolved from the ordinary L.C.T. hull. By utilising the tank hold in these craft, a considerable stock of ammunition could be carried. The only defect of these conversions was their slow speed; but they could of course keep up with the other L.C.T.s on the run to the beaches.

The Landing Craft Barge (L.C.B.)

After carefully reviewing the requirements outlined by the Staff for any form of cross-Channel operation on a large scale, C.C.O. foresaw in early 1942, that there would be a far greater requirement for craft than even the most optimistic estimates could provide. Further, the time available was short and, no matter what exertions could be made in construction, the shortage of craft would always be a bottle-neck.

However, the Port of London was not working to full capacity owing to the action of the German Air Force, and therefore a very considerable proportion of the dumb barges used in the port were idle. Here then was an excellent source of craft suitable for beaching, and the matter was taken up with the appropriate authorities. In due course, it was decided to requisition 1,000 of these craft.

A dumb barge has, as its name implies, no means of propulsion and, further, the goods which it carries are, in the normal course of events, hoisted in and out by cranes.

Designs were produced in C.O.H.Q. whereby doors could be fitted at the stern of a barge to allow vehicles to be driven in and out. To overcome the propulsion difficulty, it was decided to fit a proportion with large outboard self-contained units. These had to come from the United States.

The work of conversion was undertaken in small yards on the banks of the Thames and in Southampton Water; it was both quickly and efficiently done. By the target date, 30th June, 1942, 925 had been converted to carry vehicles and guns, 25 as fuel carriers and 15 were under conversion as repair barges.

When, in early 1943, the date for the invasion of France had to be postponed, it was decided to convert a proportion of these to fulfil special tasks, some for carrying anti-aircraft support weapons, some for landing craft repair facilities, whilst others were equipped as water, petrol or oil barges and a few even converted into floating kitchens.

About 200 of the barges were powered by Ford engines, and others had outboard motors, but the remainder had to be towed, generally by trawlers.

At Normandy, the Landing Barge Force, which was split between the British and U.S. Forces, did invaluable work in providing an essential feature of the ferry service after they had discharged their initial cargoes. They were also used at Le Havre and later in the Scheldt Estuary. Nevertheless, barges can only provide a makeshift contribution to short range amphibious warfare. They are useless for assault purposes; very dependent on good weather, both for the crossing and beaching; and, finally, cannot operate efficiently in non-tidal waters.

The Development of Minor Landing Craft

Landing Craft Mechanised (L.C.M.)

The original L.C.M. was built in 1920 as a result of requirements put forward in 1918. Requirements then were:

> To land a light tank, or a platoon, on moderately shelving beaches.
> To have good power of retraction.
> Protection against small arms fire.
> To be capable of being hoisted by the derricks of existing merchant ships.

The first boat built in 1920 differed little in dimension from the L.C.M. (1) of World War II. She had a very low freeboard, carrying the load on a deck above the waterline and discharging it by a bow door with a double folding action. She had 10-lb. bullet-proof bulwarks and a protected conning position. Her light weight was just under 20 tons. Because of the retractability requirement, she had water jet propulsion (Hotchkiss). This system of propulsion though sound in theory, was ineffective.

The design was repeated with minor improvements in 1930 and again during the Abyssinian crisis when several craft were built. They still had jet propulsion, but a different type (Gill).

One of their defects was the way in which the deck, if flooded, drained into a sump and, if the sump was not pumped out, it overflowed back on to the deck and the craft lost stability and capsized.

Another defect was the very poor speed, which was not more than 5 knots despite two 60-h.p. petrol engines.

In 1938 the L.C.M. was redesigned (by Thornycroft) on the instructions of the Inter-Services Training and Development Centre.

The new craft was designed to meet the same requirements, but with propeller drive and a single ramp. She then had a much longer clear deck within the same overall dimensions and no sump. A speed of just over 7 knots was obtained with the same engines. This craft, like its predecessor, had a wooden deck as it was thought that tanks could not be driven on steel.

A number of vessels of this design with minor improvements were built in the U.K. under the name of L.C.M. (1) and used in every European operation during the war. Their chief duty was the discharge of stores during the build-up phase, but a limited number were used for assault purposes to carry high priority stores and small vehicles.

During the war the trend of design was towards greater carrying capacity, greater stability and higher speed. These qualities all increased their displacement and precluded the possibility of being able to hoist such vessels from davits; this requirement was therefore dropped.

An intermediate type, L.C.M. (3), was designed and produced in the U.S.A. by Messrs. Higgins of New Orleans in 1941. This L.C.M. was modified, in November 1941, as a result of British suggestions and a large number of these craft were subsequently used by both British and U.S. Forces in all theatres as ship to shore ferries. The L.C.M. (3) was capable of lifting 30 tons of stores or small vehicles.

When supplies of L.C.M. (3) from America became difficult, production in the U.K. was switched to the L.C.M. (7), which was a slightly larger version of the L.C.M. (3). It was designed to be large enough to carry a bulldozer without being too large to be hoisted and carried in a merchant ship.

Staff requirements were:

> To carry a 30-ton tank or vehicles.
> To be capable of being hoisted out of a merchant ship fitted with a 25-ton derrick.
> Speed 11 knots.
> To land vehicles on moderate beach slopes.
> No protection.
> Reliable compass.
> Endurance, 200 miles.

The design was worked out by Messrs. Thornycroft, who also built the prototype. The builder's trails were successful but later experience showed that the ramp, as fitted, was too short, and the hand winch, used for the kedge and for hoisting the doors as in the L.C.M. (1), was not reliable.

The later deliveries had separate winches for the kedge and doors and a surf breakwater at the stern.

The L.C.M. (7) were not completed in time for use in World War II operations, but they remained, after the war, the standard L.C.M. in the U.K. It seems certain that this type of vessel cannot be entirely satisfactory unless it is also capable of carrying armour into the assault or across rivers. In these circumstances the L.C.M. (7) has proved too small and there is little doubt that future designs will have to be much larger.

Landing Craft Assault (L.C.A.)

In 1939, two prototype L.C.A. were completed to meet requirements laid down by I.S.T.D.C. One was designed and built by Fleming Propulsion Ltd., and the other by Thornycroft.

The two boats were similar in that the engines and conning position were aft, and the troops were carried in a hold compartment forward. They sat on low benches, fitted a few inches above the keel and disembarked over a bow ramp. Protection was fitted on the sides of the boat on the half-deck and on the deck abaft the engine room.

The Fleming boat was built of a metal called Birmabright, the Thornycroft of wood. The Thornycroft boat was a better sea-boat and much better silenced, which for raiding purposes was a very important consideration. This boat was adopted and formed the basis of the staff requirements, which then became:

> Total loaded weight not to exceed 10 tons so as to enable boats to be lifted at merchant ships' davits.
> Speed 10 knots.
> Low silhouette and silent running.
> To carry thirty-five men, plus a crew of five.
> To have bullet-proof protection to the sides and deck.
> Draft not to exceed 1 ft. 9 in.
> Endurance, 90 miles.

From 1941 onwards various slight modifications and improvements were made, but the design remained substantially the same throughout the war.

L.C.A.s were used successfully in raids and in the assault phase of every major British operation. It was inferior to its American counterparts, L.C.P. (L.) and L.C.V. (P.), in speed, manoeuvrability and seaworthiness, but had the advantage of greater protection and troop-carrying capacity, also disembarkation could be carried out from the L.C.A. more quickly and it was more silent and had a smaller silhouette.

Landing Craft Personnel, Small (L.C.P.(S.))

This boat was ordered early in 1942, as a "second flight assault craft". The idea was that it should be of such a size that it could be carried at the average liner's lifeboat davits, or inboard under the standard L.C.A. davits, and that it should be of simplified construction so as to facilitate production.

The staff requirements were:

> To carry twenty-five men.
> To have minimum crew.
> To be easy to produce.
> Speed 6 knots.
> Weight unloaded not more than 3½ tons.
> Length not to exceed 30 ft., slings at extreme ends.
> Draft, load not to exceed 1 ft. 9 in.
> No protection.

To meet these requirements a plywood planked, flat-bottomed design was adopted (the first all-plywood boat to be approved by the Admiralty). The craft had a pointed bow, a transom stern and the boat obtained a speed of about 8 knots with a single L.C.A. engine. The propellor worked in a tunnel. The first few L.C.P. (S.) were very poor going astern but after a slight modification to the tunnel they were generally satisfactory. They were never used as intended, but they served the invasion fleet as trot boats for which their robust construction suited well.

Later, some of these craft were converted as "water ambulances" and were fitted with stretchers which could be hoisted at the davits in hospital ships, but were not satisfactory as they were very wet boats in a seaway.

Landing Craft Personnel, Medium (L.C.P.(M.))

This boat was specially designed towards the end of 1941 for assault and raiding operations on rocky beaches in Northern waters. It was based on the Northumbrian fishing coble.

Staff requirements were:

> To carry thirty-five men in addition to crew.
> To be hoisted at L.C.A. davits.
> Very good sea-keeping qualities and high standard of manoeuvrability on shallow draft.
> Single screw.

Robust construction so as to suit it for rocky landings.
Good retractability.
No protection.

The design of the boat finally adopted resembled the coble very closely. It was clinker-built with a high pointed bow and transom stern. The screw worked in a tunnel. A kedge anchor and hand-winch were fitted it was propelled by a single Scripps engine, which gave a speed of about 9 knots, and the boat was provided with steps on the inside and outside of the bow instead of a ramp for disembarkation of troops. They were never used in the capacity for which they were designed but ultimately, they became despatch and trot boats to assault forces.

Landing Craft Personnel, Large (L.C.P.(L.)

Early in the war, consideration was given to obtaining a fleet of small craft that could be used for raiding purposes.

There was no surplice building capacity in the U.K. and recourse was had to the U.S.A. After investigation of a number of different types, an initial order was placed for 50 "Eureka" boats. These boats were built by Higgins Industries of New Orleans. It is alleged that they were originally designed for the rum-runners operating off the coast of Florida and therefore were fast (20 knots), drew very little water and were capable of jumping a bar or submerged log.

The boats were mass-produced on somewhat novel lines, with sides of bonded and laminated plywood. They were fitted with a single engine of 250 h.p. and proved magnificent sea-boats. The coxswain had control of the throttle and gear levers as well as the steering wheel.

The first craft from the British order was delivered at Portsmouth in November, 1940, and was sent to H.M.S. *Tormentor* for trials, as a result of which it was decided that the following modifications were necessary:

Silencers and sound-proof padding round the engine casing.
Self-sealing petrol tanks.
Screening and bonding.
Davit hoisting eyes.
A long gang plank stowed on top of the canopy which could be launched forward over a roller in the bow in order to enable the troops to disembark quickly on beaching.
Stronger cleats and rope fenders.

It was not possible to have these modifications carried out in the U.S.A., so arrangements were made to take all craft in hand on arrival, although it took about two months to carry them out.

At that time the craft were called "R" (for raiding) boats, later changed to "R" craft and later still to L.C.P. (L.).

The first craft was fitted with a Hall Scott Invader engine but, owing to shortages of these engines, the remainder of the first 150 had to be powered with Kermath 160 h.p. engines which were not nearly as satisfactory. Later, all the Kermath engines were replaced by Hall Scott, Hudson Invaders or Gray Diesels.

The initial order for 50 was increased and finally reached a total of 262 but, before these were built, Lend-Lease was in operation and the Americans were mass-producing L.C.P. (L.) for their own use. 900 L.C.P. (L.) and L.C.P. (R) were finally allocated to the British out of a total American production of 4,851, after which production was switched to the L.C.V. (P.), the American equivalent of the L.C.A.

When the U.S.A. came into the war and decided on large scale production of these craft, orders were distributed to a number of manufacturers, in addition to Higgins Industries, and the design was slightly altered. The canopy that had been fitted to meet British requirements was no longer fitted and two gun rings forward were introduced on which light machine-guns could be mounted. Although the British design was much preferred in the U.K., the American design had to be accepted.

These craft were used in all British amphibious operations as despatch craft for H.Q. Ships, as control craft and, in "Overlord", as smoke layers for the protection of the anchorages.

One of the main disadvantages of the L.C.P. (L.) compared with the L.C.A. was that there was no protection and, in 1941, it was approved to fit L.C.P. (L.) with armour (10-lb. plating), bolted on to the outside of the hull. This reduced the speed by several knots and it is questionable whether the small amount of additional protection was worth the loss in speed.

Landing Craft Navigation (L.C.N.)

In January, 1942, it was decided to convert a number of L.C.P. (L.) as navigational leaders to enable them to navigate accurately when leading raids on the French coast. For this purpose one craft per flotilla was taken in hand and fitted with an additional compass, a chart table and Q.H. 2 type radar. These craft were known as L.C.P. (Sy.) – for Survey.

Later experience showed that this was not sufficient, and in 1944 a more ambitious conversion was decided upon called L.C.N. Although L.C.P. (L.) were really too small to carry all the equipment required, they were the only craft with sufficient speed that could be carried at the davits of an L.S.I. None of these craft were completed in time to take part in actual operations, however the equipment fitted comprised:

> Standard and steering compasses.
> Echo sounding gear.
> Taut wire gear (9-mile reel).
> Bottom log.
> Trainable A/S oscillator for detection of F.H.830.
> Q.H., Loran or Decca receiver (according to the system in use in the operational area).
> Good facilities for chart work.
> W.S. radar with P.P.I. (e.g., radar type S.O.).
> W/T. Two fitted and two portable H.F. transceivers.
> Loud hailing equipment.

Landing Craft Personnel, Ramped (L.C.P.(R.))

On arrival of the Combined Operations Mission in America at the end of 1941, the firm of Higgins was trying to devise an easier method of disembarkation from L.C.P. and had produced a new design with a narrow gangway forward which led to a ramp over which the troops could disembark. Five of these modified craft (later called L.C.P. (R.)) were ordered for trial, in substitution for the last five L.C.P. (L.) then on order.

The L.C.P. (R.) were not as satisfactory as the L.C.P. (L.). When heavily loaded, they were inclined to trim by the head and to scoop water over the ramp. Before very many of them had been delivered, the design was again changed and the ramp and gangway widened to the whole width of the boat so as to enable a jeep or Bren carrier to be embarked. The craft built for this purpose was designated Landing Craft Vehicle (Personnel) short title L.C.V. (P.).

Landing Craft Vehicle, Personnel (L.C.V. (P.))

Immediately after the trials of the first L.C.V. (P.) American production was switched to this design and no more of the earlier type were built. Out of a total production of 23,051 craft, 332 were assigned to the British.

They were used by the Americans in all their operations to carry the early waves of the assault troops except when, in the later stages of the war, amphibians were used instead.

Landing Craft Infantry, Small (L.C.I. (S.))

These craft were required to lift 100 armed men, to have a speed of 15 knots and an endurance of 200 miles. The design and production was undertaken by Messrs. Fairmile in 1942.

The boat was made of wood, similar in many respects to certain coastal force craft. The scantlings were very much reduced and the side planking was of plywood. The protection was fitted in the form of plates of steel not forming part of the hull proper. Two Hall Scot Invaders, which in later boats were supercharged, were fitted to give the speed required.

The troops were accommodated in hold compartments into which the boat was divided by transverse bulkheads, and disembarked by ladders from the upper deck. Upholstered seats with accommodation beneath them for kit, were fitted. The draft was very small for a ship of its size and its beaching qualities were good. Stern anchoring arrangements were similar to those in L.C.T.s. The kedge was, however, seldom used for beaching because the hand-operated winch could not be worked sufficiently fast which meant that the kedge wire was liable to foul the propellor when the craft was retracting.

Owing to their twin out-turn screws and comparatively high speed, the L.C.I. (S.) proved extremely manoeuvrable. They were good seaboats, but not sufficiently robust to withstand going alongside other vessels in a seaway.

These craft were never used for their original purpose, raiding, as large-scale raids were no longer the policy at the time of their completion. They were however used to land the assault troops in the Normandy and Walcheren operations.

Chapter 21

THE DEVELOPMENT OF MATERIAL AND RESOURCES OTHER THAN SHIPS AND CRAFT

Bridging the Water-Gap

The Army Landing Problem
The provision of specialised ships and craft for amphibious operations gave rise to fresh problems which had not previously arisen in connection with the development of Army equipment.

The Army (and the ground elements of the R.A.F.) had designed their equipment specifically to suit the land battle and to be transportable by hitherto orthodox methods, which included facilities for assembly and organisation before being committed to battle.

The situation now demanded that they should emerge from the ships and craft on to a hostile shore, where they would be confronted with an enemy ready to receive them in prepared defensive positions. Units must therefore arrive on the shore in tactically correct formations and with their weapons and equipment prepared for immediate actions.

Thus, the requirements of large scale amphibious operations affected the modification of a great mass of equipment to a greater or lesser degree. The extent to which C.O.H.Q. was responsible for the initiation and direction of these developments varied with the nature of the equipment, and also with the evolution of the C.O.H.Q. organisation.

Initially, C.C.O. was charged with the direct responsibility for the development of material that would be needed for all kinds of landing operations but, at that time, the material resources at his disposal, in the shape of the I.S.T.D.C., were quite inadequate for any systematic or comprehensive examination of the material aspects of combined operations. This is borne out by the nature of the organisation eventually set up to deal with material matters. The Combined Operations Experimental Establishment (C.O.X.E.), when formed in August, 1942, was essentially a trials centre, not a development centre, and development work was carried on by the establishments of the Service Departments at C.O.H.Q.'s request.

Thus, while stimulus, co-ordination and suggestion were constantly applied by C.O.H.Q. in material matters, the devices designed and produced by the direct action of C.O.H.Q. were few.

Of the many problems to be solved, that of landing in tactical formations, complete with the equipment appropriate to different types of units, was met by developing the series of specialised ships and craft described in Chapter 20. The next problem was to enable the Army to cross the water-gap.

Pontoons and Associated Equipment

The water-gap consists of the distance to dry land through shallow water from the point where these specialised vessels ground.

Under ideal conditions this distance is bridged completely by the bow ramp of the vessel, whereas under adverse conditions, such as a very flat beach, some hundreds of yards of shallow water remain to be traversed.

Many beaches had slopes between 1/90 and 1/175, whereas the L.S.T. were only capable of discharging tanks and vehicles if the beaches had a slope of 1/40 or steeper. Tideless seas made the question of landing both tanks and vehicles particularly difficult.

During the latter half of 1942, the Royal Engineers produced, for trials at C.O.X.E., the Vehicle Landing Ramp. This was very heavy and cumbersome and, to compete with flat beaches, the equipment would have to consist of three sets each weighing 13 tons. This equipment was therefore discarded.

The Americans carried out trials of a Treadway Bridge. This consisted of a "roadway" supported on inflatable pontoons and was their standard Army Engineer river-crossing equipment.

To enable this to be used in North Africa, a special platform was constructed in the L.S.T. from which it was to be used and 360 ft. of bridging was hoisted on board and secured. When the ships neared their objective, the pontoons were inflated and the bridging assembled on deck. On arrival, the bridging was launched in lengths of 60 ft. and towed round to the bow door.

As the result of trials, certain modifications were introduced by the staff of D.X.S.R. and it was found possible to launch 360 ft. of this equipment in under two hours, and connect it from the ship to the shore.

During his visit to the U.S.A. at the end of 1941, the D.X.S.R. had seen the Naval Lighter Pontoon Equipment. This had been designed by the American Navy for use in establishing piers in islands, which had been seized, so that stores and equipment could be landed quickly when there were no facilities previously provided. He considered this equipment could be redesigned and modified to form pontoon causeways which could be towed by the L.S.T.

In November, 1942, when "Husky" was first broached, D.X.S.R. drew attention to the fact that the L.S.T.'s intended for this operation were not adapted for use on beaches with gradual slopes and that some special equipment would be required for the slope of the Sicily beaches.

The American authorities were advised through the British Mission at Washington and several signals passed on the matter. It became obvious, however, that this requirement was not receiving the attention that it deserved, and, in view of the imminence of the operation, the matter was brought to the notice of the Chiefs of Staff Committee who decided that D.X.S.R. should at once proceed to Washington to make inquiries on the spot and to stress the vital importance of this equipment.

The result of this visit is best described in the report made by D.X.S.R. to a meeting of the Executive at C.O.H.Q. as on his return:

> Bridging equipment for L.S.T. (2)
>
> D.X.S.R. stated that on his arrival in Washington on 4th March, 1943, no trials had been carried out with the Naval Pontoon or Army Treadway Bridge, nor had any steps been taken for the provision of this equipment, its assembly or shipment.
>
> Field Marshal Dill and Admiral Noble had, subsequent to discussion with D.X.S.R., taken up the matter with the Combined Chiefs of Staff and as a result Admiral Kirk, U.S.N., had put at D.X.S.R. disposal, two L.S.T. (2) in order that trials could be carried out with the Naval Pontoon and the Treadway.
>
> The trials were more successful than had been originally hoped. The Naval Pontoon, M.T. was landed within ten minutes of the L.S.T. grounding, while the Army Treadway was done within three-quarters of an hour. Both types of equipment could be towed from one ship to another.
>
> The present position was that Naval Lighter Pontoons were being provided for one L.S.T. in every six and a certain number of Army Treadway Bridging sets was also being provided.

All the equipment was being sent to General Eisenhower, who could re-allocate it as between the Eastern and Western Task Forces.

It was not until the campaign in North Africa had been successfully completed that the naval pontoon equipment became available to the British.

The pontoon cells were made up into rafts 175 ft. long and 30 ft. wide with shaped ends to facilitate towing. Ramps had been designed for the shore end, but were not received in time for use in the Sicily landings. Experimental ramps were therefore constructed from Royal Engineer bridging equipment and fitted to one end of each raft.

These rafts were towed to the assault beaches by L.S.T. and manoeuvred into position by minor landing craft. The rafts were a success although considerable damage was done by bad weather both en route and after arrival.

The lessons learned from their employment in this campaign were that:

(1) Ramps at the shore end were essential as an integral part of the raft.
(2) Anchoring arrangements were necessary both at the shore and the seaward end.
(3) Improved towing arrangements were necessary.
(4) It was extremely difficult to manoeuvre landing ships and craft up to the seaward end and secure without damaging the raft.
(5) Tracked recovery vehicles with winches ashore and tugs afloat were necessary as part of the team responsible for operating the raft.
(6) Several rafts could be secured together providing a causeway with extending "finger piers" to enable simultaneous unloading of a variety of landing ships and craft.
(7) It was likely that less damage to and shifting of the raft would occur if it could be sunk into position instead of floating.
(8) It was imperative that adequate "working up" should take place with operating teams, ships, craft and vehicles to be employed in an operation.

Subsequently, during the preparations for the invasion of France, a great deal of work was done in the U.K. to develop the equipment to its best advantage.

Some of these trials were carried out by C.O.X.E while others were carried out by the individual Service Ministries of the Ministry of Supply at the suggestion of C.O.H.Q. and C.O.X.E. officers.

Thus, trials were carried out to determine:

(1) How best to tow the rafts and the optimum size of rafts to stand Channel weather.
(2) The best form of ramp to use at either end of a causeway and the most effective machinery for handling the ramps.
(3) How best to maintain the equipment in operation; the crews, vehicles and small craft required.
(4) What multiples of pontoon cells could be best used for the variety of purposes to which it was proposed to put them.
(5) Comparison of floating and sunken causeways.

A considerable number of equipments were evolved as a result of all these trials and during the Normandy landings N.L. Pontoon Cells, as they were officially titled, saw service in the following forms:

(1) Causeway for bridging the water-gap between shore and L.S.T.s or L.C.T.s these were used in two ways principally, (a) as floating causeways of constant length rising and falling with the tide, and (b) as sunken causeways covering the distance across the beaches so providing a solid roadway on to which vehicles and men could be discharged at all states of the tide. The latter had the advantage that it was more easily maintained in position and was less susceptible to damage in bad weather.
(2) Large self-propelled rafts, working between ship and shore, fitted with ramps to enable discharge either direct on to the beach or on to a causeway.
(3) Small self-propelled pontoons used as shallow water tugs.
(4) Piers and landing stages.

After the invasion of France was successfully completed, attention was directed to the special problems raised by the vast distances involved in the Pacific war.

The C.O.X.E. (India) was charged with problems such as towing or carrying pontoons over long distances and operations in soft mud and narrow rivers. One of the methods tried with the L.S.T. was the side carriage method, but this did not prove very successful due to the weather, on the one trial run to the Far East, causing one of the two pontoons carried to be sunk. The end of the war with Japan put a stop to carrying out further trials. The side carrying method was, however, used by the Americans throughout all operations in the Pacific with every success.

Amphibians

A further solution to the problem of making possible a quick build-up of stores and of bridging the water-gap was the amphibian.

Two versions were developed, one tracked like a tank and the other with wheels like a normal lorry.

Both types were essentially land vehicles with the ability to float and manoeuvre in water. In consequence their seagoing performance was limited. The original vehicles were all of American design and production.

They were of exceptional value in operations against beaches which were separated from the open sea by reefs or sand bars as, for example, the Pacific Islands, or by swamps or soft mud as found on the Burmese and Malayan coasts.

The wheeled amphibians, known as the D.U.K.W., carried a load of 2½ tons with a speed on land of 50 m.p.h. and 5½ knots in the water. It could be launched into deep water from a landing ship or craft and carry its load straight across the beach to the hinterland. As it had no ramp, it was used almost exclusively as a carrier for personnel and stores. It was not armoured and, due to its light weight (7 tons), it could be hoisted at L.C.A. davits.

The tracked amphibian, known as the Landing Vehicle Tracked (L.V.T.) was evolved from a vehicle designed in the thirties to assist rescue work in the Mississippi floods. Besides carrying troops, it was also a cargo carrier, of approximately four tons capacity. The vehicle had a ramped stern and could carry small vehicles in place of personnel or stores. Being tracked, it had a superior performance over difficult terrain but was naturally much slower than the D.U.K.W., speed being approximately 25 m.p.h. on land and 4½ knots in the water. Its weight, 14 tons, precluded it being hoisted at davits; it was normally launched into deep water from landing ships or craft.

The forerunners of both these vehicles were demonstrated at C.O.D.C. in May, 1942. C.C.O. was impressed and, after later trials of both tracked and wheeled types, he recommended that they be obtained from the U.S.A. for British use.

The Americans used D.U.K.W.s in the North Africa landings in November, 1942, and the British received a number of these vehicles thereafter. They were handed over to the R.A.S.C. and were first employed by British Forces for the Sicily landings. They were most successful and played an important role in both the assault build-up and maintenance phases. The D.U.K.W. was universally popular and was widely used thereafter in all theatres in a variety of roles including: (1) Load carrier and troop carrier; (2) Air/Sea rescue vehicle where mud or sand-banks were prevalent in coastal areas; [and] (3) Casualty evacuation direct to hospital ships for personnel wounded in the assault.

Later the L.V.T. was also adopted by the British and was employed both by R.E. and R.A.S.C. units in amphibious operations. An Assault

Regiment of troops carrying L.V.T. manned by R.E. was employed in the assault on Walcheren in November, 1944, and an R.A.S.C. manned Regiment was used for the crossing of Lake Commacchio in Northern Italy in the final break-through early in 1945. Two Assault Regiments were formed and manned by the Royal Marines for the Far Eastern theatre, but the war ended before they could be employed operationally.

C.O.X.E. carried out trials and experimental modifications to all these vehicles to enable artillery equipment to be carried and fired during the approach to the beach. C.O.X.E. also successfully modified the L.V.T. to a tracked mobile workshop. The latter modification enabled damaged L.V.T. to be repaired in the forward area and so return to the battle with the minimum loss of time.

Trials were also carried out by C.O.X.E., before issue to our forces, of L.V.T. modified by the Americans as light self-propelled artillery and flame throwers.

In the meantime, C.C.O. had incorporated his requirements into the pilot models to suit them for operations in the Far East. These pilot models of both wheeled (Terrapin) and tracked (Neptune) were produced and sent to C.O.X.E. for trials and evaluation during 1945. In each case the current American equivalents were used as the standard for comparison and both British types were initially considered below standard. This was partly due to over stringent staff requirements and partially to the speed of development on account of the many pressing demands for war materials at that time for the Far Eastern theatre.

An improved Terrapin (Mark II) and a reworked pilot model of the Neptune were produced and likewise evaluated by C.O.X.E., but neither vehicle went into production due to the war ending.

In addition, C.C.O. initiated staff requirements for a larger amphibian for Admiralty use. Unlike its predecessors, this version would be basically a water-borne craft with a limited performance on land. It would have much greater load carrying capacity than any previous model and its sea performance would approach that of minor landing craft. The war ended, however, before the details of this staff requirement were finally agreed.

Waterproofing

A further approach to the problem of bridging the water-gap was that of enabling vehicles, stores and equipment to be landed through the water, direct from the bow ramp of the landing ships and craft. This would infinitely speed up the process of discharging the vessels and would reduce the requirement for pontoon causeways and shallow draft ferries. It would, however, involve movement through water between 3 and 6 ft. deep whereas most vehicles could only wade in calm water up to 18 ins. deep.

The idea was not completely original, as some light tanks had been waterproofed for training during the period 1934-1936. This enabled them to wade up to 3 ft. and to be used in conjunction with the prototype L.C.M. of that day. The idea was, however, not pursued beyond the point of enabling tanks to cross shallow fords, etc. and was not at that time applied to any other type of vehicle.

With the development of special landing ships and craft, the wading requirements came to the fore and, in 1941, was under serious consideration both in C.O.H.Q. and the Ministries responsible for design and development of vehicles.

Force 110 was, at that time, engaged in carrying out experimental work and exercises concerned with sea-borne landings and was responsible for developing the fundamental principles and original materials to enable certain vehicles to wade in 3 ft. of water.

By August, 1941, the progress was sufficiently promising to enable C.C.O. to invite all the Ministries concerned to a meeting to discuss the possibility of increasing the wading capabilities of armoured fighting vehicles, carriers and motor transport.

On 14th April, 1942, on the recommendations of C.C.O., it was agreed that armoured fighting vehicles should be enabled to wade in 6 ft. of water and all other vehicles in 3 ft.

During the early days of development, vehicles waterproofed to 3 ft. were used operationally at Madagascar in May, 1942, and Churchill tanks waterproofed to 6 ft. were used at Dieppe in August, 1942. So successful were the wading results that the vehicles of the 1st United States Armoured Division were specially off-loaded at Glasgow to be waterproofed by teams from C.T.C., Inveraray, before taking part in the North Africa landings in November, 1942.

Simultaneously, waterproofing methods were evolved for equipment, guns and small arms.

Trials and training in waterproofing materials and techniques were carried on in widely separated establishments under the direction of C.O.H.Q.; the separate Arms Branches of the Service Ministries followed by setting up training establishments overseas as, for example, in North Africa in preparation for the Sicily landings.

Development went on in this way until June, 1943. It was then agreed that to avoid confusion and duplication, the whole question of waterproofing should be centralised.

D.M.E. at the War Office was directed to take over control and he formed a new branch of his Directorate for the purpose.

A Waterproofing Committee on which C.O.H.Q. was represented, was also set up under his Chairmanship.

By September, 1943, great progress had been made and various wading depths had been agreed to cover the requirements of all types of vehicles and vessels likely to be employed by British and American Forces in France and the Far East.

In addition to depth, there was the time of immersion element to be settled. Some vehicles, notably self-propelled artillery, were required to go into action while remaining in a hull-down position in the water for up to forty-five minutes as against the six minutes required for most other types. In January, 1944, C.C.O. again studied the requirements of the different war theatres and, as a result of his recommendations, standards were set which covered all requirements on a global basis.

By this time, R.E.M.E. had developed their training resources to such a degree that they were made responsible for waterproofing the entire force employed in "Overlord" with the exception of the armoured fighting vehicles in the assault waves which remained a unit responsibility.

In December, 1944, the Combined Operations School of Waterproofing was established at Bideford to replace the various organisations which had existed hitherto, and to train personnel for the war against Japan. This school was capable of training one British Infantry Division and one Army Tank Brigade simultaneously.

It was subsequently decided, however, that all training of this nature for troops engaged in the Far East theatre would be carried out locally and not in the U.K. The school was therefore closed in September, 1945, leaving the Army solely responsible for all future waterproofing activities.

The Beach

After crossing the water-gap, there remained usually an area of difficult terrain to be crossed before reaching the firm ground upon which the Army's equipment was designed to operate. This area is termed the beach. The variety of conditions which may be encountered is infinite and almost every amphibious operation of the last war was launched over a different type of beach. In studying beach conditions, the following factors must be taken into account:

Material	Mud, firm sand, soft sand, sand dunes, clay, gravel stones or rock.
Slope	"Steep to" allow landing ships and craft to land their loads dryshod, or flat which left a

	long wade through shallow water to dry land from the point where the vessel grounded.
Width	The usable portion of beach might be restricted by natural or artificial obstacles.
Depth	The distance from the water's edge to the hinterland which would vary with tide in some areas.
False Beaches	Reefs, sand bars, and obstacles which would prevent vessels discharging direct on to the true beach.
Tides/Currents	The presence or absence of which was a vital factor in the use of any beach.

For example, the Sicily landings were carried out over fairly flat narrow beaches which had little depth and were unaffected by tide. The beaches used in Normandy, however, were very flat, wide, backed in places by dunes or cliffs and altering considerably in depth with each tide.

In the Pacific, the problem was aggravated by coral reefs which protected many of the landing areas, while in Burma and Malaya, soft mud backed by mangrove swamps created further complications.

The problem of crossing the beach fell naturally into two main categories: (1) the landing of personnel, and (2) the landing of vehicles, stores and equipment.

Each category required the development of special equipment some of which is described below.

Landing of Personnel

As a rule, the special ships and craft could discharge men on to the beach in water less than waist deep with the assistance of a simple ramp extending from the deck over the bows to the shallow water beyond. However, to facilitate operations by Commandos, underwater swimmers and special reconnaissance parties, it was necessary to develop equipment which would enable small forces to surmount, complete with their weapons, an obstacle considered impassable and thereby achieve surprise in an attack upon the enemy, or to reconnoitre unseen an enemy held area.

The extent of the development and trials work involved will be appreciated from the fact that there were, at one time, 200 different items which were not obtainable through normal Service channels.

In order to provide these items at short notice for an operation, without loss of security, it was found necessary to set up a Combined

Operations Stores Depot. This depot was established in 1942, and began to function just before the raid on Dieppe. It continued until the war ended when the individual Services assumed responsibility for all remaining equipment.

Some of the items were required on a very wide scale, such as equipment for underwater swimmers, whereas others were of limited use only, such as Commando operations where cliffs had to be scaled.

Equipment developed as the result of trails at C.O.X.E. for the Commando cliff assault requirement included: Grapnels secured to one end of a climbing rope, which could be fired from a mortar to the top of a cliff; Cliff assault Ladders, both rigid and flexible, some sectional and others extending to 60 ft; [and] Gantry and Powered Winch to enable stores and heavy equipment to be hauled rapidly up a cliff face.

Further tasks of special units were those of reconnaissance and underwater demolitions.

To fill the requirements of small specialised units, a range of rigid and non-rigid canoes was evolved, some of which could be propelled by outboard motors in addition to paddles, oars or sails. Much associated equipment was also developed for use by personnel operating from these tiny craft, such as: Wrist compasses; Waterproof torches; Miniature wireless sets; [and] Underwater writing tablets for taking notes.

Shallow water diving gear was issued to underwater swimmers and Landing Craft Obstacle Clearance Units. It consisted basically of a two-piece rubber suit joined at the waist, which covered the wearer completely, leaving only the head and hands exposed. This suit could be used by itself or with the addition of "swim fins" on the feet, to assist swimmers in shallow water operations. When required for prolonged underwater work, a self-contained breathing set could be added enabling personnel to remain submerged for about 20 minutes. Oxygen supply for the breathing apparatus was not the only limiting factor in remaining submerged, as a man's hands rapidly become numb in cold water. The use of gloves to offset this was impracticable due to the consequent loss of feeling and manipulation.

Underwater demolition charges were developed, which could be used by swimmers, with a suitable delay fuse to destroy underwater obstacles, bridge supports, enemy shipping, etc. Of necessity they were small and easily handled, and were fitted for attachment to smooth surfaces of a variety of materials such as ships hulls and concrete piers.

Landing of Vehicles, Stores and Equipment

Vehicles, particularly wheeled vehicles, required a firmer surface than that offered by soft sand, mud or loose shingle, and it was therefore necessary to provide some form of roadway from the foot of the bow ramp of landing ships and craft, through the water-gap and across the beach to the firm ground beyond.

The requirement was for something portable, both by vehicles and teams working from landing ships and craft; to be easily laid by unskilled personnel working by night or day without the use of special tools; economical to maintain; and, finally, to provide an adequate bearing surface for all types of vehicles employed in an operation.

The requirement therefore evolved into a roadway which would fulfil as many as possible of the following points:

(1) Be easily supplied from existing Service materials.
(2) Be easily transported in normal load carrying vehicles.
(3) Be portable in sections or rolls by teams of men.
(4) Be easily laid above or below water, by unskilled personnel from the point where landing ships and craft would beach.
(5) Be capable of rapid laying in the first instance so as to allow the vehicles required in the early stages of an assault to be driven ashore.
(6) Be capable of subsequent strengthening with the minimum of additional parts, to carry the heavy traffic required in the build-up and follow-up phases.

Army equipment employed to traverse sandy or swampy areas already existed, some of which could be adapted, either complete or in part, for the purpose.

C.O.X.E. (U.K.) and, after its formation, C.O.X.E (India), were charged with trying out the various materials and all their various combinations to ascertain:

(1) The best solution for each condition of beach.
(2) The best way of providing the required materials, i.e., in cut short lengths in "packs", or in rolls.
(3) The best ways of laying, maintaining and operating the roadways.

Experiments were continuous and covered the production of training and operating instructions as well as technical data and advice.

New Problems in Europe, 1945 – River Crossings

In Europe, assaults on beaches had become, if not stereotyped, at least widely understood. Suitable equipment was in the main available, as were staffs and men trained in its use. Repeated landings had been made behind the enemy lines in Italy, besides the big operations in Normandy and the South of France, and if some of these operations

THE DEVELOPMENT OF SHIPS AND CRAFT

were less successful than had been hoped, it was not because of any technical failure to get ashore in face of opposition. Difficulties of maintenance and build-up of supply across beaches were largely solved. A series of amphibious operations in the Low Countries in support of the left flank of the advancing Allied armies, of which the landings in Walcheren were the most notable, were undertaken by Royal Marine and Army Commandos. A new European problem facing C.O.H.Q. was the technique of a large scale assault river crossing. The following paragraphs appear in the records of the Yalta Conference:

> Exchange of Information with regard to River-Crossing Technique and Equipment.
>
> Admiral Leahy said that at the first meeting between the Heads of State, the British Prime Minister had raised the question of exchanging information with regard to technique and equipment employed by the Soviet Forces in river crossings. At the present time, in view of the Allied proximity to the River Rhine, this was a most immediate problem for the Allied Forces.
>
> There were now two officers present from General Eisenhower's Headquarters and it appeared highly desirable that they should meet with the appropriate Soviet experts on the subject of the technique and equipment employed by the Red Army in major river crossings which they had undertaken. Thus, the Allied Armies on the Western Front could obtain the benefit of the experience of the Red Army in this matter. He would therefore very much appreciate if General Antonov would indicate whether this could be done and, if so, would make such arrangements as were practicable for the officers from General Eisenhower's Headquarters to meet with the appropriate Soviet Officers.
>
> General Antonov said that the Soviet Army was always ready to share its battle experiences with its allies. However, at the moment there were no specialists in this technique available and he would like therefore time to look into this matter. He would furnish the required information later.
>
> Admiral Leahy thanked General Antonov for this very satisfactory reply.

Subsequent to the Yalta Conference, General Laycock (C.C.O.) and Brigadier Head, the two officers from General Eisenhower's Headquarters referred to above, went on to Moscow. There they had discussions with Russian representatives on river-crossing technique and elicited a great deal of frank and useful information on Russian methods of crossing rivers.

Mines, Beach Obstructions and their Clearance; Craft and Vehicle Recovery

The need for beach obstructions in World War II first became apparent in this country in 1940. Much of the work done was due to the policy of blocking all exits from the beaches by the use of barbed wire, concrete obstacles and mines. On the beaches themselves, large number of beach mines were laid above the high water mark. Underwater obstacles were, in general, limited to tubular scaffolding barriers and some barbed wire. In critical areas along the south-east coast, some flame barrages were installed.

Defences Against Allied Operations

When the Germans, in their turn, had to consider the defence of European beaches, a similar policy of blocking beach exits was at first in favour and it was not until the beginning of 1944, after Field-Marshal Rommel took over, that the policy of defeating the landing on the beach came into force.

There were, therefore, only natural obstacles on the beaches themselves to be overcome by our assaulting forces at Vaagso and Dieppe. In the latter operation, the beach itself was not laid with obstacles, although a few booby-traps were encountered. In this instance the beach was exceptionally well covered by accurate and well-directed fire from weapons of all calibres.

Sicily too followed this pattern, although mines were encountered towards the back of the beach. However, they gave but little concern as the bulk were still awaiting arming and laying.

Various experiments with underwater obstacles had been carried out by the enemy in 1943, and, in February, 1944, the erection of obstacle barriers was started in earnest on the North Sea and Atlantic Coast beaches.

The German intention was to create continuous belts of obstacles against landing craft along the entire length of all possible beaches, priority being given to those beaches most favourable for landings. Only rocky beaches which were considered completely inaccessible were to be left unobstructed.

Destruction by Heavy Charges

C.O.X.E. carried out trials in May, 1944, of destroying obstacles similar to the German types by means of depth charges placed by small craft. L.C.T. (4), L.C.A. and L.C.V. (P.) were all used and, on the whole, the method was fairly successful although it involved a lot of manoeuvring by each craft. The L.C.V. (P.), being easily handled, was the best craft for this purpose. This system was not, however, adopted in "Overlord".

Hedgerow

Early in 1943, experiments were carried out using an L.C.A. fitted with a number of ahead-throwing weapons on the lines of the Hedgehog mounting and using Hedgehog rounds to destroy anti-tank mines on the beaches. The L.C.A. did not, however, prove to be the best type of craft to carry these weapons (of the twenty-seven used in "Overlord" only eleven actually arrived and fired their weapons), but the hedgerow itself more than proved its worth.

Ramming

Trials were also carried out at C.O.X.E. to see if L.C.T.s could ram their way through obstacles. It was found that the L.C.T. (4) could get through two or three rows of normal obstacles (German types) with little or no damage, although the wrecks of the obstacles might still be a danger to retraction.

This method cannot, of course, be recommended when the obstacles are mined and, in "Overlord", where a lot of ramming was done, the mined obstacles did cause a good deal of damage, although most vessels still landed their loads.

Bumpers

When it was known that the Germans were using floating "Hayrick" mines and "Nutcracker" mines, light V-shaped sweeps of tubular scaffolding were designed by C.O.X.E. to fit on to the bows of minor craft and also L.C.T. (4). The sweep was intended to divert the floating mines or to actuate the "Nutcracker" mines ahead of the craft; although a number of craft were fitted prior to "Overlord", there is no record of their employment.

Following "Overlord" a pamphlet was written which included the known and anticipated problems to be encountered in the Far East, and was issued as a very comprehensive report in November, 1944. Thereafter the problem was studied at C.O.X.E. (India) where trials of a similar nature were carried out against the defences produced by the Japanese.

A much heavier bow sweep was later designed at C.O.X.E. for dealing with light obstacles likely to be encountered in Far East assaults. This was mounted on an L.C.T. (4) and controlled by two winches. In trials it was successful but was never developed owing to the end of the war.

The Americans also experimented with a heavy V-shaped bumper fitted to L.C.M.s.

Beach Recovery Equipment

Coincidental with the development of the Beach Organisation, as related in Chapter 18, were the trials and experiments to produce suitable specialised equipment for the units employed on the beaches.

Two of the great problems were: (1) To salvage and refloat landing craft which could not retract under their own power; (2) To salvage and clear the beach of vehicles which became stuck either in the water or on the beach itself.

As a further complication it was found necessary to lift beached landing craft, when re-floating them, in order to avoid damage to propellers and rudders. With existing equipment this was a tedious process as no single vehicle could at the same time lift and tow or push the craft.

The two problems were closely inter-related and were tackled respectively by the Navy and the Army working in the closest co-operation which included specific instructions to Army units to hold, on call, a percentage of their equipment for naval use.

Recovery units using normal Army equipment were first employed late in 1942 in the North African landings and clearly indicated many deficiencies.

By March, 1943, a Beach Recovery Committee had been set up within C.O.H.Q. Thereafter a R.E.M.E. Experimental Party and an American Recovery Party were established at C.O.X.E. to carry out trials in development of suitable equipment to deal with all types of vehicles, wheeled and tracked. At the same time the Admiralty formed a special detachment at C.O.X.E. to examine the problem as it related to landing craft.

In the very short time available, trials with and modifications to existing equipment was carried out in anticipation of the Sicily landings. In the event, the following equipment was employed:

> Bulldozers, light and heavy.
> 10-ton recovery trucks (American Wrecker type).
> Scammel recovery trucks (British).
> D.U.K.W.s.
> Le Tourneau Crane with tractor.

Subsequent reports indicated that the light bulldozer was not a success but the heavy version was excellent if improved waterproofing (to give deeper wading) and some armour could be incorporated.

Recovery trucks and D.U.K.W.s were all moderately successful in their roles, but there clearly emerged a requirement for a heavy, tracked armoured recovery vehicle capable of operating in water 7 to 8 ft. deep and of towing, pushing and winching.

The Le Tourneau Crane which had been adapted from civilian use, was immediately successful and largely responsible for keeping the beaches clear of stranded craft. The Le Tourneau was a tracked crane which, when coupled to a tractor that provided the lifting and motive power, was capable of lifting and moving craft requiring repair or re-floating.

As a result of this experience, trials were carried out which produced improved versions of all the foregoing and, in addition, a Beach Army Recovery Vehicle (B.A.R.V.).

The B.A.R.V. was basically a Sherman tank with its turret removed and with metal sides built on to allow continuous operation in water up to 9 ft. deep. It was very successful and was widely employed with the improved bulldozers for the Normandy landings.

In the meantime, and partially as a result of Normandy where large numbers of landing ships and craft became stranded, it was realised that equipment was required to salvage landing craft which were beyond the capabilities of any mobile crane. The Admiralty therefore developed, as the result of trials, a form of inflatable Recovery Gear. This was known during its early development in 1945 as the Sausage Slipway; it consisted of a series of inflatable fabric sausage-like bags which could be inserted below the landing craft and, when inflated, enabled the craft to be rolled either into or out of water. Trials were promising although the weight of the larger tank landing craft caused the bags to burst. Experiments were still in hand to strengthen the design and material when the war ended.

Miscellaneous Projects in Preparation for Operation "Overlord"

The Construction of Hards to Facilitate Vehicle Embarkation

In considering the Army requirements for large scale landing in France, it was apparent that even with all the port facilities on the south coast working to capacity, there would still be a need for other means of embarkation if the rate of build-up was to be achieved at the necessary speed.

C.O.H.Q. proposed that the L.S.T.s and L.C.T.s could use the sheltered beaches round the coast, but it was soon found to be quite impossible to use the beaches themselves as only a little traffic soon churned them up and made them impassable. It was therefore decided to use Hards.

A Committee under the Chairmanship of a C.O.H.Q. representative worked out a scheme by which a number of the Hards would be built under Admiralty direction.

The design of the Hards was difficult because tanks and vehicles were required to traverse the foreshore and embark between the high and low-water marks. To lay permanent concrete, except above the high-water mark, was impracticable as it was unlikely to stand up to the heavy seas in winter. To overcome the difficulty, the War Office produced a flexible concrete mattress. This was made up in sections which could be lifted by four men. Each section consisted of pre-cast concrete, reinforced with steel wire. The average hard absorbed 4,000 of these sections and hundreds of miles of this mattress was constructed and eventually used in all theatres of the European war.

The "Habbakuk" Project

The scheme was to construct one or more floating airfields in the form of giant aircraft carriers made of ice. The approximate dimensions of these novel ships were to be 3,000 ft. long and 300 ft beam, with a speed of 7 to 10 knots. The method of propulsion was to be by electric motors fitted outboard or in nacelles, and the design included refrigerating plant with pipes embedded in the outer skin to keep the walls permanently frozen.

This project, started in C.O.H.Q. by Mr. Pyke and given the title "Habbakuk", was evolved to overcome the problem of providing fighter cover for landing on the French coast, other than in Pas-de-Calais area. It was also thought that it would be useful as a floating airfield in the mid-Atlantic for convoy protection or to support American amphibious operations in the Pacific.

Very small-scale trials of blocks of ice soon showed that they lacked tensile strength to resist shock and, if bullets were fired at the block of ice, it would be shattered. So Mr. Pyke suggested using 5 per cent paper pulp mixed with the ice; the resulting substance, which was named Pykerete, had astounding qualities. It was almost as strong as concrete and, when bullets were fired at it, they ricocheted off without damage to the Pykerete. In the opinion of C.C.O. this brought "Habbakuk" within the bounds of possibility.

Following on from this, Pykerete had the advantage that all of the above water damage from bombing or shell fire, which in any case would be no greater than comparable damage to concrete, could instantly be put right by pouring in liquid Pykerete and freezing it.

A scheme for providing coffer dams to put over parts of the ship that had been torpedoed was also produced, so that liquid Pykerete could be poured down below the surface of the water. It was estimated, however, that it would take between fifty and seventy torpedoes to damage "Habbakuk" to the point of putting it out of action. A further advantage of Pykerete was that a comparatively small refrigerating plant would be necessary to keep the ship frozen even in tropical water.

At the Quebec conference in 1943, "Habbakuk" was finally withdrawn, since the three reasons for its inception were otherwise dealt with as follows:

(1) The Chief of Staff to the Supreme Allied Commander accepted that the assault on the coast in the Baie de la Seine was possible after all, and this would be feasible because fighter protection could be provided from England by using long range fighters fitted with extra tanks as originally urged by C.O.H.Q.
(2) The Allies had decided to seize the Azores, whether Portugal objected or not, and these were to be used as the mid-Atlantic airfield.
(3) The Americans had on order such a vast number of conventional aircraft carriers and had got such complete control of the Japanese submarine threat that an unsinkable floating airfield was no longer needed in the Pacific.

Power-Driven Rivers

Another of Mr. Pyke's schemes was for the construction of power-driven rivers. "Pyke's Uphill Rivers", as they were known, were to consist of 8 in. pipelines running from ship to shore and from shore forwards to the scene of an assault, up which stores could be passed to inland dumps.

As the name implied, the pipes would carry water boosted through them by special pumps set at intervals on the line. This would help solve the problem of bridging the water-gap and would have been of particular value in Far Eastern operations where they would have assisted in overcoming the obstacles of greater distances, lack of communication facilities, coastal swamp and impenetrable bush. The scheme was never progressed for a variety of reasons, the main ones being the difficulty of laying the pipeline in time for it to be effective when most needed, the packing of stores to fit it and its vulnerability.

Tank Floatation Devices

There was a requirement to land tanks very early in the assault to provide support for the infantry. It was considered that this requirement might not be adequately met by tanks wading from landing ship and craft. It was therefor decided, in August, 1940, that a swimming tank should be developed and by September, 1940, the I.S.T.D.C. issued their first concrete suggestions and commenced liaison with the Director of Tank Design and D.N.C.

In October, 1940, it was agreed at a conference of all concerned that the floatation devices should consist of buoyancy floats fitted to normal tanks. These floats were to be of a suitable size to limit the draft of the whole apparatus to 3 ft. and the beam to 21 ft. In the meantime, trials with a light tank were carried out successfully giving a speed in smooth water of 4 knots. After this, a long series of trials and discussions were pursued by I.S.T.D.C. (thereafter C.O.X.E.) and the Combined Operations Experimental Wing of the Directorate of Tank Design. As a result, it was decided during the summer of 1941, that the buoyancy float method was unsatisfactory, principally because the tank became too bulky to operate with any existing or projected landing ships and craft.

An alternative method was suggested by Mr. Nicholas Straussler and was initially tried out on a Tetrarck tank. Although only partially successful, a meeting on Tank Flotation including representatives from C.O.H.Q. decided to nominate a firm to develop the system for a Valentine tank, with Mr. Straussler as adviser.

The apparatus consisted of a canvas screen round the sides of the tank, which could be raised or lowered at will.

The advantages of this scheme were as follows:

(1) It could be used any number of times, being therefore usable for river crossings as well as the initial assault.
(2) It did not materially increase the deck space occupied by the tank and allowed launching through the bow door of the landing ship and craft.
(3) It occupied no additional space on passage over normal tanks.

This method was adopted by both the U.K. and the U.S.A., and Sherman tanks so equipped were operationally employed.

The Supply of Petrol in Containers

The question of supply of petrol to the Army engaged in amphibious operations was a source of very careful study at C.O.H.Q., commencing early in 1942. The normal method of packing for the Army was in four-gallon containers. These were of flimsy construction and, if subjected to rough handing, were inclined to leak. Thus, the petrol was not only wasted, but from the point of view of the ships in which it was transported, was a very grave menace.

Experience in the Western Desert had also shown that the vibration of the trucks in which these cans were loaded caused leakage which amounted to some 40 per cent over rough country. C.C.O. took the matter up and through the C.M.S.F. suggested that Jerricans, which were strongly made and returnable, should be adopted as the standard container. Considerable opposition to this change was encountered at first, but eventually the Fifth Sea Lord took the matter up with the Principal Administrative Officers' Committee. At a meeting of the latter, the Deputy Director of Sea Transport exhibited photographs of the holds of ships, which clearly showed the wastage and damage which resulted in the use of the standard flimsy tin. The immediate result of this meeting was the formation of a Committee to consider the production of Jerricans.

In this way certain factories were taken over and twenty million Jerricans were produced, half in America and half in Great Britain; and these became the standard method of distributing cased petrol.

It should be noted that the Jerrican was an American invention and had been adopted by the Germans with satisfactory results.

The Supply of Petrol in Bulk

Early in 1942, as part of the study of the problem of the re-entry into Europe, the question of the supply of petrol in bulk was raised. As a first solution, it was proposed that small tankers should be used to carry the petrol across the Channel and that, on arrival at the other side, they should be moored close off-shore and the petrol pumped from them into storage tanks and from there distributed as required.

Early in May, 1942, a trial of this method was carried out off Appledore (Devon) under the supervision of the C.O.X.E. which was situated nearby. As far as it went, this trial was satisfactory.

Out of this, the idea arose of pumping the petrol in bulk across the Channel. This was a very large project and necessitated both research and experiment. The idea was put up by C.C.O. to Mr. Geoffrey Lloyd, the Secretary for Petroleum, and the matter was subsequently discussed at a meeting of the Q.M.G. Petroleum Committee on 13th May, 1942. At this meeting, Mr. Lloyd reported that experiments were being conducted with a cable laid across the Medway, through which it was proposed to pump petrol at a pressure of 750 lb. per square inch.

As the idea had originated from C.O.H.Q., the D.X.S.R. stated, on behalf of C.C.O., that further experiments should be continued at high priority.

The story of the trials of the H.A.I.S. cable, as it was called, makes very interesting reading. First there were small scale trials carried out in the Thames Estuary to test the cable. These took some time but, in the end, showed that the cable would take the required pressure but impressed on everyone concerned that it must be laid by officers and men fully acquainted with the intricate nature of the work. It was therefore decided to man the cable ship, S.S. *London*, with a naval crew and commission the ship as H.M.S. *Holdfast*.

Towards the end of December everything was ready for the full scale trial across the Bristol Channel, advocated by C.O.H.Q. Accordingly, H.M.S. *Holdfast* proceeded to Swansea with the necessary length of cable embarked.

The first stage of the trials consisted of laying the inshore ends of the cable from the pumping station and to the receiving tanks. This was done by two specially fitted L.C.T.s.

On 27th December, 2,000 yards of cable were laid from No. 5 jetty, Queens Dock, Swansea and the end buoyed. Two days later H.M.S. *Holdfast* recovered the buoyed seaward end and connected it up to the main cable. She then proceeded to lay the cable from Swansea to Watermouth (near Appledore) which was accomplished without incident at a speed of approximately 4 to 5 knots. Having arrived off Watermouth, the end was dropped and buoyed about 1½ miles from the terminal in Watermouth Bay.

Difficulties then arose. The operation of connecting the main cable to the shore end delayed proceedings but in the end was successfully completed. Then damage was discovered to the main cable which had been caused by the efforts to make the joint. To add to the difficulties a tanker dragged her anchor across the cable at the Swansea end which caused further damage. The damage to both ends was eventually repaired but it was not until 31st March, 1943, some three months later, that the cable was considered satisfactory for testing.

On 4th April, pumping commenced from the British Tanker Company's pumps at Swansea and petrol was then delivered through the cable at a rate of 37,200 gallons every 24 hours.

This was satisfactory as far as it went, but the estimated requirements of the Army for "Overlord" were very much greater than this amount. Therefore other methods were investigated by the Petroleum Warfare Department.

The first one of these to be developed by C.O.X.E. at Appledore was the floating pipeline which was connected to the tanks at the shore end and then floated out to the petrol or oil carrying vessel moored off shore. This proved satisfactory and was employed at Port en Bessin in France.

In addition to the above two methods, the Petroleum Warfare Department proceeded with a design for a flexible welded steel pipe of 3 in. diameter which was wound on a large floating drum. This project, although inspired by C.C.O.,[1] was perfected under the supervision of the Department referred to above and eventually used with success in the "Overlord" operation.

The pipeline methods of supply were eventually confirmed as a requirement by C.O.S.S.A.C. and instructions were issued by the Chiefs of Staff for the provision of all necessary requirements for operating oil supply pipelines to the continent. With all methods working well, the supply of fuel reached the total of 1,000,000 gallons per day.

The Provision of Artificial Harbour Facilities for the Invasion of France, "Mulberry"

The supply over open beaches would be entirely dependent on the weather and, from statistics which had been collected over a number of years, it was found that the weather in the English Channel was very much in favour of the Germans.

As the planners at C.O.H.Q. examined this problem, it soon became abundantly clear that, to ensure any form of build-up after the initial assault, some form of artificial harbour would be required.

It was apparent that any port which could be seized would be so demolished and blocked by the Germans that it would require prolonged restoration work before it could be of use to the Allies.

The situation is well summarised in the following extract from General Eisenhower's book *Crusade in Europe*:

> Since the nature of the defences to be encountered ruled out the possibility of gaining adequate ports promptly, it was necessary also to provide a means of sheltering beach supply from the effects of storms. We knew that even after we captured Cherbourg its port facilities and the lines of communication leading out of it could not meet all our needs. To solve this apparently unsolvable problem, we undertook a project so unique as to be classed by many scoffers as completely fantastic. It was a plan to construct artificial harbours on the coast of Normandy.
>
> The first time I heard this idea tentatively advanced was by Admiral Mountbatten, in the spring of 1942. At a conference attended by a number of Service Chiefs he remarked: 'If ports were not available, we may have to construct them in pieces and tow

---

[1] Meeting on Bulk Petrol Supply at C.O.H.Q., dated 20th April, 1942.

them in.' Hoots and jeers greeted his suggestion but two years later it was to become reality.

In the summer of 1942 a study was made, leading to small scale trials in November, of a method of reducing wave height over an area. This consisted of apparatus to release compressed air beneath the water to seaward of the proposed calm area. Although successful in small scale experiments, this method was not pursued and attention was turned to the creation of a breakwater by sinking old and comparatively useless ships filled with concrete.

As the supply requirements for the forces which would be required in France became more apparent, it was found that large ships would have to be used. Consequently, a breakwater of ships would not be sufficient because they would be submerged if they were sunk in such a position as would allow deep draught ships to anchor inshore to them. This problem was given unending consideration at C.O.H.Q. during 1942 and the beginning of 1943.

In the spring of 1943, it became apparent to the C.C.O. that, *inter alia*. the provision of artificial harbours would not be pursued at high priority unless the Force Commanders stated a firm requirement, so he convinced Conference "Rattle" to obtain decisions regarding the provision of equipment in the short time available.

Investigations of the problem were taken in hand by the Director of Transportation at the War Office and under him, Brigadier Bruce White produced designs of concrete caissons which would fulfil the requirements.

Also, the Prime Minister had addressed the following note to C.C.O.:

> Piers for use on beaches.
> They must float up and down with the tide. The anchor problem must be mastered. Let me have the best solution worked out. The difficulties will argue for themselves.
> 30th May, 1942. W.S.C.

As a result of the above minute, what came to be known as the "Spud Pier" was designed, and was one of the components of "Whale" which is described later.

The actual requirement of the artificial harbours was laid down in the "Rattle" Conference which was held at Largs at the end of June, 1943.

Closely following upon the end of this conference, the Prime Minister with all his advisers went to Quebec. Among the latter was the Chief of

THE DEVELOPMENT OF SHIPS AND CRAFT

Staff to the Allied Commander (Lieut.-General Sir Frederick Morgan) who took with him the outline plan for Operation "Overlord".

At the Quebec Conference, "Quadrant", proposals for the construction of these harbours were put forward. The plan was for two of them to be built, one for the British and one for the American sector. It was decided that a joint Anglo-American Committee should be set up to study the whole project, and Brigadier Sir Harold Wernher, who had been appointed Chief Co-ordinator for this project on 6th August, 1943, was summoned to Quebec by the Chiefs of Staff. Before the Quebec Conference ended, the joint Committee had rendered their report to the Chiefs of Staff who, on 2nd September, 1943 approved it.

In addition to the actual work entailed by the breakwaters, other requirements had also arisen. These included the provision of pierheads which could rise and fall with the tide, flexible floating roadways and pontoons which were used inside the harbours for the discharge of ammunition, stores and supplies.

In anticipation of these requirements, Brigadier Wernher, acting on the instructions of C.C.O., had arranged with the Third Sea Lord for the appointment of Rear-Admiral H. Hickling as liaison officer with the Admiralty. Likewise, the Ministry of Supply had appointed members of various firms to be available for the project and the American authorities had appointed an officer in the Corps of Engineers to represent American interests. Thus, it came about that, when Brigadier Wernher left for Canada, he had assembled a team who could get on with the work without any delay.

During the absence of Brigadier Wernher, his assistant carried out a preliminary survey of all the work in connection with the project and also got into contact with the Admiralty, War Office and the Ministries of Supply and Production. When Brigadier Wernher returned, all the ground work had been completed.

Thus came into being the project which received the title of "Mulberry".

In their final form the Mulberries consisted of the following constructions:

(1) Bombardon: an outer breakwater of floating structures which were anchored in the open sea in two rows with 400 yards intervals between them and lying parallel with, and to seaward of the Phoenix.
(2) Phoenix: an inner main breakwater of concrete caissons sunk in deep water.

(3) Gooseberry: another breakwater consisting of block ships sunk in the shallow water.

(4) Whale: a number of spud piers, six American and nine British, floating up and down with the tide. These were connected to the beach by flexible floating roadways which, for towing purposes, were divided into 480 ft. spans.

Two of these harbours were built, one for the American and one for the British sectors. The original design of the Mulberry stipulated that it should last for ninety days and was to stand up to a gale of Force 6, Beaufort Scale. Actually, several years after the operation took place, the main components were still in place.

All the component parts of "Mulberry" had to be towed from England and sunk in their correct position. This constituted an operation on its own and was carried out, under the direction of the Admiralty, very successfully as far as the British sector was concerned. The harbour in the American sector never attained the efficiency for which it was planned, owing to: (1) the rapidity with which the Americans endeavoured to erect it; and (2) the fact that proper soundings were not taken prior to the sinking of the caissons, which resulted in many of the latter being sunk out of sight.

In the British harbour off Arromanches, the rate of discharge eventually reached the total of 12,000 tons of cargo per day in any weather.

Some idea of the vast nature of the task can be gathered from the fact that the labour force finally numbered between 43,000 and 47,000. Material used included 105,000 tons of steel, 850,000 tons of ballast and sand, and 144,000 tons of concrete.

Grand Admiral Raeder, the German Naval C.-in-C., stated after capture that the Germans knew something about the Mulberries but had no details. He had never believed that such a degree of perfection would be reached and, without any doubt, it was those ports which made possible the rapid and total success of the landing.

In the report[2] on the usefulness of the British Mulberries, Sir Walter Monckton, who had been ordered by the Prime Minister to hold an investigation, records the following statistics taken from Rear-Admiral Hicklings' records:

---

[2] Report by Sir Walter Monckton on The Part Played in "Overlord by the Synthetic Harbours.

Stores handled during the period ending   543,750 tons.
3rd September, 1944

Vehicles and Personnel passed through   Vehicles 47,000 and
during the period ending   Personnel 223,500.
31st October, 1944

In the final paragraph of the report quoted above, Sir Walter Monckton states: "I cannot finish my task without expressing in a single simple sentence the admiration which I have felt, as a civilian wholly unconnected with this enterprise, for the imagination, resource, resolution and courage of those who planned and carried it out."

APPENDICES

APPENDICES

Appendix I

RAIDING OPERATIONS: DIRECTIVE TO GENERAL BOURNE

Secret C.O.S. (40) 468
17th June, 1940

War Cabinet

Chiefs of Staff Committee

Raiding Operations: Directive to General Bourne

We have approved the attached directive for Lieut.-General A.G.B. Bourne, C.B., D.S.O., M.V.O., who has been appointed Commander Raiding Operations and Adviser to the Chiefs of Staff on Combined Operations.

(Signed)
R.E.C. Peirse, V.C.A.S.
T.S.V. Phillips, V.C.N.S.
R.H. Haining, V.C.I.G.S.

Directive

To: Lieut.-General A.G.B. Bourne, C.B., D.S.O., M.V.O., Royal Marines.

1. You are appointed Commander of Raiding Operations on coasts in enemy occupation and Adviser to the Chiefs of Staff on Combined Operations.

Raiding Operations

2. The object of raiding operations will be to harass the enemy and cause him to disperse his forces, and to create material damage, particularly on the coastline from Northern Norway to the western limit of German-occupied France.

3. We propose to give you within the limits of the forces and equipment available and subject to directions which you receive from time to time from the Chiefs of Staff, complete discretion in the choice of objectives and the scale of operation undertaken. The Joint Intelligence Sub-Committee have been instructed to help you in the choice of suitable objectives. You are to keep the Chiefs of Staff informed of the operations you prose to carry out.

4. Six Independent Companies and a School of Training in Irregular Operations have already been raised by the War Office. These and the irregular Commandos now being raised will come under your operational command and any administrative suggestions you may wish to make, e.g., for the organisation of units, their location in the United Kingdom, etc., will be met as far as they can be.

In addition, the War Office have taken preliminary steps to raise parachutist volunteers of whom a number will be placed under your command. When raised, they will be trained by the Air Ministry and the War Office according to your requirements and advice.

5. Should you want further independent units, over and above those already raised, you should discuss your requirements with Service Departments and advise us accordingly.

6. Certain raids by the independent companies have already been planned by the General Staff in the War Office. You should make yourself acquainted with such projects at once and take over control of any planned raids when you deem it advisable.

7. Irregular actions of various types are undertaken from time to time by the Service Intelligence Departments. There must therefore be close touch between your staff and these departments in order that your several activities shall not interfere with each other and that, on occasions, co-operation may be possible.

Combined Operations

8. Your second role will be to take over command of the Inter-Services Training and Development Centres and to act as our adviser on the organisation required for opposed landings.

APPENDIX I

9. Three brigade groups are being detailed for special training in combined operations as soon as they can be equipped. Of these, one may be made available at your request for purely raiding operations, in which case it would, of course, be placed under your command. You will, however, be responsible for supervising the technical training of all troops earmarked for combined operations.

In addition, we wish you to press on the development and production of special landing craft and equipment and to advise us, when the occasion arises, as to its allotment.

10. If it is desired to undertake a combined operation, detailed plans will be worked out by the Service Departments (through the medium of the Inter-Service Planning Staff) and the commander designate. Both will require your technical advice and help.

Relations with other Staffs
11. We are directing the Inter-Service Planning Staff to consult you whenever they receive a combined operational project for examination which implies a landing on a hostile shore.

You should maintain close liaison with this staff and also with the operational and intelligence staffs of the Service Departments and with the Inter-Service Project Board. At the same time, you will have direct access to the Chiefs of Staff Committee who will also advise you of any combined operations which are envisaged.

Headquarters and Staff
12. Your headquarters will be at the Admiralty. You should let us know as soon as possible what staff you need.

13. An officer of the Royal Air Force will be attached to your staff who will also be responsible, under the Air Ministry, for the development as far as the Air Force are concerned, of parachute troops and other air requirements for raiding and irregular operations.

Secrecy
14. You will appreciate the paramount need for secrecy.

Appendix II

CHIEFS OF STAFF COMMITTEE: DIRECTIVE TO THE DIRECTOR OF COMBINED OPERATIONS

C.O.S. (41) 166
14th March, 1941

War Cabinet

Chiefs of Staff Committee

Directive to the Director of Combined Operations

Note by Major-General Ismay

The Prime Minister has approved the amendments to the directive to the Director of Combined Operations, which were put forward by Admiral of the Fleet Sir Roger Keyes, and agreed to by the Chiefs of Staff on 11th March.
 A copy of the directive in its final form is attached.

(Signed) H.L. Ismay.

Directive to the Director of Combined Operations
The responsibilities of the Director of Combined Operations were laid down in a directive issued to Lt.-General A.G.B. Bourne by the Chiefs of Staff in June, 1940. In view of the changes which have taken place

since that date, it is desirable that these responsibilities should be re-defined.

At the same time, it is to be recognised that the division of responsibility between the Director of Combined Operations on the one hand and the Joint Planning Staff on the other is not capable of precise definition. There must always be border-line cases which will have to be settled as they arise by mutual consultations.

General Scope of D.C.O.'s Responsibilities

2. The Director of Combined Operations is responsible under the general direction of the Minister of Defence and the Chiefs of Staff, for:

(a) The Command and training in irregular warfare generally, and in landing operations in particular, of the troops specially organised for this purpose, i.e., the Special Service Troops.

(b) The supervision of the technical training in landing operations of such other troops as may from time to time be earmarked for enterprises which call for this particular type of training.

(c) The development, including experiment, research and trial, of all forms of special equipment and craft required for opposed landings.

(d) The initiation, within the general policy prescribed, and the planning and execution of operations by the Special Service Troops, reinforced if necessary, by small forces – naval, military and air – which are not normally under his command.

For the purpose of making plans, he may have any assistance he requires from the Joint Planning Staff. In this connection, the Prime Minister has laid down as a guide that the Director of Combined Operations should be responsible for the planning and execution of raiding operations which involve not more than 5,000 men.

(e) The provision of advice to the Chiefs of Staff on the technical aspects of opposed landing operations. When the Chiefs of Staff Committee are considering an operation which involves an opposed landing, the Director of Combined Operations should be present when that part of the plan is under discussion.

Similarly, when the Joint Planning Staff are directed or wish to suggest outline plans for an operation which involves an opposed landing, they should first consult the Director of Combined Operations.

Subject to:

(a) his concurrence that the opposed landing is practicable;

(b) the general nature of the project being approved by the Chiefs of Staff and Defence Committee.

D.C.O.'s staff and the Joint Planning Staff will work in conjunction; the Joint Planning Staff preparing the General Plan and the Director of Combined Operations' Staff preparing that part relative to the opposed landing. Subsequently the Commanders designate will consult the Director of Combined Operations and his staff when working out their plans.

The above does not apply to the work of the F.O.P. section, who will receive their instructions both as to what they plan and who they consult, from the Minister of Defence office.

(f) The provision of advice to the Chiefs of Staff on the tactical use and allocation of carriers and landing craft for combined operations. The Director of Combined Operations will be responsible for the training of naval personnel in so far as opposed landings are concerned, including officers and men of carriers, landing craft and beach parties.

He will have under his command and operational control carriers and landing craft for raiding purposes, which will include such transports as are from time to time allotted by the Admiralty for this purpose.

Administration
3. The routine administration of the Special Service Troops, including maintenance and movements, will be the responsibility of the War Office. The D.C.O. is, however, responsible for advising the War Office as to how these units can best be organised, armed, equipped and located, to meet his particular needs.

Special Equipment and Landing Craft
4. The Director of Combined Operations will have under his command and direction the Inter-Services Training and Development Centres.

Authority for Operations
5. The general policy for raiding operations will be laid down from time to time by the Chiefs of Staff in accordance with the direction of the Prime Minister and Minister of Defence.

Appendix III

CHIEFS OF STAFF COMMITTEE: COMBINED OPERATIONS AND RAIDS

Secret C.O.S. (41) 629
16th October, 1941

War Cabinet

Chiefs of Staff Committee

Combined Operations and Raids

Note by Secretary
The attached directive, as approved by the Chiefs of Staff, is circulated for record purposes

(Signed) L.C. Hollis.
Great George Street, S.W.1.

Annex I
Directive to the Adviser on Combined Operations

1. You are appointed Adviser on Combined Operations (short title Commodore C.).

COMBINED OPERATIONS

General Responsibility
2. Under the general direction of the Chiefs of Staff you will:
    (a) Act as technical adviser on all aspects of, and at all stages in, the planning and training for combined operations.
    (b) Be responsible for co-ordinating the general training policy for combined operations for the three Services (see para. 5 (a) below). You will command the Combined Training Centres and Schools of Instruction.
    (c) Study tactical and technical developments in all forms of combined operations varying from small raids to a full-scale invasion of the Continent.
    (d) Direct and press forward research and development in all forms of technical equipment and special craft peculiar to combined operations.

Planning
3. The procedure by which planning for large scale operations will be carried out is shown in Annex II. You will note that it is incumbent upon you to give technical advice upon all plans for combined operations at all stages from their inception to the point when they are finally approved. It is equally incumbent upon the Commanders and Staff to seek your technical advice at all stages of planning.

4. The procedure with regard to small raids will be similar to that of large-scale operations, with the exception of raids on a very small scale which are carried out by Special Service Troops only. For these operations you will appoint the Force Commander, subject to the approval of the Chiefs of Staff; and you will be responsible for the detailed plan.

Training
5. You will:
    (a) Preside over an Inter-Service Committee consisting of the A.C.N.S. (Weapons), Admiralty and the Directors of Training at the War office and Air Ministry. This Committee will formulate the training and technical policy for combined operations and will maintain close liaison with the organisation for the development of airborne forces.
    (b) Be responsible for co-ordinating the teaching at such schools of instruction or training establishments as it may be found necessary to set up.

APPENDIX III

    (c) Command the Combined Training Centres[1] at which the training of formations and units in combined operations will be carried out under their Commanders and with the technical advice of the Staffs of the Centres. This advice will be your responsibility.

    (d) Advise, as required, Commanders, subsequent to their appointment for an operation, on the technical training of their forces. It is equally incumbent on them to seek your advice on this matter.

Tactical and Technical Developments and Special Equipment
6. You will set up under the Chairmanship of the Deputy Adviser on Combined Operations an Inter-Services Committee which, under the guidance of the Policy Committee referred to in para. 5 (a), will deal with questions of detailed inspection, training, equipment and administration.

Special Service Troops
7. The Special Service Troops will be under your command. Their Administration will, however, remain the responsibility of the War Office. These troops are to be regarded, so far as combined operations are concerned, as specialists. Beyond such tasks as you may allot to them, e.g., at the various centres of instruction, these troops will be available for specific combined operations when they will be placed under the Commander appointed for that operation.

    Para. 7 is subject to early review.

---

[1] These include Initial Training Centres such as H.M.S. *Northney* and H.M.S. *Tormentor* and Raiding Craft Bases such as Brightlingsea and H.M.S. *St. Helier*.

Appendix IV

CHIEFS OF STAFF COMMITTEE: DIRECTIVE TO ADVISER ON COMBINED OPERATIONS

Secret C.O.S. (41) 732
9th December, 1941

War Cabinet

Chiefs of Staff Committee

Directive to Adviser on Combined Operations

Note by Secretary
The attached revised directive to the Adviser on Combined Operations has been approved by the Chiefs of Staff and is circulated for information and record purposes.

(Signed) L.C. Hollis
Great George Street, S.W.1
9th December, 1941

Directive to the Adviser on Combined Operations
1. You are appointed Adviser on Combined Operations. This title is always to be used when you are acting in an advisory capacity. When exercising your executive functions, you will use the title "Commodore Combined Operations" (short title – C.C.O.).

APPENDIX IV

General Responsibility
2. Under the general direction of the Chiefs of Staff you will:
   (a) Act as technical adviser on aspects of, and at all stages in, the planning and training for combined operations.
   (b) Be responsible for co-ordinating the general training policy for combined operations for the three services (see para. 5(a) below).
   (c) Study in conjunction with the Chiefs of Staff Organisation tactical and technical developments in all forms of combined operations varying from small raids to a full scale invasion of the Continent.
   (d) Direct and press forward research and development in all forms of technical equipment and special craft peculiar to combined operations.

Planning
3. You will note that it is incumbent upon the Commanders-in-Chief at Home, Force Commanders and Staff to seek your technical advice at all stages of planning and to keep you informed of their intentions.

4. In the case of operations which are carried out by Special Service Troops only, you will appoint the Commander of the Special Service Troops who will prepare the detailed plan in conjunction with you and under the Commander-in-Chief carrying out the raid. In such cases you will keep the Joint Planning Staff in touch at all stages.

Training
5. You will:
   (a) Be responsible for co-ordinating the teaching at such schools of instruction or training establishments as it may be found necessary to set up.
   (b) Command the Combined Training Centres[1] at which the training of formations and units in combined operations will be carried out under their Commanders and with the technical advice of the Staffs of the Centres. This advice will be your responsibility.
   (c) Advise, as required, Force Commanders, subsequent to their appointment for an operation, on the technical training of their forces. It is equally incumbent on them to seek your advice on this matter.

Inter-Service Committees
6. You will:

---

[1] These include Initial Training Centres such as H.M.S. *Northney* and H.M.S. *Tormentor* and Raiding Craft Bases such as Brightlingsea and H.M.S. *St. Helier*, and such other training centres or bases as it may be necessary to set up.

(a) Preside over the Combined Operations Committee which will have as members Assistant Chief of Naval Staff (Weapons), Admiralty; Director of Operational Training, Air Ministry; Director of Military Training, War office. This Committee will formulate training and development policy for combined operations and will maintain close liaison with the organisation for the training and development of airborne forces.
(b) Preside over the Combined Operations Air Committee which will have as members the 5th Sea Lord, Admiralty, or his representatives; Vice-Chief Imperial General Staff or his representatives, War Office; Vice-Chief of the Air Staff, Air Ministry, or his representatives; Air Commodore C.T.C. This Committee will examine the air requirements for combined operations. The Committee will formulate co-ordinated proposals on air requirements for submission to the Chiefs of Staff.
(c) Set up a Combined Operations Sub-Committee which under the guidance of the Committee referred to in para. 6 (a), will deal with questions of training, equipment and administration, and keep touch with progress.
(d) Set up a Combined Operations Communications Committee with representatives of the Signal Branches of the three Services to deal with all communications questions affecting combined operations.

Ships and Craft
7. The policy for the allocation of assault ships and landing craft throughout the world will be decided from time to time by the Chiefs of Staff.

All ships (other than Merchant Navy ships) and craft in the British Isles allocated for combined operations will be under your command except during such time as they are specifically turned over to the Force Commanders for an operation.

Merchant Navy ships allocated by the Admiralty for combined operational purposes will be attached to your command, or that of the Force Commanders, but will be administered by the Director of Sea Transport.

You will be required to inform the Admiralty from time to time of the state of availability of all ships and craft held for combined operational purposes.

APPENDIX IV

Special Service Troops
8. The Special Service Troops will be under your command. Their administration will, however, remain the responsibility of the War office. Beyond such tasks as you may allot to them, e.g., at the various centres of instruction, these troops will be available for specific combined operations when they will be placed under the Commander appointed for that operation.

Appendix V

OPERATIONS ON THE CONTINENT

C.O.S. (42) 103 (0) (Final)

Operations on the Continent

Memorandum
1. The Defence Committee at their meeting on 14th April, gave general approval to the proposals brought over by Mr. Hopkins and General Marshall for Anglo-American operations in Western Europe in 1942 and 1943 in the following terms:
"A policy for assigning responsibility for the development of these proposals is now required in order that planning and preparation for the operations in 1942 and in 1943 may proceed concurrently and with the maximum efficiency."
2. We propose to develop the offensive in the following stages and to delegate responsibility for planning, as set out in the succeeding paragraphs:
    (a) The conversion of the United Kingdom into an advanced base for operations in Western Europe.
    (b) The development of preparations on a front stretching from the Shetlands to the Bristol Channel.
    (c) A series of raiding operations to be carried out during the summer of 1942, coupled with;
    (d) An active air offensive over North-West Europe.

APPENDIX V

(e) The capture of a bridgehead on the Continent within the area in which adequate naval and air cover can be given during the summer of 1942 if the opportunity occurs.

(f) A large scale descent on Western Europe in the spring of 1943.

Advanced Base

3. The American proposals will involve the conversion of the United Kingdom from a defensive to an offensive footing. Many additional aerodromes will be required; extensive accommodation will have to be provided for the American troops either by new construction or by wholesale evacuation of the civilian population; the harbours, and possibly railways, in southern and eastern England will require extensive development. Skilled labour is likely to prove the bottle-neck.

4. We therefore propose:

(a) That an Inter-departmental Committee which would include representatives of Commander-in-Chief, Home Forces and the Chief of Combined Operations should be available to resolve conflicting claims which may arise in connection with the provision of sites for new aerodromes, cantonments, store parks, hards, etc.

(b) To ask the United States to provide a large part of the labour and machinery required for developing these facilities and that the War Office and Air Ministry should put forward combined requirements.

(c) To ask the United States to leave in this country all labour and equipment now engaged on construction work, such as the Rosneath base.

Offensive Preparations

5. It will not be possible to conceal our preparations from the enemy. In order to mislead them as to our real objectives, preparations for an assault will be made along the coast. Preparations for Operation "Sledgehammer" in 1942 will be confined to the south and south-east coast by lack of equipment, but, as the landing craft become available, the area from which the operation might be launched will spread northwards.

6. Responsibility for initiating these preparations will rest jointly with the Chief of Combined Operations and the Commander-in-Chief, Home Forces.

COMBINED OPERATIONS

Large Scale Raiding Operations in 1942
7. We have already provided a policy of raids to be undertaken in the summer of 1942 on the largest scale that the available equipment will permit. These raids will be carried out on a front extending from the north of Norway to the Bay of Biscay and will be planned and launched by the Chief of Combined Operations in consultation with the Commander-in-Chief, Home Forces.

Active Air Offensive
8. The Air Officer Commanding-in-Chief, Fighter Command, in consultation with Air Officer Commanding-in-Chief, Bomber Command has been charged with the task of inflicting the greatest possible wastage on the German Air Force in the West. This air action has already started and should reach maximum intensity as soon as the German offensive against Russia begins.

Sledgehammer, 1942
9. Our air offensive may in itself achieve a measure of diversion, but we must be prepared to employ land forces in order to compel a heavier diversion of air forces.

10. The situation may arise in which we shall have the opportunity to capture a bridgehead and possibly to extend this so as to include a port, enabling us to establish our forces on the Continent before the weather deteriorates at the end of September. We must clearly be prepared for such a situation.

11. The Commander-in-Chief, Home Forces, the Commander-in-Chief, Fighter Command and the Chief of Combined Operations in consultation have therefore been charged with the responsibility for working out plans for the contingencies referred to in paragraphs 9 and 10 above. Such American forces as are available in the United Kingdom will be employed as required.

Operation "Super Round-Up"
12. The Commander-in-Chief, Home Forces, in conjunction with the Air Officer Commanding-in-Chief, Fighter Command (and other R.A.F. Commands as necessary) and the Chief of Combined Operations have already been charged with the responsibility for planning Operation "Super Round-Up" in full consultation with the naval staff. This project will now be expanded on the general lines of the proposals contained in General Marshall's memorandum, and members of the United States Planning Staffs will be associated with the plans and

APPENDIX V

preparations, both in Headquarters, Home Forces and in Combined Operations Headquarters.

13. The object of "Super Round-Up" will be to destroy German forces in Western Europe. The method of achieving this object will be determined by the Commander-in-Chief, Home Forces, in consultation with the other authorities concerned.

Action by S.O. (E)
14. The action by S.O. (E) will require to conform to the general plan. A draft directive should be prepared by the Joint Planning Staff in consultation with the Chief of Combined Operations' staff.

Action by Patriots in the Occupied Countries
15. It will be necessary to organise and co-ordinate the action by the patriots in the occupied countries, both when our landing takes place and in the subsequent operations on the Continent.

Intelligence
16. A spotlight of our Intelligence system should from now onwards be focussed on the Continent. The Joint Intelligence Sub-Committee, in consultation with "C" H.Q. Home Forces and the Chief of Combined Operations' staff, should put forward proposals to the Chiefs of Staff and report any special steps for which approval is required.

(Signed) A.F. Brooke
C. Portal.
H.R. Moor.
For First Sea Lord.

Great George Street, S.W.1
18th April, 1942

Appendix VI

THE STATE OF THE COMBINED OPERATIONS NAVAL ORGANISATION

Note by the Chief of Combined Operations

The State of the Combined Operations Naval Organisation. With Particular Relation to Possibilities of Operations in 1943.

The primary calls on Combined Operations ships and craft are:
 (a) Operations.
 (b) Exercises and rehearsals for operations.
 (c) Basic training of craft crews (generally termed "naval training"). In point of time, of course, this must come before (a) and (b).
 (d) Basic combined training of military forces at C.T.C.s.
 (e) "Refresher" or "advanced" basic training for already trained forces, not specifically for a pending operation.

2. An approximately 500 per cent expansion of the Combined Operations Naval Command was commenced during the winter of 1941-42, for completion within one year. Some 3,300 British-manned landing ships and craft were called for with fully trained crews by 1st April, 1943, besides nearly 2,000 American-manned ships and craft.

3. Any such expansion programme requires a great part of new resources to be devoted to the training organisation, as they become available, and the division of the operational quota left over into first line and reserves in a proportion depending on maintenance facilities and the rate of attrition.

APPENDIX VI

In the case of combined operations expansion, a further division must be made between the naval and combined basic training within the quota of craft allotted to training; and unless the naval training can be given a certain precedence, output of crews is held back and in due course retards expansion of the whole organisation and of combined training.

4. The expansion programme has been vigorously pushed forward. But it has not been possible to observe the above conditions as much as I should have liked. Disappointments in the expected deliveries of some types of craft have cut down the quota for training.

I have kept the raids quota up in order to gain essential operational experience and provide vital incentive; but only at a cost. "Ironclad" took away resources in ships, craft and key personnel. Shortage of accommodation, accentuated by the departure of the "Ironclad" ships, necessitated for a time restricting intake of naval C.O. personnel. Maintenance facilities and spares have been a struggle to obtain. To ensure the Expeditionary Force being trained in time for "Sledgehammer", naval training has had largely to take second place to combined training in the share-out of craft; and the preparatory measures and the decision to mount "Imperator" this summer, though subsequently rescinded, interrupted basic training for some time. As events have turned out, it has not been possible to hold reserves of craft and everything has been "in the shop window".

These factors have acted early in the programme, when their consequences upon the expansion rate have been more severe than they would have been later on.

The recent unexpected loss of the Roseneath base (with its up-to-date dockyard and accommodation for 5,000), at which our whole means of expanding the naval training had just been concentrated, has been a severe blow. On the other hand, the accelerated importation into the U.K. of certain types of landing craft from America, for "Bolero", has helped to tide over some difficulties.

5. The maximum force which, after these events, it would be possible to provide operationally fit for a major cross-Channel operation in October, 1942, was calculated on 23rd July last to be as in column (1) of Appendix "A" attached [omitted]. The figures required for "Torch", and for a reduced raiding force to provide diversionary raids in the Channel, are shown in the same Appendix.

As can be seen, to meet the increased demands for "Torch", we are now providing more than we considered prudently possible even for an operation near at home, in which we would make full use of the British assault troops already trained, and continue naval training of Combined Operations personnel right up to the last minute so as to provide the maximum trained force.

6. This is being done:
   (a) At the expense of all British C.O. training, which stopped altogether on 15th August, and temporary cessation of new entries. Since that date all our training resources have been devoted to the U.S. combat teams and the R.N. active personnel for the assaults in "Torch", who have also occupied all the training accommodation left over after the loss of Roseneath.
   (b) By taking on the operation numbers of craft which are not operationally fit, and of crews who are not fully trained.
   (c) By various emergency shifts in respect of repair, provision of spares, etc., which are extravagant and cannot be repeated.
   (d) By taking all the British naval combined operations personnel there are in the U.K., including all the naval beach parties and beach signal parties, transferring L.C.T. crews to small craft as necessary; except some crews and care and maintenance parties for the L.C.T. left behind, the reduced raiding force, and the crews receiving and delivering craft as they arrive from the U.S.A. The balance of naval requirements for "Torch" have been made up by active service R.N. personnel.

7. The whole resources of C.O.H.Q., and the C.O. Establishments have for the last month been devoted to preparations for "Torch" and diversionary raids. As an instance, almost my entire navigational staff has been lent to go out in advance, and this will delay for three months or more the urgent improvements in the navigational capabilities of C.O. craft and crews which experience has shown to be so necessary.

8. These measures, as I pointed out verbally at the time, would be quite impossible if "Torch" were to be against serious opposition, or if we expected to have to mount another large operation at an early date in 1943.

The standard of training of a large part of the craft crews and assault forces is not high enough for a tough or protracted assault.

The stopping of British training and intake of new entries, devotion of all resources to "Torch" and the sweeping into that operation of so many craft for an indefinite absence, has most severely disrupted the Combined Operations Organisation and its expansion programme.

APPENDIX VI

9. The time already lost cannot be made up unless I have higher priority call than hitherto, on the facilities I shall require, especially in suitable R.N. personnel, and even then, not for some months. There have been six priorities in manning, and combined operations have had fifth priority. At the moment I have only one active service officer left on my operational planning staff. Including C.O.H.Q., the Raiding Force (Force "J"), and Instructors, but excluding the Expeditionary Force, there are now only 168 active service Executive and Engineer Officers (of whom 67 are retired officers), 83 active service Petty Officers, and 80 Engine Room and Maintenance ratings of P.O. or C.P.O. rate on whom to build up a naval assault force of some 3,000 officers and 25,000 men.

10. The position in respect of craft left in the U.K. when "Torch" has been mounted (taken as 1st October, 1942) is shown at Appendix "B" [omitted].

This also shows the estimated receipts from new British production up to the end of the year, a guess as to what we may get from America if the points in C.O.S. (W) 277 are acted upon, the quota which must be allotted to basic training if the expansion is to be resumed at once, the quota I propose to offer to the U.S.N. Authorities for training the U.S. forces in the U.K. provided the "Bolero" craft are received as shown, and the craft operationally available as on 1st January, 1943 on the basis of the foregoing.

11. It will be seen that the operational craft will amount only to a limited raiding force. In Appendix "C" [omitted] is an outline of my intentions regarding the organisation of this force, to which the Admiralty has now given approval in principle.

12. I wish to emphasise that it will be most necessary to employ this raiding force in as frequent attacks on the enemy as can be judiciously made, otherwise neither the esprit de corps nor the knowledge will be available for any future large scale assault upon the Continent, and any assault attempted without this will meet disaster.

13. It is not possible at this juncture to see clearly beyond the end of the present year. Until it is known what, if any, ships, craft and personnel will be returned to my Command from "Torch", and the condition of their material, it is impossible to assess what force could be made available for further operations in the spring of 1943. In Appendix "D" [omitted] however, are set out certain factors from which calculations

of increases in resources can be made from any given arbitrary starting point. Meanwhile it is essential to recommence basic training at the maximum possible rate, to keep pace with the production of new craft.

14. On the material side it must be realised that none of the British designs of craft is either "tropicalised", or prepared for the Arctic. In the tropics this merely leads to strain and inefficiency, if the crews are pressed. In prolonged low temperatures craft and equipment would often altogether fail to work. The American craft are virtually unprotected open boats.

On the personnel side, good service conditions, incentive, careful training, experience, and active leadership at all levels are absolute prerequisites for success in any assault on German-held territory.

15. Again, only certain types of craft are designed as assault craft; all the rest are primarily built as ferries. Military necessity may demand even the latter, particularly the craft for landing tanks and guns, acting as assault craft. They will suffer heavily, and need powerful and close fire support. The latter calls for special shallow draught bombarding and support vessels. These we have not got.

Even manning of the defensive A.A. armament clashes, in craft like L.C.T., with the call for economising crews and living space.

16. I do not wish to over-stress difficulties, but to make clear that the men and the material cannot be regarded in planning a combined operation as a matter of numbers. Their quality is all important.

The same applies to the Staffs who plan. I foresee a battle of wits between ourselves and Germany in the coming year in the development of assault and defence respectively. The defence has a long start. Only experience and the devising of new ways by special study and trial will enable us to catch up or cut the corner. The alternative, which is recourse to blunderbuss methods on traditional lines without special knowledge, can only lead to slaughter on a scale which we are no position to sustain this year or next.

17. To sum up:
   (a) "Torch" has taken more landing craft than I can produce crews for, and numbers have had to be made up from other R.N. sources.
   (b) The standard of training of a large part of the craft crews and assault forces is not high enough for a tough or protracted assault.

APPENDIX VI

(c) So large a part of the Naval C.O. Command has been given up to "Torch" that it will not be possible to train an adequate new force before the summer of 1943.
(d) The early formation of a Naval Raiding Force is an essential prerequisite for any re-entry into the Continent, and it must be given regular fighting experience.

Appendix VII

COMBINED CHIEFS OF STAFF, "SYMBOL" CONFERENCE

Report by the Combined Chiefs of Staff,
as Approved by the President and Prime Minister.

In a previous memorandum (C.C.S. 155/1) the Combined Chiefs of Staff presented their proposals for the Conduct of the War in 1943. These proposals were a broad outline, and we have subsequently examined them and reached certain conclusions on points of detail. We have also studied a number of matters closely related to these proposals. The present memorandum contains a summary of what has been accomplished.

1. Operations in the Mediterranean
(a) Operations for the capture of Sicily
We have carefully examined possible operations in the Mediterranean theatre, and we have recorded the following conclusions (C.C.S. 66th Meeting, Item 2, and C.C.S. 161/1):

(i) To attack Sicily in 1943 with a favourable moon as the target date.

(ii) To instruct General Eisenhower to report not later than the 1st March, firstly, whether any insurmountable difficulty as to resources and training will cause the date of the assault to be delayed beyond the favourable July moon, and, secondly in

that event to confirm that the date will not be later than the favourable August moon.
- (iii) That the following should be the Command set up for the operation:
  - A. General Eisenhower to be in Supreme Command with General Alexander as Deputy Commander-in-Chief, charged with the detailed planning and preparation and with the execution of the actual operation when launched.
  - B. Admiral Cunningham to be Naval Commander, and Air Chief Marshall Tedder the Air Commander.
  - C. Recommendations for the officers to be appointed Western and Eastern Task Force Commanders to be submitted in due course by General Eisenhower.
- (iv) That General Eisenhower should be instructed to set up forthwith, after consultation with General Alexander, a special operational and administrative staff. And its own Chief of Staff, for planning and preparing the operation.

The necessary directive to General Eisenhower conveying the above decisions has been drafted.

(b) Cover Plans

We intend to instruct the appropriate agencies in Washington and London and the Commander-in-Chief, Allied Expeditionary Force in North Africa, to draw up a comprehensive plan for the Mediterranean. The possibility of carrying out feints or minor operations in the Eastern Mediterranean will be examined.

(c) Command in the Mediterranean Theatre

We have agreed the following Command arrangements in the Mediterranean (C.C.S. 63rd Meeting, Item 4, and C.C.S. 163):
- (i) Sea – For operation "Husky" the Naval Commander Force X will assume the title of Commander-in-Chief, Mediterranean. The present Commander-in-Chief, Mediterranean, will be designated, Commander-in-Chief, Levant. The boundary between the two commands will be determined later. The Commander-in-Chief, Mediterranean, will, however, be responsible for naval matters which affect the Mediterranean as a whole.
- (ii) Land – At the moment to be determined after the British 8th Army has crossed the Tunisian border, General Alexander will become deputy Commander-in-Chief to General Eisenhower, the 8th Army at the same time being transferred to General

Eisenhower's command. Subject to the concurrence of General Eisenhower, General Alexander's primary task will be to command the Allied forces on the Tunisian front with a small headquarters of his own provided from the Middle East and after the conclusion of these operations, he will take charge of Operation "Husky". The boundary between the North African and Middle East Commands will be the Tunisian-Tripolitania frontier.

(iii) Air – We have agreed that Air Chief Marshal Sir Arthur Tedder shall be appointed Air Commander-in-Chief of the whole Mediterranean theatre with his headquarters in Algiers. Under him will be the Air Officer Commander-in-Chief, North-West Africa (General Spaatz), and the Air Officer Commander-in-Chief, Middle East (Air Chief Marshal Sir Sholto Douglas). We have defined the relationship and mutual responsibilities of the Air Commander-in-Chief, Mediterranean, and the Commander-in-Chief, Allied Expeditionary Forces in North-West Africa, and we have laid down certain principles for the organisation of the Mediterranean Air Command subject to any minor changes which the Air Commander-in-Chief may find necessary after his appointment.

(d) The Bomber Offensive from North Africa
We have laid down the following as the objects of the bomber offensive from North Africa in order of time:

(i) The furtherance of operations for the eviction of all Axis Forces from Africa.
(ii) When (i) has been achieved, infliction of the heaviest possible losses on the Axis Air and Naval forces in preparation for "Husky" including bombing required by cover plans.
(iii) The direct furtherance of Operation "Husky".
(iv) The destruction of the oil refineries at Ploesti.

So far as is possible without prejudice to the achievement of objects (i), (ii) and (iii) above, bombing objectives will be chosen with a view of weakening the Italian will to continue the war.

2. "Bolero" (C.C.S. 172 and C.C.S. 68th Meeting, Item 1)
(a) A study has been made of the shipping capabilities for "Bolero" build up in 1943

APPENDIX VII

With the data available at the conference and making a number of assumptions, we calculate that the United States Forces, as shown in the following table, will be available for continental operations in the United Kingdom on the dates shown. The figures given in the last column include the build-up of the air contingent to 172,000. They may be regarded as the minimum, and every effort will be made to increase the number of trained and equipped divisions in the United Kingdom by the 15th August.

	Division	Total Numbers Equipped
By 15th August	4	384,000
15th Septembe	7	509,00
15th October	9	634,000
15th November	12	759,000
31st Decembe	15	938,000

This is based on (1) the figures of 50,000 troops per division with supporting troops: (2) 45 days allowance between sailing date and availability date.

As the movement proceeds the overall number of men per division will decrease and by the end of the year it may be down to 40,000, in which case the number of divisions available on the 31st December may be 19 instead of 15. The number of divisions earlier in the year is unlikely to be increased.

(b) Amphibious Operations in 1943 from the United Kingdom

We have examined the problem of amphibious operations from the United Kingdom in 1943. There are three types of operation for which plans and preparations must be made:

(i) Raids with primary object of provoking air battles and causing enemy losses.
(ii) Operations with the object of seizing and holding a bridgehead and, if the state of German morale and resources permit, of vigorously exploiting success.
(iii) A return to the Continent to take advantage of German disintegration.

Plans and preparations for (i) above will proceed as at present. An attack on the Channel Islands is an example of the type of operation which we have in mind.

We propose to prepare for an operation against the Cotentin peninsula with resources which will be available, the target date being set at the 1st August, 1943. This operation comes under type (ii) above.

We have agreed to establish forthwith a Combined Staff under a British Chief of Staff until such a time as a Supreme Commander with an American Deputy Commander is appointed. A directive to govern the planning is in course of preparation. We intend to include in this directive provision for a return to the Continent under (iii) above with the forces which will be available for the purpose in the United Kingdom month by month.

Appendix VIII

POINTS ARISING FROM "RATTLE" CONFERENCE

No.1. Naval Fighting Instructions
Fighting instructions which are in common use in the Navy are the appropriate equivalent of "Military Standing Orders" and have a direct bearing on the handling of the military formations in the assault. Fighting instructions for the Naval assault forces to be employed in this operation are at present under revision and the Conference recommends that, when ready, they should be circulated to the Ministry and Air Commanders for their comments.

No.2. Assault and Light Scales
It is highly desirable that the British Forces there should be recognised "assault" and "light" scales for purposes of planning without prejudice to subsequent variations in these scales at the discretion of the Commander. The scales proposed by G.H.Q. Home Forces, should be used by all concerned for this operation.

No.3. Timing of the Assault
Pending a decision being reached as to whether the assault should be launched in daylight or in darkness, all Forces concerned should be organised and trained so that they could land in daylight, darkness or smoke.

No.4. Aircraft Recognition
An early decision is required as to the method by which:
(a) Our own aircraft, British and U.S., will be recognised by the Naval and Land Forces engaged in the operation.
(b) Our own aircraft, British and U.S., will recognise our own troops on the ground.

No.5. A.A. Armament for Shipping
The scale of A.A. armament proposed for shipping and craft taking part in this Operation should be reviewed with the object of increasing it to the greatest possible extent.

No.6. Armament of L.C.G. (M)
In view of the small numbers of L.C.G. (M) that will be available by the target date, the armament of the L.C.G. (M) should comprise two 17-pdr. guns instead of one 17-pdr. and one 25-pdr.

No.7. Support Craft
Early decisions are required:
(a) As to any conversion of existing L.C.T. that will be necessary in order to provide additional L.C.T. (R) or L.C.T. (L).
(b) Any special provision of other naval supporting craft that may be necessary, e.g., older cruisers and *Old Town* class destroyers.

No.8. Follow-up and Build-up
Our ability to secure the required lodgement on the Continent will depend in the initial stages on beach maintenance, and subsequently of the seizing of ports as early as possible through which alone we can hope to build up the necessary reserves that are likely to be concentrated against us. Every possible port will be required and, in addition, we shall have to create artificial ports or breakwaters, particularly in the early stages. The Conference, therefore, has recommended:

(a) That a single authority should be appointed, who, in consultation with the Service Departments, will tackle the whole problem of the construction of special piers (of which one design has already been produced) to accelerate unloading on the beaches. A decision is urgently needed as to the types and numbers required. This authority should also deal with the provision of artificial ports and breakwaters and the development of those continental ports we shall capture.
(b) That a spearhead of experienced administrative officers should be formed at once of officers of the three Services and the Ministry of

War Transport. This spearhead under the direction of C.O.S.S.A.C and the single authority referred to above, should plan the organisation of the various ports that will be used, and should eventually do the job when the time comes. A similar spearhead should be formed by the U.S. Forces. Experience in North Africa has shown that a team of this nature is of incalculable value.

If it is thought that it is prejudging the plan too much to form separate British and U.S. teams then a mixed team might be formed.

(c) That the U.S. authorities should be approached with regard to providing U.S. Naval pontoons to help bridge the water-gap with which we shall be faced when, owing to the slope of the beaches, vehicle landing craft will ground some way from the beach. Numbers required will depend on C.O.S.S.A.C.'s plan.

(d) The provision of amphibians will be of great value in bridging this water gap:

(i) Requirements of American types are under consideration but so far, no action has been taken as regards the Terrapin or any other British type. An urgent decision should be reached as to whether the Terrapin meets staff requirements and if so, how many are required. Production should be set on foot at once on the assumption that large numbers will be needed.

(ii) U.S. types of M.T. having higher and more suitable chassis than British types are more easily water-proofed. The possibility of using American types of M.T. with British Divisions should be examined.

No.9. Use of C.D.L. in Landing Craft
C.D.L. equipment mounted in landing craft should not be used in "Overlord" and C.D.L. fittings already installed in L.C.I. (S) should be removed, thus making room for more A.A. armament.

Annexure I
Responsibilities of E.-in-C., and D.C.O.(L)

Responsibility for Policy
1. The Engineer-in-Chief (E.-in-C.) is responsible for laying down the engineer policy in combined operations just as he is responsible for engineering policy in all other forms of operations

In formulating this policy, he will be advised by D.C.O. Constant and close liaison is, therefore, necessary between E.-in-C.'s Branch and D.C.O.(I.).

Communicating Policy
2. Directives communicating this policy to the combined training authorities in India are issued by D.C.O.(I.).

Research
3. D.C.O.(I.) is responsible for advising the E.-in-C. on new engineer equipment, and modifications of existing engineer equipment, which are considered necessary for combined operations. If the E.-in-C. agrees to the necessity for this equipment, D.C.O.(I.) is responsible for carrying out experiment and development, and reporting to E.-in-C.
At the same time the E.-in-C. is responsible for keeping D.C.O.(I.) informed of the latest developments in equipment that may affect him. Close liaison is necessary between the Combined Operations Development Centre and other engineer experimental establishments.

Stores
4. D.C.O.(I.) is responsible for advice to the E.-in-C. on types and scales of stores considered necessary.
Provision of stores of engineer supply is the responsibility of the E.-in-C. as for all other engineer stores required for South-East Asia Command operations.
Information on which to base provision figures is obtained by E.-in-C.'s branch in the same way as for other engineer tasks contemplated by South-East Asia Command.

Annexure II (a)
Commander-in-Chief in India

Directive

To the Director of Combined Operations (India)
12th December, 1944

Status
1. You are appointed Director of Combined Operations, India, under me as the Commander-in-Chief of India.
   In carrying out your duties you will, as necessary, have direct access to the Commander-in-Chief on all matters for which you are responsible. You will also hold yourself available to attend meetings

of the C.-in-C.'s (India) War Committee and Chiefs of Staff Committee when required. Matters affecting individual services will normally be dealt with by you through the service staff concerned.

In addition, you will act as the representative in India of the Chief of Combined Operations, and will keep him directly informed on all matters affecting amphibious operations.

Responsibility in General
2. Your responsibilities in general will be:
(a) To advise the Commander-in-Chief, in India, the Supreme Allied Commander, South-East Asia, and appropriate Commanders of all three Services on the doctrine of Combined Operations, as approved by the Chief of Combined Operations.
(b) To act in an advisory capacity as may be required by the Commander concerned during all stages of the preparation for a combined operation.
(c) To study the tactical and technical problems of amphibious warfare.
(d) To provide advice and instruction in combined operations technique to such formations, units and individuals as may from time to time be detailed to undergo amphibious training.
(e) To initiate and carry out trials and research for the modification to suit local conditions of all forms of technical equipment including ships, craft, and vehicles peculiar to amphibious warfare.
(f) To co-ordinate the development, as affected by local conditions, of communication material and inter-communication technique in amphibious warfare.

(The application of these general responsibilities is dealt with in the succeeding paragraphs.)

Preparation for Combined Operations
3. At all stages of preparation for combined operations you will be prepared and available:
(a) To give specialist advice as may be required by the Commander-in-Chief concerned, or by the Force Commanders appointed by him.
(b) To advise Commanders, as may be required, on the special training of their forces.

Further, you will advise and assist as necessary in overcoming technical difficulties which may become apparent during the preparatory stages of operations.

In carrying out these duties, you will when invited to do so, have direct access to the Headquarters of the Supreme Allied Commander,

South-East Asia Command, on all matters affecting combined operations.

Training
4. Your responsibilities will be:

   (a) To co-ordinate and direct the basic training policy for amphibious warfare in respect of all three services.
   (b) To control all combined training establishments and to ensure that the training imparted there is in accordance with the doctrine and technique of amphibious warfare as approved by the Chief of Combined Operations.
   (c) To maintain at all times intimate liaison with the appropriate training authorities in India.

5. In respect of the training in combined operations of formations or units your responsibility is limited to the provision of advice, instruction, and the necessary training facilities.

The completion of the training to the necessary standard remains the responsibility of the Commanders concerned.

Control of Combined Operations Establishments
6. In order that you should fulfil adequately your functions, certain units and personnel will be placed under your control.

These will comprise units and personnel of the three services, and together will form such combined operations establishments as may be required.

The local administration of all such establishments will continue to be the responsibility of the parent service concerned.

7. This directive is issued with the concurrence of the Supreme Allied Commander, South-East Asia Command.

Signed, C.J. Auchinleck,
Commander-in-Chief.
12th December, 1944.

Appendix IX

DIRECTIVE TO ADVISER ON COMBINED OPERATIONS

To the Director of Combined Operations, India and South-East Asia-June, 1945

Status
1. You are appointed Director of Combined Operations in India under the Commander-in-Chief in India and in South-East Asia Command under the Supreme Allied Commander, South-East Asia. In carrying out your duties you will, as necessary, have direct access to the Commander-in-Chief in India and to the Supreme Allied Commander, South-East Asia, on all matters for which you are responsible to them.

You will also hold yourself available to attend meetings of the Commander-in-Chief's (India) War Committee and Chiefs of Staff Committee, and the Supreme Allied Commander, South- East Asia when required.

You will work in closest touch with the Heads of Combined Operations on the Staff of the Supreme Allied Commander.

In addition, you will act as the representative in India and South-East Asia Command of the Chief of Combined Operations, and will keep him directly informed on matters affecting combined operations.

Responsibility in General
2. Your responsibility in general will be:
   (a) To advise the Commander-in-Chief in India, the Supreme Allied Commander, South-East Asia, and appropriate Commanders

of all three services on the doctrine of combined operations, as approved by the Chief of Combined Operations.
(b) To act in an advisory capacity as may be required by the Commander concerned during all stages of the preparation for a combined operation.
(c) To study the tactical and technical problems of amphibious warfare.
(d) To provide advice and instructions in combined operations technique to such formations, units and individuals as may be from time to time detailed to undergo amphibious training.
(e) To initiate and carry out trials and research for the modification to suit local conditions of all forms of technical equipment including ships, craft and vehicles peculiar to amphibious warfare.
(f) To co-ordinate the development, as affected by local conditions, of communication material and inter-communication technique in amphibious warfare.

(The application of these general responsibilities is dealt with in the succeeding paragraphs.)

Preparation for Combined Operations
3. At all stages of preparation for combined operations you will be prepared and available:
(a) To give specialist advice as may be required by the Commander-in-Chief concerned, or by the Force Commanders appointed by him.
(b) To advise Commanders, as may be required, on the special training of their forces.

Further, you will advise and assist as necessary in overcoming technical difficulties which may become apparent during the preparatory stages of operations.

Training
4. Your responsibilities will be:
(a) To co-ordinate and direct the basic training policy for amphibious warfare in respect of all three services in South-East Asia Command as well as in India.
(b) To control all combined training establishments, and to ensure the training imparted there is in accordance with the doctrine and technique of amphibious warfare as approved by the Chief of Combined Operations.

(c) To maintain at all times intimate liaison with the appropriate training authorities in India and South-East Asia Command.

5. In respect of the training in combined operations of formations or units your responsibility is limited to the provision of advice, instruction, and the necessary training facilities.

The completion of the training to the necessary standards remains the responsibility of the Commanders concerned.

Control of Combined Operations Establishments

6. In order that you should fulfil adequately your functions, certain units and personnel will be placed under your control.

These will comprise units and personnel of the three services, and together will form such combined operations establishments as may be required.

The local administration of all such establishments will continue to be the responsibility of the parent service concerned.

7. This directive is issued jointly by the Commander-in-Chief in India, and the Supreme Allied Commander, South-East Asia.

Louis Mountbatten,
Supreme Allied Commander.
23rd June, 1945

J. Auchinleck,
General
Commander-in-Chief.
23rd June, 1945.

Appendix X

COMBINED OPERATIONS ORGANISATION IN INDIA

The responsibilities of Directorate of Combined Operations (D.C.O.(I.)) and Head of Combined Operations Research (H.C.O.R.), need to be defined to ensure there is no overlapping and that requirements are properly met.

2. The requirements may be summarised as follows:
    (a)   Basic training, Army, Navy, Air.
    (b)   Formation training Army, Navy, Air.
    (c)   Development in technique.
    (d)   Development in material.
    (e)   Provision of special equipment.
    (f)   Provision of special personnel.
    (g)   Promulgation of information.

3. The following considerations are fundamental to any arguments that may arise on these subjects:
    (a)   Basic training is the concern of base establishments.
    (b)   Formation training is the concern of Commanders.
    (c)   Policy must come from South-East Asia Command (S.E.A.C.)
    (d)   Requirements which spring from planning must come from S.E.A.C.
    (e)   Administration must be the concern of the authority responsible for the supply of personnel and material and movement in the area.

APPENDIX X

4. In considering the functions of the two staffs, it is clear that D.C.O.(I.) is at present a "basic" or home based staff, and H.C.O.R., as a member of S.E.A.C.'s Staff, is on the level which decides policy and gives directions, but does not directly command.

Basic Training

5. All basic training in the three services is undertaken by base organisations.

The Navy – whether R.N. or R.I.N., and the Air Force undertakes all their amphibious base training with base staffs. The Admiralty and Air Ministry issue the directions, provide the staffs, and through the normal channels administer the establishments. The Army does the same in mountain warfare, jungle warfare, or normal infantry, gunner, R.E., etc., training.

6. It is suggested the basic amphibious training for the Army should follow the normal procedure. This will leave D.C.O.(I.) responsible for the Combined Training Centres (C.T.C.s), the staff training wing and the two dryshod wings. The general line on which instruction is given will be laid down by S.E.A.C. A meeting of all staffs is now planned to start at Bombay C.T.C., on 7th March, to discuss doctrine, and H.C.O.R. has been asked to attend the meeting and confirm the doctrine it is proposed to teach.

7. The direction of this basic training should, it is considered, be undertaken in Delhi where all the movements and supply arrangements for troops in India are controlled. Should direction be moved to Ceylon, it would have the advantage of being close to the next S.E.A.C., H.Q., but this advantage would be small as basic doctrine does not change much, and to attempt to control what still must be done with G.H.Q., India, by post and signal would be hopeless. Furthermore, this H.Q. in Ceylon will probably move east as operations move east. It would then become necessary to move the Basic Training H.Q. back to Delhi.

Formation Training

8. Formation training that is final operational training – is usually the concern of the Commanders of Operations. In amphibious operations the Navy and Air Force insist on final training being the business of the Force Commanders. Similarly, the formation training of the 8th Army and the 1st Army has been the concern of the Commanders of those

Armies assisted as necessary by their base organisations; movement, embarkation, etc., have to be undertaken by the Base H.Q. It would seem reasonable that this policy in India should be on similar lines. This would mean placing the Formation Training Staff under command of 11th Army and for G.H.Q., through Southern Army, to give all the assistance that will be needed to mount collective exercises.

Development of Technique

9. Technique must advance as a result of training experience, operational experience and planning. Development must immediately be available for all training organisations and must progress whether S.E.A.C., H.Q., is in Delhi, Ceylon or Singapore.

10. It is suggested S.E.A.C., that is H.C.O.R., in collaboration with C.s-in-C and D.C.O.(I.) should determine what technique should be developed. That is, the direction should come from the higher authority and it should then be farmed out to D.C.O.(I.) who is in a position to get the personnel and equipment and craft for G.H.Q.(I.) and C-in-C,, E.F., to carry out the enquiry,

11. An example is the proposal to develop the technique of a force equipped with amphibians. The directive would come from S.E.A.C. (H.C.O.R.) wherever he may be, to D.C.O.(I.); this force would be formed and mounted by G.H.Q.(I.) and be attached to the most suitable C.T.C., or be assisted by the most suitable training wing. The result would be sent to S.E.A.C. In this particular example it would be well if the G.I. of the proposed division with a small staff, undertook the experiments; he would have had no prior landing operations experience and will need the advice and help of the C.T.C.

Material Development

12. Here again, directions must come from S.E.A.C., but the work of developing is not on a Supreme Commanders level.

13. Minor developments can be undertaken by the C.O.D.C., or workshops in India. Large scale developments such as tank and craft development cannot be undertaken in India as factories and labour, particularly skilled labour, is already fully occupied. To build factories and bring labour from England would hinder projects already approved, would tend to increase inflation and would not produce the goods until probably the need for them is past.

Craft development is in any event an Admiralty responsibility, and requirements are now going to the United Kingdom for fulfilment, e.g., new design support craft. Aircraft development is similarly undertaken by the Air Ministry.

14. It is in fact difficult to be sure of policy until definite requirements arise. Alterations to existing equipment can be done by the service organisations in the East, e.g., alterations to craft by dockyard and repair staffs, alterations to vehicles by this organisation under C-in-C, India. Area aerodromes and harbour construction are only built when there are manufacturing facilities in the U.K., and U.S.A. But modifications of beach equipment can be tackled by the Combined Operations Development Centre (C.O.D.C.) assisted as necessary by G.H.Q.(I.) (India).

Provision of Special Equipment

15. The question of provision of special equipment is, in the main, answered by the preceding paragraphs. But highly specialised equipment does need a highly skilled manufacturing organisation to produce. It will certainly be quicker and more economical to send an officer to the U.K. to get something made, than to attempt its manufacture in India.

16. It is only when the demand concerns the material that is particularly available in India that it may be wise to deflect the limited productive capacity of India to the manufacture of the specialised equipment. The use of bamboo for roadway construction is an example of when India could help; should the need arise, it would be for S.E.A.C. (H.C.O.R.) to ask the Principle Administrative Officer (P.A.O.), G.H.Q.(I.), to provide.

Provision of Personnel

17. The personnel under consideration are those special parties such as folbots, S.O.E., boom breakers, swimmers, etc. It is clear that planning will decide what numbers of each type of specialist will be required. It will therefore be for S.E.A.C. (H.C.O.R.) to determine the numbers that are to be found and by what dates for the Commander-in-Chief to find and train these bodies.

18. In this connection it seems clear that all parties depending upon naval craft for training in operations should be located near Trincomalee, that they should for training and administration come

under one Officer who should in turn should be responsible to the C.-in-C, Eastern Fleet (E.F.) for their training. Parties not depending on craft for their training namely camouflage "B" and "false beach removers" could be attached to Camouflage "B" organisation in India and an already trained beach group respectively.

Promulgation of C.O. Information
19. The collation, printing and circulation of C.O. information for the use of training staffs, planning staffs, formations, landing craft and bases, Naval and Air Staffs Headquarters can either be done by D.C.O.(I.), in close touch with H.C.O.R. or by H.C.O.R. in close touch with D.C.O.(I.). Whichever does it must, however, be suitably located and have the staff to collate, print and circulate. Certainly, Delhi is the best position for the staff to be situated, except as far as the planners are concerned when they leave Delhi. While D.C.O.(I.) is at present the authority responsible for this duty because he is in touch with Chief of Combined Operations (C.C.O.) and D.C.O., M.E., and is responsible for the training establishments in India. This responsibility could hardly rest at S.E.A.C. level. Information about naval, military, and air developments is promulgated by the Departments of Admiralty, War Office, and Air Ministry, or by Commanders in the field, as the result of training and operational experience.

20. It is suggested this publication of information should continue to be the concern of D.C.O.(I.) and that the advisers for the planners should continue to come from the staff of H.C.O.R. But the close liaison that now exists between H.C.O.R., and D.C.O.(I.) must continue. The information they each get must be shared if trainers and planners are both to be served. C.-in-C., E.F., has already agreed that experience gained in exercises and operations are to be sent to D.C.O.(I.). It would be a great help if a copy of all lessons learnt, and new ideas that may arise could automatically be sent to him so that training, whether at the Staff College, in landing craft flotillas, or formations may be kept abreast of the fast moving times.

Conclusion
21. The following is a summary of the conclusions reached above:
- (a) Basic training, as required by S.E.A.C., should remain the concern of the D.C.O.(I.).
- (b) Formation training should be the responsibility of Commanders-in-Chief and Force Commanders. The formation

APPENDIX X

training staff should come under the orders of 11 Army Group and his staff should work in the closest collaboration with C.-in-C., Southern India.

(c) Technique should be approved by S.E.A.C., and should be given to D.C.O.(I.) to develop.

(d) Modifications of existing equipment should be undertaken by the Commander-in-Chief using the facilities available, or by application to G.H.Q., India (P.A.O., directly concerned). Minor special equipment will be made by or through C.O.D.C. Highly technical and quantitative equipment should continue to be produced in the U.K.

(e) The numbers of specialist amphibious personnel required will be decided by S.E.A.C. and the Commanders-in-Chief concerned will be responsible for their provision and training. All personnel dependent upon naval resources for training to be the responsibility of the C.-in-C., E.F. Remainder to join similar existing organisations in India.

(f) D.C.O.(I.) to remain the authority responsible for promulgating new information about combined operations to training staffs and establishments, naval units and forces, Army and Air Force formations, H.C.O.R. to advise planners, and H.C.O.R. and D.C.O.(I.) to remain in the very closest touch.

Appendix XI

FORMATION AND COMPOSITION – SMALL OPERATIONS GROUP S.E.A.C.

On the formation of the South-East Asia Command in 1943, Admiral Mountbatten asked the Chief of Combined Operations for several Combined Operations Pilotage Parties and Groups of the Special Boat Section to be placed under his command. C.O.P.P.7 arrived in India in August, 1943 and was joined at Cocanada by C.O.P.P.8 in the middle of November. In February, 1944, "A" and "B" Groups S.B.S. arrived. These parties all led an independent existence, although grouped in the same area.

In the meantime, it had been decided to group all such parties in S.E.A.C. together as the Small Operations Group. The object was:

(a) To reduce the number of independent organisations with which S.A.C.S.E.A. Headquarters and the Commander-in-Chief, Eastern Fleet, had to deal.
(b) To simplify administration and provide a common base.
(c) To ensure that as far as possible training and equipment of parties were standardised and that all units benefited from the experience gained in operations and training.

It was also decided to form Royal Marine Detachment 385 to reinforce the Group and to provide the Headquarters and Base Staff.

The site for the base was chosen at Hammenhiel on Karaitavu Island, off the Jaffna peninsula in Ceylon, to which the parties moved from India in April, 1944. They were joined there by C.O.P.P.4 and by the instructors under training for R.M. Detachment 385 in the following months. During this period, matters were under the control of

APPENDIX XI

Lt.-Col. H.G. Hasler, D.S.O., O.B.E., R.M. and the general layout of the camp was planned and decided; and camp construction started under arrangements made by C.-in-C., Eastern Fleet.

The Small Operations Group was officially formed on 12th June, 1944, and Colonel H.T. Tollemache arrived from England the next day and assumed command.

A Training and Development Unit was later formed as part of Headquarters, to co-ordinate basic training of units, to study new methods of operating and to carry out trials. The Headquarters and Base Staff were also increased in the light of experience. It was not until March, 1945, however, that all the new staff appointments were filled.

R.M. Detachment 385 operational ranks arrived at Hammenhiel Camp at the end of July. "C" Group S.B.S. and C.O.P.P.3 also arrived during this month.

With the arrival of the Sea Reconnaissance Unit in November, the Small Operations Group reached its maximum strength of operational units, viz: Four C.O.P.P.s, R.M. Detachment 385 of three troops, Special Boat Section of three Groups, and Sea Reconnaissance Unit of four sections.

Functions

The functions and method of control of the Small Operations Group were laid down in Supreme Allied Commander's Operational Directive No 14, to C.-in-C., Eastern Fleet. Broadly, command and administration were vested in C.-in-C., E.F., and general policy and operational control were retained by the Supreme Allied Commander.

The annex to this directive stated the functions of the group as being: "To provide small parties of uniformed troops trained and equipped to operate against enemy coastal, river or lake areas, using as their final means of approach various types of small craft (all of less capacity than 12 men), inflatable boats, paddle-boards or swimmers. The personnel of S.O.G. will not be qualified to work as agents."

This annex also stated that: "In order to prepare them to take part in such operations, S.O.G. personnel should be trained to carry out the following tasks: (a) Reconnaissance of enemy beaches, seaward approaches, beach exits and coastal defences, or alternatively, enemy territory near river banks or the shores of lakes; (b) Small scale attacks on objectives in coastal, river or lake areas, including demolitions ashore and attacks on ships in harbour; (c) The provision of markers and guides for assault landing by larger forces, which may be either sea or airborne; (d) The landing and re-embarking of agents, or stores for such agents, from small boats; (e) Seizing intelligence data and enemy equipment; (f) Providing diversions; (g) Any other type of operation which calls for basic S.O.G. training.

Component Units
C.O.P.P.s were commanded from January to March, 1945 by a Lieut. Commander and each consisted of four officers and five ratings (naval) and one officer and two other ranks (R.E.). These teams were specially trained to carry out detailed reconnaissance and survey of enemy beaches, seaward approaches and land exits and the provision of markers and guides for a subsequent assault. They included a number of fully qualified navigating and hydrographic officers. In operations, parties were transported to the area in either a submarine, H.D.M.L., or minor landing craft, depending on the task. The final approach and the task itself was carried out in canoes and by swimmers operating from them.

General Purpose Teams
The other units were considered to be general purpose units, capable of undertaking raids and patrols for general reconnaissance, demolition tasks, sabotage, capture of prisoners, attacking ships in harbour, etc. The difference between them lay more in their methods of approach than in the actual tasks for which they were trained.

(a) R.M. Detachment 385 – was commanded by a major and each troop was also commanded by a major and consisted of five officers and twenty-four other ranks. Its troops were considered operationally trained from January, 1945.

(b) S.B.S. – were commanded by a major as also were the three groups, each of which consisted of four officers and sixteen other ranks. The S.B.S. Troops were all recruited from Army sources, mainly Commandos.

The main difference in the training of these two units was that S.B.S. had more training in operating ashore and were already trained parachutists: R.M. Detachment 385 had a wider training in boat work.

(c) S.R.U. – was originally commanded by a Lieut.-Commander, R.C.N.V.R. and later by an Army Captain. Each section consisted of two officers and ten other ranks, who were drawn from all services. Although the unit was considered to be general purpose, the men had undergone special training in long-distance swimming, landing and withdrawing through heavy surf, the use of paddle-boards and underwater swimming with oxygen breathing apparatus. In addition, all men completed the Army Parachute Course at Ringway. After S.R.U. arrived at Hammenhiel Camp, the sections were trained in the use of small boats and navigation.

Limitations
The limitations of S.O.G. teams were twofold – those imposed by the training and those imposed by their establishment.

In the first instance they could be used only in roles tailor-made to their particular type of training and, in the second, they were dependent on a higher formation for maintenance. Designed to operate by air or by sea from an established base, teams possessed no general duty men and were entirely operational.

Planning
The following types of S.O.G. operations were carried out: (a) Independently Mounted Operations – in which the Commander, S.O.G. was responsible for the planning and mounting of the operation, using the facilities of all superior headquarters concerned; (b) Force Commanders' Operations – in which teams were detached to Force Commanders for use in conjunction with major operations. The Commander S.O.G. was then responsible only for the selection of the suitable teams for liaison and advice to the headquarters concerned. The planning and mounting was the responsibility of the headquarters to which they were attached.

Independent Operations
Nineteen independent operations in all were carried out, of which three were done by C.O.P.P., fourteen by R.M. Detachment 385, and two by S.B.S. These operations can be sub-divided in three categories:

(a) In connection with future operations – Reconnaissances of beaches and airstrips and deception raids.   Total   10
(b) Attacks on enemy coastal objectives   Total   2
(c) Operations for clandestine organisations – Landing or picking up of agents, landing stores.   Total   7

Under the first category, beach reconnaissances for a large-scale landing were made in North Sumatra ("Frippery"), Puket Island ("Baboon" and "Copyright") and Malaya ("Confidence"). These operations, with the exception of "Copyright", in which one officer and two other ranks from R.M. Detachment 385, together with the senior R.E./C.O.P.P. officer and an attached R.A.F. officer took part, were all carried out by C.O.P.P.s. In all cases, submarines were used to transport the party to the area of the operation and the tasks themselves were carried out in canoes.

The most interesting of these operations was "Confidence", partly because of the difficulties which were encountered in the operation itself and partly because the information was later used in the landing of 34 Corps over the Morib beaches. The object of this operation was to carry out a reconnaissance of three beaches in the area of Port Dickson and the approaches to them in order to ascertain their suitability for a large-scale landing. C.O.P.P.3 was chosen for the operation and H.M. Submarine *Seadog* was allotted for the passage to and from the area.

On the night 9th/10th June, a reconnaissance of one of the Morib beaches was carried out. Four canoes, carrying eight all ranks, were launched from the submarine for this task. It was discovered by the leader of the party at the time the canoes were due to return to the submarine that two of them were missing. They had failed to rendezvous with the "link" canoe which was fitted with "Bongle" for homing to the submarine. On return to the submarine, it was also found that they had not homed direct to her by means of their R.G. equipment. Before the S./C.O.P.P. returned to the submarine, a thorough search was carried out and the next day the submarine kept the prearranged daylight rendezvous, but in neither case was there any sign of the missing canoes. In view of the risk of compromise, the S./C.O.P.P. and C.O. of the submarine decided to cancel the remainder of the reconnaissances and to return to the base.

The occupants of the missing canoes succeeded in getting ashore further south and joining up with some guerilla forces, and returned safely. The information gained included:

(a) An accurate cross-section of the beach including underwater gradient at selected points.
(b) The bearing surface of the beach, including details of the runnels above the water level.
(c) Details of underwater runnels and of a spit off the beach, including heights of tide and rates observed on the edge of the spit.
(d) Samples of surface above and below water level.
(e) A periscope photograph showing the beach silhouette.
(f) Information about enemy coast-watchers.

As a result of the above information, plans were made for the landing of 34 Corps on the Morib beaches and the beaches between Port Dickson

APPENDIX XI

and Cape Rachado. The remaining members of C.O.P.P.3 were to have been used for marking the channel and guiding the assault craft. This was later cancelled in view of the situation.

During the planning of the two operations on Puket Island, it was decided that three deception raids should also be carried out in view of the risk of compromise. Two of these were to be done in Burma ("Bruteforce" and "Dandy") and one in N Sumatra ("Cattle"). "Dandy" was abandoned and the two others, "Clearance Able" and "Baker" (Malaya and Thailand) respectively, were planned in place; the first of these was later dropped.

"Baboon" and "Copyright" were carried out on nights 8th/9th March and 9th/10th March respectively. During these operations seven all ranks were lost. In view of the increased risk of compromise, S.E.C.S.E.A. ordered two further raids to be carried out, one in Burma ("Fairy") and the other in Nicobar Islands ("Defraud"). These operations and the ones mentioned above, namely "Bruteforce," "Cattle" and "Clearance Baker", were carried out by R.M. Detachment 385. All were successful except for "Bruteforce" in which the party was lost, and "Fairy" in which the party never got ashore.

The only operations involving attacks on enemy coastal objectives were two carried out by S.B.S. ("Spratt Able" and "Baker") of which one was successful. In this a road and a bridge in north Sumatra was destroyed.

The operations undertaken for the clandestine organisations (I.S.L.D., Force 136, "E" Group and O.S.S.) were all carried by R.M. Detachment 385 and involved landings in every country in original South-East Asia Command. The largest of these operations was "Carpenter III", in which 8,000lb. of stores were landed for the guerillas operating on the east coast of Johore, and twelve men were evacuated. H.M. Submarine *Thule* was used for the operation, the landing being carried out in nine power-driven and three dumb L.C.R.

Force Commanders' Operations
One hundred and fifty-four Force Commanders' operations were carried out, all of which took place either on the Arakan coast or on the Burma rivers. Every sub-unit with the exception of two of the troops of R.M. Detachment 385 did at least one attachment to a Force Commander. All these sub-units with the exception of C.O.P.P., who were attached to F.O. Force "W", were attached either to 14th Army or 15th Corps.

The operations on the Arakan coast included reconnaissance of defences, pre-assault surveys of beaches, interrogation through an interpreter, the bringing back of other natives for interrogation at base and acting as advanced party to a small Commando base.

In the initial stages of the Arakan campaign, C.O.P.P.8 was attached to F.O. Force "W" for a short period and "A" Group was placed under command of 3rd S.S. Brigade. From 23rd November to 16th December, "A" Group S.B.S. carried out a number of operations including reconnaissance of defences on the coast, in the Ramree Island and Taungup areas. They were relieved by "C" Group S.B.S. at the end of December. This group was placed under command of 26th Indian Division and carried out operations in the Akyab and Kyaukpyu areas prior to their capture, after which they assisted 26th Indian Division in the drive south from Kyaukpyu by operating in the area of Ramree and Taungup. Third section S.R.U. also came under command of 26th Division on 15th February and operated in the Taungup area. Finally, "C" Group S.B.S. and C.O.P.P.9 accompanied the troops carrying out the assault on Rangoon.

During this period C.O.P.P.s 1,3,4 and 9 had also been operating in the Arakan under F.O. Force "W". Their operations included pre-assault surveys of beaches at Akyab, Myebon Peninsula, Ramree Island and the area of Taungup.

The operations on the Burma rivers included reconnaissance of river crossings, river patrols, land reconnaissance patrols and "Jitter" parties across the rivers.

The first sub-unit to operate with the 14th Army was "B" Group S.B.S., who operated from 11th November to 13th December, 1944, under command of 11th (E.A.) Division. They were responsible for reconnoitring the crossing places on the River Chindwin for the assault brigade and for the remainder of the division. They also carried out several other tasks in conjunction with this information on or across the river.

The S.O.G. Units took an important part in 14th Army's crossing of the River Irrawaddy. The crossings of 20th Indian Division on 12th/13th February, 7th Indian Division on 13th/14th February and 2nd Division on 24th/25th February were reconnoitred by sub-units of S.B.S. and S.R.U., who also guided the assault troops to the correct beaches.

"A" Group S.B.S. and 1st Section S.R.U. also operated on the Irrawaddy, from 15th April, 1945 to 28th May in conjunction firstly with 7th Indian Infantry Division and latterly with 20th Indian Infantry Division. These divisions were operating in the area of Seikpyu and had been given the task of preventing the Japanese withdrawing from

APPENDIX XI

the Arakan across the River Irrawaddy. In view of weather conditions at the end of May, these sub-units were withdrawn.

Casualties and Total Number of Operations Carried Out
The total number of operations carried out was 174, and the casualties suffered were as follows:

Killed: Three officers, three other ranks.

Prisoners-of-War
In Japanese hands: Three officers and one other rank. (One officer subsequently liberated. Remainder executed at Singapore in July 1945).

Interned in Thailand: Three officers and one other rank (all liberated).

Missing: Three officers and six other ranks (two officers and two other ranks joined up with guerilla forces and later liberated. One officer and four other ranks still not accounted for).

Wounded: One officer and one other rank (both returned to S.B.S.).

Appendix XII

COMBINED OPERATIONS BEACH ORGANISATION

20th November, 1942

Under Secretary of State for War,
The War Office,
Whitehall, S.W.1

Combined Operations Beach Organisation

General
1. Experience gained in exercises and whilst preparing for operations has shown that there is a paramount need for a properly constituted unit to undertake the various duties included under the heading of "Beach Organisation".

Existing System
2. The existing system whereby an *ad hoc* "Beach Brick" composed of a number of independent units, detachments and individuals is assembled for a particular exercise or operation has proved itself to be quite inadequate for this work and almost impossible to administer. The importance of beach organisation both as regards planning, control and execution has been fully brought out in the Commander-in-Chief, Home Forces, report on exercise "Dryshod".

APPENDIX XII

Proposed New Method
3. This matter has been the subject of discussion between representatives of Home Forces, the War Office and both Naval and Army Staffs of Combined Operations Headquarters. As a result, proposals for a "Beach Organisation Group", suitable for each assault Brigade landing were proposed.

An established unit such as that now proposed should be able to reach the high standard of training and esprit de corps which is so essential if it is to work and fight as a team under the difficult conditions which can be expected on the beaches.

Functions of the Beach Group
4. Briefly, the function of the Beach Group is, in conjunction with the Royal Navy, to:

   (a) Arrange and control the movement of all personnel and vehicles from ships and landing craft to assembly areas inland.
   (b) Move stores from ships' holds and craft to dumps in the Beach Maintenance Area.
   (c) Develop and organise the beaches and Beach Maintenance Area both as regards defence, movement and administration, including evacuation of casualties and recovery of vehicles.
   (d) Provide a Beach Signal Organisation.

Beach Groups will be G.H.Q. troops allotted to lower formations as required for a particular operation. The Beach Group Commander will be responsible to the senior formation commander ashore until a Base Sub-Area is established.

Manpower Commitment
5. Attention is drawn to the fact that the size of this group is no larger than the Beach Bricks, which have been developed by First Army in conjunction with C.C.O.'s Training Staff during the past twelve months.

Responsibility for "Fathering" Beach Groups
6. As a result of recent experience, it appears essential that one arm of the service must "father" Beach Groups and be responsible for their mobilisation, both of personnel and equipment, development of the technique of beach work and training.

As a result of the foregoing, it is considered that the ideal would be met if the personnel of the whole of the Beach Groups belonged to one Corps, preferably that of the Royal Engineers; officers would be seconded to this as necessary. Should this, owing to administrative and other difficulties, not be practicable, then it is suggested that certain companies should belong to other Corps.

In either case, officers of the headquarters would be drawn from all arms.

Subsequent Employment of Beach Groups
7. Consideration has been given to the best method of employment of the Beach Groups when beach maintenance ceases. It is felt that the value of the special training and experience should not be lost by allowing them to be dispersed or retained for routine duties in the Base Sub-area; they should be withdrawn as complete units, reformed, if necessary, as a result of heavy casualties, and held available for another operation.

Number of Groups Required
8. The number of Beach Organisation Groups required will depend on the scale of any operation; in general, it can be taken that one Group for each assaulting Brigade will not be exceeded.

Training
9. In addition to units specifically allotted to the defence of the beaches there will be other units who will require to be attached to and come under command of the Beach Groups during operations.

These units comprise the following:
Detachment Field Park Company – for R.E. Stores Dump.
D.I.D. (Detail Issue Depot).
Medical Units.
Ordnance Beach Detachment.

During collective training it will be necessary for all attached units to be made available to join the Beach Groups though at other times they will be able to continue with their own technical training at their normal stations.

Summary of Proposals
10. The following proposals are therefore submitted for urgent consideration and approval:

(a) Approval in principle be given immediately to the establishment of Beach Groups, the preparation of a war establishment for the Group Headquarters and the appointment of Group Commanders and their staffs.
(b) Detailed consideration be given to the preparation of a suitable war establishment; to be undertaken by the War Office assisted

APPENDIX XII

as necessary by representatives of G.H.Q., Home Forces and Combined Operations H.Q.
(c) One Beach Group to be formed immediately in each Command in the U.K.
(d) Formation of such further Beach Groups as may then be considered necessary as a result of projected future operations.

Signed, Louis Mountbatten,
Chief of Combined Operations.

Appendix XIII

LIST OF OPERATION CODE NAMES SHOWING OBJECTIVE

Code Name   *Objective*

Code Name	Objective
Abercrombie	Hardelot.
Anklet	Lofoten Is.
Archery	Vaagso.
Avalanche	Salerno.
Baboon	Bukit Is.
Backchat	Anse de St. Marten.
Baytown	Italy.
Biting	Bruneval.
Blanket	Exercise for "Frankton".
Blazing	Alderney.
Bonus	Madagascar.
Brimstone	Sardinia.
Brisk	Azores.
Bristle	Boulogne.
Bruteforce	Zigon, Burma.
Catherine	Baltic.
Chariot	St. Nazaire.
Clearance Able	Malaya.
Clearance Baker	Thailand.
Collar	Pas de Calais.
Confidence	Malaya.
Consular	Move of Thames barges.

APPENDIX XIII

Copyright	Bukit Is.
Curlew	St. Laurent.
Defraud	Kamorta Is.
Dragoon	S. France.
Frankton	Bordeaux.
Frippery	N. Sumatra.
Greenback	In event of Russia collapse.
Huckaback	Hern.
Husky	Sicily.
Imperator	Paris via Ault.
Infatuate	Walcheren.
Ironclad	Madagascar.
Jubilee	Dieppe.
Jupiter	Norway.
J.V.	Boulogne.
Leapfrog	Exercise for "Pilgrim".
Lighter	Kupho Nisi.
Menace	Dakar.
Myrmidon	Bayonne.
Overlord	Normandy.
Pilgrim	Grand Canary.
Rankin	Operations on the Continent in event of a crack in German morale.
Rattle	Conference at Largs.
Reservist	Landing of Gen. Mark Clark in N. Africa.
Round-Up	A plan for re-entry into the Continent.
Rutter	Dieppe.
Sesame	Large scale raid of some duration on Continent.
Shrapnel	Canary Islands.
Shingle	Anzio.
Skyscraper	To establish bomber force within close range of the Ruhr.
Sledgehammer	To ease pressure in Russia.
Super Round-Up	To destroy German forces in Western Europe.
Tinder	Plan for hasty return to the Continent.
Torch	North Africa.
Workshop	Pantelleria.
Yukon I and II	Exercises for "Jubilee".
Zipper	Malaya.

Appendix XIV

DIARY OF EVENTS AND IMPORTANT DATES

1937
November — Combined Operations Sub-Committee formed.

1938
15 September — I.S.T.D.C. formed at Portsmouth.

1939
3 September — Outbreak of World War II.

1940
26 May – 4 June — Evacuation from Dunkirk.
10 June — Italy declares war on the Allies.
14 June — Lt.-Gen. Bourne appointed Commander, Raiding Operations and Adviser to Chiefs of Staff on Combined Operations.
22 June — France surrenders to Axis Powers.
17 July — Admiral of the Fleet Sir Roger Keyes appointed Director of Combined Operations.
August — First C.T.C. opens at Inverary.
22 August — C.O.H.Q. moves to Richmond Terrace from the Admiralty.
23 September — Dakar; Operation "Menace".

APPENDIX XIV

1941
14 March	Directive issued to D.C.O.
22 June	Germany invades U.S.S.R.
27 October	Commodore Mountbatten appointed Adviser on Combined Operations and Commodore Combined Operations.
7 December	Attack on Pearl Harbor by Japan. U.S.A. enters the war.
9 December	Directive issued to A.C.O.
26 December	Raid on Vaagso, Norway; Operation "Archery".
December	Prime Minister and Chiefs of Staff visit U.S.A.

1942
January	Combined Operations Advisory Committee (India) formed at Delhi.
18 March	Adviser on Combined Operations becomes Chief of Combined Operations.
28 March	Raid on St. Nazaire; Operation "Chariot".
3 April	Brigadier Wernher appointed C.M.S.F.
April	Mr. Harry Hopkins and General Marshall visit U.K. from the U.S.A.
5 May	Madagascar; Operation "Ironclad".
11 May	U.S. naval, army and air force officers join C.O.H.Q.
4 June	C.C.O. visits U.S. Chiefs of Staff in Washington, U.S.A.
July	Second visit of Mr. Harry Hopkins with U.S. Chiefs of Staff to the U.K.
19 August	The Raid on Dieppe; Operation "Jubilee".
12 October	Force "J" formed with H.Q. in the Isle of Wight.
8 November	"D" Day, North Africa Landings; Operation "Torch".
November	Directorate of Combined Operations (India) formed.

1943
14-23 January	Casablanca Conference, "Symbol".
13 April	Lt.-Gen. Morgan appointed C.O.S.S.A.C.
28 June-2 July	"Rattle" Conference held at Largs.
10 July	"D" Day Sicily Landings; Operation "Husky".
11-25 August	Quebec Conference, "Quadrant".
9 September	Italy surrenders to the Allies.

9 September	Landings at Salerno; Operation "Avalanche".
13 October	Admiral Mountbatten leaves C.O.H.Q. to take up appointment as S.A.C.S.E.A.
13 October	Bottomley Committee report forwarded to Chiefs of Staff.
22 October	Maj.-Gen. Laycock takes up appointment as C.C.O.
27 November	Directive issued to the newly appointed C.C.O.

1944

22 January	Landings at Anzio; Operation "Shingle".
26 January	C.C.O. reports to Chiefs of Staff on re-organisation of C.O.H.Q.
March-April	Re-organisation of C.O.H.Q. on functional group system.
6 June	"D" Day Normandy Landings; Operation "Overlord".
1 November	Landings at Walcheren; Operation "Infatuate".

1945

9 May	Victory in Europe.
15 August	Victory in the Far East.
9 September	Landings in Malaya; Operation "Zipper".